The Middling Sort

The Middling Sort

Commerce, Gender, and the Family in England,

1680–1780

Margaret R. Hunt

UNIVERSITY OF CALIFORNIA PRESS
Berkeley   Los Angeles   London

This book is a print-on-demand volume. It is manufactured
using toner in place of ink. Type and images may be less
sharp than the same material seen in traditionally printed
University of California Press editions.

University of California Press
Berkeley and Los Angeles, California

University of California Press
London, England

Library of Congress Cataloging-in-Publication Data

Hunt, Margaret R., 1953-
    The middling sort : commerce, gender, and the family in England.
1680-1780 / Margaret R. Hunt.
        p.   cm.
    Includes bibliographical reference and index.
    ISBN 0-520-20260-0 (alk. paper)
    1. Middle class—Great Britain—History—17th century. 2. Middle
class—Great Britain—History—18th century. 3. Middle class
families—Great Britain—History—17th century. 4. Middle class
families—Great Britain—History—18th century. I. Title.
HT690.G7H85 1996
305.5'0942—dc20   96-18063
                                                              CIP
            Printed in the United States of America

    The paper used in this publication meets the minimum
    Requirements of ANSI/NISO Z39.48-1992(R 1997)
    (Permanence of Paper)

To My Parents

CONTENTS

ACKNOWLEDGMENTS

I first became fascinated with class, gender, and families in the bosom of my own family. I thank my mother and my father for their intellectual curiosity and for permitting me to pursue my own interests largely unimpeded. Between the time I began this project and the time I finished it my father died. However, he read an early version of the book, and I know he would have been pleased to see it between covers. I am grateful to all my siblings, "natural" and fictive, for helping me stay on course; special thanks to William Hunt, Martine Lebret, Maria Elena Gonzales, and Anne Knowlton.

Margaret Jacob first showed me how exciting Early Modern Europe could be, introduced me to archival research, an activity in which she has few equals, and taught me, by example and by precept, what it was to be a historian. I am forever in her debt.

Completing my doctorate in history at New York University remains one of the premier intellectual experiences of my life. I especially thank my advisor, Darline Levy. Numerous other people taught me, read my work, found me paid work, provided financial and emotional sustenance, put me up when I had nowhere to live, and talked with me late into the night about history, women's studies, politics, and the academy. I am especially grateful to Elaine Abelson, Barbara Balliet, Thomas Bender, Patricia Bonomi; Peter Eisenstadt, Harriet Jackson, Molly Nolan, Anneliese Orleck, Claire Potter, Carl Prince, Nancy Robertson, Mitziko Sawada, Rob Snyder, Danny Walkowitz, Marilyn Young, Susan Yohn, and Ren Qui Yu.

I owe many debts to friends and colleagues in eighteenth-century English history, British studies, early modern European history, women's studies, literature, and sundry other fields. John Brewer read the manuscript at an early stage and made a number of useful suggestions, many of which have found their way into the book. At a much later stage Joanna Innes took time away from a very busy term to read a good part of the work-in-progress, to suggest some new interpretive avenues, and to save me from several missteps. At the very end, Iain Pears interrupted the writing of his own book to do a truly incomparable reading. Numerous others have given of their editorial skills, unpublished work, citations, and friendship. I want especially to thank Susan Amussen, Donna Andrew, Emily Bartels, Judith Bennett, Alan Bray, David Bush, Catherine Crawford, Anna Davin, Toby Ditz, Andrew Federer, Keitha Fine, Catherine Hall, Diane Hamer, Yukiko Hanawa, Emily Honig, Martha Howell, Julian Hoppit, Henry Horwitz, Ronnie Hsia, Jan Lambertz, Phyllis Mack, Teresa Meade, Ruth Perry, Joan Scott, John Seed, Carroll Smith-Rosenberg, Mary Springfels, Susan Staves, John Styles, Jan Thaddeus, Randolph Trumbach, Amanda Vickery, Judith Walkowitz, and Kathleen Wilson.

My two departments, History and Women's and Gender Studies, have provided me with much encouragement. I thank all my colleagues there. I am especially grateful to Rhea Cabin, who typed large parts of the manuscript and helped in countless other ways. Many other friends and colleagues, past and present, from Amherst College, the Five College Community, and surroundings, have smoothed the way or been involved in some capacity in the book project. Special thanks to Leila Ahmed, Lisa Baskin, Amrita Basu, Joyce Berkman, Bob Bezucha, Fred Cheyette, Yvonne Chireau, Barbara Corbett, Danny Czitrom, Betty Couvares, Frank Couvares, Roselina de la Carrera, Ann Ferguson, Richard Fink, Judy Frank, Bob Gooding-Williams, Margaret Groesbeck, Robert Gross, Allen Guttmann, John Halsted, Keith Handley, Hugh Hawkins, Lee Heller, Gail Hornstein, Michael Kasper, Isabel Margolin, Rose Olver, Andy Parker, Cindy Patton, Kathy Peiss, Pat Pelletier, Lorna Peterson, Peter Pouncey, Dagmar Powitz, Lisa Raskin, Walter Richard, Mary Roldan, Ronald Rosbottom, Austin Sarat, Eve Kosofsky Sedgwick, Peter Siegelman, Joyce Soucier, Kevin Sweeney, and Jonathan Vogel.

Charles Gillespie's warmth and generosity in the final year of his life will not be forgotten. Kathryn Drake put up with this book for almost as long as I did; I thank her for her decency, patience, and good cheer. The Berkshire Conference on the History of Women drew this project out longer, but kept me in mind of why we write books. Ann King provided hospitality, peace, and beautiful surroundings during the sabbatical in which the book was completed. Ruth Harris and Iain Pears offered unconditional friendship, excellent advice, and amazing food. My brother, William Hunt, proofed the manuscript serveral times and gave a week out of his life to the index, proving once more that kin solidarity is alive and well. Barbara Balliet, Michele Barale, Rhonda Cobham, Mandy Collins, Meryl Fingrutd, Mitzi Goheen, Sean Redding, and Linda Semple helped through some of the more difficult times.

Without the too often unsung labors of archivists, librarians, and bibliographers, a project like this would be unthinkable. Above all, my gratitude goes to the staff of the Amherst College Library and, especially, Margaret Groesbeck. I also thank the staffs of the Guildhall Library, London, the British Library, the Greater London Record Office, the Public Record Office, and the Bodleian. I am grateful to the New College, London, for permission to use the Doddridge Family Papers. It has been an unfailing pleasure working with the University of California Press. I want especially to thank Stanley Holwitz and Rebecca Frazier for their patience and enthusiasm.

Financial assistance toward the completion of this book has come from the Center for European Studies, an Amherst College Trustees Faculty Fellowship, the Fulbright Commission, several Amherst Research Fellowships, and the generosity of friends and loved ones.

Several of the passages on time discipline, literacy, and accountancy from chapter 2 were originally published in "Time-Management, Writing, and Accounting in the Eighteenth-Century English Trading Family: A Bourgeois Enlightenment?" *Business and Economic History* (2d ser.) 18 (1989):150–159 (copyright Business History Conference). Some of the illustrative material on domestic violence in chapter 6 originally appeared in "Wife-beating, Domesticity, and Women's Independence in Early Eighteenth-Century London," *Gender & History* 4 (1992):10–33 (copyright Basil Blackwell, Ltd). The discussion of travel writing and of Adam Smith's library originally appeared in a somewhat different form in "Racism, Imperialism and the Traveler's Gaze in Eighteenth-Century England," *Journal of British Studies* 32 (1993):333–357 (copyright North American Conference on British Studies). I am grateful to Peter Earle, Blackwell Publishers, and the Economic History Review for permitting me to reproduce a table from Peter Earle's "The Female Labour Market in London in the Late Seventeenth and Early Eighteenth Centuries," *Economic History Review* 42 (1989):328–353 (copyright Economic History Society). I am also grateful to Glasgow Museums, the People's Palace, for permission to reproduce the picture of the Glasgow Shopkeeper on the jacket.

NOTES ON THE TEXT

A good many of the people discussed in this book were self-taught or only rather desultorily educated. Often they belonged to the first generation of their immediate family to be literate. As a result their spelling tended to be eccentric and, at times, almost wholly innocent of punctuation. But since one of the themes of the book is writing and its standardization, it did not seem appropriate to censor or "correct" these peoples' efforts. Therefore original spelling, capitalization, and punctuation (or lack of it) have been retained, as have most abbreviations, with the exception of "ye" and "yt" which have been altered to read "the" and "that." Where the text is hard to follow, help is supplied in brackets.

Dates before the introduction of the Gregorian Calendar in 1752 are given in the Old Style, except that dates falling between January 1 and March 24, inclusive, are rendered with both the old and new year; for example, 28 February 1713/14.

So-called "generic" nouns and pronouns are avoided because they lack specificity. "Man" or "men" and "he" are used when males are being discussed. "Woman" or "women" and "she" are used when females are being discussed. If there is reason to think that a particular observation holds for both women and men, a gender-neutral term such as "people" or "middling sort" is used. This practice has the added advantage of being closer to contemporary usage. Eighteenth-century people were generally quite precise with their gender signifiers, and seldom used terms like "man" to mean anyone other than the males of the species. To argue that they "meant" something more universal substitutes twentieth-century mystifications for early modern candor.

Introduction:
The Middling Sort

In 1758 the readers of Samuel Johnson's *Idler* laughed with him at the character of Ned Drugget, who "began in trade with a very small fortune," married the daughter of a confectioner, worked hard and spent little, and when his fortune was made and he wished to retire to the country, found it impossible to conceive of going any farther than Islington.[1] Drugget, like all his kind, tried to ape his betters, but his horizons were simply too narrow to pull it off. A shopkeeper always wants to be a gentleman, but he never succeeds in being anything other than a shopkeeper—and what of any real interest is there to say about shopkeepers?

So runs a persistent strain of thinking both in the eighteenth century and today. In fact, Johnson's tale is a rather nuanced one. Drugget is ambivalent about both "the country" and retirement from business, which is why lodging a portion of the week in suburban Islington and living the rest of the week in the City proves the perfect solution for him. But twentieth-century historians have only recently begun to pay much attention to the ambiguities within pieces like these. They are still more likely to fix upon Drugget gazing wishfully out his window at the coaches going by than to ask why he seems so reluctant to go farther out of town.

This study starts from two rather simple propositions: that most people do not devote their entire lives to thirsting after something they cannot possibly attain, and that the culture of eighteenth-century middling people deserves more attention than it has hitherto received. A searching look at the surviving sources relating to shopkeepers, tradesmen, lower-level professionals, civil servants, and others reveals complex and conflictual family lives and patterns of sociability that are heavily marked by the experience of commerce. Such investigation suggests the signal importance of questions of gender for any understanding of early modern business, and it uncovers a rich and influential culture that grows, at least in part, out of the search for solutions to the inadequacies of a developing market society.

THE THEORY OF EMULATION

At the outset, this approach demands a critical reevaluation of "emulation," *the* central explanatory concept employed by eighteenth-century social historians in the postwar period, at least where commercial people are concerned. Emulation was seized upon in the 1950s and 1960s as a bulwark against visions of a unified, rising, class-conscious "bourgeoisie" (and, for that matter, a "working class") in seventeenth- and eighteenth-century England. Historians of the left, the right and the middle collaborated in this effort, with conservatives trying to stave off the notion that anything resembling class struggle had ever existed on British soil and Marxists trying to explain why the groups that seemed the most "middle class" were significantly less politically powerful in the eighteenth and early nineteenth centuries than they should, theoretically, have been.

Take, for example, Harold Perkin's *The Origins of Modern English Society* (1969), an essentially centrist appraisal. Perkin argues that the prime mover of eighteenth-century social and economic life was emulation, a competitive urge to out-earn and out-spend one's neighbors so as to make one's way (or enable one's children to make their way) into the ranks of England's relatively open landed elite. And since, according to this model, the central aim of all trading people was to leave their origins behind, it followed that one could not speak of an authentic commercial culture in the eighteenth century. Perkin recognizes that more "horizontal" ties, deriving from contracts, credit, and the nature of work, might act to counter the allegedly universal longing to join the gentry and that emulation might strike middling people themselves (and not just their social superiors) as a rather problematic impulse, but he does not seriously examine either issue. What coherence he finds in the lives of commercial folk derives primarily from the commitment of some of them to religious nonconformity.[2] Since publication of *The Origins of Modern English Society*, numerous others, including J. H. Plumb, Neil McKendrick, David Cannadine, Jonathan Clark, and Peter Borsay have lined up behind this rather narrow vision.[3]

A quarter-century after the appearance of Perkin's book, the social basis upon which this version of emulation theory rests seems a good deal less secure. An earlier generation of social historians knew, or thought they knew, what happened when an eighteenth-century businessman achieved success. He promptly retired from trade, purchased a country estate, married himself or his children to gentry, and set about turning his offspring into country gentlemen. Now undeniably some members of the "big bourgeoisie" did do just that. But those who did so were a minority even in the top echelons of business. Nicholas Rogers's study of London aldermen in the mid eighteenth century finds an increasingly interlocking "city patriciate," men whose fathers, and often grandfathers, had been aldermen. Although these men married gentry daughters in larger numbers than they had in the previous century, they were not typically transient in business or, in Rogers's words, at all "anxious to leave the counting house."[4] Lawrence Stone and Jeanne Fawtier Stone's *An Open Elite?* (1984) finds surprisingly few business families moving to the country, and the Stoneses' evidence suggests that landed society was far less "open" to *parvenus* than has traditionally been thought.[5]

Henry Horwitz has been critical both of Rogers's and the Stoneses' findings. His elegantly constructed study of the Augustan business elite of London demonstrates that the pattern of scions of trade moving onto the land or marrying gentry did obtain to some degree. But even he cannot show that any more than three-tenths of the eldest sons of the *top tier* of businessmen abandoned trade or the professions to become landed proprietors.[6] The "business elites" Horwitz discusses were all extremely rich men. The *poorest* men in his two main samples had at least £10,000 per annum, while more than a third of those whose incomes are known enjoyed £50,000 to £100,000.[7] This evidence raises real doubts about commercial people's supposedly universal desire to join the ranks of the landed gentry. If people who could afford to set up their sons as landed gentlemen chose, in significant numbers, not to do so, is it reasonable to suppose that smaller people, the true "middling sort," who had virtually no chance of achieving landed gentility either for themselves or their children, would live out their lives shackled to such a futile dream?

Ned Drugget does, it is true, take a limited interest in activities associated with his betters. But his story and the present study suggest more strongly the presence of a deep ambivalence among trading people toward upper-class mores—as middling people defined them, at any rate. The everyday demands of business meant few of the middling strayed very far for very long from their place of work, and fear of capital drain kept many businessmen, even very rich ones, from embracing an "aristocratic" lifestyle. Some did, of course, but often in the face of serious opposition from other family members. Ralph Davis discusses such a case in his fine study of the Levant trade in the eighteenth century. The Radcliffe family was one of those oft-celebrated "amphibious" families with ties to both land and trade. But in this family there was considerable tension about the purposes to which capital should be put, and there was little love lost between those members of the family reared to trade and those reared to be country gentlemen. Thus one trading son wrote scornfully of his gently bred father in 1714 that "by his education [he] may be esteemed incapable of the direction of our affairs in trade." And the high level of enmity between brothers in the next generation seems partly to have stemmed from the fact that when Ralph Radcliffe, the eldest son, inherited the estate in 1727, he withdrew capital from trade in order to maintain a gentlemanly life-style.[8]

Farther down the social scale, Dudley Ryder, son of a trader and studying for the bar in the early eighteenth century, vividly described the hand-wringing that went on in his family on account of his brother's insistence on dressing and socializing above his station, behaviors that seemed to his relations to signal an incapacity for business. Ryder himself, destined for a brilliant career as a jurist, engaged in some classic emulative behavior himself, but not easily or without soul-searching. Often afflicted with doubts about his choice of profession, he wondered whether he instead should not have pursued a career in trade, as did his father. And in Ryder Junior's younger days, at any rate, he claimed to have real difficulty understanding what people saw in the life of a country gentleman.[9] In another case, Samuel Thornton (1755–1838), a Bank of England director, Member of Parliament, and scion of a Yorkshire family heavily involved in the Russian trade, incurred the disapproval of his family when he bought an estate, Albury Park. His brother accused him of pretending to be what he was not, for the family was, in the brother's words, "All City people and connected with merchants, and nothing but merchants on every side."[10]

The better-off traders, particularly merchants, expected to live well and might embrace "bourgeois" variants of aristocratic practice, such as renting a "country"—actually commuter—home. Middling people, especially elderly retirees, did sometimes buy land, which was after all one of the safer investments available. We know of several active traders who wound up their businesses late in life because there was no one in their families with the inclination or the ability to carry them on. But none of these actions necessarily indicated a desire to join the ranks of the landed.[11] The world of business was an absorbing one, with personal rewards that went well beyond making money. "You see a Man out of Business becomes a Dead Letter," wrote Samuel Lowder, Bristol Customs official, to a relation in 1775, "but thank God I have been able for some days past to return to Business."[12] When an old friend of Samuel Kenrick, the Unitarian businessman, suggested he retire, Kenrick responded a trifle testily, "[I]f I was out of the bank in what respect would I be happier than I am now?" Kenrick had built up the bank from nothing with his brother, a wholesale tobacco trader, at a time when there were few lending institutions. He was perfectly content with his modest domestic regime, his work, his friends, and his library.[13]

Emulation was a real phenomenon. But it was not universal, and it was only one of a number of impulses that animated middling people. It certainly did not operate without check. Those of the middling whose job it was either to serve or to anticipate the wants of elite consumers naturally sought to acquire some of the patina of gentility, as well as a better understanding of elite tastes. But there was a distinct difference between knowledge that was likely to swell the coffers and appetites that were almost guaranteed to deplete them. Too, the need to sustain the impression of prosperity (crucial in a society that relied heavily upon credit) militated in favor of a style of life that was visibly comfortable. A reputation for extravagance could easily create the opposite effect—it could literally result in ruin.

HISTORIANS AND THE MIDDLING SORT

The eighteenth-century middling sort is a rather impoverished category from the historiographical point of view. One of the main aims of this study is to flesh out and enrich the picture we currently have of it. Until very recently the only sustained attempt to examine the lives of middling people in the eighteenth century has been Peter Earle's informative study *The Making of the English Middle Class: Business, Society and Family Life in London, 1660–1730* (1989). But the book looks only at London and does not go very far into the eighteenth century. Conversely, Leonore Davidoff's and Catherine Hall's *Family Fortunes: Men and Women of the English Middle Class, 1780–1850* (1987) unearths remarkably detailed information on the family life of commercial and professional groups but focuses largely on the first half of the nineteenth century.[14] John Smail's *The Origins of Middle-Class Culture: Halifax, Yorkshire, 1660–1780* (1994) is a welcome new contribution to the study of social class in the early modern period. Smail traces the gradual emergence in eighteenth-century Halifax of a mercantile, manufacturing, and professional group he calls the "middle class," distinguishing them from a mass of smaller yeoman clothiers ("the middling") whose roots stretched back into the seventeenth century. In the process he provides a wealth of information on the family lives, associational activities, and business and employment practices of both groups. However, Smail's book is, finally, a story about the formation of an elite; his project is not to examine the continuing history of the more extensive collectivity contemporaries thought of as "the middling sort."[15]

Although they have only recently been deemed worthy of discussion as a distinct socioeconomic category, middling people turn up in a number of studies of economic, political, and urban life in the eighteenth century—they are, in fact, difficult to overlook. Economic and business historians, especially, have contributed largely to our knowledge of specific industries and firms as well as broader economic trends. The drawback of that scholarship, from the perspective of the present study, is that until very recently it has tended to identify "work" almost exclusively with men and to deal little with the sphere of the family beyond pointing out its importance for capital formation.[16]

Similar difficulties beset a body of work that emphasizes the importance of extraparliamentary politics in the eighteenth century. The middling formed a crucial element in city "mobs," populated the lower echelons of the Tory opposition, lent their numbers to the Wilkite movement, engaged in moral or evangelical vigilantism, founded philanthropic organizations, participated in local government, and worked their way into the expanding government bureaucracy: they are not to be lightly dismissed. But political historians have shown less interest in exploring the broader family or occupational cultures out of which these pioneering urban activists came.[17]

One of the most promising recent developments bearing on the study of the middling sort is the new scholarship on consumption. Early work in this field, such as McKendrick, Brewer, and Plumb's *Birth of a Consumer Society* (1983), uncovered a wealth of information about the astounding diversity of eighteenth-century consumer tastes, the rise of shops, the birth of "modern" advertising, the relation between consumption and urban politics, even what we might term the commodification of childrearing. This research and more recent work on consumption have stressed the immense potential of early modern capitalist society to generate new institutions, new forms of desire, and, it is implied, new liberatory possibilities, at least for some. Moreover, the newest work in the field has moved considerably beyond the old simplistic model of emulation that drove much of the social history of the 1950s, 1960s, and 1970s. A different generation of scholars is stressing ambivalence and diversity and patterns of middling- and lower-class consumption that differed self-consciously from those of elites. We are discovering more about the small-scale material and spiritual ambitions that helped make up the fabric of family life and class and gender identity for people from a range of social backgrounds.[18]

In the present work I adopt the fluid analytical boundaries between individuals, families, and the market that are characteristic of some of the best studies of consumption. I also take a new look at the culture of production, somewhat neglected in the recent rush to study consumption patterns, arguing that it too had an important role to play in middling life. To emphasize production (understood here in the broadest sense), and to seek to understand how it intersects with family life, is to focus renewed attention upon the obstacles and challenges that faced early modern commercial people. One result is that the present study takes a more skeptical view of the liberatory potential of the early modern marketplace than has been the norm in some other studies.[19]

This book lays heavy emphasis upon the experience of women and families. Although social historians have abandoned many of the sentimental notions they used to entertain of premodern "social harmony," it has been harder for them to be as hardheaded about the sphere of family relations as they are about, say, labor relations, village life, or peasant agriculture. Within the subdiscipline of social and family history this persistent romanticism has manifested itself especially powerfully in the long-running debate over whether "the modern family" is a nicer or nastier institution than it was in past times. The eighteenth century has been a pivotal period for both the optimists and the pessimists. Thus, Lawrence Stone and Randolph Trumbach, in two studies published in 1977 and 1978, respectively, argue that romantic love and marital egalitarianism were, in a sense, "invented" in the eighteenth century, at least among the aristocracy and middle ranks, and then bequeathed to the modern world. Other scholars, chiefly feminists, view the eighteenth century less positively, as a time when women's position, and family life more generally, actually deteriorated as a result of wives' and daughters' declining involvement in household-based production and agriculture. This is the position taken by Bridget Hill in her recent survey of women in eighteenth-century England.[20]

For our purposes the problem is less when and where the ideal family system is to be found than the dubious belief, shared by both sides, that it is to be found at all. In fact, most social historians of the period either see family harmony almost everywhere or acknowledge tension without examining its larger significance. Thus Davidoff and Hall's *Family Fortunes* showcases a unified "middle class" and so consistently emphasizes family order and cross-gender solidarity at the expense of talking about tension and conflict of interest. Peter Earle discusses tensions arising within the family (he could hardly avoid doing so, since his chapter on marriage relies partly upon divorce court records) but fails to examine their impact either for what he calls "the making of the middle class" or for the position of women.[21] John Smail's study of Halifax paints a surprisingly harmonious picture of the family lives of elite merchants and manufacturers.[22]

The present study is agnostic about whether the eighteenth century witnessed improving or deteriorating family relations—or for that matter, a rise or a decline in women's status. I am, however, more prone than some scholars of the period to view family conflict as a central, even constitutive feature of eighteenth-century social life. This is far from an attempt to argue that family life is a perpetual war of the all against the all, or, that it does not change over time. There is much variety in the structure, function, and relative felicity of families (to talk glibly of "the family," as if all families at a given historical moment were the same, is itself deeply misleading), and this is matched by striking changes over time in all the

elements that are said to make up family life. This book's central methodological point is that families and the arena of family conflict closely articulate with the culture at large and that they are an important place for
working out individual and group identity (particularly gender identity).
In this sense, family conflict may be just as important as the intergroup
conflicts (such as class conflict) that have dominated the social history of
the period.

A good deal of eighteenth-century history writing ignores women altogether or accords them only the most token representation.[23] Two main
justifications are generally offered for this. The first is that the eighteenth-
century family (and hence women) were so separate from the world of
politics, business, and the like that political or economic or even social
historians need not feel any compelling need to talk much about them.
The second is that there are simply too few surviving sources on women to
make it worthwhile to study them. Several very recent studies have gone
some way toward overturning these assumptions. Amy Erickson's *Women
and Property in Early Modern England* (1993) explodes the belief that the
sources are silent on the lives of women and pushes us to look at new kinds
of records and examine familiar ones more perspicaciously. Linda Colley's
Britons (1992) and Kathleen Wilson's *The Sense of the People* (1995) challenge the view that eighteenth-century women had little or nothing to do
with politics, as well as the presumption that politics (and political ideology) can be understood without reference to women and ideas about
them. L. D. Schwarz's study of eighteenth- and early-nineteenth-century
London and John Smail's study of industrializing Halifax have also sought
a place for women within narratives of urban economic transformation.[24]

In historiographical terms, the most striking feature of this work is the
way most of it, if not all, either bypasses or rejects the theory of separate
spheres.[25] The notion of a progressive drawing apart of the private and the
public "spheres" over the course of the eighteenth and early nineteenth
centuries has been a cornerstone of family history and women's history in
the last twenty years, and, since Leonore Davidoff and Catherine Hall's
Family Fortunes (1987), has had pride of place in class formation studies as
well. Undeniably, the notion of separate spheres *does* plausibly represent a
very influential strain of eighteenth- and nineteenth-century prescriptive
moralizing about women. The harder question is whether the heavy focus
upon separate spheres in much writing on women's history helps or hin-
ders our efforts to understand how real early modern women lived their
lives. Does the alleged public/private dichotomy simply reify distinctions
that never (or only intermittently) existed in practice? Does it divert historians' attention from the manifold ways in which the lives of women and
men and families, politics and the economy, "interiors" and "exteriors"

merged and converged in the past? Does it impose too rigid a chronological pattern on eighteenth- and nineteenth-century women's history, especially the history of middle-class women?[26] The present study is more concerned with the ways "the market" *transcended* the so-called "public sphere" and went to the heart of family life. In that sense it flies in the face of a good deal of "separate spheres" thinking. I am also not primarily concerned with developing a stage-by-stage chronology of how urban middling family structure developed over time. I do not consider it an entirely vain undertaking, nor am I in any sense rejecting the notion of change over time.[27] It is simply that, in the present project, I am more concerned to see what can be discovered when one does *not* construe one's central task to be the establishing of a comprehensive social-historical chronology. Readers will find a great deal of dynamism and change in these pages: those looking for a larger, more exhaustive tale of causes and effects are likely to be disappointed.

PLAN OF THE PRESENT STUDY

The late-seventeenth- and eighteenth-century middling sort was the first non-elite English social grouping to generate really significant quantities of personal documents. These men and women enjoyed a high and growing rate of literacy and tended to associate "respectability" with reading and writing. They engaged in lengthy correspondences. They wrote diaries, autobiographies, travel accounts, and personal *apologia* and kept endless books of accounts. The professionally trained as well as the autodidacts wrote tracts on theology, politics, and economics. The civic-minded compiled town directories or established local newspapers. Those with artistic inclinations wrote poetry and novels. Although the bulk of this material has disappeared, some has survived, either in manuscript form or in the pages of tattered Victorian local history journals. Even more recently a few "middling" diaries and autobiographies have appeared in modern editions.[28]

The other major body of sources pertaining to this group is court records. Middling people enjoyed a high degree of sophistication when it came to dealing with legal and governmental bureaucracies. They resorted frequently to the courts to resolve business disputes, to combat crimes against their property, to extricate themselves from bad marriages, and to adjudicate problems having to do with inheritance, marriage settlements, guardianship, and debt. And, not infrequently, they got caught up involuntarily in the clutches of the law, either as criminals or as victims. The result is a rich body of court-related material, virtually all of it unpublished, that bears on some of the most intimate aspects of these peoples' lives.[29]

None of these sources is without its problems. Diaries and autobiographies, notoriously, present a highly artificial picture of the writer and his or her context. As William Matthews has pithily remarked, "most diarists pose even to themselves."[30] And any written "first-person" material from this period is susceptible to the charge of being unrepresentative.[31] Court testimony is, arguably, even more "manufactured" than diaries. Its relationship to anything resembling "real" events is often very remote indeed: it inevitably emphasizes conflict, and it has the additional disadvantage of having been recorded by often less-than-attentive court clerks. And yet, sources like these are as close as we are likely to get to the voices of middling people in the eighteenth century.

This study attempts to synthesize a fairly large and scattered body of primary material, much of it little studied in the past. In the process, inevitably, a good deal has been left out. Most provincial archives contain manuscript or printed material bearing on middling folk (typically correspondence, diaries, business records, town directories, club records, and the like); only some of these have been consulted. There are hundreds of thousands of extant middling wills, marriage settlements, and other family records scattered throughout the English archives, and the middling (including, incidentally, thousands of middling women traders and property owners) are heavily represented in eighteenth-century insurance records, which also run to hundreds of thousands of manuscript pages. Samplings rather than systematic coverage were the rule. Other very large bodies of sources (for example ecclesiastical court records, Chancery Masters' Exhibits, and Court of Exchequer records) have been sampled, but by no means systematically surveyed, and non-London courts are left out almost entirely. Newspapers, periodicals, and novels, all important sources for understanding the middling sort and eighteenth-century life more generally, receive much less systematic attention in the present study than they might have, partly because a significant amount of work has already been done on these genres by historians and literary critics, and partly because my research uncovered so many people whose "real lives" read like novels.[32]

In thematic terms, one of the most obvious omissions is middling peoples' formal political role. This should not be taken to mean that the people discussed here lacked municipal or party involvements, but the challenges of tracking specific individuals through poll books, corporation records, and like sources threatened to expand an already overlengthy program of research into the next century.[33] I also chose not to rehearse once again the excellent work that has been done on the work lives of middling men and, particularly, on eighteenth-century commercial and manufacturing firms. The relationship between the middling sort and their servants, workers, and slaves goes largely undiscussed, not because these are not key to the study of the historical dimensions of class, gender, race, and national identity, but because several fine studies have recently been published or are on the verge of appearing which cover these topics in detail.[34]

The chapters follow a fairly straightforward plan, one that, at least for the first six chapters, roughly parallels the middling life cycle. Chapter 1, "Capital, Credit, and the Family," describes the climate of late-seventeenth- and eighteenth-century business, and introduces the theme of the intrusion of credit networks and indebtedness into middling family and kin relations. It explores an apparent shift, somewhere around the beginning of the eighteenth century, from religious to more secular, or at least more utilitarian, explanations for business failure. It looks at the obstacles placed in the way of the pursuit of "possessive individualism" by the nature of middling family life. And it endeavors to paint the backdrop against which the insistent eighteenth-century middling concern with prudential morality arose.

Chapter 2, "A Generation of Vipers: Prudential Virtue and the Sons of Trade," examines the rearing of sons of trading families. It explores the practical and epistemological significance of the heavy emphasis on reading, writing, and accounting for middling boys and also looks at the ways more "prudential" virtues, among them sexual restraint, fitted into the making of the successful businessman. It discusses some of the numerous extrafamilial methods of socialization that arose in the eighteenth century, some of which were quite coercive in character. It also goes in some detail into the ways tensions over money, morality, and parental control acted as a solvent on family ties.

Despite some common features in the rearing of middling sons and daughters, in the final analysis middling girls' position within the family and in society differed profoundly from that of boys. Chapter 3, "To Read, Knit, and Spin: Middling Daughters and the Family Economy," explores the reasons for and some of the implications of this divergence, paying special attention to the constraints placed upon women by the combination of contemporary notions of gender, on the one hand, and the demands of the family economy, on the other. Girls tended to receive a narrower education, less capital, and less encouragement than boys. However, this regime was not universally followed, and even when it was some girls rebelled against its strictures.

The Reformation of Manners was an early and important experiment in civic activism that attracted large numbers of urban middling supporters. Chapter 4, "Just in All Their Dealings: Middling Men and the Reformation of Manners, 1670–1739," examines middling men's participation in the movement, with a particular emphasis upon religious societies for middling youth, and reformers' attempts to clear the streets of prostitutes and homosexuals and to suppress Sunday trading. It delves into the reasons for the Reformation of Manners' popularity among the trading classes, explores the question of why the movement was so heavily male, and examines the extent to which it helped define a public, political role for urban middling men.

Chapter 5, "Eighteenth-Century Middling Women and Trade," deals with general questions about adult middling women's work while focusing particular attention on a small, if buoyant, female trading sector. Beginning with the question of why women's trading activity tended to be on a smaller scale and more marginal than that of men, it goes on to explore the relative impact of women's limited access to capital and married women's disadvantageous position vis-à-vis the establishing of good credit. It looks briefly at the conditions under which some women (most of them spinsters and widows) built up truly successful businesses. Finally, it surveys long-term changes in the social and economic milieu within which women traders sought to operate.

Chapter 6, "The Bonds of Matrimony and the Spirit of Capitalism," examines intersections between the institution of marriage and the concerns of trade and traders. Middling people tended to make large claims for their ability to form ordered, harmonious families. In practice, marriage was an especially conflictual area of middling life. Disagreements over marriage portions, personal expenditures, women's separate property, and sexual matters all worked to disrupt family life. The parlous conditions in which most widows lived showed, in the starkest terms, the long-term results of the tendency in middling families to concentrate resources, notably capital, in the hands of men.

Chapter 7, "Print Culture and the Middling Classes: Mapping the World of Commerce," examines some of the intersections between print culture and middling culture. Printed books flattered commercial peoples' sense of self-worth, emphasized their closeness to God, and underscored their supposedly distinctive ways of looking at the world. Growing literacy gave middling people entré to specialist (often professional) bodies of learning while encouraging more secular modes of understanding and analysis. Finally, commercial ephemera, from printed account books and appointment calendars to town directories, helped disseminate new urban and commercial visions while fostering greater conformity to behavioral and moral norms.

Chapter 8, "Private Order and Political Virtue: Domesticity and the Ruling Class," looks at the ways moral concerns, fueled by the experiences and insecurities of trade, helped to redefine traditional notions about political agency and the ruling class. It discusses the tendency, alive and well in the eighteenth century, to assume a close connection between private (family) order and public (political) virtue. Finally it examines in more detail one response to this: the effort by some moralists to "invent" virtuous aristocrats who, by imitating the middling ranks in the realm of family governance, could reform their peers and their inferiors and solve the problem of emulation once and for all.

CLASS QUESTIONS

Few people would today argue that a class has to be both autonomous and consistently oppositional with respect to the class above it in order to be worthy of the name. Marxists and conservatives alike have been at pains to point out that such a rigid notion of class cannot be reconciled with serious examination of any of the groups that have been said to carry its banner: peasants, working-class people, people of commerce, or, for that matter, elites.[35] It is not so much that these groups (or, more likely, subgroups within them) cannot, at times, be found behaving in classically "oppositional" ways. It is rather that, as Pierre Bourdieu recently put it, "the potency of economic and social differences is never so great that one cannot organize [historical] agents on the basis of other principles of division."[36]

In recent years, however, those "other principles of division" have threatened to drown out claims based upon class. It had been standard for intellectuals on the left to dismiss, say, identification with "a nation" as a sort of conspiracy to divert people from their real problems, a position that, at least in the case of the more militaristic species of nationalism, may not be far wrong (the same argument works rather less well for religious affiliation). But categories such as race and gender—joined more recently by sexuality—have proved considerably harder to reduce to the status of a plot, and the result has been that since the 1970s the analytical field has grown a good deal more complex and the solutions, correspondingly, very much more elusive.

To emphasize race, gender, and sexuality *along with* class is to have to come to terms with collectivities that are riven with internal conflict, that exploit even as they are themselves exploited (and even organize their "culture" precisely around keeping other members of their own group, for instance their women, in a subordinate position).[37] The "membership" of these groups often has widely divergent interests, and their "oppositional" stance may have more to do with hating Jews, Frenchmen, or homosexuals, or (in latter days) shutting the borders to West Indians and Pakistanis, than it does with promoting the class struggle.

A further assault upon the notion of class has come from postmodernism. The issue for this study is neither the fortunes of a group of French intellectuals of the last three decades or so (few of whom, unless I am very much mistaken, are systematically read by most eighteenth-century English historians) nor the often abstruse debates that have raged around the status of the subject, essentialism versus social construction, and the like. Postmodernism is understood here as a broad series of analytic and aesthetic maneuvers common, to a greater or lesser degree, to all the humanistic disciplines in the last twenty-odd years. Perhaps its most characteristic move has been to cast doubt upon analytic and organizational categories that were previously taken for granted. Those categories that have, in postmodern parlance, come under the heaviest interrogation are, precisely, groupings clustered around class, race, gender, nationality, ethnicity, and sexuality. Within the discipline of history, one result of this has been an updated form of empiricism that, at its best, is a good deal less committed to the maintenance of the status quo than the empiricism of the 1950s and 1960s had been.[38]

If the notion of class is in such a bad way, why does this study bother to resuscitate it? Class in the orthodox Marxian sense (or sens*es*, for it was always a contested concept) may be obsolete, but many of the historical questions that have traditionally surrounded it are not. It is perhaps worth reminding ourselves that the notion of class originally arose in the late eighteenth and early nineteenth centuries not as a preemptive strike against Tory historians but as a way to make sense of contemporary experiences, observations, and problems. Karl Marx, David Ricardo, and even, at moments, Adam Smith, may have defined their terms too rigidly, emphasized particular aspects of social existence to the detriment of others, or adopted overelaborate cyclical schemata.[39] But their ideas about class drew heavily on eighteenth- and early-nineteenth-century inquiries about the meaning of social collectivities. To jettison class is to turn one's back upon a rich body of contemporary observation and debate.

Class, as the term is used here, is a more contingent, more insecure category than it was for most late-eighteenth- and nineteenth-century theorists. There is enough evidence of "homogeneity of conditions" among people in roughly the middle rank of eighteenth-century English society to justify lumping them together for heuristic purposes under rubrics such as "the middling sort" or "the trading classes."[40] A central part of these people's individual and collective story had to do with the negotiation of identity in an unfamiliar and in many ways inhospitable economic environment, and perforce this gave rise to numerous commonalities in their experiences and concerns, particularly their moral concerns. At the same time, their "identities" were powerfully divided. The middling sort was not a unified group, either at the political level or at the level of the neighborhood, the family, or the married couple. The story of premodern English capitalism, and of the people who were centrally involved in overseeing its birth, was fundamentally one of conflict, insecurity, and uncertainty, not of unity or group consensus.

In keeping with its emphasis upon conflict, this is a study of the fortunes of middling families rather than a story about how a "class" made itself. Here my approach differs from that of John Smail, among others. My reluctance to make class formation central to my story does not derive from a principled belief that the topic cannot or should not be studied. Rather it is a question of preference and the nature of the sources used. People do form social and political clusters and collectivities, and they do (albeit temporarily) arrive at cultural consensus. I talk about these where appropriate. But this study focuses on the way individuals struggled (and often failed) to make their way more than on their ephemeral achievement of a particular kind of group identity. I also agree with Smail that class formation can only really be studied, and may only "happen" at the local level.[41] The people and families examined in this study came from cities and towns all over England. Their responses to historical stasis and change were powerfully influenced by local conditions, differences of rank and income, individual (and family) idiosyncrasy, and fickle fortune. They resist assimilation into a new "grand theory" that aims to show precisely when, how, or why the "English middle class" emerged.

DEFINING THE MIDDLING SORT

The terms *middling sort, middling classes, trading classes,* and *commercial classes* are used in this study—as they were used in the eighteenth century—more or less interchangeably to refer to shopkeepers, manufacturers, better-off independent artisans, civil servants, professionals, lesser merchants, and the like. These people were beneath the gentry but above the level of the laboring classes; most of them worked for a living, although a growing number lived wholly or partially on rental income and other investments.[42]

The composition and outline of the middling sort is, and must remain, somewhat vague. Let us try for a little more specificity in demographic terms. Rank is never purely a function of income, but it is seldom utterly divorced from it, either. Individual circumstances varied, but at the bare minimum an urban householder in the eighteenth century needed £50 to £80 a year to sustain a lifestyle and a level of "independence" commensurate with middling status.[43] By contrast, a female servant might make little more than a few pounds a year, plus room and board, while the wages of a day laborer or journeyman might range between £8 and £35 a year. At the other extreme, some hereditary aristocrats were bringing in as much as £20,000 a year in 1700 and considerably more a century later.[44] Most middling people had incomes between £50 and £2,000, and the bulk of these were concentrated within the range of £80 to £150. However, increasing numbers of commercial people, especially in the larger urban centers such as London or Bristol, were able to top £10,000 through involvements in long-distance trade, wholesaling, finance, real estate, industry and office-holding. Indeed, a few made £100,000 or more, rivaling or even exceeding the richest aristocrats. When a trader's income goes much above £5,000 or so, a term like "middling" begins to seem more than a little strained. On the other hand, it should not be assumed that all commercial people who competed with the upper gentry in terms of income necessarily adopted their mores wholesale.

"Now I pray you, what is a commercial nation, but a collection of commercial towns?" asked George Chalmers, author of *An Estimate of the Comparative Strength of Great Britain.*[45] This study does focus largely upon commercial people in the towns, yet one might with some justice ask, *pace* Chalmers, how appropriate it is, even very late in the century, to identify the middling classes so narrowly with urban centers. All western European economies in the early modern period were heavily reliant upon the movement of foodstuffs, raw and finished materials, luxury goods, and labor forces between the rural hinterland and the towns. Many urban middling folk had relatives and trading connections in more rural areas. Quite a few of the middling were themselves amphibious, hailing from yeoman or smallholder stock, or were from the threadbare lesser gentry and hanging on to ancestral agricultural land even as they plighted their troth to the world of commerce. Just as towns and cities took in agricultural products, raw materials, and immigrants in search of jobs or apprenticeships, they busily exported "urban" culture to the countryside in the form of newspapers and periodicals, fashions, novels, traveling theatrical troupes, political programs, and religious movements. This study focuses on the middling in towns and cities for three reasons. First, urban centers contained high concentrations of such people. Second, they were centers of rising literacy, publishing, and record keeping (many of these records are still extant). And third, they tended to encourage such predominantly middling institutions and enterprises as moral reform societies, trade directories, newspapers, and proprietorial schools.[46]

As all social historians know, towns and cities were socially disparate, with large contingents of the laboring poor, many of whom were arrivals from the countryside, and small but socially and politically prominent scatterings of gentle folk, who were sometimes connected by marriage to local captains of commerce. What percentage of the average town was made up of people who might be termed "middling"? For the early period all we have is guesswork, derived through extrapolation from somewhat firmer late-eighteenth-century estimates, themselves based primarily upon the not entirely satisfactory criterion of income. Leonard Schwarz, working from London tax assessments, places some 2 to 3 percent of the London population in 1798 in the "upper income" bracket (average £200 a year) and 16 to 21 percent in the "middling" bracket (£80 to £139 a year). The remaining 75 percent is comprised of a diverse body of small shopkeepers, smaller independent artisans, wage laborers, and the unemployed.[47] Peter Earle, in turn, uses these figures and other data compiled by Schwarz as a rough indicator of the "class" breakdown in London for the period 1660 to 1730. He suggests that 20 to 25 percent of London's population was made up of people in the "middle station."[48] London is not necessarily representative—cities and towns varied greatly in size, function, and relationship to the surrounding countryside—yet a 20 percent figure (the lower end of Earle's range) for the number of middling people in the average town seems a plausible, if conservative, guess.

What might this have meant in national terms? Between 1700 and 1800 the English population grew from approximately five million to roughly eight and one-half million. If one considers an urban center to begin at 2,500 people, as does Penelope Corfield, the English *and Welsh* urban population together grew from about 970,000 (19.4 percent of the total population) in 1700 to 2.7 million (31.4 percent of the total population) a century later.[49] E. A. Wrigley, who takes as his cutoff point for an urban center a population of 5,000, estimates that the total urban population of England rose from 850,000 in 1700 (17 percent of the total) to 2.38 million in 1801 (27.5 percent of the total). By either measure, the number of English people living in cities rose sharply over the course of the eighteenth century, with almost two-thirds of this growth occurring outside London.[50] Piling estimates on other estimates begins very quickly to seem a fanciful enterprise, but let us press on nonetheless. We can, starting from the above figures, estimate that there were perhaps 170,000 *urban* middling people (defined, in this case, solely on the less than satisfactory basis of income) in England in 1700 and, perhaps, 475,000 by 1801. These figures leave out an indeterminate number of people in villages and smaller county towns who may have differed little in cultural terms from the people living in areas of more concentrated population.[51]

The main benefit of such demographic artifacts is that they permit us to make some broad comparisons with other social groupings, most notably with the gentry and aristocracy, who made up a very much smaller proportion of the population. The middling may not have been a huge group, but in sheer numerical terms they dwarfed the gentry and aristocracy. There were 173 peers in 1700 and 267 in 1801.[52] The gentry were more numerous, of course, and are also more difficult to pin down as a category. G. E. Mingay estimates that in the eighteenth century there were some 1,000 families in the upper gentry, perhaps 2,000 in the lesser gentry, and as many as 10,000 in that more amorphous—and expanding—group who called themselves "gentlemen": lesser esquires, men of respectable lineage who had lost their estates, the better class of professional men, retired military officers, former merchants, and the like.[53] In short, the middling constituted a quite large group in comparison with their social superiors. More significantly, they were a group which, fueled by the spread of commerce, a rising standard of living, the appeal of towns, and an expanding government bureaucracy, was growing very fast indeed in the eighteenth century.

THE MIDDLING AND THE WORLD OF TRADE

The establishment of the Bank of England in 1694 was both a highly significant moment in the development of the English state and a splendid piece of public relations for commerce and commercial people. England in the 1690s already possessed a fairly buoyant economy (drooping in some sectors, it is true, under the impact of war), but the founding of the Bank was a resounding vote of confidence for the projectors, for the notion of paper investments, for the charging of interest, and for commercial men conceiving their commercial plans and talking their commercial talk. It is possible to exaggerate the pace of economic growth in the ensuing three-quarters of a century.[54] Nonetheless, over the course of the eighteenth century, England came to look like a modern nation in many ways, partly as a result of the growth of state finance. The civil service so grew in both size and efficiency that by the century's end no part of England was untouched by the power of the state. New, more "modern" forms of commodity distribution led to the demise of a good many, although certainly not all, of the more localized productive and distributive networks. Cities grew at a faster rate in England than anywhere else in Europe, spawning new consumption patterns, impressive building projects, and a considerable increase in businesses that provided services, from eating establishments, hairdressers, and hackney-coaches to, late in the period, commercial banks, libraries, and infirmaries. In 1759 the Excise Office counted 141,700 shops, *not* including stalls at fairs, purely wholesale outlets or alehouses, or "shops above stairs."[55] Finally, the opening of new markets and shipping routes across a far-flung empire drew a surprising range of people into the business and the ethos of overseas conquest and expansion.

Economic growth, then as now, required personnel. More shops demanded more shopkeepers and also more wholesalers. A growing state apparatus meant more civil servants, and because one of the big growth sectors was customs and excise, there was a thriving demand for men who possessed some knowledge of commerce. The task of carrying an increased volume of goods across long distances spawned agents, financiers, hostelers, warehousemen, shipbuilders, and canal engineers. Eighteenth-century English people adopted new manufacturing processes with less alacrity than scholars once thought, but there is no doubt that the demand for specialized technical and scientific knowledge increased. The growth in overseas trade and the expanding financial infrastructure provided jobs for people who could manipulate numbers, anticipate demand, organize business networks, and cope with the intricacies of the law. And, finally, the personal needs, thirst for knowledge and culture, and moral and religious concerns of people with money in their pockets supported an expanding body of lawyers, doctors, educators, journalists, artists, musicians, and clergymen.[56]

The "middling professional" demands some additional discussion. The center of gravity of the middling sort (and the focus of this study) was families that were engaged directly in trade or commerce. On the other hand, many professionals were so caught up in the social and cultural milieu of commerce that it would be absurd to exclude them. It is unquestionably the case that some professionals possessed an income, a level of prestige, and a range of connections that placed them on a par with elites. Sons of the gentry, moreover, were more concentrated in the professions than they ever were in trade.[57]

The real growth sector in the eighteenth-century professions, however, lay in providing services to the urban middling sort. Medical men, largely physicians, who could confine their practices to "Society" were few and tended to be located in London or the richer provincial cities. The middling patronized apothecaries and surgeons and helped, over the course of the eighteenth century, to make these professions more respectable. By the same token, most lawyers were not majestically and lucratively associated with the prestigious London-based courts. They were humbler and less lavishly remunerated men who earned their daily bread arranging conveyancing, doing probate work, drafting marriage settlements, brokering business deals, serving in municipal office, doing business in the numerous local courts still to be found throughout England, and investing other middling peoples' money for them. Generally, such men went through a regular apprenticeship to a practicing proctor or solicitor (although some did not even do that) and their firms were often hard to distinguish from other types of businesses.[58]

One of the largest, although hardly the most prestigious, growth sectors among the eighteenth-century professions was that of schoolteacher. Schools *were* businesses, and they often "failed" in just the way other businesses did. As the only "professional" occupation that included women, schoolteaching was an especially variegated category. Old women who taught reading and writing at a few pence per student, spinsters or widows who kept boarding schools for girls, accountants who taught bookkeeping on the side, those who organized full-scale academies (such as the well-known clergyman, the Rev. Philip Doddridge)—all were in some sense schoolteachers. And most, although not all, of these people would have served a predominantly middling clientele.[59]

The clergy was a diverse body. Many of them, Anglicans as well as dissenters, came from trading backgrounds, ministered almost exclusively to trading people, and were thoroughly immersed in urban business culture.

We find such men dedicating their tracts to businessmen, building their sermons around the crudest of mercantile analogies so as to make them more relevant to their trading congregations, and speaking explicitly to the moral and sometimes, the business concerns of people of commerce.[60] A good many professionals, journalists and clergymen preeminently among them, were in a real sense "public men." They actually made a living by writing and speaking in an age in which respectable people avidly followed both printed literature and sermons. It would be too much to call such men (and very occasionally women) spokespeople for the middling: there is copious evidence to show that nonprofessionals among the middling were fully capable of speaking for themselves. Still, professionals did constitute the intellectual fringe of the middling sort. Possessed in a good many cases of a more expansive education than other middling people, often including a knowledge of Latin, they were in an especially favorable position to mediate between the workaday culture of tradesmen and the more genteel culture of their betters.[61] Most professionals remained linked to the world of commerce by breeding and by the men and women they served, yet they also retained some additional prestige by virtue of their status as purveyors of specialist knowledge.

CONCLUSION

The middling sort comprised the people who conceived and executed the bulk of the projects, large and small, successful and unsuccessful, tangible and intangible, that combined to make up the world of eighteenth-century commerce. Everyman and everywoman they were not: beneath them stretched a sea of the less fortunate, a good 70 or 75 percent of the urban population and an even larger percentage of the total population, who, when they could get work at all, labored on someone else's materials or in someone else's fields, household, or manufactory. The middling prided themselves, not without a covert glance over their shoulders, on what they called their "independence." Even that growing number who were technically employees—of the state bureaucracy, of the new municipal institutions, of a body like the East India Company—liked to believe that they possessed an independence of intellect and expertise not given to their inferiors.

Trade was a fickle master, and the instability of commerce and investment cast a mantle of anxious foreboding over the eighteenth-century middling classes, claims of independence notwithstanding. Edward Gibbon, author of *The Decline and Fall of the Roman Empire*, admirer of Roman civic virtue, and indefatigable chronicler of the precariousness of human projects, may have had one of his earliest introductions to the latter through the example of his grandfather, one of those same "big bourgeoisie" of

Augustan London and a director of the South Sea Company, who in 1720, in the midst of the South Sea fiasco, was stripped by Parliament of a fortune exceeding £100,000. As Gibbon was later to put it, in a marvelously intertextual moment, "[H]e was buried in its [the South Sea Company's] ruins, and the labours of thirty years were blasted in a single day." It is to that latter species of trauma, one with which even the cream of the commercial classes was familiar, that we now turn.[62]

CHAPTER ONE

Capital, Credit, and the Family

[Of Credit]
I cannot now enter into her private Recesses, when she concerns her self with
Families, Persons, and Things—Long Accounts might be given of her there; there
she blesses and blasts just as she pleases.
DANIEL DEFOE, *REVIEW OF THE STATE OF THE BRITISH NATION* 6, NO. 35
(25 JUNE 1709)

A Prison will pay no Deatt.
FRANCIS FISHER, STOCKING PRESSER, FROM DEBTOR'S PRISON, TO ONE OF HIS
CREDITORS, JANE FRANKLIN, SOAPBOILER IN VAUXHALL, 4 NOVEMBER 1722[1]

In 1759 Philip Eliot, a London merchant and underwriter, lay dying. As
the old man moved fitfully in and out of consciousness he dreamed a
dream that struck his nephew so forcefully when he heard of it that he
took the trouble to write it down in his journal:

> A man came to arrest [my uncle] for debt and pushed him into a corner.
> "Wait," replied he, "I have money to pay you." "Oh," said the man, "that is
> not the thing, this debt is not to be paid with Money." When he awoke he
> recounted this dream to his nurse and said that he knew well that the person
> who had appeared to him was Death and that his time had come.[2]

The metaphors the unconscious reaches for in its hour of distress speak as
much to the daily concerns of the living as they do to the fears of the dying.
This dream actually follows a quite standard pattern, articulated as early as
1600 in Christopher Sutton's *Disce Mori; Learne to Die:* "Death comes like a
sergeant in an action of debt, at the suit of nature to attach and arrest us
all."[3] This chapter will describe some of the particular anxieties that came
with living in and attempting to profit from an underdeveloped society
and economy, one in which there was little structural support for capitalist
endeavor and in which what ideological support there was competed furi-
ously with older ways of looking at family, society, the economy, and God.

FAMILY SOLIDARITY AND CAPITALIST RISK

In the seventeenth and eighteenth centuries people accumulated investment capital almost exclusively through personal connections. There were

very few lending institutions capable of responding to this need until very late in the period. Consequently, people wishing to set up in business most often relied on inheritance, their wives' dowries, loans from relatives and "friends," and credit extended by other traders.[4] The fact that business risks were shouldered for the most part by individuals and families rather than banks or investment firms was echoed in a legal system in which the distinction between business liability and personal and family liability was extremely vague. Limited liability is an accumulation of legal principle, institutions, and practices, aimed at distinguishing sharply between personal or private assets and liabilities and business assets and liabilities. As a problem in the history of ideas, the rise of limited liability has been relatively little studied; were it to be investigated it would undoubtedly tell us a great deal about the ways capitalist institutions worked their way into British life and British minds. But the fact remains that, for much of the period covered by this study, impounding household goods for the payment of business debts and imprisoning people for insolvency—practices which failed to distinguish between "private" and "public" spheres—were the rule rather than the exception.[5]

What were the implications of this for the relationship between trade and families? It meant that it was very difficult for people with even very peripheral involvements in trade to remain detached from the insecurities of commerce. Many individuals or families who were not themselves in trade had surplus funds tied up in relatives' enterprises. Often, especially in middling families, they were also bound as personal sureties for additional debts. The landed classes could mortgage their estates on extremely favorable terms, but few of the middling possessed freehold land, and among such people creditors relied instead upon the presumed strength of kin ties to ensure ultimate payment. If catastrophe struck, the moral onus was on kin to try to stave off eviction or the seizure of a relative's goods or, at the last resort, to get the family out of debtor's prison. Early modern English business activity relied upon the willingness of ordinary families to shoulder risks that most middle-class people today would view as unacceptable.

It is also the case that the bonds of kinship extended more widely and more deeply than they tend to do today. A considerable amount of evidence suggests that in the eighteenth century many people, and not just the middling, took extremely seriously their responsibility to contribute, if it was at all within their power, to the setting-up costs and ongoing capital needs of relatives as far removed as cousins or nephews, and sometimes those even more remote.[6] Apparently the expectation of profit was only one motivating factor: there appears to have existed a strong presumption that one should contribute even in cases where the ability of one's relative to realize a profit or even remain solvent was questionable. Of course, relatives were sometimes denied assistance, but one refused them only at the risk of gaining a reputation for being self-centered and miserly among one's kin and the community at large. Equally, by denying aid, one endangered or even forfeited one's own place in the network of mutual assistance.

Loyalty to kin had functional and symbolic importance in premodern societies. As an ideal, and no doubt to a lesser extent in practice, it helped people to make sense of a society in which bureaucratic structures were few, authority was for most intents and purposes lodged in households, and social valuations at all levels of society were often more related to blood and ancestry than to individual merit. At the level of the nuclear family unit it provided some reassurance to parents that they would be supported in old age. It also gave them moral leverage with respect to the important matter of disposing of the labor of their children. Loyalty to more extended kin provided a framework on which to base the sharing or swapping of scarce resources. It also constituted a kind of insurance policy against being left entirely alone, as well as a way of ensuring that most people at most times of their lives would be under someone's guardianship. This was a matter of no small moment in a society in which a staggering proportion of people were half or full orphans from a very early age, and where it was by no means uncommon to have had all one's children die before one reached old age.

Although often beneficial, close kin ties were full of potential for friction, particularly when the issue at hand was the distribution of scarce and coveted resources. Close ties based on kin, and especially kin-based resource sharing, had undoubted advantages for early modern entrepreneurs. In the first place they provided investment opportunities. Opportunities for safe investments were few in the early modern period, and family businesses were one option over which one could, or felt one could, have a certain amount of control, if only because there were moral sanctions that could be used against relatives if they defaulted or absconded which were not available with nonrelatives. It was also the case that internal discipline within trading communities with respect to the payment of debts, honest dealing, prompt remittances, and the like, was low, and may even have declined with the waning of medieval guild controls. From the perspective of the smooth operation of trade in general, kin-based loyalty helped to distribute risk by placing a heavy load of guilt and community disapproval on those people who did not help relatives by paying their debts in time of dire need. Kin-based systems of moral enforcement and resource sharing helped compensate for the absence of a developed infrastructure of business ethics, commercial law, finance, and communication.

The latter part of the seventeenth century saw some important changes in the context within which both moral enforcement and resource sharing took place. One new development was the rise of investment opportunities that were more secure than were investments in a family business or in trade generally. In symbolic terms the most important of these was the Bank of England, which began inviting subscriptions for loans and selling annuities in 1694.[7] By 1700 there were a range of annuity schemes, and lottery, stock, and municipal bond options available to the man or woman with money to invest. The subscribers to these schemes, although they included members of the landed classes, were throughout the entire first half of the eighteenth century drawn disproportionately from the London mercantile and professional classes and from government office holders. According to P. G. M. Dickson "they were merchants, bankers, brokers, jobbers, clergymen, doctors, lawyers, shopkeepers, artisans."[8] A fairly typical investor would have been a man like Samuel Jeake of Rye, who moved in the 1690s away from money-lending, marine insurance, and trading in products such as hops, honey, and French cloth (Jeake's trade was heavily dependent on family networks in the City of London and Southwark) in order to concentrate the bulk of his money in the funds, notably in Bank of England and East India stock and at least one lottery scheme.[9]

Tens of thousands of trading people speculated in the financial market in the eighteenth century and many more became urban rentiers, another sector that was becoming increasingly popular with the lesser investor.[10] But the scale of their involvement must have had the effect of diverting funds from other sorts of investments, including lending to family members. And this, in turn, might well be expected to have had some impact on contemporary notions of what it meant to belong to a family. It may not be entirely coincidental that, in the opening decades of the eighteenth century, at least one well-known moralist could be found arguing for the legitimacy of refusing assistance to imprudent and extravagant relatives.

The Reverend William Fleetwood (1656–1723) was a lecturer at St. Dunstan-in-the-West, Fleet Street, and, from 1714, Bishop of Ely. His well-known tract of 1705, *The Relative Duties of Parents and Children, Husbands and Wives, Master and Servants* contained a discussion of disinheriting that turned on just this issue of personal morality and resource distribution between relatives (in this case between generations). Confronted with the problem of "notorious vice" in an heir, Fleetwood declared:

> There is no body thinks that the compassions of Nature, (which are oftentimes its weakness) should carry it above the considerations of Virtue and Goodness; i.e., that a Child should without dispute, succeed to all the advantages of Honour, and Estate, let him be never so vicious and immoral . . . only because he happened to be born of such Parents.[11]

At first sight this looks like old-style patriarchalism. However, in the same discussion Fleetwood presented a startling critique of one of the traditional grounds for disinheriting: a child abandoning a parent in captivity when he could "with his ease" have saved him.[12] This stricture dated from an entirely different era, one, presumably, in which upper-class feuding did sometimes place people in the position of having to ransom relatives, and it clearly bothered Fleetwood. After all, in his own time the most common reason for imprisonment was nonpayment of debts, and Fleetwood was inclined to think that in such cases the moral liability of children for their parents was rather diminished:

> We must not hastily conclude, that all children offend against their Duty, who do not pay their Parents Debts and deliver them from bonds and imprisonment; for sometimes the Children are just able to live themselves, and have Families of their own to maintain, and if they should discharge their Parents Debts must contract new ones of their own: and sometimes Parents are so extravagant that there would be no end of paying for them, and therefore all things must be well considered, before we condemn the Children who suffer their Parents to lie in Prison or Captivity.[13]

Thus a child should discharge a parent's debt only if he could do so with no great inconvenience, and he was permitted, indeed encouraged, to take into account the parent's character in deciding whether to lend assistance.[14]

Fleetwood may not have been representative of attitudes on disinheriting at the turn of the eighteenth century, and his position on the conditions under which one could refuse to pay for one's parents' release from prison may even have been rather radical for its time. It is notable that, like most family tract writers of the period, Fleetwood continued to conceive of families and households primarily in terms of the duties of members toward one another, particularly the duty of inferior members of the household (servants, children, and women) toward the head. It is only occasionally that anything resembling "economic individualism" is permitted to contravene these duties, and in such cases the justification is not couched in individual terms at all, but in terms of the survival of one patriarchal family group in preference to another. Debt and insolvency raised these kinds of tensions about individual, as opposed to family, duties (and also duty to one's immediate family versus duty to extended kin) in an especially emotionally charged way.

What was one to do when one's relatives were unable to pay their debts and appealed for help? In 1701 the pious and learned Elizabeth Bury (1644–1720) of Clare, Suffolk, was faced with just this problem:

> In perplexing Difficulties about the Relief of my poor Relations, for fear of dishonouring GOD, by intangling myself in Debts, or in denying what Help might be in my Power to the Afflicted.[15]

Bury readily equated personal financial loss with dishonouring God, a position that could help to justify what others might term selfish conduct (that is, failing to provide help) but that also reflects an era in which bankrupts, at least among dissenters, faced not just disgrace but, in some cases, excommunication. Bury's "perplexing difficulties" also hinted at some larger issues. For some the fear of dishonoring God was beginning to pale when compared with the fear of losing everything else: credit, friends, reputation, much of one's property, and even one's personal freedom. What profits a man if he gains his soul and loses the world? Bernard Mandeville was to put it somewhat differently. "Men seem to repose no greater Trust in Providence than they would in a Broken Merchant," he remarked only a few decades later, admittedly in the face of an especially shocking demonstration of the strange workings of Providence in the sphere of business.[16]

How in practice did people justify refusing to invest their capital in their relative's enterprises? And what sanctions were available on the part of families to keep individuals from shirking their responsibilities toward their kin? Samuel Marriott was a clerk of the London Guildhall who had received a small inheritance from his father. In the 1720s or earlier he struggled with his conscience about whether to invest in his brother's hosiery and ironmongery business in return for a 9 percent annual payment. A lonely and somewhat obsessive man with little to recommend him to the outside world save a handsome copying hand, Marriott described his mental torments in a small octavo volume, illuminating, as few other contemporary documents do, how considerations of risk, as well as of profit, could erode older conceptions of responsibility to kin. Torn between "the higher Duties we owe to intimate Friends such as Trust & Familiarity and venturing our Lives and Fortunes for them, and espousing their interests with particular zeal and concern" and the knowledge that investing in the Corporation of the City of London offered "a better Security, than that of any one single Person whatsoever," he finally opted for the City Corporation.[17]

This young clerk's travails of spirit speak volumes about the more personal side of the rush to invest in the public funds that followed on the Glorious Revolution. Driven to justify a decision even he suspected was unnatural, Samuel Marriott filled some 150 manuscript pages with the wrongs previously done to him by his brother, wrongs of such magnitude (cheating him out of his rightful inheritance and the like) that he could, in conscience, treat him as an enemy rather than a brother and invest elsewhere. Conveniently for Marriott, this was an issue that seems to have been in the air. A number of learned divines had recently been drawn to the theme of the impracticality, especially to businessmen, of overstrict interpretations of biblical injunctions such as "love your neighbor as yourself," "love your enemies," and "turn the other cheek." The burden of the clerics' argument was that loving your neighbor as yourself was *not* meant to suggest that you should let your neighbor take advantage of you. Nor did it mean (and here some of the examples specifically addressed the problem of "neighbors" who were also brothers or other close kin) that you were duty-bound to put your relative's economic well-being above your own.[18] Not too surprisingly, Marriott seized with relief upon authorities such as these.

Perhaps the most telling part of this whole episode, as Marriott had foreseen, was the response of his relatives to his decision to invest in the Corporation of London rather than in his brother's business. The move cost him the good will of all the rest of his siblings as well as an aged uncle who later virtually disowned him. Some years earlier this uncle had taken offense when Samuel obtained a bond from his father to ensure that he would not change his will in Samuel's brother's favor (Samuel, although the eldest son, was partially crippled, and because of this disability his father had vacillated about how much to leave to him). When Samuel, rather understandably, sought legal means to protect his own future security, his uncle accused him of being a "vexatious & litigious person and Lover of Law & Trouble" and argued that to require a bond from one's own father was "an unnatural thing . . . [and] invallid in the law."[19] Eventually Marriott was shamed into burning the bond, an unwise move since his father almost immediately seized the opportunity to change his will in the brother's favor. Now Samuel's refusal to invest in his brother's business supplied another excuse for persecuting him. At family dinners the uncle, who had apparently inherited the role of family patriarch, took a perverse delight in accusing Samuel of being "nothing but self" and of having a "greedy and covetous temper"; other relatives were less direct but just as wounding. Possessive individualism in this early-eighteenth-century extended family was practiced at a considerable psychic price. For Marriott the conflict between his own interests and those of his brother and the suspicion that he might really be the covetous person his family claimed he was seem to have poisoned a good part of his adult life.[20]

Almost identical arguments about one's duties to one's brother, or more precisely about the question of where one's obligation ceased, are found in a piece by a contemporary of Marriott's, Roderick Mackenzie (fl. 1711–1725). Mackenzie's "Apologia," originally intended for publication, outlined his reasons for committing his own brother to prison for a £750 debt.[21] It was written in response to his brother's "more scandalous Emissaries & Partizans" who

> have rais'd a most hideous *out-cry* against me, upon the foot of my pretended *Cruelty* & *unnaturality* to my own *Brother*, and an *Older Brother* too: what? to detain him in Prison, all this time? If he ow'd me ever so much money his very imprisonment ought to be deem'd a full & satisfactory Revenge: but to

continue him there! This is such *Cruelty* as no good man who had any Bowels of Compassion would be guilty of & c.[22]

Mackenzie was willing to own that the prisoner was his brother ("tho not my eldest"), but he maintained he was "commanded *to love my Brother, or my neighbour as my self*, not better than myself." He had actually hurt his own and his immediate family's well-being, he claimed, by his ill-considered generosity and compassion toward a brother who paid him back with treachery, breach of trust, perjury, and lies, finally contriving to utterly "murder my *Good Name, Reputation, Credit & Interest.*"[23] Like Marriott, he could no longer persuade himself to call his adversary his brother: "by your abominable ingratitude . . . you have too justly forfeited . . . that appelative."[24]

These unappetizing family disputes provide powerful evidence for the continued strength of community norms that opposed a single standard of economic practice for both kin and non-kin. It was standard procedure for creditors to resort to imprisonment to enforce payment of debts, but one was not supposed to imprison one's relatives even if the debt was quite large. Having violated these norms, Mackenzie was forced to argue that his brother's extravagant immorality actually dissolved the "natural" duties and responsibilities that contemporaries understood to accrue to kinship. The Reverend Fleetwood had the luxury of theorizing; Mackenzie and Marriott experienced in their own lives the conflict between two value systems, one stressing obligations toward kin, the other concerned with individual profit and loss. In the long run the process by which individualistic economic behavior came to be normative owed much to the rise of large and fairly impersonal business institutions and investment opportunities that allowed some people to escape with their money from the psychic morass of family needs.

BUSINESS RISK AND PERSONAL CREDIT

Reliance on relatively unsecured capital from family and friends, lack of supporting institutions such as banks or insurance facilities, and virtually unlimited liability of individuals and families for debts contracted in the course of business were a feature of trade at least since the middle ages.[25] But the late seventeenth century was a very different place from the twelfth or thirteenth centuries. Not only had there been a significant increase in population; proportionally fewer people were now engaged in subsistence agriculture and far more lived in towns or in locales where they were required to obtain foodstuffs and other necessities by exchange. The opening of trade routes to the Far East and the colonizing of the West Indies and North America not only opened up new markets for English goods but also created a range of new consumer demands at home that could only be satisfied through trade. Moreover, significant numbers of the English were better off in material terms than their counterparts had been a century earlier, and they often responded to this by buying things that their ancestors had once produced themselves.[26]

Around 1650, agricultural production, manufacturing, and overseas trade appear to have begun expanding at a considerably accelerated pace relative to the previous one hundred years.[27] This growth was to be sustained through the period of industrialization, and it soon enabled England to eclipse her main mercantile rival, the Netherlands, in foreign trade, to build up the largest merchant marine in the world, and, after about 1675, to enjoy an almost continual national surplus of grain, an important factor in giving England one of the highest, perhaps the highest, standard of living in Europe.[28]

The relatively favorable economic climate of much of the eighteenth century did not mean that the average market actor had an easy time of it. To understand both how middling people responded to social and economic developments in the late seventeenth and early eighteenth centuries and how they helped to shape them, it is necessary to look in more detail at some of the ways early modern businesses actually functioned.

A chronic problem afflicting England throughout the period was a shortage of coin. The growing volume of business demanded far more money than the treasury, still geared to a more sluggish economy, was able or willing to supply. And a proliferation of clipped and counterfeit money and private tokens of questionable worth, plus the fluctuating value of precious metals, eroded still further public confidence in coin as a medium of exchange. As a result, traders and others relied heavily on bonds, notes, cheques, and book debts—that is to say, on paper credit.[29] These instruments were extremely unreliable unless secured by a fairly stable and responsible institution. Such institutions were in short supply, and it appears that the bulk of business was carried out on the basis of credit secured only by the reputation of the debtor or the debtor's family, or worse, on nothing but the knowledge that the person demanding credit would only do business on those terms.

Thanks to research by Andrew Federer it is now possible to say quite a bit about the day-to-day operations of urban traders and manufacturers, and particularly about the ways in which networks of credit and debt affected the organization of work as well as the continued viability of individual businesses.[30] In eighteenth-century Westminster, very much a zone of expanding market activity, hard cash was in such short supply as to represent a less important medium of exchange than was credit in terms of defining the structure of work.[31] In one coachmaking business that Federer subjected to microscopic analysis, book debts (that is, outstanding debts owed the firm by customers) for the period between 1769 and 1785 fluctuated between three and more than four times the firm's liquid assets (cash in hand and stock) for the entire time.[32] This meant that, at any given time, the firm was, as Federer puts it, "so finely poised" between its current obligations and the funds it actually had available as to render the business very insecure.[33]

Coachmaking, because of the elevated character of its clientele, was more likely to carry an extremely large debt burden than some other trades.[34] But weighty and delicately balanced structures of credit and debt characterized most trades, even if they did not cater to the elite.[35] Personal accounts by traders from the late seventeenth and eighteenth centuries attest to the fact that the problem of overstretched credit was virtually omnipresent in trading communities across the length and breadth of England. Heavy reliance on credit or problems of insolvency were not, of course, confined to persons in trade. However, because traders stood at the hub of the exchange system they tended to be affected in a very direct way by reversals in any sector. One well-known case will suffice to show a pattern that was virtually universal. In 1697 William Stout, a Lancaster grocer and ironmonger did a ten-year accounting of business profit and loss and found that in the previous nine years' trading he had had to write off debts totaling £220 by 248 insolvent debtors. Since in that time he had made an average yearly profit of £100, desperate (uncollectible) debts were equivalent to two years' profit. There is no reason to think Stout's experience was unusual.[36]

The shaky structure of trade and enterprise coupled with the lack of clear boundaries between the family and entrepreneurship lent a special precariousness to English middling life. A closer look at William Stout's career demonstrates this at almost every turn. He began in business with certain advantages: he had £50 and a parcel of land inherited from his father worth another £69.10s. He had also received a fairly thorough education and served an apprenticeship with a Quaker ironmonger and grocer. (Stout himself became a Quaker convert, but his industrious and very improving parents were "of the communion of the Episcopal Protestant religion and observant of the rites and ceremonies thereof.")[37] Preparatory to setting up shop in 1688, Stout liquidated all his assets and borrowed another £22, £10 of it from his sister. He then set off for London with £120 to buy goods, getting, as he tells us, "of sundry persons goods to the value of two hundred pounds or upwards and paid each of them about halfe ready money, as was then usual to do by any young man beginning trade." Before Stout ever concluded a single sale he was already in debt for at least £100. Had he been robbed on the trip down, had the ketch in which he transported his goods home been sunk, had there been a fire in the shop, he and his family would have been plunged into destitution. As it was, by the end of the year he was in red by £40: "I had been too forward in trusting [extending credit], and too backward in calling [demanding payment], as is too frequent with young tradesmen." He was forced to borrow the money at interest and, in typical fashion, the lender insisted that both his brother and his cousin be bound with him as surety for the repayment of the loan.[38]

By dint of very hard work, an abstemious lifestyle, and assistance from his sister Ellin, coupled with a concerted effort to settle balances with debtors once a year so as to "get in what money I could without borrowing," traveling to London with packs of tradesmen for protection against robbers, sending goods by land (which, although dear, was safer than risking loss to the privateers), and saving fuel costs (he had become inured to extreme cold in his childhood), Stout managed to stay afloat and eventually realize a profit of £100 a year. All about him, however, other tradesmen and their families were coming to grief, their tribulations as well as their moral failings forming one of the primary leitmotifs of Stout's narrative.[39]

Stout's feats of self-discipline were, if not precisely typical, not especially unusual either. However, one is still struck by the risks he took, and the way in which his extended family, largely without protest, shouldered the liability. This was the other side of the urge for improving, especially when it involved moveable and hence, in this period, largely uninsurable property.[40] There are many comparisons with Stout's own parents, who had through much effort increased their acreage in the 1660s and '70s from twelve to sixteen unencumbered acres and acquired other small parcels of land.[41] Stout's siblings and cousin were in one sense merely living out patterns of family solidarity observed from their parents—Stout's account of his childhood reveals a family in which every member made some contribution. Still, there is little doubt that trade represented an extremely anxious sort of enterprise and one in which instinctive kin solidarity could prove singularly ill-advised.[42]

The potential pitfalls were exemplified by one of Stout's apprentices to whom he later sold his business. Although the boy was well-versed in writing and arithmetic and active in business, with a mother who was "a discreet and good manager of her estate and affairs,"[43] once he was his own master he became negligent and dissipated the profits. Eventually, "despite his mother's pains and care" he went broke, and having got his brother bound in bonds with him, also "broke" him, which "caused his mother's sorrow till death and broke the famely—which had been as much in substance and reputation as any famely in Overton or the neighbourhood."[44] As this story and many like it suggest, when failure came it struck straight at the heart of family survival, depriving people of the basic necessities of life, sending men, women, and children into exile or debtor's prison, crushing the innocent and the charitable among one's relations as well as the extravagant or imprudent. The degree to which people's "private" lives were enmeshed with business can seem incredible today, and the lengths to which they would go to avoid insolvency correspondingly extreme. Witness a letter of 1763 regarding a debt owed to the surgeon and merchant G. A. Gibbs or one of his family by one Mr. Kelly. In desperation Kelly was offering to sign over one half of "Mrs. Kelly's £4,000" (presumably a jointure or other monies held separately for her use), "Wch is to belong to him after her Death without issue. The hazard that will thereby be run [by the creditor]," the writer goes on, "is Mrs. Kelly's having a child."[45]

Today the context within which the capital-owning classes invest their money is a very different one. One of the primary defining features of the "middle class" in today's Western industrialized countries is privileged access to processes and institutions designed to minimize the impact of business risk (and also serious illness, death, or "acts of God" as some insurance instruments still quaintly put it) upon those most basic conditions (food, clothing, home, ability to maintain one's children adequately) without which the family becomes enormously more difficult to sustain. It is of course true that the thrust of much social legislation over the last century has been to temper similar sorts of insecurity in groups other than the middle class. However, not only is access to insurance, pension schemes, and the like substantially lessened the farther one goes down the social scale, many of the institutions that help to guarantee the considerable autonomy of some families from economic risk, or that permit them to invest as well as consume, are in practice closed to people who do not conform to certain standards recognizably more common to middle-class people than any others.[46]

In addition to basic things like insurance, there are a number of other institutions that similarly favor people whose income is above a certain point, who engage in business, or who own a home. Among these are, in most Western countries, tax breaks for business losses, including uncollectible debts, limited liability laws that are extremely charitable to business owners and less so to defaulting customers, and bankruptcy procedures that tend to favor homeowners (often they permit the bankrupt's family to continue living in the same place, and, within reason, at a similar standard as before). This is one part, but an important one, of the complex accretion of law and custom sometimes referred to as "welfare for the middle class."[47]

Eighteenth-century middling people lived in a very different and less hospitable world. One of the reasons it is so difficult to recapture the ethos of the early modern trader is that it is hard for many people to conceive of families engaged in investing capital in the absence of most forms of property insurance, health insurance, credit bureaus, generally agreed-upon and highly systematized methods of securing debts, and bodies of law, including bankruptcy law, that assume a quite remarkable separation between personal or family property and business assets and liabilities. These are the institutions and procedures that today literally sanctify the middle-class family, separating it not just from risk, but from those less fortunate families that live outside the charmed circle.[48]

It is impossible to say just how many eighteenth-century families of "substance and reputation" were brought low through ill-advised involvements with the likes of Stout's apprentice. The image of whole families failing owing to the fact that they had imprudently provided money or security for relatives is one of the master narratives of middling culture. It recurs over and over in letters, diaries, and autobiographies of urban non-elites of the period. It hovers in the background of numerous novels and journalistic enterprises. And it is difficult to find *any* good runs of personal records from tradesmen's families between about 1650 and 1800 that do not record failures (often multiple failures) among friends, family acquaintances, or business connections.[49]

Yet well into this period and beyond there survived the strong presumption that one should assist close friends and relatives in distress, supply them with capital loans, especially setting-up costs if it was in one's power to do so, and provide them with jobs in the family business. One would have to search far for any successful early modern English trader who set up business without some sort of significant assistance from relatives or patrons. The entirely self-made man or woman was in this as in other historical periods largely a figment of the moralist's imagination.[50]

This, then, was the substance of the dilemma that faced not only families directly involved in trade themselves, but any individual or family with connections to persons in trade. To profit, to improve, required capital, and capital under ordinary seventeenth- and eighteenth-century conditions meant having to rely on those relatives who were willing or felt duty-bound to provide help. But to supply a loan or to be a signatory to a bond was to take on a portion of the risk at a time when business loss cut right to the heart of household viability. It was out of this quandary that many of the most characteristic middling institutions and ideals were born.

GOD AND CAPITALISM

In the seventeenth century it was still common to explain financial success and failure by reference to Divine Providence or magical intervention. Early modern people were prone to see the hand of God at work in everyday occurrences, and the peaks and troughs of business lent themselves readily to supernatural interpretation. As late as 1700 the possibility was bruited about that witches might be to blame for many of the evils commonly attributed to human management or blind chance. It was apparently not uncommon throughout this period for businessmen to resort to astrology to help them make their decisions. Keith Thomas cites several seventeenth-century cases where people sought the aid of magicians to extricate themselves from debt: one man got a charm from a cunning woman, along with an assurance that, when he wore it, "he need not fear what money he owed, for no bailiff could take hold or meddle with him"; another went to a magician in 1654 for advice on whether it would be advisable to ask his family for a loan.[51]

By the early eighteenth century most people in commerce (or the literate city-dwellers at any rate)[52] were ceasing to credit business failure and like problems to supernatural forces and beginning to attribute them either to a moral or prudential defect on the part of the failed person, or to immoral, imprudent, or meretricious behavior on the part of someone with whom he or she was connected either as creditor or debtor. Of course the shift was neither a sudden nor a straightforward one. A distinctly prudential streak had been discernible as early as the sixteenth century in some manuals designed for the trading classes.[53] By 1635 William Scott, a citizen of London, was already complaining about men who failed and then blamed Providence when the real culprits were sloth and shoddy bookkeeping.[54] Even spiritual explanations tended to include moral features—God's ways might be unknowable but they were seldom arbitrary. Fires in the business district, failure, and even downturns in trade were often read as punishment for such transgressions as unfair dealing, trading on Sunday, or avarice. Sir Simonds D'Ewes ascribed the fire that destroyed his father's business premises in 1621 to God, whose ire was provoked when D'Ewes's father and his colleagues "[kept] short the gains of their under clerks . . . to advance their own" and then compounded their sin by doing business on Sunday.[55] Considerably farther down the social scale, Nehemiah Wallington, a London turner, attributed the burning of a house in Honey Lane in 1634 to the fact that the family had been "gadding forth" on the Sabbath. In a more positive vein, Richard Baxter urged listeners in 1681 to model themselves on the virtuous London businessman, Henry Ashurst, whom God kept from breaking when everyone around him was going under.[56] Comparable advice was still issuing from England's pulpits in the aftermath of the South Sea Bubble of 1720.[57]

The phenomenon of failure also fit fairly smoothly into providentialist frameworks, although these were different in kind from what Adam Smith was later to champion. Few before the middle of the eighteenth century viewed business failure as part of the normal working of an essentially self-correcting system, but seventeenth-century people routinely argued that it was really a blessing in disguise, an opportune punishment designed to wean the individual sinner from worldliness and ensure his or her salvation. Oliver Heywood (1630–1720), a nonconformist minister, exemplifies the ease with which religious and secular explanations for business failure could coexist in the same brain. Heywood's father, a dealer in fustian, had been a classic improver. He began by purchasing the land on which the family had lived as tenants for life and went on to build houses and barns, sink coal pits (which however "brought little profit"), establish a paper mill and fulling mill, invest in additional real estate, and diversify into woolens.[58] Around 1650 he failed, and the Reverend Heywood was sufficiently traumatized by the experience to devote a special section of his own autobiography to an analysis of the reasons.

Although his father had been "sparing, and forecasting and witty [i.e., intelligent] enough for his calling," the final foray into woolens proved his undoing. Adding up the factors that resulted in his father's final ignominy, Heywood included the expense of supporting two wastrel sons in London, dishonest subordinates, and advancing senility. But behind it all, Heywood was certain, lay the hand of God. His father had

> sinned in changing his calling [from fustian to woolen trading], in too eager pursuit of the world, in unfaithful dealing, in not keeping his word, in pleasing himself with hopes of riches or imagining a kind of contentment in worldly injoyments.[59]

Any one of these was sufficient to draw divine retaliation. Heywood also glimpsed a providential side to this sorry train of events. His father learned by his loss to distance himself from worldly things, and it was noticeable that God waited until all Heywood's siblings were educated or married with portions before taking the family's riches away.

God hovered for some time about the periphery of economic affairs, occasionally using the scourge of failure to chasten sins that might or might not be peculiar to business. But literate public opinion was moving perceptibly toward the view that failure could be adequately explained in terms of proximate or immediate causes rather than remote, occult, or unknowable ones. The factors that were behind this new, more secular attitude toward market processes will never be known precisely. They certainly included a yearning for new standards and new justifications for moral uniformity at a time when consensus on ultimate causes had begun to break down. And they reflected the growing interest in natural explanations that seems to have characterized such a wide spectrum of educated opinion in the seventeenth and eighteenth centuries. As will be seen, contemporaries were much occupied with trying to uncover why people failed. The matter turns up frequently in diaries, autobiographies, and letters, forming, indeed, a central focus of moral concern among people active in commerce, as well as among those clergymen who claimed to speak to the spiritual needs of urban trading communities.

One of the striking features of late-seventeenth-century efforts to plumb the proximate causes of business trends is the emphasis on individual morality. Graft, corruption, and stupidity are endemic to market societies, perhaps societies in general, but economic historians looking back at the period have been less likely to focus on individual moral turpitude than on liquidity problems, lack of protection from even very localized economic disruptions, problems of liability, chronic undercapitalization, poor transport and communications, relatively low demand, and relatively inefficient methods of production. Seventeenth- and eighteenth-century traders were only dimly aware of what would today be considered "impersonal" economic forces: when they took it upon themselves to explain why failure occurred they persisted in tracing the problem to immoral acts on the part of parties to business transactions.

Accordingly, there was a strong tendency to believe that the solution to failure and most other business ills lay in a general reformation of social mores, essentially along what we are accustomed to call Puritan lines, although in fact they were more urban and commercial than uniquely Puritan. From the late seventeenth century, traders, whatever their religious affiliation, were almost unanimous in believing that failure came as a result of extravagance, lack of industry, and especially inattention to one's accounts, keeping bad company, lending to or otherwise supporting people who were untrustworthy or "in declining circumstances," drunkenness, illicit sexual activity, and maintaining extravagant family members, especially sons. None of these was a strictly new explanation;[60] what was unusual was that these vices now seemed in and of themselves to supply a sufficient explanation for the phenomenon of failure. Thus the diagnosis was accompanied by a tendency to disparage the sins of extravagance and the like (increasingly they were termed "vices"—a significant shift) more because they impinged upon individual or family survival, business success, or the public good than because they offended against God's law. Late-seventeenth- and early-eighteenth-century thinking on business failure, despite the protests of such equivocal figures as Richard Baxter ("the great curse of a carnal mind is the failure to relate everything to God"), tended more and more to conceive of economic issues within a secular rather than a religious frame.[61]

It is somewhat unfashionable these days to make such a claim. The last few years has seen a reaction on the part of some historians to what they see as an exaggerated emphasis on eighteenth-century secularization. Thus, David Spadafora's long and scholarly study, *The Idea of Progress in Eighteenth-Century Britain* (1990), seeks to "push forward" *English* secularism, at any rate, to the very late eighteenth and early nineteenth centuries.[62] Spadafora's argument is forcefully made and valuable, but he also somewhat overstates his case. Spadafora adopts a very restrictive definition of "secular" in order to argue that science that is linked, even tenuously, to some sort of overarching religious vision (as most early science was) was not secular, or even secularizing, but part of an "expanded Christian vision."[63] On the surface this is simply an issue of interpretation, an insistence that the vial of holy water is half full in the face of someone who claims that it is half empty. But at a deeper level it makes some quite unreasonable demands upon eighteenth-century people, requiring them to possess a level of philosophical rigor and rhetorical consistency that would have been quite foreign to most of them (and that may indeed still be hard to find today). Contemporary rhetorical strategies routinely buttressed religious argument with secular evidence and justified secular actions by recourse to scripture. But the ways in which individuals negotiated these conventions was already highly individualized, ranging from sheer opportunism to deep belief, with every gradation in between.

A graver difficulty lies in the narrow sample upon which Spadafora bases his conclusions. It is not, perhaps, surprising that the divines and theologians (and professional intellectuals more generally) with whom the book is almost exclusively concerned tended to share a strongly religious view of the world. The problem lies in taking these men, even if implicitly, to stand for everyone else in a much more complex society. What would the result have been had Spadafora spent more time studying people whose bread and butter derived from activities other than expounding the Word?[64]

Early modern traders, who assuredly did make their living on a more earthly plane, also tended to view the world in increasingly secular ways. But it is important to be clear about what this did and did not mean. The new approach did not necessarily mean a more optimistic outlook on life. In the eyes of most improving folk in the late seventeenth and early eighteenth centuries, commerce was poised perpetually on the brink of chaos. To a man like George Boddington, a Levant Company trader who in the early eighteenth century recorded, retrospectively, the "breaking" of his own grandfather ("who wasted a good estate by gaming"), a son-in-law, and a brother,[65] the world was a precarious place indeed and commerce a potentially deadly series of moral choices. At any moment, the decision to game, to live extravagantly (as one of his sons was to do), or to borrow with no prospect of ever having the money to repay the debt could tip over the mechanism and plunge everyone in one's orbit into insolvency. It has been argued convincingly that at least some seventeenth-century economic theorists were fully capable of abstracting the working of the market from the human or social context.[66] There is little to show, however, that the average man or woman actually engaged in trade possessed such an ability. For most traders such underlying order as the market possessed derived neither from a belief in Divine Providence (in the economic sphere at any rate), nor from a sense of the uniformity or predictability of self-interest. Instead it relied upon a rather cynical hope that the penalties for transgressions such as not paying one's debts were so dire that people would go to almost inhuman lengths to avoid them. Commerce was embedded in and inseparable from society, and it required the constant sanction not only of the law, but of families, clergymen, and community opinion for its continued maintenance.

This position was expressed with particular clarity by the Reverend William Fleetwood. His sermon *On the Justice of Paying Debts* was originally preached in the City on the occasion of "the failing of some eminent Citizens," and some years subsequently, in 1718, it was published. Fleetwood dedicated his tract to the worthy citizens of London, who he said had urged him to make his remarks public, and he expressed his hope that by obeying their wishes he might be of some service to "the Trading-Part of the whole Kingdom." [67]

The true cause of most business failure, according to Fleetwood, lay in living above and beyond one's means. Hence, it was in great measure within people's power to prevent such "miscarriages" by being sober, frugal, diligent, and careful. [68] The great tragedy of failure was that it seldom stopped at one individual or even one family:

> Almost every Day brings us account of, I know not how many sad Families, that are either ruined, or much endangered, by the Credit they have given their Neighbours; in *most* of which cases, there must needs have been some notable Failure, in Point of Justice [i.e., some sort of malfeasance involved on the part of the debtor]. [69]

By its very nature, maintained Fleetwood, commerce presents us with a dilemma. No "extraordinary advantages," that is, profits, accrue to any man who does not first take risks. It is "to this purpose, [that] Men must use the Credit and Wealth of other People, because their own is not sufficient." And it is precisely because capital formation ordinarily follows this pattern that virtues such as sobriety, industry, prudence, and frugality are so essential if the whole system is to operate smoothly. [70]

Fleetwood, like most of his contemporaries, thought the acquisitive impulse could get out of hand, with individuals jettisoning their own and their families' security, as well as the good of society, in the rush to get rich. It was, he wrote,

> endeavouring to make great Fortunes in a little time by most immoderate and excessive Gains that makes a few Men become the Ruine of many families. [71]

On the other hand, Fleetwood viewed the instinct toward self-betterment as both natural, and, on the whole, positive for both the individual and society. However, it had always been the intention to remain consonant with Christian principles, its inherent potential for deteriorating into mere rapaciousness kept in check by those virtuous principles that God had made as efficacious in business as they were in religion.[72]

The question might be raised as to whether Fleetwood's views represent those of actual traders. The evidence suggests that he was closely in touch with the views of businessmen, and, if the dedicatory preface of *On the Justice of Paying Debts* is any indication, prided himself on being a spokesman for their moral concerns. No doubt opinion, like individual practice, differed but it is hard to imagine most businessmen of the period publicly embracing a philosophy that argued for the unbridled pursuit of private gain. The assumption, common to so many personal accounts, of a tight, highly interdependent system in which individual immoral acts almost invariably caused chain-reactions of economic disorder must have militated strongly against such a philosophy.

In contrast to some later capitalists, seventeenth- and eighteenth-century traders did not feel they could afford to sit back and let the market, trade organizations, or the law weed out the rash and imprudent, the defaulters on loans, or the criminals. The market was not yet conceived of as orderly in any sense. Nor did market acts harmonize automatically with each other. The only order the market possessed was that which was imposed upon it by conscious human agency in the form of community pressure aimed at convincing as many people as possible to conform to similar standards of frugality, honesty, industry, and prudence in lending, borrowing, and account keeping.

DEBT AND THE SOCIAL HIERARCHY

The acute sense eighteenth-century people possessed of the interdependence of transactions in the market led to tension in a society still characterized by rank and special privilege. It seems that eighteenth-century traders, as much as any other group, shared in the rejuvenated respect for social and political hierarchy that characterized the English scene after the Revolution settlement. But hierarchical systems require marks of status, and a number of the traditional marks of high status, such as gentlemanly negligence in paying bills, lives of relative leisure, conspicuous expenditure, and somewhat less inhibited forms of sexual expression than those of other people, were potentially highly disruptive of a well-regulated market. "[The] misdemeanour I have been guilty of is a crime half the nobility are *daily* guilty of," wrote a young man named William Jackson from Retribution Hulk in Woolwich, where he languished under a sentence of transportation for having drawn upon a banking house without having any effects there. He was exaggerating of course, but the barb hit a tender spot.

In Jackson's view, running up debts he had no way of paying was no disgrace at all, since the best people in the land behaved the same way and, usually, got off scot-free. But the shopkeepers whom he had bilked of substantial sums saw things rather differently, since this kind of reasoning, if writ large, would place the whole precarious structure of commerce in jeopardy.[73]

Characters like William Jackson provide part of the explanation for why middling people in this period were so drawn to images of self-mastery. Middling, and later middle-class, offensives against the laboring classes, aimed at inculcating obedience, clock discipline, and a willingness to work hard for low wages, have been much studied by historians. But in the period prior to the establishing of the factory system, middling people were, arguably, more concerned about the morals of people who were roughly their equals, at least in contractual terms, than they were with the morals of their social inferiors.

This is not to say that poverty and the poor went unnoticed by the more fortunate. The period beginning in the late seventeenth century was an extremely fertile one for generating new ideas about the rationalization of work and the productive potential of the poor, as well as for founding new institutions for the purpose of re-educating and reforming the laboring classes, preferably from as early an age as possible.[74] What came, rather later, to be called "middle class values" initially emerged less from an urge to organize other people's labor more efficiently than as a result of common experiences with regard to credit and the mechanisms of commerce and investment. The poor disturbed the peace, failed to pay their small debts, stole, begged, ran away from their places, and cast themselves and their offspring upon the parish. But it was people of one's own rank, especially one's own family, to whom one lent really substantial sums of money or on whose behalf one had oneself bound surety for loans. These were the people on whom one depended for scarce capital, on whose industry and "fair dealing" one relied, and whose moral lapses were the most potentially devastating to the social order.

It should not surprise us then that one of the paradigmatic acts of heroism for eighteenth-century middling people became that of braving extreme hardship to pay off one's own or one's relative's debts. Elizabeth Ashbridge (1713–1755), originally of Cheshire, was a Quaker convert, whose picaresque travels took her from England to Ireland to Pennsylvania and finally back to Ireland. When her second husband died around 1740, he left £80 in debts. Because her husband's assets at the time of his death were negligible, Elizabeth was not legally obligated to pay off his creditors. But the creditors immediately complained, arguing that they had only trusted the husband for his wife's sake. In order, as her last husband and biographer put it, "that truth might not suffer," she engaged her word to pay them all, and by steady application to her needlework and running a school, she managed, in time, to do so.[75]

William Gray, a provincial lawyer, was on the verge of bankruptcy for three years in the 1780s on account of the extravagance and misconduct of the favorite nephew of one of his partners. He worked desperately to save the firm, a heroic labor that permanently cost him his peace of mind, but "the credit of the office [was] preserved."[76] David and James Fordyce, two influential contemporary moralists, gave special laurels in their allegorical *Temple of Virtue* (1759) to "one who ruined has worked himself up again,"[77] while in Mary Hays's heavily fictional *Letters and Essays* (1793), one Melville, a businessman driven to extravagance and bankruptcy by an unsupportive first wife, first surrenders his effects to his creditors, then goes to America and slowly retrieves his finances. He succeeds in paying off his creditors "both principal and interest" and is only then permitted to court the heroine, the virtuous and learned Cecilia.[78]

CREDIT AND DEBT IN OTHER SOCIAL RANKS

By the late seventeenth century, creditor and debtor relations pervaded all ranks in the country as well as the city. Laborers sometimes waited months or even years for their pay and had to manage in whatever way they could in the interim, including buying on credit. In urban areas the poorer classes purchased all their food and other necessities in the market, usually by a combination of credit and pledging their meager belongings (often their clothes) to the neighborhood pawnbrokers and moneylenders. At the other end of the social spectrum, aristocratic indebtedness reached alarming proportions, especially after mortgage collateral arrangements were worked out that ensured that landed elites were unlikely ever to lose their lands.[79]

Did middling peoples' experience of indebtedness really diverge significantly from that of anyone else in eighteenth-century England? Traders, merchants, shopkeepers, manufacturers, and professionals differed from the poor in having a substantial stake in eighteenth-century society. They could aspire to a comfortable style of life and even, in some cases, riches. Their high rate of literacy permitted them to cultivate connections to clergymen, journalists, publishers, and other local literati, and to articulate often distinctive views on family life, work, politics, morals, and business.[80] They were in a position to seek a return on capital invested, rather than to have to pawn their clothes to feed their families. They could afford to rent four or five rooms or a whole house and outbuildings instead of a garret or cellar. They could send their sons and sometimes their daughters to school, rather than having to send them out to work almost as soon as they could walk.

And yet, their status was hard won and extremely insecure. In this they differed significantly from the aristocracy and a good portion of the gentry. The perception of stability and the social prestige that accrued to land and pedigree (and especially to titled pedigree), combined to make the terms on which the landed elite borrowed extremely favorable. The staggering debt burdens that some of them accumulated, the indulgence with which even the most profligate peers were treated when they fell into financial difficulties,[81] and the very small number of landed families who ever actually went under for financial reasons (as opposed to failure to produce heirs) in the eighteenth and even the nineteenth century all confirm this.[82] Some aristocrats did involve themselves in trade and industry and, especially, transport. But their connections to the market were cushioned considerably by their social position, their ownership of large tracts of land, and their sheer wealth. Among the middling, who were generally devoid of land to use as collateral, who operated, in most cases, on a smaller scale and engaged in riskier enterprises, who were more reliant than the landed on personal sureties and more vulnerable to imprisonment for debt and other extreme judicial measures, indebtedness was a very different matter.

There was more blurring of boundaries between the middling and the lesser or declining gentry. There were financially embarrassed families among the gently bred, and gentlemen did sometimes end up in debtor's prison.[83] Nor was it unknown for gentry families to rent their estates and flee to the Continent to avoid their creditors. The landed were also hampered by their inability to declare bankruptcy, unlike a good many tradesmen. Popular stereotypes about the difficulties of getting gentlemen debtors to pay had their counterpart in a venerable body of opinion that took the side of gentlemen against rapacious traders and moneylenders. William Fennor's *The Compter's Common-Wealth* (1617) is written partly to keep young heirs "out of books and bonds, which oftentimes are the main cause of their overthrow." According to Fennor, gentlemen are seduced by extortionate tradesmen or "spent-Gallants" into signing bonds, and then, when they cannot pay, they are consigned to debtor's prison, memorably described as "a costive creature, that surfets almost all the yeere long, yet very seldome doth purge itselfe; and when it doth it leaveth abundance of ill humours behinde." The greed of creditors and imprisonment for debt are depicted as prime causes of the beggaring of old families and the dissipating of inherited estates.[84]

Accounting handbooks marketed specifically to the upper class, such as Roger North's *The Gentleman Accomptant* (1714), also took this tack, as did advice books apparently intended for the gentry and aristocracy, such as Francis Osborne's *Advice to a Son* (1656). *Advice to a Son* would hardly have been acceptable to many middling folk on moral grounds. Osborne disparaged marriage and advised that if a young man must enter the bonds of matrimony (that "Clogge fastened to the neck of Liberty"), he should marry for money rather than for love, virtue, or beauty. Extramarital sex with one's social inferiors was, in Osborne's view, perfectly acceptable (for elite men, at any rate) so long as one neither fell in love with the woman in question nor married her. And lastly Osborne advised his readers never to oppose any established religion "how ridiculous soever you apprehend it."[85]

Some of Osborne's other advice would have been perfectly congenial to many among the middling. For example, he recommended early rising (although not at anything like the inhuman hours suggested by bourgeois writers: it was enough not to "lye long abed"), thrift, and the avoidance of gaming. On getting into debt and the conduct of business he was quite peremptory: Never buy except with ready money. Never stand security for friends or even for relatives, for "experience [has] recorded many . . . that have, by *Suretyship,* expired in a Dungeon." Do not lend to the government, for you will likely not be repaid. Write down all contracts, "for where Profit appears, it doth commonly cancell the Bands of Friendship, Religion, and the memory of any thing that can produce no other Register than what is verball."[86]

Traditions like these evidence the degree to which market relations, and more specifically credit relations, had already passed well beyond mercantile communities, if they had ever been confined to them. They also point to the presence of a common reservoir of cultural attitudes, from which people could pick and choose according to their needs. The ethic of good stewardship of one's estate, particularly in a time of rising costs, could look very like the middling championing of thrift, care, and good accounting. But aristocratic or gentry commitment to such ideals was never as visceral as it was among the middling. Middling people, especially if they or their relatives engaged in trade, took more risks than their betters, and they had far less protection from the vagaries of the market. A member of the gentry who took a long time to pay his bills, kept a mistress, and was overfond of leisure pursuits was only displaying his status and living up to expectation. A working tradesman who did the same was courting a visit from the bailiffs. In the end, prudential values that seemed to promise a better-regulated market (and also greater individual success within the market) had more resonance for the middling than they did for any group either above or below them.

CONCLUSION

The culture of the middling classes in eighteenth-century England was heavily marked by the peculiarities and inadequacies of the early modern marketplace. But it is not enough to say that this culture emerged purely and simply out of the marketplace. Even capitalists are never purely economic people, nor are they impelled solely by crude considerations of profit and loss. Any "culture" is a shifting amalgam of ideals (those people live by and those they honor in the breach), customary practices, institutional flux, and internecine conflict. Eighteenth-century middling culture was no exception.

To call the values and way of life described in this book "middling" is to say that it is out of the experiences of the middling that they most authentically derive. It is not to say that they had no appeal for people in other ranks, particularly those contemplating entering the more risk-prone sectors of the market, or those intent upon upward mobility. The realm of commerce was an ill-understood and understandably fearful place to seventeenth- and eighteenth-century people, but it was one that, in theory, also offered impressive opportunities for social mobility and personal and dynastic enrichment. In the course of the period from approximately 1680 to 1780, middling people, especially, developed novel ways to analyze their relationship to the market. They developed new value systems and more utilitarian cosmologies. And they began the process of building institutions that would both facilitate capitalist activity and soften the impact of capitalist risk on themselves and their families. The middling inherited a world that was significantly more fearful and insecure than the one middle-class people inhabit today. In their efforts to come to terms with it they were inevitably changed.

CHAPTER TWO

A Generation of Vipers:
Prudential Virtue and the Sons of Trade

[Of the Illiterate Man]
He is unable to take or keep any just Account of his own Affairs, of the Encrease
or Decay of his Estate; much less can he be useful to others, which is always a
comfortable thing, and sometimes beneficial.
RICHARD STEELE, M.A., THE TRADES-MAN'S CALLING. BEING A DISCOURSE
CONCERNING THE NATURE, NECESSITY, CHOICE &C. OF A CALLING IN
GENERAL. DIRECTIONS FOR THE RIGHT MANAGING OF THE TRADESMAN'S
CALLING IN PARTICULAR 1684

Chuck-Farthing like Trade
Requires great care
The more you observe
The Better you'll fare
EIGHTEENTH-CENTURY CHILDREN'S RHYME

George Boddington (1646–1719) of London was a prosperous Levant merchant and staunch Presbyterian. In the 1690s he sent his son, also named George, who was then in his late teens or early twenties, to Aleppo to represent him in trade. There, as his father tells it, he fell in with some friends who

> incouraged him in Extravagant liveing . . . [so that he] minded not the busi-
> ness *wch* greatly grieved me in not wrighting me as [he] ouh[t] nor giveing
> me an Acct. of my Effects for many monthes.[1]

In desperation his father sent a second son to Aleppo to "call him to ac-count," but it was at least another four years before George the younger reappeared in England. He spent the intervening time careening across Europe ("an Extravagant & Expensive Journey," his father huffed) and took up with a papist whom he later married. In his commonplace book the elder Boddington reckons up the money his son spent on this ill-starred journey down to the last shilling.[2]

Boddington's judgments of his sons' worth were based narrowly on their abilities in business and whether they proved a drain or an asset to family finances. John Boddington (1676–1695) was one of his favorites and the

46

following comprised his father's epitaph for him (the unpunctuated style
is characteristic of all the elder Boddington's writing):

> John Boddington my son was borne 1676 ... and Dyed ... [in] 1695 to
> my great greiffe being a dilligent comfortable child Very understanding in
> business he for some time in a vacancy of A Treasurer to the Greenland
> Company supplyed that trust to theire intier content for *wch* they gave him
> A Gratuity.[3]

Another of his "good" sons was Benjamin (1692–1779), described by his
father as "dutifull & dilligent" and "very exact" at keeping accounts. Like
the rest of his brothers, Benjamin was taken into his father's counting
house at the age of fourteen, and at twenty he was sent off to the Levant.
There he avoided the example of his older brother, worked hard, and managed to foil an embezzlement scheme aimed at his father's stock. To his
father's gratification, by the age of twenty-one he had already formed a
five-year partnership, "*wch* was prudently done and to his advantage," and
had begun trading on his own account.[4]

It was an ancient commonplace that youth was a time of hot-blooded-
ness, riot, and sensuality. But since virtually no records of non-elite family
life survive from before the mid seventeenth century it is difficult to say to
what extent or in what ways families and masters felt it necessary to control
these alleged tendencies in practice. Nor are we in a position to say to
what degree the vices of youth were systematically linked to specifically
commercial, as opposed to, say, religious, concerns before the late seventeenth century.[5] The fairly significant numbers of non-elite family papers,
including letters between parents and children, that become available
from the mid seventeenth century suggest that among the middling (although not necessarily *only* among the middling), feelings of financial vulnerability were focused disproportionately on adolescent or young adult
males.[6] Families reposed great hopes in their sons, but they were also extremely fearful that they would become liabilities in terms of maintaining
family credit and reputation. The main dangers here, none of them new
to the seventeenth century, included sexual entanglements, getting into
debt, and "keeping bad company." Landed families also worried about
their sons establishing inappropriate sexual liasons, imitating people with
more money, getting into debt, or dissipating the family estates. However,
the need to give them the gloss of good breeding, the aversion felt by a
good many, if not all, gentle families toward "base and servile" skills, as well
as the continued attachment to public school educations,[7] often defeated
attempts to teach greater self-discipline before they began. Within middling families, however, the content of socializing messages strongly reflected the prevailing orientation toward trade and the lower-level professions, as well as, increasingly, the civil service. That is to say that it focused

heavily upon thrift, hard work, and the acquisition of business-related skills.

But the early sources on middling families (from approximately 1660 to 1700) pose some methodological problems. Most crucially, they are heavily weighted toward dissenters and especially Quakers, and it is difficult to say how representative they are of middling people in general. On the one hand, contemporaries, both those who conformed and those who did not, tended to attribute unusual moral strictness to dissent and sometimes even to argue that dissenters' feats of self-discipline made them unusually well-fitted for trade. This association was to persist through the eighteenth century. On the other hand, there were some Anglican families even in the late seventeenth century whose attitudes toward their children, and especially their sons, would have been hard to distinguish from those of dissenting families.

The problem is further complicated by the fluidity of confessional affiliations so evident in middling and gentry families during the Restoration and beyond. The shopkeeper William Stout's parents were Anglicans, but they apprenticed their son to a Quaker and in time he converted to that religion. By contrast, the antiquarian Abraham de la Pryme (1671–1704), of French Huguenot extraction, abandoned the religion of his parents for a clerical career in the Church of England.[8] There were many such cases in this period. Few serious readers of the highly moralistic devotional literature of the time confined themselves to Anglican or nonconformist writings alone—or even necessarily to Protestant ones. Mixed marriages were quite common.[9] And the passion for sermon-going among urban middling people could be eclectic as to its object. On one Sunday in January 1733 Stephen Monteage, Jr. (1681–ca. 1764), a London accountant, attended a Quaker meeting, services in Westminster Abbey (part of the thrill certainly lay in the contrast), and a sermon at "St. Martins." That spring Monteage was off to hear open-air sermons by the Reverend Whitefield, and he also visited a Jewish synagogue "where I heard them at their Devotion finely illuminated wth Wax Candles being there Passover time." In the same year he read William Wollaston's *Religion of Nature,* a freethinking tract, and got through the Old Testament twice. Monteage undoubtedly ranged more widely than some, but there is plenty of evidence of other middling city dwellers who were similarly ecumenical in their spiritual interests.[10]

As one moves into the eighteenth century, the sources not only begin to encompass a wider variety of religious groups (Anglicans, Catholics, Jews) but show that the prudential virtues associated, at least by repute, with dissent were, by now, widely dispersed outside these communities. Some methodological problems still remain (how representative of any period in history, particularly one where literacy is nowhere near universal, are families who keep diaries, write to one another, *and* save the letters?), but the sheer range and the diversity of the surviving documentation after about 1700 make generalizations somewhat safer.

This chapter is concerned primarily with the content of socializing messages to sons in the period approximately 1660 to 1800. Advice to the young always has more to do with what a given community aspires to be than it does with "real" behavior. Nonetheless, if used with caution, letters of counsel from parents, conduct books, and the like can give us important clues to contemporary attitudes. Let us begin, then, with a brief and necessarily speculative look at some of the differences between trading people in the late seventeenth or early eighteenth centuries and medieval urbanites. Apparently an important virtue in the London merchant community in the period approximately 1300 to 1500 was what Sylvia Thrupp has called "sensitivity to differences in status." This meant being able to muster the range of appropriately deferential or authoritative behaviors to permit one to operate relatively freely, as a trader had perforce to do, within that belligerently status-conscious society. Youths were enjoined, above all else, to learn to keep their tempers in the presence both of inferiors and superiors. More familiar concerns of urban traders, such as sobriety, sexual abstinence, and avoidance of gambling already had their place in the moral discourse of the medieval urbanite, but they apparently played a more peripheral role than they did later. Significantly, in these times there appears to have been nothing approaching the glorification of work which is so striking a part of middling thought in the period covered in the present study.

The merchants Thrupp studied did not place much stress on literacy or mathematical skills. Double-entry bookkeeping was not introduced into England on a significant scale until the seventeenth century, and while other accounting methods were in use prior to that time, they were not accompanied by the propaganda campaigns about good bookkeeping that were so prevalent after about the mid seventeenth century. In medieval cities uncontrolled violence represented a greater threat to social order than did unpaid bills or the other forms of disorder specifically associated with commerce, and the vices and virtues most stressed by those responsible for the socialization of youth tended to reflect this.[11] As we will see, the world of the late seventeenth and eighteenth centuries looks very different.

PROFLIGATE SONS

By the eighteenth century the erring son was a stock character in trading life, a potent symbol of the failure of parents to effectively inculcate virtue into their children, as well as of the manifold temptations that, in a newly consumption-oriented society, could block the way to secular success. In the minds of people of the time, the vices of youth were closely intertwined one with another. Looseness in lending and borrowing was but a short step away from sexual looseness, and extravagance a short step from theft. While the profligate could inspire pity, more often he inspired real fear and disorientation.

For if wayward youths epitomized the dangers of emulation, they were also walking proof of its wide appeal. In this hierarchical, status-oriented society, there were real advantages to acquiring an air of gentility. Middling people who served (or aspired to serve) a high-class clientele profited from a familiarity with the latter's ways and tastes. And those who wished to be thought prosperous and credit-worthy by their peers might, up to a point, adopt genteel patterns of consumption (wearing better clothes, acquiring another servant, attending balls, etc.), for these were universally associated with wealth.[12] Nor were the middling immune to the appeal of gracious living for its own sake: luxury was routinely condemned in the eighteenth century, but ostentatious asceticism was not an alternative many championed. The problem, of course, was how to summon up the self-discipline to keep emulative impulses firmly oriented toward the demands of business, reputation (especially credit-worthiness), and a reasonable degree of ease, while avoiding having them degenerate into efforts to imitate the ruinous habits of the naughtier nobility. Youth, that age when self-discipline is at its weakest and the desire to impress at its height, was indeed a dangerous time.

It is difficult to find an eighteenth-century middling family for whom records have survived that was not preoccupied with anxieties of this sort: the moralism was hardly less intense among nondissenters than among dissenters, and it even extended to Jews and Catholics. Indeed, the small family dramas of indiscipline and betrayal to which this regime gave rise could be powerfully complicated by minority status. This is well illustrated by the case of Moses Marcus (fl. 1724), the eldest son of an East India Merchant who had been a founder of the Hambro' synagogue in London. On his mother's side he was the grandson of Glückel of Hameln, woman merchant and one of the most significant Jewish memoirists of the seventeenth century.[13] To the Marcus family's profound distress, young Moses turned profligate and converted to Christianity, apparently in order to take advantage of a law that forbade Jewish parents to disinherit or withhold financial support from children who became Christians. Moses launched a lawsuit against his father aimed at forcing him into compliance with the law, published a bid for public support, *The Principal Motives and Circumstances that induced Moses Marcus to leave the Jewish, and Embrace the Christian Faith, with a Short Account of his Sufferings Thereupon* (1724), and spent some time in debtor's prison. In private he vacillated wildly in his attitude toward his parents, at one point begging them to pardon the folly I committed[.] I never had Committed it if several people had not perswaded me to it telling me by turning Christian I could oblige you to give me a sum of Money but as I was born a Jew so I will Die a Jew[.] I go here [in Amsterdam] to Sinagogue & Live as a Jew ought to do so I hope God Allmighty will pardon my sins likewise I beg pardon of you.[14]

With respect to issues of credit and debt the situation of Jews in trade did not differ very much from that of the Christians with whom their business affairs often overlapped. Family letter collections show Jews to be as afflicted with problems of credit as other people, and it is notable that both Sephardic and Ashkenazic communities maintained special charities for the relief of imprisoned debtors that paralleled those maintained by Christians.[15] Relatively little is known about Anglo-Jewish family relations in this period, but what evidence there is suggests that credit relations loomed just as large as they did in Christian families. However, as the Marcus case shows, commonplace problems with debt, filial obedience, and the like could be greatly exacerbated by the legal disabilities Jews faced in eighteenth-century English society.

The temptations associated with wealth, perhaps aggravated by the fact that the family were recusants, brought another London family, that of the woolen draper William Mawhood (1724–1797), literally to blows in the late eighteenth century. The dispute arose initially after the elder Mawhood purchased a commission for his son and namesake, William. The officer corps, which boasted strong gentry and aristocratic participation and was renowned for its libertine mores, was viewed with considerable suspicion by trading parents, even those who could afford to buy their sons good places. In this case the fears were justified. Son William was posted to America sometime in the 1770s and not long after he was accused of sheepstealing, a quite serious crime. A letter quickly ensued from his father, full of standard eighteenth-century expressions of parental outrage: If his son would review his earlier letters he would find that his father's first advice to him was to keep good company and live a sober life. Instead, William has selected as his friend the most abandoned person in the whole corps, and Mawhood Senior will not be surprised to hear his son's dying speech cried in London. Mawhood begged his son to reform his conduct, and outlined the pressures under which the family was laboring:

> For God & yr own Sake take great care that yr conduct and whole deportment be such as may Establish yr carracter, this often does more than money . . . Trade is very bad[,] More Bankruptcys than Ever and mony Exceeding scarce. I am oblig'd to be as saving as possable, and I recommend it to you and I hope you keep good Company and take particuler care you are not drawn inn to marry, for then you are ruin'd for Ever.[16]

Shortly thereafter Mawhood senior began soliciting reports from business acquaintances traveling in America about his son's behavior. One of them advised in 1781 that "Your son is naturally extravagantly inclined" and recommended that he be made to live on a strict income, for "if you give him latitude and the privilege of drawing on you for his expenses you will do him an injustice."[17] More parental threats followed:

> I trust you will be so prudent as never to run in[to] Debt with anyone [again] . . . for if you do your [army] Commission must be sold, and you are ruined; for my own part I shall distribute Equall justice to all my children, but my fortune will not permit any extravagance.

> And so son you have keep a Horse, Kep't a whore, Spent yr Company's mony and ruin'd yr Constitution: yr Soul I shall say nothing of.[18]

In 1782 son William returned to England, where his father had his coachman report regularly on his movements. Another son, Charles, now allied himself with his brother, and the next ten years are a record of their gradually deteriorating relations with their father. The elder Mawhood had them watched for sexual irregularities and, belatedly, forbade them to keep horses or dogs. Charles and William accused their father of placing all his affections on their sister Dory, to which Mawhood retorted, "I shou'd place my Affection on those that pleased me."[19]

The situation steadily worsened. William stayed out all night, threatened and assaulted his father, and refused to be disciplined. Mawhood remonstrated with his son, threatened to cut him out of his will, and refused to allow him any spending money: "Wrote to son Wm [that] I had returned his D[raft] for 100£ & should return all he might draw as long as he was dissipated." Charles was barred from becoming a partner in the family business on the grounds that he had shown a lack of application. By this time the continuity of the family business was in serious jeopardy. Mawhood sought advice from friends and business associates as to what to do: "Mr. Crofts advises me if my Children are untoward to quit & sell my Trade" reads a memorandum of 1784. Other friends advised the elder Mawhood to liquidate his assets and leave everything to his wife so she could control Charles after his death, also "to charge son Wm. with what he has had [i.e., debts paid by his father], & [these] to be deducted from his share [of the estate]."[20]

Not long after this, William the younger had to flee England to avoid imprisonment for debt, and while in France he eloped with the daughter of a count. In a penitent letter of 1791 he informed his father of his desire to return to England in disguise to see his father on his sickbed. But the elder Mawhood, now in decline, proved obdurate in his refusal to favor his sons in his will. Consequently, in 1796, William and his brother Charles, joined by a sister, Maria, swore out a commission of lunacy on their father that focused on the peculiarity of his having excluded his sons from inheriting. The elder Mawhood defended his sanity with the expert testimony of several doctors and counterattacked with a detailed account of his sons' moral failings, including Charles's neglect of his father's business and the allegation that his son William had struck him and threatened him with pistols. The case was finally brought to arbitration, but not before this family had been literally torn apart—as contemporaries would have had it—by the power of emulation and the ungovernable passions of youth.[21]

TIME DISCIPLINE

It is time to look in greater detail at some of the more positive messages that parents sought to convey to their sons. In the last fifteen years a series of important works have established the historicity of modern conceptions of time. For the most part these have focused on the imposition of clock time on the working class.[22] Surprisingly, little attention has been paid to the question of how the capital-owning classes internalized clock time. And yet, the moment, apparently somewhere in the late seventeenth century, when it became *de rigueur* among trading folk to inculcate a deep respect for clock time into their children is surely an important one for the overall history of work and work discipline.

The precise relationship between attention to time and the diffusion of clocks and watches among this class of people remains uncertain. In the late sixteenth century, merchants already were known for their strict attention to time, and advice books from the same period exhorted apprentices to rise early, avoid "unprofitable" activities, and carefully plan how they organized their days.[23] It is clear that for some people the use of personal watches followed on, rather than preceded, the stricter observance of time. "[On the] 10th of April 1666," wrote the Levant merchant George Boddington in his commonplace book, "I bought me a Watch which cost me 5 £." It seems that this purchase merely confirmed his already highly time-conscious style, since he earlier remarked that "I was dilligent being Generally first and last up in the House in the yeare [16]63."[24] Still, the purchase obviously had great symbolic significance for this budding merchant. In a folio volume detailing the major events of his life, this watch is virtually the only thing he bought for himself that he ever saw fit to mention. The use of clocks and watches obviously bore some relationship to new attitudes toward time, but the connection was not a simple one.

More disciplined attitudes toward time were not just a straightforward development from the Calvinist notion of calling, as some have suggested. Nehemiah Wallington, the Puritan turner, was scrupulous about allocating time to religious devotions but quite ambivalent about applying the same discipline to more worldly activities. Traders who were "up early and late, very industrious and careful and painful in use of all means, taking hold of all time, seasons, and opportunities" simply had less time to devote to God, and what, Wallington would have asked, did earthly labor do for one's immortal soul?[25]

The rural Lancashire shopkeeper, Roger Lowe (fl. 1663–1679), a considerably more worldly man, although nominally a Presbyterian, showed no more interest in time and work discipline than Wallington did. Lowe was no layabout: he acted as amanuensis for other villagers, helped lobby for a school, went about collecting pledges for the relief of victims of the Great Fire of London, and spent much time cementing alliances among his neighbors and friends. He also worried a good deal about his status and reputation, the condition of his finances, the prospect of casting up the accounts of his master's shop, and his fickle sweetheart and undependable friends. And once or twice he felt a qualm about attending a cock fight or going to the nearby town of Prescott "on an idle occasion." But it seldom occurred to him to worry about how he spent his time, and it seems never to have crossed his mind to account for it systematically. All in all, Lowe spent as much time in the alehouse and going about the countryside with his friends as he did keeping shop.[26] Was it temperamental unfitness for trade, inadequate rearing, rural backwardness (in the case of Lowe), or simply that time and work discipline had not really yet generally caught on that makes Wallington and Lowe seem so distant from traders of the next century?

Whatever its typicality, it was this rather haphazard approach to both time and work that Richard Steele (the nonconformist divine, not the more famous playwright and journalist) was challenging when he urged, in 1684, that tradesmen apply the same discipline to their earthly vocation as they did to religion. They should, "after due consideration of all Circumstances, and of [their] necessary business within doors and out," fix times to pray, read, and hear sermons, *and also* times for working and bargaining. "Hours having wings," asserted Steele in a phrase that was to reverberate through the next century, "every moment flies up to the Author of Time, and carries news of our usage of it."[27] This was a very different ethos from that of either a Wallington or a Lowe.

In the eighteenth century more and more traders do appear to have begun to worry seriously about time in relation to their work. Early in the century, Reformation of Manners tracts often recommended better secular time management. A diary penned by an anonymous London wigmaker between 1707 and 1709 is full of self-flagellating notations about his "slackness in [his] duty" and his tendency to "waste time" on the job.[28] By mid century printed appointment calendars were being advertised,[29] and letters of advice to children being bred up for trade standardly included exhortations about better management of time. Let us look in detail at how one early-eighteenth-century mother attempted to get a young son destined for trade to internalize time discipline along with other business-related skills. In 1712 Sarah Savage, wife of a prosperous farmer, wrote to her son Philip, then in school, that she was pleased with

> the account they give that yr time is close filled up with wt is useful and profitable, that there will not bee room for those trivial diversions wch Wrenbury [where he had previously lived] was too full off.[30]

Soon after she was advising him to study in the morning for "the manna . . . was to be gathered only in the morning—afterwards it was melted and not to bee found."[31] Around this same time the Savages began finalizing plans for Philip's further education:

> Since you went yr Fa. [father] & I have had some careful discourse about you and hee seems very clear that yr next step should bee to Chester to be a while at Sis. [Sister] T. if it be but one Quarter & ly *wth* the Dr. and improve in writing and Casting account.[32]

Business skills were closely linked to morals, thus in this same letter Philip was admonished to "Remember to be sober minded and flee youthful lusts and vanity." And some eight months after that his mother writes, "W[he]n the schollr [scholars'] Bell rings [sic] this morn. I could not omit thinking of you—*who I hope need no such Call among the rest of the Childish things which you put off.*"[33]

The Savages' child rearing was highly systematized, future-oriented, and prudential. It aimed to inculcate sober-minded application to the task at hand and saw profitable and highly conscious use of time as crucial to this process. There are frequent allusions to scripture in these letters, yet the ends (at least where this youth was concerned) were secular and tied to specifically economic fears and insecurities. The remainder of Sarah Savage's correspondence leaves little doubt as to the kind of temporal pressures that existed in her community. It is a world where every local catastrophe contains some cautionary message, and where the most common failures of self-discipline are related either to sexuality or personal finance—or both.

> Co[usin] Y . . . has griev'd & sham'd her Friends by marrying a young Rakish lad . . . pp. [people] cry out shame on her—150 p.a.y. [pounds a year] joynture—as they say but only 15 p.a.y. that she can dispose off [evidently a separate estate]—& [she] ow[e]s 300 p[ounds]. [N]obody knows how she could spend it all.

> Poor Wid[ow] Leicestr is below *wth* sorrowf[ul] Complaints—her son-in-law & Dau[ght]er have all [been] seized for debt and [she?] will be turn'd out a May—& she has not so much as [a] bed left.[34]

Early eighteenth-century middling parents were keenly aware of the speed with which secular ruin could strike. The emphasis on internalizing clock time, early rising, avoidance of unproductive activities, and steady attention to one's calling was a bid to improve work efficiency. It was also an attempt to forestall expensive and less-than-creditable diversions on the part of the young. The relationship between moral prescription and action is always a troubled one, but there is no doubt that eighteenth-century people were remarkably prone to associate promptness with rectitude.[35] There are also signs that youths from middling families were beginning to chafe against the restrictions that time discipline imposed, which suggests that it had more than just a prescriptive reality.[36] But the major significance of eighteenth-century prescriptions concerning the proper use of time does not lie in whether people followed them; it has rather to do with what these prescriptions imply about competing systems. All middling attempts to influence the use of time implicitly set their morality against "upper-class" attitudes that emphasized at least the appearance of leisure, and "lower-class" attitudes that seemed in the view of the respectable to keep the poor perpetually oscillating between menial labor for brute survival and criminal idleness. When middling groups (sometimes joined by the more reform-minded among the gentry) sought to differentiate themselves, both from their betters and their social inferiors, the use of time was a central concern.[37]

READING AND WRITING

The ability to read and write, and especially to write a good hand, was also a matter of major import to trading parents. Reading represented the key not only to serious bible study but also to a wealth of educational opportunities ranging from shorthand and foreign languages, to the more abstruse realms of mathematics. Writing was just as important. As business grew more complex in the late seventeenth and eighteenth centuries, the need for clerks grew apace. There was no longer a respectable place within early modern business or government for the illiterate, however retentive a memory or ingenious a mind he or she might possess. If parents had any doubts about this, they had only to look at advertisements for positions. This typical one appeared in *Aris's Birmingham Gazette* in 1760:

> Wanted, a sober steady young man of 18 or 20 of mean parentage but honest and unexceptional [*sic*] character, able to write a good hand and understand accounts and willing to do any business he shall be sent about[,] to be employed for a term of 5, 6, or 7 years.[38]

Parents who wanted to see their sons succeed encouraged them to attain standards of competence in writing that far surpassed what had been required of them by their own parents. This is reflected over and over again in almost any letter collection spanning two or more generations, virtually throughout the period. Written records of older people from the trading classes generally display significantly worse spelling, syntax, and general legibility than do younger ones. Those apprentices or would-be apprentices so unlucky as to hail from families who failed to insist on a neat writing hand and exact mathematics tables could easily find themselves without prospects—even seriously declassed. One Richard Maris of Worcester wrote his sister Mercy (who happened to be the wife of the prominent Presbyterian divine, Philip Doddridge) a pathetic letter in this vein in 1765. There he complains that his children had had no schooling for the last seven years; he also betrays in his own orthography and syntax some of the disadvantages under which his children labored:

> [The boy] could have [wrote *or* wrighten(?)] well, and was very Forward in Accounts and Now can do Neither, hes grone almost a man and yeat fit for no maner of Bisnes what to do with him I cant tell.[39]

Other youths, even carefully reared and educated ones, failed to attain the standards of proficiency that business (and their parents or masters) now demanded of them. In the 1770s young Adam Prattinton's grocer father briefly entertained hopes of educating him to one of the professions; he even considered investing in a living for him in case he displayed clerical leanings. Alas, Adam turned out to be a young man without intellectual pretensions of any sort, and this misfortune was compounded by the fact that he showed little aptitude for business either. Sent to work in his father's shop when his schooling was finished, he could not get along with his father's chief assistant and showed a striking lack of application. Family friends sought, in the rather heavy-handed style of the time, to reason with him. Thus, one Colonel Holmes

> expressed much concern at [Adam's] not attending to business and says if he does not leave off Childish amusements and stick to matters of more importance, he shall take little notice of him.[40]

Another friend advised Adam's father to have the youth set to "Copy Letters, to Examine and Copy bills of Parcels and invoices etc." as the best way of teaching him accounts, but after only a few months of this Adam developed "a weakness in his right hand" that at least temporarily incapacitated him for business.[41] This story illuminates some of the origins of that bitter animus so many late-eighteenth- and early-nineteenth-century middle-class youths held against the world of business.

Writing involved the systematic ordering of data on a page with a particular end in view. One could arrange information in abstract patterns, or, freed from lapses of memory, contextual interruptions, or intrusive mnemonic metaphors, one could watch for the patterns that grew from the material. Seventeenth-century commentators were convinced of its epistemological significance. Richard Steele, the nonconformist minister, thought reading and writing so essential for the conduct of everyday life that "he who is unaccomplished with them is scarce to be reckoned among rational creatures."[42] Some modern researchers have been more cautious about claiming causal links between literacy and changes in cognition, but to the relatively recently literate among the eighteenth-century commercial classes its potential for ordering and expanding knowledge seemed almost limitless.[43]

ACCOUNTING

The most characteristic "middling" skill of all was bookkeeping, and the ability to keep accurate accounts soon became the centerpiece in the education of youths from trading families.[44] "Know then that my Parents were very careful to cause me to learn writing and *Arithmetic*," wrote the anonymous female author of *Advice to the Women and Maidens of London* (1678), a passionate call for women to learn bookkeeping,

> for without the knowledge of these I was told I should not be capable of Trade and Book-keeping and in these I found no discouragement for though *Arithmetick* set my brains at work[,] Yet there was much delight in seeing the end, and how each question produced a fair answer and informed me of things I knew not.[45]

Accounting involved "mak[ing] inspection into that, that is to keep me and mine from ruine and poverty."[46] It was an art that allowed one to divine at any time where one's money was going and thus forecast disaster in time to avoid it. When we compare the regular keeping of accounts with other contemporary methods of predicting and hence controlling the future, we can begin to see why people waxed so enthusiastic about it. In the seventeenth century, as we saw, people sometimes resorted to magicians or charms to safeguard them from their creditors.[47] By contrast, the principles of bookkeeping were both simple and accessible: they relied on no secret formulas, esoteric symbols, or charismatic practitioners. Compared with astrology, water divination, or efforts to influence the course of romantic love, they were dry and mundane. Yet what bookkeeping sacrificed in glamor it made up for in the uncontroversial character of its results and in the fact that anyone who could add and subtract with fair competence could learn it. A democratic mystery in the best Baconian tradition, it promised its initiates an unprecedented sense of control over the intimidating universe of credit, debt, and cash-flows.

For some, accounting held out still grander possibilities. Propaganda in favor of better instruction in bookkeeping found its way into some of the numerous seventeenth-century tracts devoted to teaching the English how to better the Dutch in trade:

> The education of Dutch Children, as well Daughters as Sons; all which, be they of never so great quality or estate, they always take care to bring up to write perfect good hands, and to have the full knowledge and use of *Arithmetick* and Merchants Accompts; the well understanding and practice whereof, doth strangely infuse into most that are the owners of that quality, of either Sex, not onely an ability for Commerce of all kinds, but a strong aptitude, love and delight in it." [48]

So wrote Josiah Child in 1668 in *Brief Observations Concerning Trade and Interest of Money*. For Child the wide diffusion of this kind of knowledge would render all of trade more comprehensible and ordered and would have incalculable national benefits.

The interest in accounting also crossed class lines. Textbooks on landed estate management and advice books for the elite often recommended that the nobility and gentry learn accounting, and some elites certainly did learn it, although many of the latter must have contented themselves with a rather passive knowledge of the art. Younger sons intended for trade were generally encouraged to learn accounting by their gentry parents, just as were sons who hailed from trading families. [49] But involvement with accounting was deeper and more all-pervasive in trading families. In some of these families the keeping of accounts became a sort of consecrated collective activity, akin to, and perhaps actually replacing, family prayers. The anonymous author of *Advice to the Women and Maidens of London* was given the job of keeping household accounts by her father, who "made it my Office to call all persons to an account every night what they laid out, and to reimburse it them, and set all down in a book." She thought all parents should require their children to keep household accounts, so that they would be "train[ed] up . . . to be regular and handy in Accounts of greater Moment." [50]

In fact, although girls did learn accounting, the skill was deemed more crucial for sons, the prime economic actors of the rising generation. One way to sweeten the pill was to give boys small sums of money to invest in order to give them a taste of what business was like and to instill in them good bookkeeping habits. Looking back at the significant moments in his life, George Boddington made particular mention of the day and year when he first began to keep his own books: "[On] 25 March 1664 [at the age of eighteen] though [I] was possessed but of a very small Sum wch had binn given me I begann a pare of Bookes for my selfe and bought a Small parcell of cotton." In turn, he gave his son Benjamin the care of all the firm's cash ("in the keeping of which he was very exact") when he was fourteen years old, just as his own father had done.[51]

At a more mundane level, a commitment to teaching sons accounting, generally coupled with attempts to train them early to be vigilant about their personal expenses, became an established part of the education of middling youth. In 1771, when Adam Prattinton was only ten years old, his unoffical guardian was already planning "to promote his improvement" by introducing him to expense accounting, which happy day would come "as soon as he is made acquainted with his pence Table."[52] Thousands of other youths must have experienced similar pressure.

Correct and neat accounts were aesthetically pleasing in themselves (often the headings were richly decorated and the bindings of embossed leather), but they also formed a necessary backdrop for the virtuous trading life, to which increasing vigilance and the ability to forecast one's present and future assets had become as critical and as morally obligatory as work itself. People who failed to keep good accounts were already deeply suspect in some circles by the end of the seventeenth century,[53] and by the mid eighteenth century there were even scattered attempts to make the accountant into a sort of latter-day folk hero. Thus a cheap novelette of 1758 featured as its protagonist a young man who, "as he was designed to follow his Father's Business[,] closely applied himself to the perfect Knowledge of Merchants Accompts, of which he is justly esteemed to be . . . the compleatest Master in *Great Britain.*" This was a long way from Robin Hood or Guy of Warwick.[54]

Did celebrations of accounting translate into well-kept books, or indeed any books? A significant campaign was commenced in the seventeenth century to popularize accounting. Numerous accounting manuals were published, and the fact that many of them went through multiple editions suggest that they were bought.[55] But as in all such campaigns, the ideal often fell short of the reality. Historians of business have often pointed to the low standard of accounting still prevalent in the eighteenth century.[56] Daniel Defoe, among other things a champion of accounting, claimed in 1727 that he had heard sceptics assert that they knew of

> several men in great business . . . that keep no Books at all, or that very little Book-keeping serves their turn; and yet . . . those men thrive and flourish, go on in their trades, and grow rich.[57]

But the future clearly lay with better bookkeeping. Defoe, indeed, argued that "ancient commerce," with few middlemen and substantially less reliance on credit, had required much less in the way of bookkeeping; conversely, in the modern world of the eighteenth century, where everything was credit, it was folly to neglect it. Defoe quite explicitly associated the failure to keep accounts with the smaller, less respectable sort of tradesman:

> If there comes to me a Tradesman upon reading these sheets and tells me, Sir, I trade all for present money; I give no credit, and I take none; I go with my money in my hand to buy, and I take all ready money in my shop, for I give no trust by retail, and I let no body keep or come at my cash but my self, what occasion have I of keeping any Books? To such a man I shall readily answer, none at all, Sir, you are a person qualified to trade without Books; but you are the only man in the world that is so, except any other whose trade is so very small, that he can keep every thing he trusts in his head.[58]

As Defoe well knew, there were still traders who kept everything they owed (or were owed) in their heads. But the culture of trade, the culture of the middling sort, was already moving to appropriate bookkeeping as a symbol of rationality, honesty, and control—in a word, of superior virtue. Some had done so a good deal earlier. "I set to make some strict rules for my future practice in my expenses, which I did bind myself in the presence of God by oath to observe," wrote Samuel Pepys, not normally an especially religious man, in 1662.

> And I do not doubt but hereafter to give a good account of my time and to grow rich—for I do find a great deal more of content in those few days that I do spend well about my business then in all the pleasures of a whole week, besides the trouble I always have after them for the expense of my money.[59]

He capped these good intentions by commencing on a program of figuring up his accounts at least once a month.

During the seventeenth and eighteenth centuries economic theorists from Thomas Mun and William Petty to Josiah Tucker and Adam Smith worked out many of the basic principles of classical economics and began formulating "laws" of economic motion.[60] But humbler people could attain to a superior, even godlike, comprehension of their own small microcosm of trade, they could "discover," as did that anonymous London woman of the trading classes, "things I knew not," simply by attending carefully to their account books and making their business decisions on the basis of the "objective" data they found there. More instrumental and systematic ways to manipulate time, language, and numbers seemed to promise real control over an extremely anxiety-ridden area of daily life. Whatever their actual cognitive impact (or impact in terms of verifiable changes in behavior), these skills assumed tremendous paradigmatic importance for the middling themselves, symbolizing new ways of looking at the world that were more utilitarian, more comfortable with abstract approaches to decision making, and, although this point was seldom explicitly acknowledged, less psychologically dependent on the direct intervention of God.

Western Europeans have not always been uniformly enthusiastic about advances like these. The Renaissance educator Juan Luis Vives had complained about a tendency in the study of numbers that "leads away from the things of life, and estranges men from perception of what conduces to the common weal."[61] Restoration playwrights twitted citizens on account of the rigid way they managed their time and their preference for future profits over present pleasures.[62] Middling moralists were routinely accused of preaching virtues no human being could practice consistently. And numerous Europeans, well into the nineteenth century, worried that broad access to reading and writing would lead to social leveling. But for many literate non-elites in early modern England, reading, writing, and accounting, whether of one's money or one's time, became the prime exemplars of that most enlightened of ideals, "the rational."

EDUCATIONAL INSTITUTIONS

These various efforts to prepare youths to play a creditable part in life took root amid an atmosphere of anxiety and suspicion, for every false step carried the potential for collective, not simply individual, ruin. "How many Parents in this Congregation are afflicted by their own children? . . . [by] Enemies . . . aris[ing] against them out of their own Houses?" the dissenting minister Philip Doddridge queried darkly of his parishioners around 1734, and he went on to liken such children, in a dramatic scriptural tag, to "a generation of vipers."[63] The notion of family metamorphosed into enemy was one of the great tragic themes of eighteenth-century middling family life and Doddridge's words must have struck a powerful chord among his largely middling listeners.

One common response to such uncertainties was to insist on a good education, and eighteenth-century parents (including numerous non-elite parents) became more demanding consumers of education than an earlier generation had been.[64] Among the middling, opinions varied as to what kinds of schools were most appropriate. Some better-off boys, those destined for the clergy or the law, were sent off to the elite public schools and later to university to gain polish and contacts. But the moral reputation of places like Westminster and Eton (much less Oxford or Cambridge) was extremely low in the eighteenth century, and the treatment of tradesmen's children allegedly poor. Such institutions hardly fitted youths for the world of business, either in terms of skills or in terms of general outlook, and could, by teaching them poor morals, incapacitate them for all other useful vocations as well. And thus we find a middling advice monger like R. Campbell fulminating at length against public school vice and luxury, the uselessness of learning classical languages, and the deep incompatibility of an upper-class education and a profitable and virtuous business career. As Jos-

iah Wedgwood put it: "The ideas of a long school[ing] & classical education & the company kept, & habits acquired there, are almost imcompati-
ble with a life of drudgery . . . & application to business afterwards."[65]

To be sure, some trading families did succumb to the lure of the public
school (although in many such families the sons did not board and only
went for a year or two), but this was certainly not the case with any but a
trickle of youths of this class.[66] Alternatives included the lesser grammar
schools, which still stressed classical languages, the odd local school with a
more vernacular focus, and two fairly new phenomena, the dissenting
academy and private proprietorial schools designed to teach literacy, languages (usually French), and business skills. A surprising number of better-
off middling families also sent their sons to schools in Geneva or Amsterdam, cities known for their relatively high moral tone, their commitment
to trade, and their Protestantism.[67]

The dissenting academies possessed a particular appeal because of their
strict attention to morals, and in the eighteenth century they drew both
Anglican and nonconformist applicants from all over the British Isles.
Thus in 1747 the aunt of a prospective pupil wrote from Edinburgh to the
Reverend Philip Doddridge, director of one of the most respected of the
dissenting academies, about her nephew, then aged sixteen ("a very criti-
call period for Boys"). She was deeply concerned lest he get a taste for idle
company, and she wanted him to go to Northampton "as I hear you admitt
of none into your Academy but such as bear a good Character and will
submitt to the most exact Rules of Sobriety and good order."[68] The boy
was admitted to the academy, but to his aunt's (professed) shock and dis-
comfiture he managed to get into debt, an offense punishable by expul-
sion. The aunt appealed to Doddridge not to expel her nephew for his
extravagance ("sending him away from your House . . . I am persuaded
would be his utter Ruin") and strongly implied that if the boy's uncle
found out about his misdeeds he might be disinherited: "[His uncle] being
a man of the strictest morals, it might do poor David a hurt that could
never be recover'd again."[69]

Almost certainly, the vast majority of middling youth were educated in
the private proprietorial schools that mushroomed all over England in the
eighteenth century. These enterprises—and enterprises they were—were
an authentically middling response to the expanding need for literate and
numerate men. Generally run by businessmen or the families of businessmen, often as a side business or domestic enterprise, these schools were
thoroughly utilitarian in outlook. Thus in 1756 Reeve's Academy on Bish-
opsgate Street in London, one of the more "genteel" of these schools, advertised itself as a place in which "Young Gentlemen are instructed in the
Several Branches of Science, necessary to qualify them for Employment,
whether the Compting House, Public Offices, Se[a], Army, & c." and noted

that "the Pupils may either Board in the Academy, or daily attend the Hours of Instruction."[70] These schools were all fundamentally similar: they emphasized accounting, learning to write with a clear, consistent hand, and, in the better schools, French, the language of international trade. Very large numbers of middling youths attended such schools for a few years before being apprenticed, partly, no doubt, to make them more desirable to prospective masters. For others, the proprietorial school actually replaced the traditional apprenticeship. The former's flexibility recommended itself to youths (and parents) who did not want or could not afford to wait out a costly seven-year apprenticeship, and it was ideally suited to producing a body of semipermanent clerks, employees who, unless unusual luck or particular merit lifted them above the common herd, would not be expected to graduate much beyond routine paperwork. Over the long run the proprietorial schools played an important part in the formation of a kind of lower-middle white-collar class, although numerous more fortunate boys also had their start there.[71]

EDUCATING PROFESSIONALS

Families in the upper reaches of the middling classes often preferred to send one son for a professional education while apprenticing the rest to trade. The decision to groom a youth for one of the more elite professions was generally entered upon only after serious consideration as to his moral fortitude. George A. Gibbs, an Exeter surgeon with involvements in international trade, had sent his son Vicary to Eton with the intention of having him go up to Cambridge. In 1769 he wrote to another son, George, who was apprenticed to trade, of his concern about exposing Vicary to moral contagion:

> When I reflect on your brother's situation, I foresee a great deal of solicitude & anxiety on his account. He will be exposed to a variety of temptations, from which you, my dear, will be exempted.[72]

Other families decided not to educate their sons for the professions because they seemed to lack the steadfastness to withstand its temptations. At a certain point Philip Doddridge the younger ("Philly") was attracted to the law, but his friends and relatives had already discerned in him evidence of a lack of moral fiber. A family friend wrote anxiously to Philly's mother about it:

> The more I see of [Philly] & observe wt a ready Tincture his sociable Temper takes from the company he frequents, & how great a Hazard he would run of being linked in with some giddy & extravagant youths the more I dread his settlement in a large Town [such as would be required by a clerkship].[73]

Samuel Lowder of Bristol advised his kinsman, a grocer in Bewdley, that he would be "exposing [his son] to great danger" by sending him to university because of the latter's "volatile [and] lively" temperament. Lowder thought the boy should be placed "in such a Station as he may not run [to] such lengths as tis so likely to fear would be the case was you to send him a Commoner to the University" and recommended instead that he be bred, like his father, to the grocer's trade.[74]

Vocational fitness notwithstanding, a professional education had a strong appeal for middling groups in the eighteenth century. Emulation of the gentry and aristocracy has been overemphasized and certainly over-simplified as a motivating force in the lives of middling people, but emulation of professionals has not received the attention it deserves. The professions had long been seen as constituting a kind of aristocracy of merit. In the eighteenth century several factors conspired to make this "aristocracy" appear more accessible than it had been previously. First, the professions grew significantly in numbers in this period while also diversifying, particularly at the lower levels. There was both a wider range of options for training and more modes of entry for bright boys from undistinguished families than there had been before. Second, the professions began to shed at least some of their association with arcane knowledge. A professionally trained individual in a largely illiterate world is a very different creature from one in a subculture that is highly literate and in which fairly ordinary people standardly read books on medicine, the law, and theology.[75] Third, while *training* for the professions was fraught with danger—in no small part because so many morally suspect sons of elites were concentrated there—once attained, a professional career combined a level of prestige seldom attained by men of commerce and a powerful commitment to hard work, usefulness, and "rationality." This powerful combination was to have enduring appeal for trading parents and their sons, even in the face of the moral danger posed by the professions' intermediary status in eighteenth-century society.[76]

PRISON

Despite their families' care, many youths signally failed to live up to their parents' expectations. Impressions can be misleading: problem children, then as now, took up disproportionate amounts of their parents' time and thoughts, and hence are mentioned more frequently in family papers than children whose rearing was comparatively uneventful. Obstreperous offspring were, moreover, to be found in all ranks of society. Still, the sheer numbers of problem youth among the middling, as well as the nature of their rebellious behavior, suggest that a substantial proportion of sons of trade responded very badly to the new time discipline, the self-restraint, the glorification of work, and the exaggerated orientation to future success that were becoming such a feature of the world of trade. If this period is viewed as a phase in the internalizing of "bourgeois" habits of time discipline, rationalization of work, and so on, values later imposed to such effect on an industrial work force, it may not be unreasonable to see parallels between some of these recalcitrant middling sons and the crowds who later rioted against machine speedups and the imposition of time clocks.

The fascination English travelers had for the coercive institutions of other lands points to a growing sense of the inadequacy of ordinary families when it came to socializing youths who were already "hardened in vice." Travelers to the Dutch Republic in the late seventeenth century were sent into transports of enthusiasm by the "Verbeteren Huizen" (literally, reform or improvement houses) set up in Amsterdam, The Hague, and elsewhere to, as one observer put it, "receive, detain, and chastise Extravagants, Deboshees and reprobate, wicked and lewd Children."[77] Reform houses were not introduced on a large scale in England, at least in part because imprisonment for debt was so common. But not a few parents appear to have used debtors' prisons as if they were private bridewells. Far from taking steps to secure their sons' immediate release, they used the experience to encourage penitence and a reformation of morals.

One such unfortunate prodigal was Jean-Baptiste Grano, musician, imprisoned for debt in 1728 by his long-suffering landlady. Grano roomed in Marshalsea prison with Mr. Blunt, "a Cloatherer," Mr. Sandford, "a young Fellow, the son of a Rich Man but under the displeasure of his father," and Mr. Blundel, "an unfortunate jeweler."[78] Grano's own family remained resolutely deaf to his increasingly frantic appeals. His sister-in-law intercepted his letters to his brother and sent them back unopened. Other relatives pleaded poverty but, to Grano's annoyance, managed to find the money to pay a clergyman to come to the prison and "arraign my past follies."[79] Finally, a full four months after he was imprisoned, his parents sent along a gentleman bearing a few books and some money to help pay Grano's keep. "He kept me at least two hours, giving me both Spiritual and Temporal advice and assuring me I should never be foreseaken of my Friends" wrote Grano sardonically in his journal.[80]

Not surprisingly, this section of Grano's journal is full of meditations about the universal undependability of families and especially his brother's "deceitful ungratefulness" for past favors.[81] Grano was beset with nightmares and millenarian forebodings, and he confided to his sweetheart his belief that

[w]e Approach to the Disolution of the World according to St. John's Revelation where he observes, that for a token of the Grand Judgements' drawing

nigh things would in their turns be revers'd[,] a Day in highest winter in summer[,] Friend against Friend[,] Brother against Brother[,] Son against Father &c.[82]

Clearly, Grano was experiencing very profound doubts about the strength and durability of blood ties. A case like this suggests again that the insistent rectitude around which so many trading families aspired to organize their lives, and which, no doubt, commended itself to even greater numbers in times of family crisis, coexisted uneasily with older conceptions of loyalty to one's kin.

There is plenty of evidence that family patronage and mutual assistance between kin continued to play a far greater role throughout the early modern period than many today would view as either normal or desirable.[83] On the other hand, the virtues that were stressed by a good many "responsible" parents and clergymen (and youths themselves) were more individualistic and more prudential. Implicitly they set themselves above other ethical systems, including ones that emphasized high levels of kin reciprocity. The natural attachment assumed to exist between parents and children, or the natural sense of duty one had toward one's relatives, was ceasing to be an *a priori* good, at least when it conflicted with the newer virtues. Resort to coercive institutions to buttress the education and socialization functions of families is one indication of this shift.

SEX AND MANHOOD

In the late 1790s Miss Richenda Gurney, from an upper middle-class Quaker family, spent a day with some young beaux. Later she confided to her diary how "superior to bank boys" they were, concluding, "What a surprising difference rank and high life make in a person's whole way and manner, it is most pleasant being with people who have been brought up that way."[84] Power and rank held considerable erotic appeal for both women and men in the eighteenth century, and few middling people had any illusions about that fact. This was the guilty knowledge that lay behind the fear that middling youths would be "seduced" into immorality by associating with or attempting to emulate their betters. Middling people had to establish new, nonaristocratic definitions of "manliness" that could "seduce" (but more productively) in their turn.

Sexual reputation in early modern England had never been as closely identified with men's core identity as it was with women's. But an illegitimate birth was a drain on community resources, and, if paternity was proved, it carried with it loss of reputation and financial and personal liabilities (such as being forced to marry the woman in question). Edith Gelles reports a case where rumors of a youth's inattention to his studies, alleged sexual promiscuity, and reckless spending caused the family of his intended to break off his engagement to her. This kind of thing may not have been all that unusual.[85] From the perspective of middling parents the main drawback of illicit sexual activity seems to have been its expense, closely followed by the alleged risk to health, and much propaganda was devoted to the claim that whole families were being daily ruined through the blandishments of whores and the moral frailty of husbands and sons.[86] For our purposes the key point is that whoring (and the term was used broadly to refer to almost any extramarital sex) was seen as a sort of magnet vice, one that led inexorably to gaming, criminality, extravagance, and nonpayment of debts.

Another "magnet" sexual vice was masturbation. The sin of Onan garnered a good deal of attention in the eighteenth century, especially after the publication of the best-selling *Onania; or the Heinous Sin of Self-Pollution,* around 1710. There is a considerable historical literature on this and similar tracts: indeed, masturbation is by far the best documented of eighteenth-century sexual practices.[87] The discussion surrounding masturbation closely resembled the one that had grown up earlier around whoring, in that it focused upon the potential expense, the consequences to health, and the threat to the integrity of families. But because the "solitary vice" was just that, extra ingenuity had to be expended to establish a plausible causal link between it and financial ruin: there was no malignant prostitute waiting in the wings to persuade a previously reliable husband and father to neglect his trade and cast off his family.

Two things came to moralists' rescue. One, ironically, was the relatively open way in which the actual act of masturbation could be discussed. Thanks to the fairly explicit character of the relevant biblical passage (Genesis 38:9) the secret was, as it were, out. Ready to hand was a rich store of stimulating analogies between barren spillage of seed and wasteful expenditures of both money and physical and mental vitality. The second boon to moralists was that youths were not, on the whole, thought to happen on the solitary vice all on their own; rather, they were initiated by older boys or by servants. This struck a chord for several reasons. In the first place, it was sometimes true. The autobiography of John Cannon, a Somerset excise officer, contains a graphic description of a scene that took place when he was ten or eleven, in which another boy, a seventeen-year-old, taught a group of younger boys (including Cannon himself) how to masturbate, touting it as a remedy for lustful thoughts and noting helpfully that "altho the first act would be attended with pain yet by frequent use they would find a deal of pleasure [from it]."[88] The main reason moralists insisted upon the social origins of the solitary vice was that it offered an excellent opportunity to emphasize the danger of moral infection from without, specifically from groups above and below the middle ranks on the social scale.

It is no surprise that one of the chronic concerns about public school was that older boys would teach the younger ones how to masturbate, thereby destroying their innocence, launching them upon a career of licentiousness, and ruining their health.[89] The masturbation scare slipped easily into a larger moral discourse that emphasized the need for ever greater degrees of parental involvement in children's upbringing and that promoted the view that the virtuous, who were increasingly, if never wholly, identified with the middling sort, were under moral siege from forces beyond themselves.

In many societies lack of sexual restraint is associated metonymically with a more general loss of control. However, what is defined as lack of restraint, who is imputed to display this lack, and which other forms of loss of control it is used to represent can vary enormously across cultures. Eighteenth-century middling people were in the process of developing new ways to control themselves and their environment. They were also seeking to come to terms with a political culture and a politically powerful class to whom they felt strong traditional loyalties, but whose ascribed values were, at certain crucial points, antithetical to their sense of their own security. Not surprisingly, divergences in sexual mores and attitudes, whether real or imagined, came to function as powerful symbols both of difference and of middling superiority.

Sixteenth- and seventeenth-century English people appear to have shared a belief in a kind of universal impulse to libertinism. The vice was concentrated most strongly, it is true, in certain cohorts (Catholics, citizen's wives, widows, Quakers, youth) and locations (the Inns of Court, the theater, the Royal Court), but it was, to a degree, present across society. As the Restoration gave way to the renewed moralism of the period after 1689, accusations of licentiousness seem to have become directed more and more at the aristocracy, both male and female. This shift, if it is a shift, can be discerned in contemporary pornography, in Reformation of Manners sermons, in middling advice books, in feminist tracts, and in contemporary novels. And it is a commonplace in middling discussions about the rearing of children, especially sons.[90]

In many societies male sexuality is a powerful marker of masculinity, and it is often envisioned as a species of conquest, whether of women or other men (or boys).[91] This association is never unproblematic, since it is seldom in the interests of any society to permit entirely unrestrained male sexual activity, still less among the young and those of lower rank. Still, the widely accepted linkage between sexual potency and manhood posed a practical problem for those seeking to argue, as many late-seventeenth- and eighteenth-century reformers did, that any and all forms of sexual activity outside marriage, all the way from masturbation to actually keeping a whore, were fundamentally reprehensible. Essentially they were forced to come up with other measures by which to establish a solid claim to masculinity—and to do so at a time when simple appeals to godliness (one of the staples of an earlier generation of sexual reformers) had lost a good deal of their power. Moreover, they were competing with a class of men (the gentry and aristocracy) who both possessed greater license than others to indulge their appetite for sexual conquest *and* who possessed the erotic *frisson* of political potency—"Real Men" indeed.

There were a number of ways by which middling youth (assisted by their families and interested moralists) sought to establish their manhood. One was to form all-male societies devoted to the pursuit of virtue: associations that differed from the traditionally masculine, aristocratically marked, and libertine venues of the army or parliament. (This topic is discussed in depth in a later chapter.) Middling youths also asserted their masculinity by distancing themselves from behaviors alleged to be characteristic of women, and they often did so in ways that also permitted them symbolically to affirm the complementarity of gender roles and, by extension, heterosexuality. A fine example of this subtle series of maneuvers is found in the correspondence of the young Gervase Leveland, son of a woolen draper. The time was the 1760s and Leveland's friends, most of whom appear to have been in their mid to late teens, were a close-knit group, prone to romantic crushes on each other and addicted to writing letters in a comical mixture of elevated English and bad French.[92] They were also much given to loaning money back and forth among themselves (one suspects without the knowledge of their parents), and the self-conscious and highly emotional language in which they do it suggests both the fear and the fascination that this authentically adult type of social interaction could engender.

But within the homoerotically charged atmosphere of Leveland's circle there were nevertheless clear rhetorical limits, and Leveland himself came up against them in an exchange with his friend Worrell. Leveland had written a "tender, praiseful letter to Mr. Worrell" which has not been preserved. A week later Worrell replied with a thinly disguised rebuke:

> Much Dear Gervase could I add in praise of your sensibility of heart, were I to take up the subject where your modesty induc'd you to quit it; but I hold it very idle in two he fellows to be complimenting each other on the possession of a quality in which the [other] sex so far outdo the most feeling of us all; the Girls, the dear Girls, my friend, feel more in half an hour, than Men do in an Age, 'tis their delicate sensibility that tames our fierce passions & softens the steely temper of our minds, and our bodies too i'faith.[93]

A young man of less than steely temper, Leveland had overstepped the boundaries and, in a moment of what Eve Kosofsky Sedgwick would call "homosexual panic," was having to be reined in.[94]

Other efforts to uphold middling masculinity were more public, if no less rhetorical. Middling moralists obsessively identified traits that were alleged to be aristocratic (luxury, interest in things French, lack of application, moral laxity) with softness and effeminacy.[95] Conversely they identified any and all values alleged to be nonaristocratic (plain speaking, usefulness, perseverance in the face of adversity, rationality, systematic pursuit of virtue) with masculinity. "He that applies himself to virtue, and strongly addicts himself thereto, never commits anything unbecoming a Man, nor contrary to right reason," wrote young Gervase Leveland piously.[96] A schoolmaster wrote to the father of one of his pupils in the 1770s, "I have great hope that we shall have the satisfaction of seeing your son enter upon life with manly and virtuous principles and a cultivated understanding, and supporting a respectable and useful character in the world."[97] Women prefer a man who displays "blunt freedom of behavior" and who "has sense and spirit enough to act in that manner [to] which his reason and understanding direct him in which he would always be inflexible, but at the same time an affectionate husband," asserts the upright (and unusually sexist) "Freeman" in a dialogue of 1765.[98]

Erotic attraction, however, is an unpredictable thing. In their erotic relations with their betters, as perhaps the novelist Samuel Richardson showed best, the middling classes were hopelessly torn between attraction and repulsion. Although individual members of the middling sort, beginning in the late seventeenth century, launched what was to be one of the longer-lived propaganda campaigns against extramarital sex that the West has seen—a campaign that lasted, with ups and downs, all the way through the Victorian era—they were never able fully to stamp it out. None of the various projects associated with the eighteenth-century middling classes were fully successful at the time, because many of them were simply too ambitious. But sexuality was to prove an especially intractable problem: even as it summed up with particular acuteness the subtle interplay of danger and fascination at the heart of middling peoples' view of their betters, it also revealed a large field in which their best efforts at self-control seemed often to be for naught.

CONCLUSION: SUCCESS ITS OWN REWARD

"[T]he mind of a young person cannot be more profitably employ'd than in revolving the principles of right action," George Gibbs, the Exeter surgeon, wrote rather sententiously to one of his sons in 1769. Foremost among those principles was the agreeable belief that "Providence never fails to give the virtuous and industrious man such a share of worldly blessings as are sufficient to make him contented at last." Later Gibbs put it in slightly more social terms, "Consciousness of virtue," when combined either with "the innocent pleasures of an opulent fortune" or with "a more moderate one," is the prime source of human happiness and the basis of social order.[99]

This was perhaps the most secular of the various visions of prudential morality that commended themselves to middling parents and their sons in the seventeenth and eighteenth centuries, and it exudes an optimism and a utilitarian spirit that place it authentically within the broader stream of the European Enlightenment. At almost precisely the same time, the young Jeremy Bentham, product of the union of an attorney turned real-estate speculator and a shopkeeper's daughter, committed a rather terse note in his commonplace book to the effect that the purpose of education was to "inspire a general habit of applauding or condemning actions according to their general utility." He was perhaps twenty-two at the time.[100]

Moral advice to young men was not to move in an uninterrupted upward sweep toward modern "bourgeois" secularism. Instead it bifurcated under the influence of Evangelicalism and the French Revolution, the main route being a retrenchment in the direction of rather more pietistic approaches to personal morality than most of the ones described in this chapter.[101] The results have been described masterfully in Catherine Hall and Leonore Davidoff's *Family Fortunes,* and they go well beyond the chronological scope of the present study.[102]

But it is also the case that none of the moral directives of the period from the late seventeenth century into the nineteenth century, whether evangelically or otherwise inflected, diverged all that far from one another. Safeguarding one's credit, avoiding the temptation to spend extravagantly, applying oneself diligently to business, remaining sexually chaste, keeping good accounts, writing a good hand, maintaining rational self-control— these were the primary measures of middling male respectability all the way through the eighteenth century, and they continued to be touchstones of middle-class masculinity in the nineteenth century as well. As this chapter has shown, all this restraint and moralism did not always receive a positive response from the rising generation. As a value system it was in perpetual competition with other systems that retained their own not especially discreet appeal, and it ran up against all the errors of judgment, incompatibilities, personal weaknesses, and twists of fortune that go to make up both family and business life. The fears it engendered were painfully close to the surface. Some of its most enduring features are not ones many of us have much sympathy for today. Nonetheless, middling morality taken *in toto* does represent a kind of monument to a moment in the formation of modern Western capitalist society when rigidly enforced discipline seemed to many to be the only defense against moral and economic anarchy.

CHAPTER THREE

To Read, Knit, and Spin: Middling Daughters and the Family Economy

Miss Harriot is here: she is so grown I scarcely know her—She is a fine girl & her meekness is a recommendation to her.

CALEB DICKINSON, 14 DECEMBER 1752 [1]

[I was] sometimes grieved at my not being a boy, that I might have been [a minister] believing them all to be good men, and therefore beloved of God.

ELIZABETH ASHBRIDGE, *SOME ACCOUNT OF THE EARLY PART OF THE LIFE OF ELIZABETH ASHBRIDGE* (CA. 1755)

The artist-engraver William Hogarth executed *A Harlot's Progress* and *A Rake's Progress* in 1730–31 and 1734–35, respectively, intending them to form a semicontinuous narrative of moral decay and retribution first in a young woman and then in a young man.[2] The two protagonists' stories can be briefly told. On Moll's arrival in London from the country she is met by a procuress. In short order she is raped, seduced into prostitution, and becomes the mistress of a rich Jew, to whom, however, she is unfaithful. Although initially she lives in some style, she is soon reduced to a common prostitute and is arrested, imprisoned in Bridewell, and forced to beat hemp (one of the standard punishments for whores and vagabonds). Finally, with one illegitimate child already and another on the way, she dies of syphilis. In the final scene we see her in her coffin, being desultorily mourned by a group of whores and their customers.

Tom Rakewell is likewise a new arrival to London. His miserly father, a merchant, has recently died, and Tom has come into his fortune. He immediately casts off his pregnant mistress, Sarah Young, and sets out to live the life of a gentleman. He collects bad art, is bilked by his numerous servants, and keeps company with prostitutes, gamblers, and highwaymen. He marries an old woman for her money, gambles that away, and is imprisoned for debt. Shattered by his misfortune Tom goes insane. In the final scene he has been confined to Bedlam, where we see him almost naked, raving and in manacles while the still-faithful Sarah attends him.

Both series concern young people who betray respectable middling origins to pursue the sensual gratifications more often associated with their betters. The fact that Moll is female and Tom is male makes for very considerable divergence in their stories. Moll's worst sin is unchastity, the original sin of women, and it is this that ultimately leads to her downfall. Tom, on the other hand, is profligate, the paradigmatic sin of young men of the trading classes. (He is also lewd, although this is of secondary importance for his story.) Moll's imprisonment in Bridewell for prostitution and Tom's in the Fleet for debt[3] are the climaxes of the two series and represent key statements of what is really at stake in moral terms for each. Although both stories explain their protagonists' destruction through an artful mix of individual propensities, bad luck, and bad influences, the choices available to each are very different.

While the viewer is left in no doubt that Moll's taste for luxury, her deceitfulness, and her social pretensions all contribute to her destruction, it is also quite plain that she has no real choices available to her once she has taken the fatal first step. Harried by the law, mother of an illegitimate child, on the edge of poverty, and totally dependent financially upon the whims of men, her only friend is her bunter who profits from her prostitution. If there are jobs for young women like Moll other than prostitution, the artist gives no indication of them. Moll's relatives manifestly fail to assist her. And respectable marriage is no longer an option. In *A Harlot's Progress* there is no real way out.[4]

Conversely, as feckless as Tom is, it is clear that he possesses a degree of agency that Moll does not and that there are real choices available to him. *A Harlot's Progress* chronicles a series of largely passive encounters on Moll's part with the procuress, with the forces of the law, with the wardens at Bridewell, with the doctors, with death.[5] By contrast, in *A Rake's Progress,* Tom makes numerous choices. Granted, some of these are empty, as in plate 2, where he is seen "choosing" between different forms of entertainment, none of which will ultimately redound to his benefit. Other choices are very real. Tom chooses to cast off his mistress who truly loves him. He chooses immoral companions when he has the money to associate with whomever he pleases. He chooses to dissipate a fortune in gambling, whoring, purchasing fine clothes, and employing a retinue of useless servants when he could have put his money to more productive uses. In plate 4, given the opportunity to repent and take up once more with the faithful and hardworking Sarah, who has just paid off a creditor who was about to arrest him, he lets the opportunity slip away. When his funds are exhausted he chooses to contract a marriage with a rich old woman, then gambles her money away too. Although Tom is self-deluded, unworthy, and often taken advantage of by the people around him, he is not a victim in the way that Moll is: he has plenty of choices, but he consistently chooses foolishly.

Unlike Moll, he has at least one real friend, Sarah: his salvation, at least for the first six plates, is always at hand if he would only reach for it.

Prescriptive writing (and prescriptive art) in the eighteenth century tended to portray most women as largely passive in the face of men, biology, and fate, and this presumption of passivity has, in turn, become firmly established in the eighteenth-century historiography. Only very recently, with work by Katharine Rogers, Leonore Davidoff and Catherine Hall, Keith Snell, Bridget Hill, Donna Andrew, Amy Louise Erickson, and Kathleen Wilson, has any serious effort been made to overcome this legacy, and it remains uncertain to what extent the notion that women can possess real historical agency has made its way into most historians' views of the period.[6] Some of this is simply a function of the relatively small body of scholarship that exists for eighteenth-century English women's history, as compared with the relative riches for some other periods. A good part of the problem derives from the fact that many historians' views of eighteenth-century women come directly from prescriptive writing—and a very small number of writings to boot. It is certainly reasonable, if only to find out what some eighteenth-century people thought women *should* be like, to spend time on the ubiquitous Addison and Steele, Lord Halifax's *Advice to a Daughter* (1688) (reprinted numerous times throughout the eighteenth century), James Fordyce's *Sermons to Young Women* (1767) (reprinted fourteen times before 1814), Dr. Gregory's *Legacy to his Daughters* (1774) (reprinted at least twenty-three times by 1877), or Hannah More's popular *Strictures on the Modern System of Female Education* (1799), with its milquetoast feminism and what Katharine Rogers aptly terms its "vigorous iteration of conventional principles."[7] It is harder to fathom the almost total neglect of more ambiguous texts like Sarah Fielding's prescriptive novel for girls, *The Governess, or Little Female Academy* (1749), which was reprinted almost continuously throughout the eighteenth and early nineteenth century, or a resolutely prescriptive children's book like *Little Goody Two-Shoes* (1765), which was probably more widely read in the hundred years after its publication than all the rest of this list combined.

Since Addison and Steele, Halifax, Fordyce, Gregory, and More have received wide exposure elsewhere[8] they will be discussed here only briefly. With the partial exception of Halifax's cynical and mildly libertine *Advice to a Daughter,* these books differ little from one another. They argue for companionate marriage, better education for girls so that they will be equipped to be good wives and mothers, and a tempered form of male supremacy allegedly based upon nature and designed for the greater utility and happiness of both sexes. Respectful of domestic order and family privacy, they are hostile to the sexual double standard, and, in most cases, suspicious of high rank. Without exception these authors locate the highest happiness for rational women in thoroughgoing economic and emotional dependence upon a man. In consequence, they slight or entirely ignore friendships among girls and women in order to focus on current or future heterosocial[9] and heterosexual relations. The moralists omit any discussion of alternatives to marriage for women, fail to provide information on ways girls might pursue training for independent employment, and ignore or condemn attempts by married (or soon to be married) women to maximize control over their own assets.[10] They leave out a great deal that was important in real women's lives, and they smooth over or reduce to euphemisms much that was neither simple nor especially appetizing about the female condition. Let us look at two sources that suggest a more complicated picture.

SARAH FIELDING: A LITTLE FEMALE ACADEMY

Sarah Fielding's *The Governess, or Little Female Academy* (1749) is one of the very first full-length novels for children and the earliest of what was to become a long-lived and much-loved genre, the Girls' School Story. The book was extremely popular in its time, going through at least eleven editions in the eighteenth century and taking on a new lease on life in the 1820s and '30s in the form of a "modernized" rewrite by Mary Martha Sherwood, that prolific writer of books for children. Thoroughly didactic, *The Governess* is also one of the subtlest accounts of the rearing of girls of the middling to lower gentry rank produced in the eighteenth century. Fielding's book is a good deal less hysterical than Hogarth's *A Harlot's Progress*, but it resembles it in that it emphasizes the risks to which girls and women were likely to be exposed. Unlike Hogarth, however, Fielding attends closely to the ways girls and women could exercise agency in their own lives while describing with clarity the constraints likely to be placed upon them.

The novel is set in a small boarding school for girls. The framing device is a childish quarrel among the girls, which is resolved by the end of the book into harmonious relations. The girls are taught greater consideration for one another through listening to a series of didactic fairy tales, by relating and reflecting upon their own "life histories," and by observing the exemplary behavior of their governess and Jenny Peace, the head girl. The "little female academy" is an idyllic place—calm, well-appointed, and supportive of female endeavor. Its students, once past the unseemly lapse in manners that opens the book, are loving and sweet tempered almost to a fault. Mrs. Teachum, their governess, is rational, affectionate, and all-knowing.

Hidden behind this utopian scene are some less palatable realities. Mrs. Teachum is the widow of a clergyman. Within twelve months of his death her two children died of a fever and she was plunged into penury owing to "the unforeseen Breaking of a Banker, in whose Hands almost all her Fortune was just then placed."[11] A victim of the improvidence of men, she has taken up teaching in order to support herself. Males, young and old, appear as a decidedly unreliable element in the novel. For instance, the girls are advised to love and revere their brothers, as one girl notes:

> [M]y good Mamma bid me remember how much my Brother's superior Strength might assist me in his being my Protector; and that I ought in return to use my utmost Endeavours to oblige him; and that then we should be mutual Assistants to each other throughout Life.[12]

But the boys who actually do appear in the novel are torturers and killers of animals, and men are often distant, undependable, capricious, or abusive.[13]

The promotion of loving and supportive relationships among women could be said to be the *raison d'être* of the novel as a whole (in this respect it differs profoundly from more conventional prescriptive literature), yet the friendships depicted, passionate and meaningful as they are, are vulnerable and short-lived. Men try to destroy them in order to monopolize women's affections for themselves.[14] Families disregard girls' affection for one another in planning for their future. And women are corrosively envious of other women for precisely those things—beauty, rank, income, a winning disposition—that make it possible for them to wield some power in the world of men.[15]

In reality, the little female academy is less a utopia than a liminal space, a place apart from men, boys, and families, into which girls temporarily withdraw to examine together what life is really about. What they discover is that it is possible to submit to others' mistakes and all-too-frequent lapses from virtue and rationality and still retain one's self-respect. One can— and it is a very stoic moral—still possess virtue and rationality oneself, even when the men and women around one are capable of neither. A more covert message is that even in a world where women are constantly at risk from the errors of judgment and cruelties of the other sex and the envy of their own, a few of them can still hope for and, like Mrs. Teachum, occasionally achieve economic independence and some degree of personal fulfillment.

The book contains some touching tributes to conjugal love and feminine retirement, yet the final pages of the book suggest a more ambivalent vision of adulthood than that found in the better-known prescriptive writers. The girls are devastated when Jenny Peace, the most popular and virtuous of the girls, reaches the age of fourteen and is abruptly taken out of school by her aunt. We the readers, like Jenny's schoolmates, know with such certainty that she will be married within a few years that it is unnecessary to say the words. Jenny masterfully sums up one of the major messages of the novel with these words: "Let us submit chearfully to this Separation . . . because it is our Duty so to do." She then rather unreassuringly remarks to her distraught friends that she hopes "a Friendship, founded on so innocent and so good a Foundation as ours is, will always subsist, *as far as shall be consistent with our future Situations in Life.*"[16] In fact, Jenny never returns to the school again, and her connections to her former friends are henceforth confined to letters.

Clearly submission to duty is the most important lesson a girl has to learn in her years at school, but the reader is left as well with a distinct sense that the world outside the female idyll of the little academy is not likely to be anywhere near as agreeable. Sarah Fielding would have argued, at least in public, that marriage was essential for most women (although she herself did not marry), but she also sought to emphasize that the reality of marriage generally fell well short of the ideal. It was natural for women to subject themselves to men, yet the way men exercised their authority was seldom rational or virtuous, and sometimes it was frankly abusive. Unlike Hogarth or the male moralists, Fielding does assume that women have some agency in their own lives; she even allows for the possibility that their actions do not consistently have to be for the benefit of a man. Mrs. Teachum (out of cruel necessity, it is true) starts a successful school. Jenny Peace teaches the other girls to be good through the use of stories, including one in which an extremely authoritative female fairy reclaims a wayward daughter. Women develop friendships with one another that are supportive and emotionally fulfilling and that contribute to their moral maturity. Yet, agency is hard-won for women, and is itself constantly at risk. Self-sacrifice for the benefit of others and obedience to authority remain for Fielding, as for other moralists, the central aims of female socialization.

LITTLE GOODY TWO-SHOES

The most popular children's book of the period, indeed one of the most popular of all time, was *The History of Little Goody Two-Shoes.* Originally published in 1765, *Little Goody Two-Shoes* ran through at least twenty-eight British editions and twelve American ones before 1800. More than sixty-six British and thirty-five American editions were issued between 1800 and 1850. Of unknown authorship (Oliver Goldsmith is one candidate), the tale of Margery Meanwell, also known as Goody Two-Shoes, artfully combines the themes of female agency in the face of adversity, the pursuit of literacy and virtue, honest woman's work, and successful social mobility.[17]

Margery is the daughter of a well-to-do farmer named Meanwell who is ruined through the harassment and depredations of an enclosing landlord and soon after dies. His wife survives him by only a few days, and Margery and her younger brother Tommy are cast penniless upon the world. Ig-nored by their relatives ("[o]ur relations and friends seldom take notice of us when we are poor; but as we grow rich they grow fond"),[18] they are helped by a local clergyman who buys them clothes and sends Tommy off to sea.

Meanwhile, little Margery teaches herself to read and becomes so adept that she begins teaching other children, using alphabet blocks she devises herself. A lengthy section of the book describes her rounds as an itinerant reading teacher. Margery also becomes a sort of child-sage, advising a bil-ious gentleman that he should rise early and eat sparingly if he wants to regain his health, combating superstitious beliefs, and preventing a rob-bery aimed at the house of her father's old enemy and former landlord, Sir Timothy—thus demonstrating her capacity to return good for evil.[19]

In time, Margery's reputation earns her the position of schoolmistress of the local school. There she continues to teach children to read using her alphabet blocks, combining this with preaching obedience to authority and the efficacy of early rising and hard work. She inveighs against cock-throwing, torturing insects, and whipping horses and dogs, and she contin-ues to dispense wise advice to villagers and to spread rational problem solving wherever she goes. In the fullness of time a gentleman falls in love with Margery and marries her, at which point brother Tommy fortuitously reappears, having made a fortune in Africa, and endows her with a rich settlement. Margery is widowed after a mere six years of marriage and thenceforth uses her large fortune to encourage piety, succor the poor, and promote matrimony, although she herself never remarries. She finally dies, lamented by all.[20]

Goody Two-Shoes is a self-possessed and appealing heroine. She re-sponds to adversity in the best enlightened style, through virtue, active ra-tionality, and reading. Her adventures as an itinerant reading instructor and, later, local schoolteacher make her one of the more credible independ-ent working women of eighteenth-century literature. And the story of her rise to power and influence in her village is to some extent believable, even if her brilliant marriage and sudden riches are not. In *The History of Little Goody Two-Shoes*, as in most eighteenth-century prescriptive literature, sud-den changes of fortune and the world of risk are seldom far away. Margery teaches submission to Providence with a parable about a young servant who rises to mercantile riches through hard work, scrupulous account keeping, and marriage to his master's niece, only to lose everything to his creditors when he fails to properly insure a fleet of ships.[21] Although Mar-gery emerges as a powerful character, she does not seriously threaten the traditional view that women should exercise power only in a moral capac-ity. Margery's frequent advice giving puts her in a class with Defoe's trades-man's wife, who encourages her husband to cut expenses, Richardson's

Pamela, who reforms a rake, the delicately influential women of the *Tatler* and *Spectator,* and Mrs. Teachum and Jenny Peace, who bring harmony to their school.[22]

The problem of preparing middling girls for womanhood was not a simple one. Both *The History of Little Goody Two-Shoes* and *The Governess* give due attention to the risks of being a woman, whether deriving from others' abuse of power, from simple incompetence, from the corrupted values of social superiors, or from the workings of fate and the market. The authors address the topic of female agency with far greater subtlety and flexibility than do the better-known authors, while giving due emphasis to the fact that girls *did,* in reality, have fewer options than boys and frequently found themselves in an economically precarious position as a result. Sarah Fielding's novel also stresses (although without exaggerating its durability) an aspect of women's lives that is virtually ignored in most conduct books: their friendships with other women. Both *The Governess* and *The History of Little Goody Two-Shoes,* the latter more strongly than the former, also suggest the possibility of women achieving economic independence from men through self-education and work. Since, as we will see in the next chapter, the eighteenth century was the first century in which a significant number of middling women did just that, often by engaging in activities like school teaching, this is an especially apposite theme.

GIRLS AND THE FAMILY ECONOMY

Prescriptive literature depicts a world of relatively clear choices (or, as we have seen, absence of choice) and very clear punishments and rewards. Its characters are stereotyped and conventional; its narratives predictable. It is often difficult to separate what the author thinks *should* be done from what he or she thinks *is* being done. Family and court records show us a less predictable and less orderly world.

Ellin Stout was the sister of William Stout of Lancaster (1665–1752), the Quaker ironmonger and grocer whose early career was discussed in an earlier chapter. Their parents were of industrious yeoman stock, anxious to improve their estates and their posterity. They educated their sons with some care. However, Ellin, the single daughter of six children, "was early confined to waite on her brother," that is, taken out of school to provide childcare so as to permit her mother to do farm and household work.[23] The boys went on to the free school in nearby Boulton, where they stayed until about the age of twelve or fourteen. As they grew older, they too were sometimes taken out of school to do farmwork. Stout reported that this meant he made "smal progress in Latin" and that his brothers "got little learning except to read English and some little writing." Yet their education remained a higher priority than was their sister's, and the pattern of expected labor contributions was quite different.[24]

The distribution of resources in the family showed a similar pattern. The boys received small estates to the value of £100 to £200 each, with the oldest son getting the family home and farm. William Stout got a small parcel of land and an apprenticeship premium. Ellin got £80, but since the family decided her health was not such as to permit her to marry, this money became a source of low- or no-interest loans for her brothers' businesses. (One has to wonder whether the unwelcome prospect of losing both Ellin's dowry *and* her not inconsiderable labor power to another family played a role in the family's decision to discourage her from marrying.) Ellin spent much of the rest of her life acting as unpaid housekeeper and shop assistant to her brother William. She also assisted her other two brothers, Josias and Leonard, in their trades. Her early training as "a good and diligent assistant to her mother" set the pattern for her life.[25]

Middling boys tended to be placed in positions from which they could learn skills that would be useful in their future careers, give them social contacts, and make them money. Middling girls, on the other hand, worked as companions, housekeepers, seamstresses, nursemaids, shop assistants, and the like. Their labor represented a family resource that could be deployed by fathers, mothers, or brothers to supplement the family income, shore up kin connections, and free other family members for more specialized work or to attend school. When William Stout's sister Ellin died, William Stout noted that "my brother Leonard sent his 2d daughter, Jennet, to keep my house till I was otherwise provided." The cycle had started again.[26]

Although girls' schools catering specifically to the middling classes proliferated in the eighteenth century, the habit of keeping middling girls at home died hard. The result was a hit-or-miss education for many girls, since their female relatives, who typically supervised their educations, were less likely to be literate than men of a similar rank. Middling girls' rearing was organized around the assumption that their individual needs and aspirations could be subordinated to the labor needs of the family group, and this pattern was supposed, in theory, to hold for the rest of their lives, whether or not they married.

Boys too were expected to make a contribution, but they were also allowed greater independence of action. More time and care was taken over their education, they were taught more diverse skills, and the governing assumption was that they would take what they learned in childhood and adolescence and strike out on their own. Much of the discussion of "individualism" in the early modern period has suffered from the failure of too many commentators to recognize the obvious—that some people (women, servants, slaves) were simply expected, liberal theory or no, to be significantly less "individualistic" than others. For girls this fact of life was established early.

"[L]ove is, such a friend as is desired everywhere and without which a comon weal, nay, a family would not subsist," wrote the Lancashire shopkeeper Roger Lowe in a diary entry for 13 July 1663.[27] By modern standards girls received a worse deal than did their brothers, but that did not mean they were any less loved. Much work on the seventeenth and eighteenth centuries adopts the view that affection, or even deep love, is automatically accompanied by egalitarian treatment. Now there is no doubt that in many, perhaps most, middling families, girls were "loved" just as boys were. It is also clear that girls were a lower priority when it came to distributing family resources, whether of a material or symbolic kind, and that this relative lack impeded them for the rest of their lives. In eighteenth-century middling families, love (and the threatened withdrawal of love) were key ways of ensuring the obedience of subordinate members. Especially for girls and women, love, self-sacrifice, duty, and subordination were inextricably linked both in life and in the advice books.[28] Lawrence Stone and Randolph Trumbach are two of the most important proponents of the notion that love translates into practical egalitarianism. Where they err is in failing to recognize that girls and women were supposed to make sacrifices precisely *because* they loved those who benefited from their actions and knew themselves to be loved in return. Familial affection is not reducible to a way of manipulating others, nor is it simply a sop to inferior family members. By the same token it is far too complex a phenomenon to be viewed unproblematically as a path to liberation, especially for women.

Seventeenth-century middling people encouraged both boys and girls to be loving. But they were much more explicit in the case of girls, whose working lives, in theory at least, would be recompensed within a primarily emotional, rather than monetary, economy. In reality, of course, mothers as well as fathers pocketed the earnings of their children, there were complex financial dealings between husbands and wives, and daughters acted dutifully toward their parents partially in expectation of a monetary reward on marrying or on their parents' death. Moreover, as a later chapter makes clear, large numbers of middling women, married and single, worked at paid employment, and some must have defied family pressure in order to do so. But the belief that middling women "should" operate within an economy of emotion rather than of money continued throughout this period to justify a range of economies in their education and training.

One of the most potent symbols of girls' familial role was the attention given to teaching them sewing. Ellin Stout was "early taught to read, knit and spin, and also needle work" and was soon set the task of providing the clothes for her younger siblings. Charlotte Charke, writer and actress, detested womanly chores and refused to learn how to sew, but she left a revealing account of the home of her relative, the physician Dr. Hales, where cooking and sewing formed the bulk of the instruction for the girls of the household.[29] Mothers often started their daughters with the mending of their brothers' school clothes (work which deftly symbolized the role girls were supposed to embrace with respect to boys and men), and they were supposed to graduate from this to overseeing larger, but equally family-oriented, and home centered projects. In the 1650s the daughters of Ambrose Barnes, a Newcastle merchant, were set to sewing by their mother, who seized the opportunity provided by the sedentary character of needlework to "put them in mind of a tortoise, the emblem of a woman who should be a keeper at home, as the tortoise seldom peeps out of its shell."[30]

Early introduction to sewing was by no means confined to the middling, but it had a somewhat different resonance in middling families than in the upper gentry or aristocracy (lesser gentry women hovered somewhere in between).[31] Undoubtedly, middling girls spent less time on fancywork, and their sewing was often essential to clothing their families. The key difference, however, was that very many daughters of middling families actually made their living partly or wholly by their needle at some time in their lives. The rub was that the needle trades tended, with few exceptions, to be a low-paying, low-status field; the fact that huge numbers of women learned to sew made for a permanent glut on the market. The low remuneration that resulted from this surplus in turn played a role in keeping many women close to home, since other options were so few. It is a paradigmatic case of the ways in which the extremely narrow range of skills and activities to which girls were exposed both symbolized and perpetuated their inferior status within the family and society.

MOTHERS AND DAUGHTERS

It is a vexing problem to disentangle acts or practices designed and executed by superordinate groups to keep their social inferiors in subjection from acts of complicity or apparent complicity on the part of members of the subordinate groups themselves. Several decades of intensive work on slave societies, master-servant relations, lords and peasants, colonial subjects, women, and other groupings has made clear how very complex such systems are.[32] Subordinate groups have their own internal hierarchies that intersect intricately with "larger" systems. Superordinate groups successfully encourage these and other divisions by rewarding inferiors who demonstrate a commitment to the prevailing system, thus, inevitably, setting up competing "ladders of success." At the same time, subordinate groups tend to be expert at ambiguous acts, and they often speak an insider and resistant language among themselves and a language of compliance in the presence of their superiors. On the other side, there is no doubt that in most hierarchical societies some members of socially inferior groups *do* embrace the dominant ideology in whole or more likely in part, up to and including an at least partial belief in their own intrinsic inferiority.

Mothers (and stepmothers) bore a direct responsibility for the rearing and socialization of daughters in seventeenth- and eighteenth-century England, and an important part of this task involved instructing their daughters on the terms of their subjection to men. Girls learned early to express verbal support for male supremacy, particularly—here almost reflexively— if they were doing, or planned to do, anything that could be construed as unconventional. It is harder to tell to what extent women and girls actually internalized these beliefs, and there must have been much variation. Some mothers urged their daughters to obey their fathers while, at the same time, slipping them money that would permit them to defy them. They encouraged young women to defer to their husbands, yet they often bequeathed their money to their female relatives, including their daughters, for their "separate use," that is, in such a way that their husbands could not, in theory at least, get hold of the funds.[33] And when obedience and deference failed to ensure decent treatment for themselves or their daughters, they could be quick to seek remedies—even, at times, to resort to the law.[34] At the same time, other mothers either showed little or no interest in their daughter's welfare in the first place or were too mired in passivity or in their own difficulties to take any steps on their daughters' behalf.[35]

Inegalitarian societies present a difficult series of choices for parents. One condemns one's offspring to perpetual inferiority, with all the risks that entails, if one simply tries to fit them for, and reconcile them to, the sort of future most people of their gender (class, race) are expected to lead. But to train a child for some other future and encourage her or him to expect something better greatly increases the risk that, as an adult, that individual will be punished, at times savagely, for going against prevailing norms. Equally, she or he might fail to overcome the other obstacles to a better life or be unable to be reconciled to the disappointment. Faced with this unpleasant set of choices, many parents tacked uneasily between, on the one hand, trying to teach their daughters to excel in the traditional female role and to be at least outwardly subservient to men and, on the other, working to pass on to them saleable skills, self-reliance, and money of their own.

LITERACY AND NUMERACY

Evidence from the written records of private families, as well as quantitative studies of marriage registers, signatures on petitions, and the like tend to confirm what the advice books suggest, namely, that one of the most fundamental changes that took place in the rearing of middling girls between the mid sixteenth and the late eighteenth centuries was the popularizing of the new or relatively new skills of reading and writing. It is well known that far fewer women than men were literate in the early modern period. David Cressy estimates that perhaps 1 percent of women and 10 percent of men were able to read and write in 1500, and R. S. Schofield thinks that about 40 percent of women and 60 percent of men were able to do so three hundred years later.[36]

Schofield and Cressy have both shown that, in the case of males, literacy was highly occupationally specific in the seventeenth and eighteenth centuries. Far from being evenly distributed across the population, male literacy was heavily concentrated among the gentry, professionals, government officials, retail traders, and skilled tradesmen.[37] Can something similar be said for women? Early forays into the historical study of literacy tended to provide occupational breakdowns only for men while lumping all women into a single category. More recently there have been some attempts to treat women as the heterogeneous group they are. The most important of these has come from Peter Earle who has compared rates of female literacy in London during the years 1665 to 1725 to such variables as age, origin (immigrant or London-born), working or nonworking status, and type of occupation. In terms of the last he finds a wide spread: women who did personal service work (domestic service, nursing) had a literacy rate of 40 percent or less, women in the needle trades reached 70 percent, and shopkeepers, midwives, and schoolteachers reached 80 to 100 percent. We would expect literacy rates to be lower outside London, but it is likely that the proportions were roughly similar elsewhere. Middling women were beginning to enjoy very high literacy rates indeed.[38]

It was high and it was rising. Between 1650 and 1800 overall female literacy in England increased from under 15 percent to about 36 percent. By 1840 it had risen even more precipitously, to around 52 percent.[39] It is almost certainly the case that most of this increase, particularly in the eighteenth century, was among urban middling women, though the crude figures conceal much variation. Quaker and Methodist women were more likely to learn to read than were other women,[40] and younger women more than older ones. Women in retail sales learned to read in larger numbers than did women in service or like fields. Family records overrepresent individuals who could write, but it is suggestive that it is in the late seventeenth and eighteenth centuries that one begins for the first time to find significant numbers of writings, published and unpublished, by women in commercial and professional families.

In the sixteenth and early seventeenth centuries a real hostility toward the idea of women learning to read or write at all is evident in some sources. (This was matched at times by an antipathy to non-elite men learning to read.) A common complaint during the Reformation was that women were taking down sermons in shorthand, a practice that threatened (male) clerical authority and dovetailed dangerously with the alleged religious credulity of women. In the seventeenth century moralists charged that women were reading and writing bawdy verse, a practice that was said to stimulate their naturally lustful temperaments.[41] Concern about lower-class women learning to read, and especially to write, persisted well into the eighteenth century and beyond.[42] By the latter part of the seventeenth century however, most urban people, at least, seem to have come to see literacy among respectable women as a positive asset, and in the eighteenth it became a clear status marker for women of the urban trading classes and above. The content of what women read continued to raise fears, however, more so than was the case with men, and this anxiety was to last well into the modern era.[43]

Girls were taught to read with the presumption that other people would be the primary beneficiaries. As the previous chapter shows, in the latter part of the seventeenth century respectability and worldly success among the middling became much more directly contingent than it had been upon the ability to read and write. There was a great deal more literate or numerate "work" to be done inside and outside the family proper than had been the case before. One result was that the daughter or wife who assisted her father's or husband's intellectual labors by reading to him, copying for him, organizing his papers, doing translating, and so on became a common sight among the eighteenth- and nineteenth-century *literati*. But daughters and wives of more ordinary middling families—shopkeepers, manufacturers, lower-level professionals, civil servants—also kept their male relatives apprised of the news (often by reading to them), did their accounts, wrote letters for them, and provided almost every other conceivable type of clerical assistance. Women became part of a complex exchange of cultural information that both assisted the growing self-esteem and confidence of the middling classes generally and represented a significant creative arena for the reader or writer herself.

In her illuminating study of women and the eighteenth-century periodical, Kathryn Shevelow talks of literate women becoming part of a "community of the text."[44] When whole families committed themselves to a culture of reading and writing, a good many of the more tedious or painstaking aspects of the work fell to women, particularly lower status women within the family. But like the more intricate or ornate varieties of sewing, tasks requiring a fairly high level of literacy demanded skills servants did not, or were thought not, to possess. The shared literate, if not always literary, projects of what we might call, after Shevelow, "the family of the text" were to a large extent class-exclusive, which is to say that they included the middling nuclear family and their relatives by blood or marriage, but much less often their servants. For this reason these tasks became an important marker of group identity.

On a more prosaic note, many middling families depended on teaching for at least a portion of their livelihood. Again, girls were groomed from childhood to make a contribution. Zelophead Vincent, a hotpresser and sometime schoolteacher whose career spanned the late eighteenth and early nineteenth centuries, wrote in 1813 to his daughter Jemima criticizing her writing hand which in his view exhibited "hurry, perturbation & impatience," not "calmness, placidity and steadiness." Vincent wanted his daughter's penmanship to suggest the stereotypically feminine (and also middling) virtues he hoped she would strive to acquire. Her command of writing also had a specifically economic meaning within their domestic economy: a fine writing hand was essential for Jemima because

> if Amelia leaves the Concern [i.e., the school he ran] I am sure your own good Sense must not only see the necessity of continuing the School, but of the Impossibility of Phebe being in it alone, as also the folly & impropriety of giving it up. And I should hope you see the Circumstance clear that if Amelia leaves[,] the Bounds of your habitation will be fix'd by the will of Providence who orders all things for the good of his Creatures who resign themselves to him and confide in his management & direction.[45]

Jemima would replace her sister when the time came, and the subtly coercive combination of parental concern, appeals to "good sense" and propriety, and a suitably paternalistic rendering of Divine Providence was designed to ensure that she would do so with the minimum of trouble.

Vincent also kept a close watch on his two sons, but here the expectations were quite different. He was less than delighted with the progress of one of his sons, Isaac, who "is inattentive to business [and] shows little desire to learn & less to exercise care." By contrast, his other son, Stephen, who was working for merchants who sold by commission, was "all eagerness for pushing on. He would never have the patience to wait the dull round of [a] seven year apprenticeship, but wants to feel his ground immediately."[46] For his sons the watchwords were "pushing on" and "eagerness," traits that might, today, be termed aggressive pursuit of individual opportunity. There was no question but that Vincent's daughters would work too, but he took it for granted that their labor would be deployed by him, and later by their husbands, and that any "pursuit of opportunity" should and would directly benefit him and the rest of "his" family, and only indirectly the girls themselves. As chapter 1 shows, eighteenth-century middling family life also raised obstacles to men's pursuit of "possessive individualism," but the barriers placed in the way of girls and women were considerably more difficult to overcome.

Because girls were not typically expected to use their skills to advance themselves outside the confines of their natal family or, later, the marital home, they were not, as a rule, encouraged to advance beyond a certain point in their studies, and often were actively discouraged from doing so. The learned old maid whom men were afraid to marry was already a stock figure in the eighteenth century.[47] The rather stunted education many girls received in school as well as at home was designed as much to render them useful to, but not competitive with, men as it was to fashion them into ornaments to their families and class.

The ability to read and write could not always be regulated by convention. Up to a point, literacy increased a woman's value and therefore her bargaining power; moreover, the ease with which some women picked up such skills could cast doubt upon the widely held presumption that women were intellectually inferior. Some women were certainly aware of this. Eleanora Hucks wrote to her daughter in 1778 urging her to practice her letter writing, "as nothing debases a Woman so much as being defficient [in writing]." Besides, she went on, as "Men in general have but a mean opinion of our understanding[,] do not let us by neglect [of our minds] verify that notion, let us show them they have no other advantage than education." In the next breath, however, as if frightened by her own temerity, she reminded her daughter of the necessity of "still bearing in our Minds the natural subordination [of women to men] nature at first design'd."[48]

The ability to read and write was a saleable skill in the early modern period, and once having mastered it, some women were not content to live the rest of their lives laboring on behalf of, and being dependent upon, families or husbands. Although very few women seem to have had access to clerks' jobs, the major growth sector for literate men (even though at least one contemporary feminist writer thought such jobs would be ideal for women),[49] female schoolteachers and women who wrote for money proliferated in this period. And there are numerous cases of women who used their earning power to establish full or partial independence from their relatives or to avoid marriage. The way was arduous and risky, but some girls undoubtedly saw literacy as a partial escape route from the stultifying narrowness and the real psychic, physical, and financial risks attendant upon the established female life course.

The ability to read and write allowed girls and women to maintain emotional connections with a far-flung network of male and, especially, female friends. It also gave them new tools with which to influence their male and female kin, place their mark upon the historical record, and even engage in polemical writing.[50] More and more women wrote their autobiographies, and some of these women were willing to describe in very explicit terms the mental or physical abuse they had suffered at the hands of men and other women and to detail lives that departed very far indeed from

conventional norms.[51] The eighteenth century also saw a striking proliferation of poems, novels, history, travel writing, devotional tracts, and even
feminist writing emanating from the ranks of middling and gentry women.
Female agency and feminine social critique can and do exist independently of literacy, and one cannot assume *a priori* that what women wrote
down once they were capable of doing so was qualitatively different from
what, prior to the arrival of widespread female literacy, women merely
talked about. Nonetheless, here, as elsewhere, literacy supplied opportunities to learn about the world in a more independent and self-directed way,
to influence others, and, occasionally, to chart a new course.[52]

The spread of accounting skills among women is, unlike literacy, virtually impossible to quantify. Anecdotal evidence suggests that it became a
desirable skill for girls of middling and gentry families beginning some
time in the mid to late seventeenth century.[53] Again, the acquisition of this
new skill came initially in response to family labor needs. The anonymous
author of *Advice to the Women and Maidens of London* (1678) was set by her
father to the task of keeping the accounts for the entire household.[54] In
1717 John Thomlinson, a worldly young clergyman in the market for a
wife, "had thoughts of Sir G. Wheeler's youngest daughter and a very managing woman, keeps accounts of all matters of house and husbandry etc."[55]
Such a woman, trained early to assist with, in this case, the family estate,
might well be a desirable mate for a young man ambitious of improving
himself. William Stout, the Lancaster ironmonger, remarked disapprov-
ingly of his nephew's wife that "she was a gentlewoman, and knew nothing
of business or housekeeping to encourage a trade, so that I have small
hopes of their doeing well in any busines or trade."[56]

Like a good writing hand, the ability to keep accounts and to do so
systematically throughout one's life became, for women as well as for men,
a mark of respectability. It is likely that accounting improved some wom-
en's confidence in their own abilities as businesswomen, but except in
rather unusual circumstances, this did not mean that they would have access to the kind of capital enjoyed by men of their class. As a previous
chapter showed, it was customary to give middling boys small sums of
money for the express purpose of having them invest it in some small-
scale trading venture, thus encouraging them to keep good accounts and,
ideally, giving them a taste for turning a profit. By contrast, a girl was
schooled to think of money in terms of her future dowry, a sum of money
that would go with her when she married, to be used by her future husband
or his family to capitalize *their* business. Men got capital; women were, at
least in theory, merely a conduit for capital to flow to other families. Still,
accounting remained an important badge of belonging for eighteenth-
century middling women, linking them in symbolic terms both to the world
of trade and to the class that traded.

WOMEN AND APPRENTICESHIPS

Fathers and mothers were aware of the disadvantages under which girls labored, and some of the more provident among them—sometimes at the urging of daughters themselves—did take steps to train their daughters to be self-supporting. A presumably typical case comes from the 1740s. One John Birkett of Poolbank, a dissenter and trader, apprenticed one of his daughters to a mantua maker because she was "always much dissatisfy'd with a Country Life tho' otherwise sober and tractable," and when she wished to move to the city for "improvement" he made inquiries about getting her a mantua making position in Northampton. Eventually he set her up, along with another daughter, in a partnership. One relevant factor here may have been the untimely death of their only brother at the age of about ten, shortly before he was to embark on a lengthy and costly course of education. This was a family with surplus capital to spend on daughters.[57]

We know from other sources that middling families did apprentice their daughters to trades. In a survey of nonparish indentures in five counties (Surrey, Sussex, Bedfordshire, Warwickshire, and Wiltshire) in the first half of the eighteenth century, Keith Snell found that 562 out of 11,555 indentures, or an average of 4.9 percent, involved female apprentices. He also uncovered some interesting differences between nonparish girl apprentices (that is, girls whose parents or guardians paid the apprenticeship premium and so would probably qualify as middling) and poor girls (those for whom the parish paid the apprenticeship premiums). First, poor girls were apprenticed in much larger numbers. In Snell's study of parish apprenticeships in the southern counties women averaged as many as 34 percent of all the indentures issued between the beginning of the seventeenth century and about 1834. Among non-parish indentures (ordinarily better-off households), however, only about 4.9 percent were women. Second, poor girls were apprenticed to a wider range of trades, including a number of trades commonly associated with men (blacksmithing, carpentry, shoemaking, and the like). Middling girls, on the other hand, tended to be apprenticed to "genteel" trades such as millinery or mantua making.[58]

Parents, guardians, or anyone else wanting to find out more about training and apprenticeship options for girls in the eighteenth century would not have had much to go on. The majority of advice-book writers had little or nothing to say on the subject of giving young women saleable skills beyond what they would need to be wives or fall-back domestic labor in the houses of their male relatives. And the growing number of publications designed to help middling parents raise and train their children for productive careers concentrated almost exclusively on boys.

A refreshing exception is Joseph Collyer's *Parents & Guardians Directory and the Youth's Guide in the Choice of a Profession or Trade* (1761). Collyer supplies valuable information on the trades most often entered into by middling girls, including the prerequisites in terms of skills and apprenticeship premiums and, occasionally, estimates of the costs of setting up an independent business. Here is his entry for cap makers, a desirable employ for middling women. In this case, part of the appeal, as Collyer makes clear, was that even if a woman failed to raise the money to set up independently, she could still make a comfortable salary and enjoy diverse employment opportunities as a journeywoman:

> Their apprentices should be smart girls of a genteel appearance; they should work well at their needles and be ready accomptants. Their friends must give with them [as an apprenticeship premium] from 10–30 £ in proportion to the trade carried on by the mistress. They serve only five years [instead of the usual seven]; and are kept the first part of their time close to the needle. Those who cannot set up [independently in business] may get 15 or 20 £ a year and their board as journeywomen, they being qualified not only to serve capmakers but may be shopwomen to milliners, the haberdashers or any buying and selling trade proper for women.[59]

Here is his entry for pamphlet-shop owners, an occupation that did not involve a formal apprenticeship, but did require capital:

> This business is principally carried on by women ... it is easily learnt and requires no abilities but writing, accounts and an obliging behaviour ... 100 £ will enable him or her to get a good support.[60]

Collyer's directory provides descriptions of most of the jobs to which middling girls would have been encouraged to aspire, as well as the skills prospective entrants were expected already to possess (not surprisingly, accounting is prominent).[61] But what it shows most plainly is the dearth of remunerative occupations for women in comparison with men. The vast majority of jobs in which women were likely to be found were low paying and insecure. Those who worked at livery-button making, for example, were "chiefly women who are paid by the dozen and are able to get but a poor living"; broom makers were "men and poor women who get from 8 to 16s a week."[62] It seems likely that the scarcity of options was a disincentive for many girls (or their families) to consider special training. It also seems reasonable to suppose that many middling girls and women, both married and single, experienced downward mobility in occupational terms when they attempted to strike out on their own. Even if they came from solid middling families (with say, a father who was a moderately prosperous shopkeeper or professional) they might well end up as servants or in low paying by-employments that would yield a respectable standard of living only if combined with a tolerable man's income. They also had much less access to capital than did their brothers, and even if they had funds of their own, say from a bequest, there was strong pressure for them to put the money into a male relative's business, not their own enterprises.

CHASTITY

It was a common conceit of the time that a woman's whole worth lay in her chastity. In fact this was never true in the strict sense, and certainly not in middling families, where girls' and women's labor was often essential. Still, it is true that a reputation for unchastity was a signal disadvantage that could outweigh a woman's other assets. The problem for the historian lies in finding out under what circumstances it was likely to do so.

It is not difficult to find cases where pregnant women were let go from their places, excommunicated by dissenting chapels, forced to post bond against going onto the parish rates, or cast off or divorced on grounds of adultery by husbands who suspected the child was not theirs. And these things happened to daughters of middling families as well as the daughters of the laboring poor.[63] But it is by no means clear how severely or how consistently even an obvious manifestation of sexual misconduct, such as bastard bearing, was punished, especially if the girl or woman could rely on her family or herself for support rather than the parish, if she could be conveniently married off, or if the baby miscarried or died in infancy.

Nor were miscreants necessarily made to suffer in perpetuity for their transgressions. In 1746 the Limestreet Independent Church in London excommunicated Sarah Bryan for having become pregnant out of wedlock, which was standard practice in such cases. The minutes of the church meeting report that Sarah was "deliver[ed] up to Satan . . . for the Destruction of the Flesh that her Spirit might be saved in the Day of the Lord," which certainly has a ring of finality about it. Remarkably, less than two years later Sarah Bryan was petitioning for readmission to the fellowship. Apparently she was not readmitted, but the fact that she thought she might be is revealing.[64] If a congregation that excommunicated members for associating with scandalous people and for not paying their debts, as well as for a range of specifically sexual sins, could consider readmitting a woman like Sarah, what does this suggest about attitudes in less morally repressive settings? Certainly this sounds very different from the uncompromising dualisms of virtue and depravity found in *A Harlot's Progress*.

The difficulty of establishing the significance of chastity in real life (as opposed to in sermons and conduct books) makes it hard to say how related fears affected the rearing of girls. There is copious evidence to show that adult women who attempted to enter the "male" public sphere, say by writing or engaging in political discussion, or taking on conspicuously "public" roles of any kind, were extremely likely to have their chastity challenged as a result.[65] The obsession with chastity also worked to constrain the mobility of girls by giving families, as well as communities, an incentive and a right to watch over daughters and unmarried women more closely than they did sons or unmarried men.[66]

Chastity was more than simply an idea foisted upon women. There is no doubt that the fetishizing of female sexual "purity" was preeminently a way for individual men and families to control the reproductive capacities of women. But it was double-edged. It also supplied women with a way to partially protect themselves against sexually predatory behavior, at least that of men not their husbands. This simple fact ensured a rather high degree of support for the ideal of chastity from many women. It is impossible to say what the prevalence of rape was in the seventeenth or eighteenth centuries, but there is plenty of evidence that much rape, although not all, including the rape of extremely young children, was winked at, viewed as funny, or thought to depend upon female complicity, that is, not to be raped at all.[67] Certainly it was very inconsistently punished, and in those cases where it was punished, the central issue was often the property rights of male relatives and the maintenance of social hierarchy rather than the welfare of the victim herself. Women's often aggressive defense of their own and others' "virtue" provided one of the relatively few points of stability in an extremely confused discursive field.

The whole issue of chastity thus represents something of a dilemma for the historian. Sexual violence was real, but the pretense that keeping girls and women confined within the patriarchal family would protect them from it (and the corollary belief that women who entered the world of men were inviting violence and deserved what they got) was probably more constraining than the violence itself. Eighteenth-century views on such matters were also based upon some highly ideological understandings of what sexual violence was. Although we know little about this aspect of sexual coercion, it is likely that in the eighteenth century, like today, most sexual violence was perpetrated by employers, friends, relatives, household members, and husbands rather than rakish aristocrats or the various strangers and "others" who populate the better-known eighteenth-century narratives of rape: far from being an attack on the family, as it often appears in, say, eighteenth- and nineteenth-century melodrama, sexual coercion thrived at the family's very heart.[68]

Female chastity symbolized many things. Its violation was a powerful indication of a failure of patriarchal control. The man who was unable to guarantee his daughter's or his wife's purity hardly deserved to wield power. Loss of reputation drastically lowered a woman's worth in the marriage market and meant a net loss in terms of her relatives' ability to marry her off in such a way as to accrue them social influence and business connections. Yet the pervasive concern about allowing girls to run about freely and about gender mixing that one sees in contemporary advice books seems to suggest that such dicta were as often as not honored in the breach.[69] The problem of keeping girls close to home was akin to the problem of keeping women at home. They had work to do elsewhere. Although girls were burdened with more time-consuming and mobility-constraining jobs than boys (most notably, of course, sewing and baby minding), if they went on errands, went to market, helped their mothers with their paid work, participated in standard patterns of neighborhood sociability, or went off on family missions (girls were often sent off to assist aged relatives or otherwise stand in for their mothers), they could hardly have spent all their time at home. The various prohibitions on girls functioned less to keep them at home in the strict sense than to restrict their aspirations and keep them out of activities reserved for boys and men.

REBEL GIRLS

Oppressive systems certainly spawn timidity, servility, and internalized self-hatred in some people. But they can equally result in (or at very least be consistent with) remarkable strength of character. The main form of female rebellion in this period to receive much attention from historians has been young aristocratic women's apparently growing refusal to submit to arranged marriages and their new insistence on marrying for love.[70] Even if this represents a real trend in aristocratic families, which does seem likely, it is not clear how much it says about the 99 percent of English families who were not aristocrats. And the focus on a few women's increased freedom to marry for love is in one sense unfortunate, because it perpetuates the fiction that even the most aspiring women could look no further than romantic love and reproduction.

This final section discusses two eighteenth-century middling girls who rebelled in much more thoroughgoing ways. Historians often seek to establish typicality, but there is an equally strong argument for looking at the singular, the unconventional, the people who do not fit the mold. Outsiders often have a more critical and a more sophisticated view of a given society than insiders do. They tend to be expert at codes and symbols, at the "theater" of the everyday; often they have an especially subtle understanding of the workings of power. Nonconformists frequently break the unspoken rules, often at some cost to themselves, but in so doing they tell the historian a great deal about what those rules were. Because prescriptive writings are the most accessible sources we have on women in past times, they have been allowed, to a very great extent, to define what historians think gender norms actually were. Gender nonconformity tells us another, sometimes corroborative, sometimes contrasting, story about what norms and expectations were and how they operated in real women's lives. Finally, people who do not fit in tend to spend a good deal of time pondering the question of why that is the case. The two gender insurgents discussed here both reflected deeply on their girlhoods, and in doing so provide valuable evidence about the limitations that convention, an inferior education, and lack of job skills placed upon middling girls, as well as about the conditions under which some could challenge the status quo.

Elizabeth Ashbridge (1713–1755) was born in Middlewich, Cheshire, the daughter of a surgeon. Largely educated at home by her mother, from an early age Elizabeth chafed at the dearth of opportunities for girls. Had she been a boy from the same background she might well have been educated for the ministry, for she had powerful spiritual leanings and was apparently good at her studies. She relates in her autobiography that as a child "[I was] sometimes grieved at my not being a boy, that I might have been [a minister]; believing them all to be good men, and therefore beloved of God."[71] Instead she stayed at home and learned to sew, contenting herself with sampling a range of religious denominations, a quest that was to continue well into her adulthood.

At the age of fourteen Elizabeth took one of the relatively few options available to young women, albeit one filled with risk: she gave way, as she later put it, to "foolish passion" and eloped with a stocking weaver. Her husband soon died and she was left a penurious young widow, her father having reacted to his daughter's attack on his prerogative by casting her off. Her more forgiving mother assisted her secretly with a small grant, and she left for Dublin, ultimately taking passage for Pennsylvania. She arrived in the New World in 1732, aged twenty-one, worked as an indentured servant for a master who harassed her sexually, and finally bought herself out of her last year. Eventually she married again, to an alcoholic schoolmaster who physically abused her: as she puts it, "I had got released from one cruel servitude, and then, not content, got into another for life."[72] Now she too began teaching school, and finally, over the violent objections of her spouse, she joined the Society of Friends. After her second husband died, she supported herself by school teaching and sewing (this was one woman whose early introduction to sewing proved a blessing). A few years later she married for the third time, this time to a much more congenial man, also a Quaker, and she became a prominent woman preacher within that fellowship. In 1753 she was called to Ireland on a missionary trip, a project her husband is said to have fully supported, and she died there two years later, having come as close as an eighteenth-century woman could to her childhood dream of becoming a minister of God.[73]

Elizabeth Ashbridge's life up to her twenties was a patchwork of commonplace female burdens: unrealizable childhood dreams, an authoritarian and vengeful father, a sexually abusive master, cruel and impecunious husbands, poverty, and limited job opportunities. In her late twenties, from a combination of good fortune and real courage and ability, her situation changed. The fact that she had never had children gave her mobility she would not otherwise have had. Emigrating to America put her back on the path to the respectable status that she had lost when her father disowned her. The death of her second husband freed her from an abusive and constraining relationship. Her association with the Friends gave her opportunities to exercise her very considerable rhetorical skills and exposed her to a community that practiced greater sexual egalitarianism than was the norm. And her third husband proved to be both loving and supportive. Elizabeth Ashbridge was a rare example of someone who rebelled against patriarchal convention and still managed to achieve respectability, material comfort, and the fulfillment of a lifelong ambition. But the circuitous and boulder-strewn path she took to achieve her goals speaks powerfully of the forces that circumscribed most women's lives.

Charlotte Charke (1713–1760) was the youngest daughter of Colley Cibber, the well-known actor and theater impresario. Charke's 1755 autobiography contains some of the most detailed information on an eighteenth-century middling girl's childhood that survives today. It is as informative as it is largely because Charke experienced major difficulties conforming to female role expectations and was alternately indulged and punished by her parents because of it. Charlotte described her education as "not only a genteel, but in fact a liberal one, and such indeed as might have been sufficient for a son instead of a daughter." By this time her father was at the pinnacle of his profession, and her education was one of which a gentlewoman would not have been ashamed. She attended a fashionable girls' boarding school from the ages of eight to ten where she learned Italian, music, geography, and Latin (the last, it is true, was somewhat unusual for a girl). Then she spent several years at home learning languages, music, and dancing. Finally, around the age of fourteen, she was sent to board with a relative, one Dr. Hales, ostensibly to learn housewifery.[74]

Charlotte's childhood up to that time, at least as she tells it, had been one long challenge to traditional expectations for girls. At the age of four she dressed up in her father's wig and a waistcoat in order to play the gentleman. She got into numerous scrapes with her playfellows, usually, according to her, leading the pack. And when her social-climbing father leased an estate in Hillingdon, Charlotte went shooting every day, until "one of my mother's strait-laced old-fashioned neighbours, paying her a visit, persuaded her to put a stop to this proceeding, as she really thought it inconsistent with the character of a young gentlewoman to follow such diversions." Charlotte was deprived of her gun but got her revenge by stealing a hand gun from over the kitchen mantlepiece and endeavoring to shoot down the woman's chimney with it.[75]

Given all that preceded it, it is not surprising that Charlotte's mother's belated attempt to teach her femininity and womanly skills by sending her to Dr. Hales' family failed to bear fruit. As Charlotte puts it,

> While I staid at *Thorly*, though I had the nicest Examples of housewifely Perfections daily before me, I had no Notion of entertaining the least Thought of those necessary Offices . . . nor could I bear to pass a Train of melancholy Hours in poring over a Piece of Embroidery, or a well-wrought Chair, in which the young Females of the Family (exclusive of my mad-cap Self) were equally and industriously employed.[76]

Charlotte was obdurate in her refusal to learn feminine skills. While the rest of the girls were employed at housewifery she spent most of her time in the stables or, having conceived a passionate interest in medicine, riding about the countryside assisting Dr. Hales with his practice. When she returned to Hillingdon two years later she set up her own dispensary from which she gave out prescriptions for free, using Salmon's *Practical Physick* and Culpeper's *The English Physician* as her guides. This went on until her father discovered what she was up to and instructed the widow who was supplying her with the drugs to stop extending her credit. For a time Charlotte continued her practice using herbs and potions made of crushed snails. But when the family gardener was sacked she switched her attention to gardening, doing her best to persuade her family not to replace him so that she could take over the job.[77]

Charlotte Charke was drawn to the freedom of mobility of men as well as to the respect they enjoyed, the virtues they were expected to embody (courage, heroism, rationality), and the easy authority that professional men, skilled tradesmen, or men who worked with animals gained through their work and through specialized knowledge not typically available to women. She was acutely aware, from a very early age, of the narrow range of skills and opportunities open to girls of her rank, the tedium and triviality that so often characterized their lives, and the low valuation placed upon their persons and their work relative to those of boys and men. In response, as so many women, by no means all of them especially "feminist," have done throughout history, she tried to gain access to the same information, the same respect, and the same right to exercise authority. She did this by modeling herself after certain types of men and by avoiding those tasks (like sewing) which were not only dull and confining but in her view also uncomfortably emblematic of the enforced narrowness of spirit and lack of authority that was the lot of most women.

Charlotte Charke charted an unconventional course through the rest of her life. Like Elizabeth Ashbridge, she married young and disastrously, and she too ended up permanently alienating her powerful father.[78] In contrast to Ashbridge, she came out of her short-lived marriage with a child and, apart from a mysterious second marriage to someone with whom she apparently never lived, most of her subsequent attachments seem to have been to women. Unlike Ashbridge she was never able to make a secure living. Although Charke worked at numerous jobs, apparently posing as a man some of the time, her rearing had left her with few saleable skills appropriate (as contemporaries would have seen it) either to a man or to a woman. Nor, as far as one can tell, was Charke able to find a consistently supportive community of the sort that Quakerism provided for Ashbridge, although the theatrical community, and at one particularly low point the Covent Garden coffeehouse women, performed some of those functions in her life.[79]

More thoroughly unconventional than Ashbridge, in ways that struck not just at male authority but also at the conventions of gender and hetero-sexuality, Charke suffered obloquy, poverty, and rejection throughout lengthy stretches of her adult life. Her autobiography poignantly illustrates the personal costs of gender transgression in a rigidly sexually bifurcated world: it swings erratically between brilliant insights into what one might call the "theater" of gender, appreciative anecdotes (often embroidered) about her exploits in the nether world between male and female, and the most painful kind of self-denigration. In the end Charlotte Charke seems unable to decide whether the Cibbers should have knocked femininity and womanly skills into her by force from infancy, or, conversely, given her the systematic training, the comparatively looser rein, and the capital that would have been the standard lot of a boy of the same class. Unlike Ash-bridge, Charke had a deep sense of her own inadequacy, coupled with a rather pathetic sense that the only person able to appreciate her was her-self.[80] Such was the price of really thoroughgoing gender nonconformity in the eighteenth century.

Elizabeth Ashbridge and Charlotte Charke were unusual people, but the broad outlines of their lives were not. The most unexpected thing about them is that they wrote autobiographies that have survived, not that they antagonized their fathers, attempted to support themselves independently, traveled widely, insisted on determining their own love lives, or attempted to encroach upon the social and cultural monopolies of men. Countless other girls and women in the early modern and modern periods did simi-lar things. We now know, for instance, that in the early modern period women attempted to pass as men in far larger numbers than was once thought, often precisely for the purpose of escaping their families, support-ing themselves independently at higher paying and more interesting jobs than the ones women were usually able to obtain, gaining skills to which they would otherwise not have had access, and escaping the pressure to marry.[81] Far larger numbers of women did not cross-dress, but did set up in independent trades, travel long distances to improve their employment opportunities, or marry (or, as the case might be, not marry) against the advice of their families and friends.

The lives of Ashbridge and Charke exemplify the difficulties faced by women who tried to overcome the limited opportunities, narrow training, and typically inferior or inconsistent education that girls of all classes, including the middling classes, tended to receive. They also show something about the new possibilities for self-expression provided by the ability to read and write. Both these women penned their autobiographies in the 1750s; a hundred years before, these two adventurers would have been significantly less likely to be literate, and the likelihood of their having been able to leave personal accounts of this caliber would have been close to nil.

CHANGE OVER TIME

From the end of the seventeenth century to the end of the eighteenth century, feminists complained, with reason, about the low level of education girls received and the dearth of choices and multiplicity of personal risks that ensued from their inadequate early training. Both at the beginning of the period and at its end (and indeed, into the nineteenth century, as Davidoff and Hall have shown), middling girls were groomed to contribute to their families but not to strike out independently from patriarchal control and "protection."[82] Middling girls continued to be educated at a lower standard than their brothers throughout the period. They were educated at home more often, and they were expected to contribute greater amounts of labor service, partly so as to permit their brothers to go to school. They were given significantly less access to skills that would make them independent, and when they did learn skills, these tended to be in a very narrow range of traditionally female activities.

And yet, the almost totally passive antiheroine of Hogarth's *A Harlot's Progress*, who opened this chapter, gives a misleading picture of middling women of the time, just as do the inert and acquiescent woman implied in so much of the social history of eighteenth-century England. The clearest evidence of this is in women's own writings. Over the course of the eighteenth century most middling women learned to read and write, and with these skills they gained an ability to contribute to the historical record, as well as the chance to appropriate new kinds of power and authority that few non-elite women before them had possessed.

As is so often the case, however, gains in one realm were offset by losses in another. A more equivocal development occurring over the course of the same period was the sharply declining number of women who never married, from the very high late-seventeenth-century figure of around 25 percent to a low of around 6 percent by 1800. It is axiomatic that a society in which virtually all women marry is one in which girls (or their families) see few other options available to them. Wrigley and Schofield theorize that the extremely high rates of spinsterhood in the late seventeenth century were due mainly to the prevalence of clandestine marriages and to falling real wages.[83] At the other end, Keith Snell attributes the rising nuptiality and declining age of marriage after 1760 mainly to a decline in service and apprenticeship opportunities for women, a trend that resulted in part from deepening male unemployment and growing hostility to the notion of women getting the better jobs. Although Snell is here speaking primarily of women of the laboring classes, some of his conclusions certainly apply to middling women as well.[84]

Inequality is found in one form or another in most societies. But the way inequality is organized differs enormously from place to place and time period to time period. Despite membership in a group that was palpably better off than the laboring poor, middling girls were among the most vulnerable members of their class. In middling families everyone was bound up in a web of duties and obligations: no one had the room to maneuver that middle-class people today see as their birthright. But the situation was not identical for boys and girls. Middling girls often played an important, if only intermittently acknowledged, role in the family economy, yet they were seldom trained to be more than dutiful assistants to their mothers, brothers, fathers, and husbands. Because education, job-training, and resources were systematically channeled toward boys in most families, middling girls could expect far fewer choices in later life than could their brothers. In a class whose hold on respectability—or at least solvency—often depended upon its ability to shift and diversify, girls and women held a particularly disadvantageous position simply by virtue of their limited access to the skills and qualifications that an increasingly complex society demanded. It is an endlessly fascinating question, in any inegalitarian society, how those with less power are cajoled, constrained, or, where necessary, coerced into putting out more in terms of emotional or physical labor than they ever get back in palpable benefits. In the loving yet exploitative gender-system of the eighteenth-century middling family, a system suffused with contention as well as complicity, one can glimpse the ways that the hierarchy was maintained and, just occasionally, the places where it was vulnerable to attack.

CHAPTER FOUR

"Just in All Their Dealings": Middling Men and the Reformation of Manners, 1670–1739

There is a natural tendency in Vice to ruin any Person, Family, City, or Nation, that harbours it. It engenders Sloth, Variance, Profuseness, Pride, Falshood, Violence, and a Neglect and Betraying of the Publick Good. It dulls the Understanding, takes away the Sense of Honour, dispirits Manhood, cuts the Nerves of Diligence, and destroys the true Principles of Commerce and just Dealing. And by these means it directly tends to undermine and overthrow the Prosperity of an City, or Publick Body.

JOSIAH WOODWARD, *AN ACCOUNT OF THE RISE AND PROGRESS OF THE RELIGIOUS SOCIETIES IN THE CITY OF LONDON &C. AND OF THE ENDEAVOURS FOR REFORMATION OF MANNERS WHICH HAVE BEEN MADE THEREIN,* 1698

The Reformation of Manners was an intensely moralistic series of campaigns that swept through English cities and towns toward the end of the seventeenth century and lasted well into the eighteenth century. A full-fledged movement with a mass following and highly placed propagandists, the Reformation of Manners was also a cast of mind in common to many journalists, clerics, petty tradesmen, and large capitalists of the period, not to mention the reigning monarchs from 1689 through 1714. The movement had its critics as well, although they have been less studied. The most famous of these, the high church Tory and demagogue *par excellence* Henry Sacheverell, delighted his followers with his denunciations of, as he saw it, the reformers' hypocritical intrusions into the lives of ordinary city-dwellers.[1]

There is a large secondary literature on the Reformation of Manners. Its relationship to the history of civil liberties has been argued over, and its influence on eighteenth-century literature, especially on Defoe, Addison and Steele, and Richardson, has been explored. Elite offshoots of the movement, notably the Society for Promoting Christian Knowledge, have an important place in the history of eighteenth-century Anglicanism. The movement has also been treated as part of an increasingly sophisticated series of efforts to control the lives and mores of the poor. For historians of sexuality, Reformation of Manners activists' attacks upon prostitutes and their attempts to infiltrate "sodomite" meeting places constitute a paradigmatic "lay" effort to define and confine "deviant" sexual communities and practices.[2]

Overall, the Reformation of Manners of the late seventeenth and early eighteenth centuries injected a greater specificity and a new urgency into discussions of moral reform. It could be said to have defined the field in institutional and ideological terms both for elite reformers and for humbler people for at least the next one hundred years. This chapter looks, quite narrowly, at only one of its aspects, although a relatively underresearched one: the heavy participation of middling men in two out of the three branches of the movement, the Religious Societies and the Societies for Reformation of Manners, and the links between the message of reform and contemporary trading morality.

The Reformation of Manners has often been portrayed as a backward-looking movement. According to Harold Perkin, its campaigns were merely a "traditional attempt to bolster the old social system by improving the morals of rich and poor."[3] T. C. Curtis and W. A. Speck conclude that its strategy of involving the whole community in self-regulation represented "a return to the sixteenth century," and they suggest that the movement faded because it conflicted with more secular notions of society and more professionalizing trends in law enforcement.[4] In contrast, I see the Reformation of Manners as a buoyant and essentially modernizing movement that involved middling people, with elite patronage, in a thoroughgoing attempt to "reform" themselves and others. As will be seen, the reform movement owed part (although certainly not all) of its commitment to moral uniformity to the now familiar middling urge to understand and better control the social world in which commerce was conducted. But the Reformation of Manners was more than simply an inward-looking project. The novel methods of moral surveillance that the reformers pioneered, and that they used on both their own cohort and their social inferiors, constituted one of the earliest systematic efforts by groups of middling people to remake the urban environment. The various societies spawned by the movement helped forge new relationships between trading folk (specifically trading *men*) and the judiciary, opened up new cross-class alliances, and looked forward to middling peoples' increased participation in a political nation. The movement presaged later endeavors—the Freemasons, the literary and philosophical societies, the Wilkite clubs, the Sunday schools, and the societies for the prevention of felonies, among others—institutions that combined sociability, the ostentatious pursuit of virtue, and urban activism. Like these later groups, the reformation societies helped make middling males into more "public" men.[5]

THE THREE WINGS OF THE REFORMATION OF MANNERS

The present discussion centers on two of the three most visible organizational arms of the movement: the so-called Religious Societies, which emerged in the late 1670s and lasted, in some cases, into the nineteenth century, and the Societies for Reformation of Manners, appearing in the early 1690s and subsiding in the late 1730s (although the latter was reincarnated several times in the mid and late eighteenth century). The Religious Societies were almost exclusively middling in their social composition; the Societies for Reformation of Manners, on the other hand, had a diverse membership that included parish elites, ministers (both Anglican and dissenting), constables, magistrates, and justices of the peace, and a broad assemblage of middling tradesmen who appear to have done much of the actual legwork.[6] The third arm of the movement, an influential elite and clerical organization called the Society for Promoting Christian Knowledge (SPCK), was founded in 1698/99. The SPCK will not be examined here in any detail because its membership did not, for the most part, extend to middling people. But this omission should not be understood as suggesting that the Religious Societies and the Societies for Reformation of Manners existed in a sort of vacuum, bereft of support from the Anglican hierarchy or from lay elites. In fact, the middling men in the Religious Societies, and even more the Societies for Reformation of Manners, boasted many links with highly placed clerics in the SPCK, as well as with law-enforcement officers, municipal elites, and at least some reform-minded gentry.[7]

Activists were linked by a shared belief that England (and English cities in particular) had experienced a serious decline in morals and that this had major implications for the spiritual and material welfare of the nation as a whole. Society was beset by vicious people, intent on ensnaring the weak and leading them down the path of secular and spiritual ruin. If this problem were not immediately and aggressively addressed, more comprehensive kinds of social disorder, either as a result of divine intervention or deriving from the domino effect of temporal ills, were likely to ensue. All the organizations tried to remedy this perceived crisis. While the Religious Societies tended to focus on promoting virtue among their own membership, the Societies for Reformation of Manners busied themselves in accosting and convicting the publicly lewd (especially prostitutes), Sunday traders, tipplers, swearers, and the like and distributing large numbers of reform and religious tracts. The elite wing of the movement, comprising the members of the SPCK and other well-placed clergymen, also disseminated reform tracts and were heavily involved in founding charity schools, through which the laboring classes would be taught Christianity and good morals.

THE RELIGIOUS SOCIETIES

The Religious Societies were the oldest of the reform organizations, predating the Societies for Reformation of Manners by up to a decade and a half. They will receive fuller attention here than they are usually accorded by historians of the larger movement. The Religious Societies were formed for the purpose of group prayer and the discussion of "serious" (i.e., moral and religious) subjects. The kinds of topics covered, according to a description of the Societies dating from 1698, included just dealing (the text was Thessalonians I, 4:6, "That no man go beyond and defraud his brother in any matter: because the Lord is the avenger of all such"), subjection to magistrates, improvement of opportunities of doing and receiving good, the duty of parents and children toward each other, and the duties of husband and wife.[8] Meeting once a week in a private house, alehouse, or church, the typical Society collected dues, sometimes on a sliding scale, and relied heavily for its continuity on a system of fines charged to members who missed meetings.[9] The money was used for charitable purposes and, in some Societies, to finance public sermons or lectures by visiting clergymen (in one probably typical London society the costs included an honorarium for the preacher, advertising, candles, and fees for the use of the church or chapel). Some Societies also hosted a sumptuous dinner once a year in which the supply of alcohol and tobacco seems to have been unstinting.[10]

The membership of the Religious Societies consisted overwhelmingly of young men of the trading classes: apprentices, journeymen, and small masters. A manuscript list of Religious Societies in London and Westminster in the year 1694 contains the particulars of fifteen Societies comprising altogether 236 men. Their occupations range across almost every conceivable mercantile or skilled trade, and men in trade make up all but a score of names. (The remainder consist of half a dozen law clerks and another ten or so persons for whom no occupation is listed.)[11]

The Religious Societies (and the Societies for Reformation of Manners after them) were an early manifestation of a larger disposition for associating together into clubs and societies that swept England and Scotland from the late seventeenth century on.[12] In recent years there has been a revival of interest in the phenomenon of eighteenth-century sociability. Among other things, it seems to have facilitated the flow of ideas back and forth from elites to non-elites and to have been important in the popularization of the New Science.[13] On another level it apparently represented a stage in the evolution of more secular, or at least more prudential, values, since most of the societies (and the Religious Societies were no exception) focused far more attention on the pursuit of virtue than they did on religious doctrine.

There was a good deal of fear in the last quarter of the seventeenth century, presumably exaggerated by the mid-century upheavals, of societies and "associations," especially those with non-elite memberships. This explains part of the reason for the persistent suspicion directed toward the Reformation of Manners by the government and a good many members of the elite. But people of the time also possessed an apparently inexhaustible faith in the efficacy of societies for promoting the social good. Moral reformers were convinced that the vicious were already combining together to subvert the commonweal and that the only way to combat them was to adopt the same tactics and form what one clergyman called "combinations and public confederacies in Virtue."[14] The Religious Societies were one such "combination," a constructive response to the chorus of complaints about the dangers of bad company and aimless leisure pursuits that, as we have seen, pervaded the moral discourse of the late seventeenth and eighteenth centuries. Like the slightly later Freemasons and a multitude of other organizations that sprang up during the first half of the eighteenth century, the Religious Societies were anything but aimless, and, almost without exception, they took great care whom they inducted into their fellowship. The vast majority of eighteenth-century men's (or youth's) societies, although differing in many ways, shared the characteristic of having voluntarily placed themselves under rules, laws, or constitutions and of seeing themselves as individually and collectively engaged in the pursuit of virtue. It was this primary emphasis on virtue that set them off from guild associations, from which they had taken such organizational features as money fines for missing meetings or for declining office.[15] Moreover, because young men from diverse trades mingled freely in the Societies, when economic or business-related issues entered into their discussions it was in a manner that tended to reflect their common identity and interests as tradesmen and prospective tradesmen and not any "vertical solidarity" based on a particular trade.[16]

In part, the Religious Societies reflected a groundswell of discontent on the part of young middling men at the inadequate job their families were doing to prepare them for the world. Prudential morality was clearly "in fashion" among the business classes in the late seventeenth century, but human nature being what it is, we can be on firm ground in asserting that plenty of people did *not* follow such systematic methods. In a good many cases members of the younger generation were more aware of changing business standards, as well as changing conventions of personal morality, than were their parents or masters. The Societies show many of the features of a surrogate family. Like families they were insular and highly selective about who gained entrance to the group, but in their case the primary, even sole, criteria for entry were moral and religious. Men admitted to the Religious Society at St. Giles, Cripplegate, had to "serious[ly] Resolve to apply themselves in good earnest to all means proper to make them rise unto Salvation," and they were not allowed to subscribe their names until "Due Enquiry [had been made] into their Religious purposes & manner of life."[17] The Religious Societies, like the Freemasons after them, emphasized their familial character by referring to themselves as "brethren" or "brothers"; they also encouraged a kind of instant intimacy that included both physical displays of affection ("Scarce any natural Brothers are so vigorously Affectionate") and the right to watch over and admonish other members in ways that would have been considered only marginally acceptable from a non-relative.[18]

Probably there were other "familial" elements to the Societies. One suspects that there was much borrowing and lending among the membership, in addition to the making of business and social contacts.[19] Once one had been, as it were, adopted into this fictive family, one's primary aim became the pursuit of virtue for oneself and one's fellows. The members of the St. Giles Society took an oath to encourage one another in what they called "Practical Holiness." Anyone who absented himself from a weekly meeting was fined sixpence and received a visit from one or both of the "Stewards" (elected by majority each half year), who were to "enquire into the reasons of such members absence and desire him to be more frequent in Meeting his brethren for each others mutual advantage."[20] Members pledged themselves to shun unnecessary resort to alehouses and to wholly avoid all alehouse games and playhouses.[21] They were to be "just in all their Dealings even to an Exemplary strictness" (the main concern here was specifically business dealings), to "take care of their words and give not way to foolish Jesting," and to shun evil company and "all foreseen occasions of evil." They were "Modest and Decent in Apparel," and they frequently read good books, especially the Bible.[22]

Despite (or because of) these strictures, virtue was difficult to achieve, so another order provided

> that every Member in this society look as near as he can after each others conversation and if they [sic] find any that walk disorderly, let him Admonish him privately by himself and if it prove inefectual let him be reprov'd before one or two more and if this prove inefectual also, let him be reprov'd before the whole society and if this reclaims him not let him be Excluded.[23]

Obviously the model for much of this behavior was the dissenting conventicle, and the St. Giles Society membership, and the sponsors of this and other Societies among the Anglican clergy, were perfectly aware of this. Given the atmosphere of suspicion that greeted all attempts to associate, it was crucial to fend off the accusation that the Religious Society membership were really dissenters slipping back into the church in disguise. Thus there are unmistakable signs of efforts to dissociate the group from the excesses of puritan demeanor: members were charged "to watch against censuring others" as well as to "shun all manner of affectation and morossness and . . . be of a Civil and obligeing Deportment to all men."[24] Moreover, a polity apparently indebted to dissent did not preclude obsequious orthodoxy in other respects. None was admitted unless he was willing to take the sacrament in the Church of England, and members pledged to "partake of the Lord's supper once a month at least if not prevented by a Reasonable impediment."[25] In their Society devotions these young men used prayers approved by the Lord Bishop of London, and the accounts for 1712/13 show disbursements for three quarts of canary and other expenses on the occasion of a diocesan visitation, which suggests that the group had no objection to supporting episcopal pomp.[26]

Despite their ostentatious orthodoxy, the Societies showed little interest in the finer points of Anglican doctrine. The orders and rules of the St. Giles Society did not require that the members subscribe to the thirty-nine articles, or indeed to any dogmatic statement whatsoever. Order 3 provided that at meetings

> there be no dispute about controversial points [i.e., points of doctrine], State Affairs or the concern of trade and worldly things, but the whole bent of the Discourse, be to the Glory of God: and to Edifie one another in Love.[27]

The vagueness on doctrine was in stark contrast to the specificity in morals and conduct; it is also notable that provisions for "exclusion" or for receiving reproofs were based narrowly on nonattendance at meetings and "walk [ing] disorderly" and not on points of faith. A parallel set of orders, outlined in Woodward's *Account of the Rise and Progress of the Religious Societies* (1698) was similarly nonspecific, demanding only frequent communion and humble deference to ministers.[28]

In effect, these tradesmen seem already to have embraced that ethical and "rational" Christianity so favored by the low-church wing of the Anglican church. It is striking, however, that greater latitude in matters of religious belief went along with a new (at least for Anglicans) exclusivity based upon communally defined and enforced norms of (largely) secular virtue. An earlier chapter explored the fear among trading families (not, of course, confined to them alone) that youths were unusually vulnerable to baneful influences and that such influences came primarily from vicious people, as opposed to, say, spirits or other supernatural sources. The Religious Society membership concurred with this view, for their carefully written-out orders and rules were all of a piece with the moral advice that more prudent trading families were already dispensing to their sons. The Societies, too, were convinced of the contagiousness of vice. In fact, they represented an attempt to quarantine the virtuous from a world teeming with "bad company," who included people who set extravagant standards in dress or failed to "apply themselves in good earnest to all means proper to make them rise unto Salvation," who did not display "exemplary strictness" in their business dealings, who frequented alehouses, alehouse games, and playhouses, who lacked the self-discipline to attend a weekly meeting and who would inevitably entangle their intimates in debt.[29]

Virtue not only required that one eschew most of the traditional pleasures of the young but implied an entirely new discrimination in the sharing of resources. It is unlikely that Religious Society membership did much if anything for the problem of importunate relatives, but it did supply an ingenious solution to the problem of spendthrift friends within one's peer group. The Societies went beyond the rhetoric of countless sermons and moralizing tracts to supply an alternative use of leisure time that was emotionally satisfying and, in theory at least, free from moral temptation. At the same time, they refrained from intruding unduly upon the actual conduct of business. Trade being what it was, one might often find oneself doing business with less than exemplary individuals. As Josiah Woodward, the most important contemporary champion of the Societies, hastened to point out when he spoke of the need to avoid bad company, "I speak not of civil *Conversation,* nor of Intercourse by way of *Trade* and Commerce, but of our chosen and delightful company." It was leisure time, the time when one was *not* working, that was most dangerous. Committed Religious Society members used that time to spread the word to others hungering for virtue. Woodward describes them, "after their Shops have been shut," commonly walking four or five miles "to give Instruction and Encouragement to a new-planted *society.*"[30]

The membership of the Religious Societies may not always have achieved virtue, but they all knew precisely what it was, and, at least within their own microcosm, what the penalties were for transgressing its bounds. They also knew where to turn for sympathetic advice and encouragement: the surviving membership lists for Societies show blood relations, fellow apprentices, next-door neighbors, and journeymen working under the same master.[31] The people one conversed with at a weekly meeting were a subset of the people with whom one lived, worked, and socialized the rest of the week. The difference was that this group had separated itself from the rest by the seriousness of its commitment to virtue and by the fact that it had sworn to uphold a very explicit, written system of values. As Josiah Woodward put it,

> whilst vicious and profligate *Youths* afflict their Friends, defile their Consciences, becloud their Understandings, wound their souls, bring Temporal Judgements upon their Country and Eternal Plagues upon themselves: You will rest *quiet from the fear of Evil* in both Worlds; being sensibly interested in the favour of God, and in his promises relating to *the Life than now is, and that which is to come.*[32]

It is of no small significance that these young men wrote out their orders and rules and placed themselves under them by oath. The Religious Societies (and, as will be seen, the Societies for Reformation of Manners) reflected the prevalent tendency to attribute to reading and writing a special power to temper the insecurities of this life and the next. The St. Giles Society had their "orders and rules" read aloud each week, and careful accounts were kept of all the Society's income and expenditures. Some societies required prospective members to explain in writing their motives for wanting to join; some assembled small libraries and were involved in setting up or supporting charity schools. All this suggests that for these youthful reformers the ability to manipulate letters and numbers had become a mark of virtue in itself.[33] A later voluntary organization, the Freemasons, would actually put into their 1723 written "Constitutions" a proviso excluding the illiterate from membership on the grounds that they would be unable to fully grasp the "rules" of the order and could therefore not achieve true virtue.[34]

Unfortunately, the haven from vice provided by the Societies was partly an illusory one. The conscious pursuit of virtue, even with the considerable sanction of a community of serious-minded brethren, could have little immediate effect on the world in which the membership operated from day to day. The Society records show that economic insecurity followed the membership into the Societies, and, as we shall see, in the St. Giles Society the distinction between membership and recipients of charity visibly faded.[35]

Beginning in 1713 we find in the steward's accounts a series of expenditures on behalf of Mr. Alexander Dussty, leather dresser from Coleman Alley, and his family. The notations in the accounts make it clear that Mr. Dussty (or Dusty), a former steward of the Society, was seriously in debt: on 22 July 1714 almost £10 was paid out to four of Mr. Dussty's creditors as well as 4s 10d "Expenses on the creditors." On 3 December of the same year, £2.17.1/2 went to the Dusstys' landlord. Again on 4 January 1716/ 17, 2s 6d went to Mrs. Dussty "in money to buy her children some necesarys." In June 1717 the Society paid a Mr. Meares £2.13 to apprentice Jonathan Dussty and provide him with clothes, and it continued to make periodic payments to Dussty or his creditors from 1717 to 1720. In 1720 Dussty began paying the Society back in 2 shilling increments, but later that year it again paid for coal for his family and for getting him to the hospital. More payments to the Dussty family appeared in the accounts from 1721 to 1724, including contributions for their rent, and on 18 November 1725 "(to) Mrs. Dussty five shillings and a further supply if occasion be spent in collecting Mr. Brooks money." The last notice of the family was on 7 June 1726 when the Society gave 10s "towards burying Mrs. Dussty."[36]

Alexander Dussty apparently maintained his membership in the Society throughout this whole period, as a "Declaration of being well-affected to King George" appearing in the front of the steward's book, and presumably dating from around 1715, bears his mark. It is somewhat puzzling why he alone among the membership should have been the object of such largesse; possibly he had fallen into debt through an unusual mishap or sudden disability which had aroused the special sympathy of the membership.[37] Presumably other members fell in and out of financial difficulty during this time, although we cannot know for sure because the roll books for this group have not survived. Roll books for 1732 to 1762 for a second Society, originally affiliated with Christ Church, Cripplegate, make frequent note of members not able to pay their quarterly contributions despite a system of sliding scales. Sometimes these people quietly drop off the register shortly after. The Michaelmas 1743 notation on Henry Gaywood reads tersely, "broke and gone." Several years before, the St. Giles Society elected Mr. Abraham Holbeech steward, only to have him fail and be unable to serve.[38]

A financially stretched membership also made for problems in internal discipline—even in societies committed to the pursuit of virtue. In the Christ Church Society in 1735 a Mr. Walbancke failed to account for monies supposedly spent on behalf of the Society. On 14 July 1736 he "left the school [presumably where he worked] and went away Deficient in his Acco[un]t . . . 4.13.9." Shortly afterwards a Mr. Pincke made good part of Walbancke's arrears with the Society, but the rest appears never to have been paid.[39] Given the membership's intimate knowledge of failure, it is not surprising to discover that one of the St. Giles Society's entries into parliamentary politics (albeit on a very minor scale) was to vote a small contribution in 1713 toward an act for the relief of insolvent debtors.[40] These acts were periodically passed, often just before the cold season set in, to clear the prisons of petty debtors by paying off a percentage of each person's debts. This small gesture nevertheless displays the tension that lay at the heart of the attempt to influence market forces by moral means.

The logic of reform demanded strict and consistent punishment of deviations from virtue, whether with ostracism or, in another context, by shutting someone up in debtors' prison for nonpayment. Hence it was in each individual's interest to be sober, chaste, thrifty, prudent, forecasting, and so on. Yet like many in the early modern period, these small tradesmen could not reconcile themselves to the full implications of this doctrine. Despite all their earnest efforts at virtue and their determined insularity, the plight of the man or woman imprisoned for debt might at any time be their own. So they were willing to contribute toward the release of a group of debtors about whose characters they knew nothing in addition, in some cases, to supporting their own membership about whom, one presumes, they knew a great deal. They faced very similar dilemmas to the families discussed earlier in this study, and their efforts to impose a homogeneous system of values on their membership was equally unlikely to achieve complete success.

GENDER AND THE RELIGIOUS SOCIETIES

The most striking way in which the Religious Societies differed from the dissenting sects was the fact that the former, but not the latter, were composed almost entirely of men. The 1694 list of 236 Religious Society members appears to contain no women's names at all, although some of the original pages have been torn out.[41] A later roll book for the Christ Church Cripplegate Society, on the other hand, lists three women members in the 1730s and '40s, a Mrs. Anne Deane, a Widow Turner, and a Mrs. Jones, all of whom appear to have been related to men in the Society. This was not typical, however, and by 1752 even this small number of women had disappeared.[42]

What lay behind this exclusion? In the late seventeenth century we know of a number of cases of women congregating informally to pray or to discuss religious questions. But in this early period there seems to have been very powerful and long-standing taboos against women meeting together in a formal manner, whatever their purpose. Almost the only adult women's organizations of the time were the Women's Meetings of the Society of Friends, which met from the 1660s on. But even in that most egalitarian of Protestant sects, the women found themselves forced to defend their "right" to associate by appealing to "feminine" virtues such as domesticity and subordination.[43] Girls' schools were less threatening, presumably because they catered to children rather than adult women, but schemes to set up separate colleges,"protestant nunneries," or other organizations for women met with hostility throughout the period.[44] These taboos were only partially overcome in the 1780s, when women's charitable organizations began to appear.[45]

All this goes a considerable way toward explaining why no women's organization sprang up to match the men's Religious Societies. But why not mixed-sex organizations, more along the lines of the dissenting sects? The central obstacle seems to have been the abiding concern of the Reformation of Manners movement with controlling sexuality, one strand of which, it is true, fastened upon homosexual practices but the bulk of which had to do with fear of out-of-control heterosexuality. We may wonder, though, precisely how sexual fears begot all-male societies. The answer is of some moment, since male-exclusive organizations devoted, at least rhetorically, to the pursuit of virtue and masculine sociability are still prevalent today; indeed, they are, arguably, one of the more enduring monuments to early

Enlightenment culture. Let us begin with one of the more basic sexual fears of the late seventeenth and early eighteenth centuries, the fear of prostitutes and prostitution.

Efforts to eliminate or control prostitution are often linked to efforts to redefine repressive norms of sexual expression for all women, and this campaign was no exception.[46] One does not have to look far in reform propaganda before encountering a high level of suspicion and fear of women in general and female sexuality in particular, for which the figure of the prostitute merely functioned as a proxy. In Josiah Woodward's *Rebuke to the Sin of Uncleanness* (1720), for example, fornication is compared to "the Filth of a Dunghil serv'd up as an *Entertainment*," and he ransacks the Old Testament for passages like the following: "[T]he Unclean Person abuses his *own Body:* He has given his strength to Women, and his Years to the cruel"; "The Mouth of a Strange Woman is a deep Pit, they that are abhorred of the Lord shall fall into it"; "The Woman whose Heart is Snares and Nets"; "Her House inclineth unto Death . . . None that go unto her return again." Like much purity literature, Woodward's *Rebuke* is overtly misogynist and borders on the prurient: recurrent themes include the eating of excrement, bestiality, lingering death, and being trapped for eternity in dark pits or labyrinths overseen by predatory and sexually insatiable females.[47]

Against feminine sexual subjectivity, which he abhorred, Woodward set monogamous marriage. In his view it advanced the "mutual Delight, Confidence, and Satisfaction of the Man and Wife" and was ordained by God for "tha [*sic*] Peace of Mens Minds, the Quiet of Families, and the Happiness of Societies."[48] Although Woodward was the most important clerical supporter of the Religious Societies and closely involved with their affairs, it is difficult to say for certain to what extent he represents the views of the young men of the Societies. But there are good reasons for considering his writings as emblematic. Many, perhaps most, of the young men of the Religious Societies were still unmarried. For such a youth, that happy and fearful nuptial day would, if all went well, bring with it a key influx of capital and entry into a potentially crucial new set of kinship relations; it might also form the basis for a good part of his labor force in coming years. For good or for ill, it would determine the shape of his future.[49] The problem was to get there safely. Undoubtedly these young men worried about their own sexual reputation, for prospective in-laws were likely to use it as one marker of worth. But their anxiety was more visceral than that, incorporating fears that illicit sex, that notorious transgressor of the boundaries of rank, would drag them down into the social depths.[50]

Sexuality was a fraught issue for at least three additional reasons. First, fornication was a sin against God, and of all sins it was the one most likely to bring down "collective judgements," of which the destruction of Sodom and Gomorrah was the most notorious. (The lesson of these two corrupt cities was not, by the way, thought to apply only to sodomites.) The continued currency of both popular and elite millenarianism, coupled with the highly visible and apparently officially sanctioned character of vice during the Restoration and political and military instability as well, ensured sexual sins a prominent place in the moral rhetoric of the day.

Second, unbridled sexuality was the ultimate paradigm for a breakdown in discipline, whether patriarchal discipline or self-discipline. As such it led to a wide range of other sins and irrationalities. "[B]rutal Lusts will bear no Government, Decency, nor Restraint," intoned the Reverend Woodward, going on to link sensuality to the coveting of others' property, intemperance, rape, murder, atheism, and the destruction of civilized society. Woodward also thought that sensuality "sullie[d] . . . the Beauty and Activity of the rational faculties of men." In his view the lewd individual was

> just like the beast that perishes, he can only look down on his present Pasture, and try a while the fatal Experiment of putting by the Thoughts of Eternal punishment by Short and momentary sensuality.[51]

The sensualist was utterly unable to defer present gratification for future profit whether on earth or in heaven.

Third, moral discourse had by now thoroughly absorbed older fears about venereal infection. Woodward refers several times to what he calls "loathsome diseases," and the earliest of the Societies for Reformation of Manners named as one of its motives the fear of prostitutes infecting householders with sexually transmitted diseases. The "French Pox," as it was called in common parlance, was not only considered a divine punishment on fornicators and adulterers, it also crystallized fears of foreign, and particularly French, contagion and invasion.[52]

The unbridled sexuality of which Woodward and others spoke was, in the first instance, feminine in origin. But seventeenth-century people did not see it as being confined only to prostitutes: it could work itself in subtle ways into the very fabric of "normal" family life. Part of the exaggerated concern about indulgent mothers current from at least the sixteenth century derived from the fear that women's excessive fondness for their offspring (and mother love was commonly believed to have a distinctly erotic component) would encourage children to develop sensual tastes and weakened powers of self-discipline.[53] Maternal indulgence was traditionally linked to an inability to effectively discipline children. Late-seventeenth-century theorists found it additionally problematic because it flew in the face of rational and goal-oriented approaches to childrearing. The overindulgent mother simply would not be able to proceed with the steadfastness of purpose that all the experts of the period claimed was absolutely essential to bringing up a child, especially a son, to virtuous and successful adulthood.[54]

The Society membership itself clearly subscribed to the belief that earnest groups of men could contribute as much, if not more, to supporting one another on the path of virtue as could their families. Moreover, their men-only policy, so different from contemporary dissenting groups, suggests that they found it hard to reconcile the feminine presence with the course of rational self-discipline they had set for themselves. Masculine virtue, at least at that dangerous stage of life, required an at least partial separation from women.

It is important to note that theirs was not the final word on this matter. John Wesley, the Methodist, pushed strongly for single-sex bands, but in his case he added the much more radical innovation of women's bands.[55] And while exclusively male organizations devoted to the pursuit of "masculine" virtue and the socialization of teen-aged boys continue to flourish to this day, a strong strain of thought in the eighteenth century also pressed for readmitting chaste women into the company of young men of roughly the same age. The argument for the latter was, essentially, that given men's strong need to impress women, they would naturally behave in more moral and refined ways around them.[56] But the members of the Religious Society could not take this chance. As far as they were concerned the best way for young men to pursue the path of virtue was through "rational" male-only sociability, to be followed by virtuous heterosexual marriage. This model was to place its imprint upon a good proportion of middling public culture for many years to come.

THE SOCIETIES FOR REFORMATION OF MANNERS

The Societies for Reformation of Manners proved more short-lived than the Religious Societies, even though, in this first incarnation, they still lasted almost fifty years. The earliest of the Societies was the Tower Hamlet Society, founded in 1690 or 1691 by a small group of Anglican gentlemen.[57] Tina Isaacs's impressive study of the Societies for Reformation of Manners outlines the hierarchy of organizations that soon evolved. At the top was the original founding group, bolstered by the addition (or behind-the-scenes support) of certain reform-minded lawyers, justices, and members of parliament. The next level was composed of a society of (presumably) better-off tradesmen. This is the group that published the blacklists of sinners and the annual reports and was probably responsible for record keeping. A third level was made up of associations of constables, themselves almost invariably middling men, who met frequently to discuss problems that came up in the course of suppressing vice. The bottom tier consisted of "lay" groups of tradesmen and shopkeepers, who did the actual work of combing the city for criminals and informing on them to the justices and who garnered most of the hostility from the critics of the movement.[58]

In the early years, public lewdness was a major preoccupation of the Societies. The attack upon it took two primary forms: first, arrests of prostitutes, especially street walkers; second, raids on "molly houses," that is, public houses and taverns catering to men with homosexual tastes. The objection to prostitutes has already been outlined: they were said to "allure and tempt our sons and servants to Debauchery," to invite divine retribution on the people and cities who harbored them, and to ruin families.[59] One of the manifestos of the first Society was also concerned lest they indirectly transmit diseases to the innocent:

> Here [among prostitutes] 'tis that Bodies are Poxt and Pockets are picked of Considerable sums. . . . Here 'tis that many a Housekeeper is infected with a venomous Plague, which he communicates to his Honest and Innocent Wife.[60]

The activist bent of the Societies, as well as their sense of having turned the tables on vice, is well captured by Josiah Woodward: "behold *young men* (not led by ill women to the *correction of the stocks*) but leading them [the women] to a just correction."[61]

The attack on homosexuals, referred to at the time as "mollies" or "sodomites," was a reaction to the increasing visibility of what had apparently become a thriving, albeit largely clandestine, urban subculture, with its own styles of dress, cruising areas, social mores, and even the beginnings of a distinctive argot. Society for Reformation of Manners members seem to have systematically infiltrated certain molly houses, helped carry out large scale raids, and gathered evidence to assist in convictions.[62] During the same period propagandists for moral reform, along with sensationalist journalists, labored in their sermons and tracts to establish connections between sodomy, foreignness (especially Catholicism), luxury, and effeminacy, on the one hand, and conjugal heterosexuality, Englishness, Protestantism, plainness, and masculinity on the other. Homosexuality thus became a potent symbol of foreign invasion in the moral, commercial, and military realms. By contrast, heterosexuality became a defining feature both of English manhood and of what the English, as a people and a nation, most fundamentally were, or could be, if only the moral rot could be cut away.[63]

The suppression of public lewdness continued to be of central ideological importance for the Societies throughout their life span (they lasted into the late 1730s): the membership's antipathy to prostitution, playhouses, homosexuality, and obscene publications may have played some role in facilitating the transition from the relative sexual openness of the Restoration to the more buttoned-down style apparently characteristic of mainstream literate culture in the teens and beyond. Carefully prepared raids on molly houses and brothels continued intermittently at least through the

1720s, and the names of people convicted of public lewdness were printed up and passed around in the streets up to 1707.[64] After about 1705, however, probably because of the intense opposition they were beginning to inspire among the popular classes, the rank and file of the Reformation Societies retreated somewhat to focus more of their attention on sins such as drunkenness, swearing, and sabbath violations.

Lesser sins these undoubtedly were, but they had real significance for trading people. A series of "arrest and conviction" registers generated between 1704 and 1716 by some especially active reformers documents thousands of arrests for these sorts of offenses.[65] Attacks on public lewdness had targeted the poor, especially poor women; attacks on Sunday traders and swearers not infrequently netted other middling people. There is some debate as to how much to make of this. Robert Shoemaker has shown that the more zealous Reformation of Manners informers, who were almost all from the ranks of skilled craftsmen, tended to focus their attention on people having a status lower than their own—specifically, the victuallers, bakers, and fruiterers who were the people most prone to trade on the Lord's Day.[66] Shoemaker uses this evidence to argue *against* the view, expressed by several other scholars, that the reformers were engaged in a kind of self-policing program among their own class.[67]

In fact, the Sunday trading issue demonstrates the ways that social control and what we might call "group police" were intertwined in middling urban activism. Judicial procedures in the late seventeenth and early eighteenth centuries, as Shoemaker himself shows, were highly class determined, and there is no reason to suppose that the membership of the Societies for Reformation of Manners (or, for that matter, the justices whom they had to convince to take the complaints) possessed anything other than conventional views of social hierarchy. But the issue of Sunday trading was a good deal more than simply another excuse to harry lower-status or more marginal people. It tugged at the sensibilities of the middling precisely because it had to do with the limits of entrepreneurship more broadly conceived.

The concern about Sunday trading represented the residuum of the belief that God would punish in kind those who scoffed at his laws, while rewarding those who revered them. "Is it not absolutely necessary to our *Prosperity* (as well as *Salvation*) that the *Holy Name and Day* of the Lord be Sanctified?" asked Josiah Woodward, summing (and summoning) up a venerable body of thinking in trading communities.[68] Sunday trading was popularly thought to contribute to fires in the business district, commercial failures, and other disorders whose effects would be likely to extend beyond the individual malefactor. It could even have national consequences, or so the Reverend William Stukeley argued in the early 1740s when he sought to convince the House of Commons that the Revolution of 1640 had been a punishment for sabbath violations.[69] Sunday trading was a quintessentially commercial matter, having everything to do with whether Divine Providence favored or failed to favor business undertakings, both individually and in the aggregate. That, at least, was the reformers' side of the argument.

The other side, less often articulated, can be inferred from a petition of 1701 from a group of victuallers to the Lords Justices asking to be allowed to follow their trade on Sundays before and after the sermon. Transparently an attempt to head off Reformation of Manners activists, this petition shows that not all the people who felt themselves to be at risk from the reformers' intrusions were marginal or politically disenfranchised. It also suggests that there existed a good deal of disagreement within the trading community itself about the role of Providence in everyday business dealings and perhaps even a gathering conviction that, in the end, God favored free enterprise, even on a Sunday. Undeniably, Sunday trading statutes were enforced most readily against more marginal people, but this was also a debate *within* the middling class itself, about its own behavior.[70] Middling men who set themselves seriously and against considerable opposition to the task of defining and enforcing standards of conduct for themselves and others like them, *as well as* for their social inferiors, were the heart and soul of the Societies for Reformation of Manners.[71]

THE RATIONALIZING ETHOS

The ethos of the Societies was an overwhelmingly urban one, reflecting the outlook, as well as the ideals, of men who had known little else but trade. One of the Societies' more remarkable features was their attempt to systematize and keep account of their activities, using techniques that were clearly indebted to accounting. The minutes and registers of the Societies afford a fascinating glance at the mental world of these pioneer urban organizers and would-be petty bureaucrats. By at least 1704 some of the Societies were systematically collecting data on their effectiveness, using bound, multiple-entry ledger books printed especially for that purpose. Every intervention was noted down in parallel columns with printed headings: name, address and occupation of offender, date, person signing the warrant, type of offense, informer, and final disposition of the case. Offenses were assigned standard abbreviations, printed, as a reminder, at the bottom of each form: "S" for profane swearing, "E.T." for unlawfully exercising a trade on the Lord's day, "P.T." for permitting unlawful tippling, and so on.[72]

There were two practical reasons for this data gathering. The first, and most important, was that it permitted reformers to check on the performance of parochial officers at quarter and petty sessions, the main venues in which these so-called "crimes" were adjudicated. Reformers, not without reason, were convinced that some members of the law enforcement hierarchy were winking at vice, even benefiting from it materially. Their statistical accounting was supposed to give them both the evidence and the moral authority to intervene.[73] Second, the registers were used as the basis for printed annual statistical reports that testified to the Societies' success in combatting vice. Thus they had an important public relations function.

It is unclear who originated these data-gathering procedures. All the surviving registers date from the period after the formation of the Society for the Promotion of Christian Knowledge (SPCK), which had a strong commitment to the accumulation of useful data, coupled with an interest in directing the activities of the local Societies.[74] The immediate prototype for the summons journals, as Tina Isaacs has pointed out, can be found as an appendix to a reform pamphlet of 1700.[75] What is most interesting about the registers from an administrative point of view is the fact that they were actually used. Members of the Societies conscientiously kept up the data gathering for years, apparently experiencing no difficulty with either the concept or the forms. Given the challenges that day-to-day data gathering still pose for social services and criminal justice professionals, this was no mean achievement. An orderly, standardizing, efficient spirit had apparently pervaded the Societies almost from the beginning, at least eight years before the founding of the SPCK. Early Societies for Reformation of Manners agreements from London show that efforts were made from at least 1693 to impose a consistent system of organization over the entire city, and special arrangements were made to facilitate the making of complaints—"that the Informer may not loose his labour in comeing"—such as providing standardized complaint forms and making sure officers were frequently at home to receive information.[76]

Internal discipline in the Societies was tight. The Tower Hamlet Society had a rotating committee of nine persons elected monthly to cope with day-to-day administration. Like some of the Religious Societies, it charged its members fines for nonattendance and had an elaborate system of collections and organizational accounting.[77] The unadventurous orthodoxy of the Religious Societies had its secular counterpart in the Societies for Reformation of Manners' narrow definition of their brief: they confined their activities solely to the execution of existing laws. This is especially evident in one group, consisting of "Divers Constables and other Officers of London" that met every week at a coffeehouse near the Royal Exchange to discuss remedies to the problems they encountered during the week in the course of suppressing vice.

As in other Societies, religious and reform, Society proceedings were kept secret[78] and individuals were only admitted to the group after inquiries had been made about their moral character. Much of the discussion in this Reformation of Manners Society revolved around ways to avoid offending the sensibilities of the public while more efficiently fulfilling one's constabulary duties.

> [Q]uere . . . can [a] constable take the money if the offender offers to pay the fine on the spot, so as not to be arrested?
>
> *Answer:* yes, but cautiously and before witnesses only.
>
> *[Q]uere* . . . can constables act outside their constablewick in the aforesaid way?
>
> [*Answer*]: no, unless an offender runs into another constable-wick to escape.[79]

Stewards in the Tower Hamlet Society were categorically forbidden to take money for informing and were instructed not to inform against anyone "they have had any personall difference or quarrel w*th*." The desire to maintain a posture of disinterestedness had precedents. By at least the sixteenth century certain city officials were required to swear oaths to the effect that they would not permit private animosities to influence the discharge of their public duties. The fact that it was taken up as an ideal within a voluntary society and coupled with such a subservient attitude toward due process and the letter of the law reflected the growing conservatism of the reform impulse and presaged its assimilation into the mainstream of middling associational life.[80]

THE RISE OF PUBLIC MAN

The overlap between at least some representatives of the state and municipal law-enforcement apparatus and the Societies for Reformation of Manners constitutes one of the most interesting features of the movement, for it suggests its potential for expanding the range and scope of acceptable public sphere activity for middling men. Because we currently know little about individual members of the Societies, it is difficult to say how this might have worked in practice. But clearly the membership developed a greater-than-average knowledge of the workings of the judiciary, cultivated all sorts of links with their social superiors in both law enforcement and the church, and engaged in forms of public activism unusual for non-elite people. It is quite possible, although we have no specific evidence for this at present, that some then went on to parlay these experiences and these contacts into positions of greater authority in their parishes, neighborhoods, or trade associations. One of the great assets of the Reformation of Manners was the support it enjoyed in high places. William and Mary as well as Anne issued proclamations calling for moral reform, and Anne's proclamation of 18 August 1708 actually urged magistrates to assist rather than to hinder informers. To the otherwise undistinguished rank and file of the Societies, royal backing must have seemed powerful encouragement to move beyond the usual sphere of influence of a tradesman.[81]

Royal support notwithstanding, there was much opposition to the Societies from high and low. Sinners objected strenuously to reformers coming into their neighborhoods and making an issue out of activities they had engaged in since time out of mind. Not a few fought back violently. One reformer was killed in 1702 while trying to arrest may-fair revelers, and another died attempting to arrest a prostitute. In 1725, when a Covent Garden molly house was raided, the mollies, many of them in transvestite garb, violently resisted arrest attempts.[82] The reformers commented frequently on the hostility of average folk to their activities.

At the same time, more highly placed critics objected to the kind of ethos that had permitted the Duke of Norfolk to be fined £5 for gaming on a Sunday. The Societies seemed a throwback to the days of the puritan ascendancy in the 1650s and there were suspicions that what they were really about was social leveling.[83] Jonathan Swift objected to the Whiggish complexion of the Societies and to the fact that they were nonsectarian (unlike the Religious Societies, the Societies for Reformation of Manners included dissenters). Like many of his confrères he distrusted the reformers' motives, claiming that they were simply seeking to enrich themselves with rewards and bribes at the public's expense. The movement for reform, he suggested in 1709, had "dwindled into factious Clubs; and grown a trade to enrich little knavish Informers of the meanest Rank, such as common Constables, and broken Shopkeepers." Henry Sacheverell pressed hard with the argument that the reformers were hypocrites, bent on undermining the discipline of the established church.[84]

But others felt the Societies did not go far enough. Daniel Defoe and Edward Stephens both criticized the Societies for focusing on the petty sins of common folk rather than the vice and corruption pervading the corridors of power. Stephens called upon the Societies to stop harassing poor people and train their sights on larger targets—such as reforming the House of Commons. He had in mind eliminating rotten boroughs, banning mercenary elections, and forcing M.P.s to listen to petitions. Stephens was just as scathing about another body in sore need of reform, the Church: "I know not a more Insignificant Body of Men upon the face of the Earth than the present Bishops." In Stephens's view the "things fit to be consider'd by such as pretend to attempt a National Reformation" were the central institutions of late-seventeenth-century governance.[85]

Middling people must have been sorely divided. For some the Reformation of Manners represented a clear-cut attack upon their livelihood. Thousands of city folk made money directly or indirectly from what the reformers liked to define as vice: running taverns, brothels, and gaming houses, renting rooms to prostitutes, and trading on Sundays.[86] But people with less tainted incomes were not necessarily in favor of the Reformation of Manners either. A libertarian streak ran deeply through this precariously independent class. Even when they approved of a good many of the reformers' principles, they often objected to their intrusive tactics, their sanctimoniousness, and their disdain for older methods of keeping the peace.

Despite, or because of, the unpopularity of some of their measures, the Societies for Reformation of Manners were narrowly, even priggishly lawabiding. Their ordered, rational reformism left barely a crack into which a subversive impulse could creep, and as such it set the tone for middleclass voluntary activity for a considerable time to come. Their stress on disciplined organization, precision with respect to a given code, and systematic, standardized gathering of numerical data with which to evaluate past actions and "forecast" future ones represented the transferring of values and practices learned in shops, storerooms, and countinghouses into the sphere of public surveillance.

More concretely of course, the Societies for Reformation of Manners were comprised of real individuals who emerged from those same shops and countinghouses and turned their attention to society. It was certainly not the first time such people had placed their mark somewhere other than in an account book, but the Societies for Reformation of Manners were, in a sense, a coming of age. Like the Religious Societies, they helped redefine the urban moral inheritance by subtly altering the ways ethical and behavioral norms were enforced. Reared to respect order, accuracy, and planning, their members were men to whom moral nonconformity represented a breakdown of the code that kept a precarious system going. In a sense, as contemporaries recognized, the Reformation of Manners was simply another of the vast number of "projects" (coinage reform, credit banks, insurance, and dozens of others), dating from precisely the same period, that attempted to systematize and control the world and render it safe for commerce.[87]

The Societies for Reformation of Manners and the Religious Societies were committed to building ideological and practical links to government (especially the judiciary) and the church. They saw themselves as participants in a larger polity, working as active agents within the system to reform it in a way that they were convinced was universally beneficial. They aspired to become more moral people themselves, but they also sought to watch over others' behavior, not simply in their own neighborhoods but in the nation as a whole. It is of no small significance that in its most long-lived form, the Religious Societies, the movement was predominantly Anglican: It clearly helped make moral interventionism on a grand scale legitimate for those who conformed as well as those who did not. Even more significantly, these Societies helped to link rational surveillance to public service and public service to membership in civil society, while restricting that ever more complicated universe almost exclusively to males.

What the movement meant to women, who were after all the traditional overseers of morality in both the family and the neighborhood, is less clear. The hysteria about sexuality and effeminacy and the confining of active membership in this movement (and many that came later) largely to men would seem to leave little opening for an increase in women's power or moral authority. "The whole universe is harnessed to men's attempts to force one another into good citizenship," wrote Mary Douglas in a classic study of the ways theories of contagion and impurity work to organize and stratify societies.[88] In this case men really were doing the forcing, and the definition of "good citizenship" was very much up for debate.

If the exclusion of women from civic participation was one of the (presumably unconscious) aims of Reformation of Manners activities, it was not fully successful.[89] Attempts to set up women's organizations in the early part of the eighteenth century fell upon stony ground, it is true. But by the end of this period, women's philanthropic endeavors were becoming an accepted part of middling urban life, and in the next century female voluntarism played a central role in the birth of feminism and in a more general expansion of the public role of middle- and working-class women. Still, the Reformation of Manners was, in this respect, less a holding action than an expression of an enduring ambivalence and even fear (the latter articulated particularly strongly around sexuality) about female influence within spheres men preferred as far as possible to monopolize.

How successful, in a more general sense, was the Movement for Reformation of Manners? Clearly it did not succeed in eliminating vice, either in the short or the long run. On the other hand, the idea of reform was to have an enduring appeal. The Reformation of Manners Societies, the most famous manifestations of the reformation impulse, were dead by 1738, but they were to reemerge in various guises at several points throughout the century. The Religious Societies were much longer lived, and they probably exerted a strong influence, organizationally and theologically, on early Methodism. More shadowy linkages probably connect the Religious Societies and the Societies for Reformation of Manners to a range of other predominantly middling voluntary activities in the mid to late eighteenth century, from the founding of institutions for the religious education of the laboring classes to the numerous local societies devoted to the apprehension of felons. One of the more distinctive features of the Societies for Reformation of Manners (although not of the Religious Societies) was their willingness to include both Anglicans and nonconformists and, for that matter, whigs and tories in their ranks, and this set a precedent for a rather striking degree of cooperation across confessional and political barriers within many urban communities in the eighteenth century—at least when it came to what Donna Andrew has called "philanthropy and police."[90]

How did this early movement compare with the Reformation of Manners movement of the late eighteenth and early nineteenth centuries? The issues with which the two movements concerned themselves were similar, in some cases identical. A good many of the tactics were the same. Yet there were at least two important differences between the two movements. The first was the strength of the link the Evangelicals forged between morality and religious conversion. The late-seventeenth- and early-eighteenth-century middling ranks could compete for devotional zeal with anyone. Still, religion often seemed a more compartmentalized affair for them than was the case for a later generation of the middle-class pious. Eighteenth-century middling morality contained great potential to degenerate into a body of tediously utilitarian prohibitions set within an essentially Arminian framework. Wilberforceian Evangelicalism, by contrast, added drama and a larger purpose. Taking a leaf from earlier efforts, both Anglican (the Religious Societies and Methodism) and nonconformist, it sought to create a religious "family" of the disciplined, but one that shared pure morals and direct experience of divine grace.[91]

The second major difference between the earlier and later movements lay in the fact that the Evangelicals seem to have enjoyed the support of a wider spectrum of the population. In the late-eighteenth-century movement, ironically, women featured prominently as propagandists and even participated in some of the reform organizations.[92] Thanks, in large part, to William Wilberforce's organizational talents and extensive connections, the later movement proved far more successful in attracting gentry and aristocratic involvement than the earlier movement had been. This success was made possible in part because, by the late eighteenth century, societies and organizations composed of middling people, of elites, even of middling women, were very much more common and seemed far less threatening to the status quo than had been the case in 1690. (The main exceptions here, as E. P. Thompson and others have shown, were societies that boasted significant laboring class participation, or that agitated for radical political reform.) In the late seventeenth century it was still the case that any and all organizations were suspect—liable, in the eyes of the authorities, to be a magnet for any real or imagined subversive ideas abroad in the land. Over the ensuing three-quarters of a century the authorities learned to distinguish between voluntary moral reform or philanthropic associations, which came to have a respected place in the firmament of conservative reformism, and more "dangerous" organizations.

The Reformation of Manners of the late seventeenth and early eighteenth centuries constituted an early and important experiment in urban activism, middling associationism, and practical theology. A cross-class movement at least to a degree, it appealed most powerfully to, and implanted itself most fully among, the urban middling. To these people it offered a message and a sphere of activity that affirmed their own deeply held moral assumptions, offered new scope for their skills, and flattered their sense of their own importance. Never fully successful, the movement nevertheless bequeathed to future generations a model for action and a vision of order that was to have enduring appeal. The Reformation of Manners then and later was never an entirely middling project, nor was it confined only to the world of trade and commerce. Later reformers, however, were to find it virtually impossible to contemplate projects for reform without strong middling (or later middle-class) participation. Hannah More's famous dictum "Most worth and virtue are to be found in the middle station" was actually delivered as part of a back-handed critique of middling luxury, especially of women who adopted elegance above their station. Sentiments like these, from the pens of prominent Evangelicals (a number of them, like More herself, of gentry stock), nevertheless confirmed and paid tribute to a century of middling moral activism, at home and in the marketplace.[93] By the late 1790s, when More wrote these words, this activism had become a familiar part of the urban landscape; one hundred years before, when the first Religious Societies and Societies for Reformation of Manners came into being, they were a less than universally welcome innovation.

CHAPTER FIVE

Eighteenth-Century Middling Women and Trade

*Alas, Alas, why wou'd you not put some confidence in me, your not doing so has
undone both you & my self, you I fear, in the loss of your debt, or a great part of
it, & me in the everlasting anguish of mind, in not fulfilling my engagements, so
very separate from Mr. Holl, that many of my Cred[itor]s did not even know I was
a married woman, & it was upon my Industry & the punctuality of my payments,
that my Credit was founded.*

MARY HOLL, LONDON MILLINER, TO ONE OF HER HUSBAND'S PRINCIPAL CREDI-
TORS AFTER HER SHOP GOODS AND FIXTURES WERE SEIZED TO PAY HER HUS-
BAND'S DEBTS, 1778

In December 1686 Thomas and Alice Cryer took John and Elizabeth Jonaway to court, alleging that Elizabeth Jonaway had cheated Alice Cryer out
of some money when the two were partners in trade. Seven depositions
were filed in the case, six of them by women, and all of these by women
who were part of Alice Cryer's and Elizabeth Jonaway's social and trading
network (see table 1). The women involved were probably typical of London women traders of the period. Four of the six were married to men
who lived by entirely different trades from those of their wives; two of the
six were spinsters. The younger of the two spinsters was apparently a servant (the most common occupation of unmarried women in their teens
and twenties), whereas Margaret Cooper, aged fifty-four, maintained herself by selling tea. Only two of the six could sign their names (Margaret
Cooper was one), clearly reflecting the lower literacy rate of women, and
all were rather reticent about defining themselves specifically by a trade or
occupation. All the married women mentioned their husbands' occupations, but they did not name—although they gave many other details
about—the separate trading activities that took up the bulk of their own
time and that may well have been their major source of income. Finally,
these women fit a pattern familiar to anyone who studies early modern
women traders either in England or on the Continent, in that their trading
activities were on a fairly small scale and involved small lots and retail
selling.[1]

It is often assumed that middling women dropped out of gainful

TABLE 1.   Woman Deponents in Cryer v. Jonaway (1686)

Name	Age	Marital Status	Occupation	Literate
Joyce Fisher	24	spinster	unknown, a servant?	no
Margaret Cooper	54	spinster	sells tea	yes
Ann Bunce	34	married	sales (unspec.)	no
(husband a citizen and plasterer)				
Elizabeth Brewster	32	married	sales (unspec.)	yes
(husband a citizen and mason)				
Ann Covent	45	married	sales (unspec.)	no
(husband a citizen and weaver)				
Elizabeth Anderson	47	married	sells silk	no
(husband a surgeon)				

SOURCE: CLRO MC6/462A-B.

employment some time in the course of the eighteenth century, and, indeed, a good deal of the prescriptive literature of the time suggests discomfort with the notion of respectable women working. But in actual fact there is no good statistical evidence either to support or to disprove this theory. Conversely, there is much evidence that large numbers of women continued to work, both in their husband's shops and in their own trades, through the end of the century and beyond. It is quite conceivable that some method of plotting long-term changes in eighteenth-century women's work-force participation will be developed in future; the field is still young and there is quite a bit of available evidence, albeit of a scattered sort. But this chapter takes on a different and less researched problem, that of exploring and describing the parameters within which middling women's work took place.

What kinds of work did middling women do during the late seventeenth and eighteenth centuries? What sorts of methodological and especially classificatory problems attend attempts to find out? How did women's work intersect with family life, and in what ways was it affected by larger economic shifts? Early modern people tended to be more deeply embedded in families and households than is the case today, and, as previous chapters have shown, this raised a particular set of problems for those also engaged in trade. Women, moreover, encountered unique problems that derived specifically from the patriarchal character of family relations. This chapter explores what those were. It also looks at some women who, despite the obstacles, persevered in trade. Whether middling women did or did not desert the world of work is, at present, a matter for speculation, and I am not loath to add my opinions to the pool. But the more fundamental aim here is to chart the ways middling women's relationship to the market was molded and formed.

Let us begin with a closer look at the dispute between Alice Cryer and Elizabeth Jonaway. Alice, whose age is not given, had already been in business buying and selling silks, muslins, chinaware, tea, chocolate, and sundry other things for three or four years when Elizabeth, then in her early thirties, persuaded her to take her into partnership. Presumably Elizabeth was to contribute some capital, while Alice, in return, was to "instruct . . . her in the way of trading & to goe along with her to Gentlemen's houses to observe her way of dealing." Witnesses describe them "discoursing between themselves concerning trade," going out to buy wares together while their husbands stayed at home, counting up their profits ("[they] did comonly every night accompt together at . . . [Elizabeth Jonaway's] house, touching the profits of the goods sold"), and reimbursing each other for out-of-pocket expenses. Their husbands are presented as uniformly supportive of their wives' enterprises.[2] In time, though, things turned very sour, with Elizabeth concealing payments made to her by customers, boasting in an alehouse of having "mumped" (cheated) her partner, and attempting to suborn Alice's friends (or so it was claimed). The conflict soon spilled out into their dealings with others in their trade network with the result that some of the rest of that group had trouble recovering their debts from the pair. At length the two couples found their way to court.

Traders like Alice Cryer and Elizabeth Jonaway tended to deal in light luxury items, especially imports. They were attuned to the convenience of their better-off customers and well placed to take advantage of the growing demand for consumer goods already evident by the late seventeenth century. This case shows women banding together to compensate for their relatively lesser access to capital. It suggests the relatively informal but still "contractual" ways women passed on skills and contacts, a specialized knowledge of which they were proud and that they knew was worth something in terms of money and prestige. It shows women operating as a matter of course in the marketplace, a realm that encompassed their own homes, where they figured up their accounts, stored their merchandise, and "discourse[d] about trade"; the wholesalers' warehouses where they bought their goods; the streets and alehouses where they met other women traders, talked business, and occasionally divulged secrets they would have been better off keeping to themselves; and finally the "gentlemen's houses," where they practiced the ancient and subtle art of persuading customers to buy. Cryer v. Jonaway gives a glimpse of the microeconomy of two typical urban middling families: diversified (that is, engaged in at least two, and possibly more, separate enterprises each) and thoroughly immersed in the world of exchange.

This picture bears little resemblance either to a binary model that associates men with production and women with reproduction and consumption or to a unitary model that puts preindustrial women laboring alongside their husbands in household production. Assumptions about women's need to stay close to their homes and children are central to both models, but the depositions in Cryer v. Jonaway suggest that these women may have been less tied to their homes than their husbands were.[3] And yet, interpretive problems persist. Although women like Alice Cryer and Elizabeth Jonaway played an indispensable role in urban commodity distribution throughout the early modern period, there are other senses in which their activities look strangely marginal. The women who made up this small trade network may well have spent the bulk of their time involved in trade-related activities, yet the married women in the group defined themselves not as independent traders but as "the wife of a citizen and plaisterer" or "the wife of a surgeon." Their money-making activities lacked either the formal or the symbolic structure, from apprenticeship and guild ritual to occupational identity and trade consciousness, that would have characterized their husbands' occupations.[4]

In the late seventeenth century and the early eighteenth century the majority of urban women, including many women of the middling or trading classes, supported themselves in full or in part by paid work at some point in their lives. In a recent study of witnesses in the London Consistory Court between 1695 and 1725, Peter Earle found that 81 percent of spinsters, 60 percent of wives, and 85 percent of widows described themselves as wholly or partially maintained by their own paid employment.[5] Figures of comparable quality for urban women's paid work-force participation for the later eighteenth century or for areas outside London are scarce, but it seems likely that most women continued to work for pay for much of their lives.[6] Middling women present a special case. Earle shows that the higher a woman's status (and presumably income level), the less likely she was to report working for pay. Moreover, he found that being married was itself highly correlated with not reporting work for pay. His data show 40 percent of married women reporting no income above what their husbands brought in, suggesting not only that many middling married women did not work but also that the nonworking wife could be found in the laboring classes as well.

It would however be unwise to conclude from this that middling women, including middling married women, did not work. This was a class of women especially likely to identify themselves with their husbands' trades even if they also worked independently (as Cryer v. Jonaway and other examples show). By the late seventeenth century there were already status problems associated with several of the traditional types of women's work, notably doing laundry and selling goods on the street or door to door, and

there is a strong likelihood that more status-conscious women did not report such work even if they engaged in it. Conversely, of the women married to "Gentlemen" in Earle's sample, almost half, 15 out of 32, worked
for pay; a number of these seem to have been in more prestigious trades,
most likely with fixed premises (one wonders how many were helping to
finance their husband's "genteel" status). At the same time, women never
reported certain other types of women's work, particularly keeping board-
ers, which was a very extensive practice among middling families in the
seventeenth and eighteenth centuries. Although Earle shows that it was
relatively uncommon for women to report that they worked in the same
occupation as their husbands, it is also clear from other sources that the
wives of shopkeepers very commonly assisted their husbands with retail
sales. In this case they were not bringing in money independently, and they
would not turn up in Earle's tabulation; yet they were certainly, in one
sense, women in trade. Finally, the data show that if a woman was either a
spinster or a widow, or if her husband had absconded or failed, she was
very much more likely to report working for pay.[7] Earle's study is the best
account we possess on eighteenth-century women's work-force participation, but it may tell us more about how women defined work, and themselves in relation to it, than what they actually did with their time.

THE GENDERING OF THE MARKET

A large body of scholarship on the history of women in England, the Continent, and America has shown the striking persistence of occupational segregation by sex in the West. Throughout medieval and early modern times
urban women were clustered in a very small number of occupational categories, notably personal care (nursing, midwifery, domestic service), the
needle trades, petty sales, and preparing and selling food and drink.[8]
Women in early eighteenth-century England appear to have conformed
fully to this model. Is there any solid evidence of much alteration in this
pattern as the eighteenth century wore on? Again, hard statistics are elusive, but the evidence suggests that, while the nature of middling women's
work changed relatively slowly if at all, some larger shifts were underway
that had important implications for the way women's work was received
and understood.

Table 2 presents data from the *Manchester Directory* of 1772, not incidentally compiled by an energetic businesswoman named Elizabeth Raffald,
who, at various times in her life, was a cook, the proprietor of a confection-
ers' shop, a tavern-keeper, the author of one of the best-selling cookbooks
of the eighteenth century, and mother of sixteen daughters.[9] There were
ninety-four women with trades listed in Raffald's directory: they made up
a little more than 6 percent of the total number of traders listed. It is clear

TABLE 2.   Women in Trades in Manchester (1772)

Only trades containing two or more women are listed

Baker (2)
Blackworker (2)
Boarding School for Young Ladies (3)
Calenderer (4)
Cloth-presser (2)
Glover (2)
Grocer (6)
Hosier (3)
Huckster (9)
Inn-keeper (5)
Linen & Woolen Draper (5)
Mantua Maker (4)
Midwife (2)
Milliner (4)
Tea-dealer (2)
Toy & Hardware Shop (2)
Victualler (13)

SOURCE: Raffald, *Manchester Directory for the Year 1772*

that Raffald did not include the vast majority of working women (or work-ing men) in Manchester, and it is likely that only widows and spinsters appeared by name in her compilation. Forty-six of the women she lists are widows, a suspiciously large proportion, and she puts her own trade under her husband's name, although she kept her own shop at the time.[10]

Here, unlike in Cryer v. Jonaway, women (albeit, it seems, widows and spinsters only) *were* identified explicitly with a trade. But, again, they were heavily concentrated in victualling, the needle- or cloth-related fields (in this case the lower end of cloth manufacture), and petty sales (hucksters). Women who would have had shops were concentrated in an even smaller number of trades and they were almost exclusively grocers, milliners, and mantua makers. The only "professional" positions for women were teach-ing and midwifery. A look at men's trades points up stark differences: there were at least ten times as many job categories in Raffald's directory for men as there were for women, and there were either no women or a tiny num-ber in the building trades, manufacturing (with the exception of a few of the less prestigious and less remunerative branches of cloth manufacture), transport or any other activity involving animals, agriculture-related ser-vices, wholesale dealing of any sort, skilled occupations outside of sewing and cooking, and most of the professions.

Like many directories of the time, Raffald's *Manchester Directory* contains two sections, an alphabetized list of traders and members of the town elite and a sort of gazette that presents, in schematic form, the major commercial, governmental, religious, and philanthropic entities of the town. The gazette clearly represents an idealized picture, but it also reveals a good deal about the gendered nature of town life.

There were no women among the large capitalist cloth manufacturers who were, even then, turning Manchester into a notable industrial center, and only one woman, the matron, among the officers and professional staff of the city infirmary and lunatic asylum. There was one woman stagecoach owner (a widow) out of a total of forty-eight, no women in shipping, and no women bankers. Obviously there were no woman sheriffs or justices of the peace, but there also were no woman subscribers to the Committee for the Detection and Prosecution of Felons. Needless to say, women had no formal positions in the church, municipal government, or Parliament.[11] The real significance of the directories is the way they highlight what women were *not* doing in late-eighteenth-century towns and cities. Very much in evidence in the directories, especially in the "gazette" section, is a substantial "industry" devoted to managing the junctions between manufacturing, marketing, finance, long-distance transport, law and government, and civic and commercial activism. Each of these sectors had its own role to play in the prolonged transition from primarily local economies to a developed national and international market economy and a modern state, but the articulating of the various parts was a cultural project of at least equal importance. The assemblages of individuals exhibited in the directories, whether actual civic bodies or merely fictive groups of alphabetized names, are a powerful testimony to the complexity as well as the symbolic power of this achievement.

Middling men monopolized virtually all this integrative work and at the same time benefited from the numerous perquisites that accompanied it: trade opportunities, jobs in the national or local bureaucracy, cultural prestige, political power and connections, opportunities to learn new skills, and access to "insider" knowledge. The directories suggest that as the flow of both trade and information extended its reach, women traders and the neighborhood networks that formed their economic base became, in cultural terms at least, more and more marginal. The growing prestige of larger networks, assiduously promoted by the directories and other bourgeois forums, spelled a corresponding loss for local systems, which often were small scale, retail, based on oral transaction, and, not coincidentally, populated heavily by women, the lower reaches of the middling and artisanal classes, and the laboring classes.

The directories also indicate another facet of the gendering of the market: the rise of men's civic associations. Although the significance of such associations clearly goes well beyond the sphere of commerce and municipal affairs, one purpose must have been to provide the social glue that knit various sectors (business, finance, government, the church) together. Male solidarity is not always a given, and in any case it does not, by itself, necessarily lead to effective collective action. Nonetheless, the men who staffed these various sectors were sufficiently diverse socially, educationally, religiously, and experientially to benefit from the egalitarian atmosphere, the social contacts, and the sense of shared purpose that could be supplied by a Masonic lodge, a town betterment society, or a charitable foundation.[12] These organizations had the further advantage of bypassing the more local, more feminine, more socially conglomerate, and more tradition-bound networks of family, neighborhood, and church—precisely what supported the small-scale trading activities in which women could be found. Even though these associations shed neighborhood connections they still managed to offer their membership a strong sense of community and, in some cases at least, mutual support. Ultimately we may discover that fewer major changes than were previously supposed took place in the eighteenth century with respect to the kinds of work middling women did and the proportion of women who did them. But the *meaning* of women's work, the way it fitted into a larger surround, and the degree of authority and power it brought with it almost certainly did change, in ways that still need to be fully explored.

WOMEN AND THE CONSUMER SOCIETY

Let us examine a different kind of source. The eighteenth-century registers of the Sun Fire and Royal Exchange insurance companies contain thousands of policies from spinsters, widows, and independent tradeswomen from all over England. Many women policyholders were insuring their dwellings or property they had rented out (among other things the policies testify to the large number of eighteenth-century rentier women); others had property insured for them under the terms of a trust. There were, however, tens of thousands of women traders. Table 3 shows the female-owned businesses insured by the *smaller* of the two companies, the Royal Exchange Assurance, during a twelve-year period in the 1770s and 1780s.

Despite the pervasiveness of gender segregation, these data demonstrate that there were some trades in which women could consistently be found and a few in which they actually predominated. Although many traditional women's trades are represented here, some are new arrivals. Pawnbroking and the relatively "new" trades of china, glass and earthenware dealing and house chandlery testify to the increasingly consumer-oriented nature of the eighteenth-century economy and the centrality of women in a culture and an economy of material objects.[13] The relatively large number of woman shopkeepers shows that they were holding on in general

TABLE 3.   Female Owned Businesses Insured with the Royal Exchange
Assurance, 1775–1787 (England-wide)[14]

Type of Business	Total Number of Businesses Insured	Number Owned by Women	Percentage Owned by Women
Milliner	127	77	60.6%
Mantua Maker	19	11	57.9%
House chandler	27	5	18.5%
Pawnbroker	62	10	16.1%
Haberdasher	155	19	12.3%
Tea dealer	44	5	11.4%
China, glass and earthenware dealer	34	4	11.8%
Shopkeeper	895	103	11.5%
Saleswoman	72	8	11.1%
Fellmonger	28	3	10.7%
Glover	44	4	9.0%
Innholder	763	60	7.9%
Linen and Woollen draper	336	24	7.1%
Victualler	1032	68	6.7%
Stationer	75	5	6.7%
Wine and spirituous liquor dealer	30	2	6.7%
Farmer	936	59	6.3%
Grocer	630	35	5.5%
Baker	540	28	5.2%
Hosier	116	6	5.2%
Draper	468	23	4.9%
Bookseller	90	4	4.4%
Hatter	47	2	4.2%
Mercer	235	10	4.2%

NOTE: Businesses of which fewer than 4 percent of the total were woman-owned have been omitted from this table.

SOURCE: Microfiche index of the Fire Insurance policies of the Royal Exchange Assurance 1775–1787 in London Guildhall (indexing project financed by the Economic and Social Research Council).

retail as well. Indeed, if we assume, following the Royal Exchange Assurance figures, that 11.5 percent of shopkeepers were women (and that figure is almost certainly too low) there would have been considerably in excess of fifteen thousand women shopkeepers operating during the period 1775 to 1787 alone.[15]

It is important to make clear that the Royal Exchange Assurance policies represent only a tiny fraction of the actual numbers of women engaged in trade in England during this twelve-year period. The Royal Exchange

Assurance was not the only insurance company and was not even the largest, and many, probably most, women did not insure their businesses. These data overrepresent the better-off traders, those women who owned, as opposed to rented, their premises. They exclude most married women who, although they might well have pursued a trade, would not, for the most part, have insured property in their own name. They do give us a considerable amount of information about how women carried on their trades. Among other things the data reveal that many women set up in trade with other women (sometimes their sisters, sometimes not), probably in an effort to compensate for their relatively lesser access to capital in comparison with men and perhaps also to safeguard their title in case of marriage. Most eighteenth-century middling people still ran their businesses out of their own homes or adjoining buildings; not surprisingly, the insurance registers show that women were especially likely to do so. On the other hand, some women set up in purpose-built (or purpose-renovated) business premises, which would seem to indicate a quite high degree of identification with their chosen profession, not to mention access to capital.[16]

The social dimension of the insurance evidence is perhaps even more striking. Numerous policy-holding women lived by themselves or with another woman in their own houses or apartments and with their own possessions, which often included substantial book collections. They routinely supported themselves by trade or rentals or both, and they did not necessarily choose to reside with male relatives. The insurance policies, in short, reveal some of the personal implications of some women's involvement in trade, and they refute the widely held assumption that middling women could not respectably live on their own and be self-supporting. One sees here evidence of the first substantial body of independent, literate, and self-supporting women in English history.[17]

We have not yet hit upon a way to make the existing sources yield unambiguous statistics about the rise or decline of middling women's trade participation over the course of the eighteenth century. The sources do show that a far larger number of eighteenth-century women operated as traders than received wisdom would have it, and they give us a considerable amount of detailed information about the kinds of trades women engaged in and the conditions under which they operated. Finally, the sources can yield an, admittedly, impressionistic picture of the larger changes taking place in urban polities and of the ways women, as traders and as citizens– manquées fit or failed to fit within their purview.

THE FAMILY ECONOMY OF TRADE

Up through the late 1970s historians writing on women and work in late medieval and early modern Europe laid heavy stress upon the allegedly "cooperative," "mutually supportive," and "unindividualistic" character of the preindustrial household. The pattern was, of course, set by Alice Clark's classic 1919 study, *The Working Life of Women in the Seventeenth Century.* Clark herself thought family solidarity around shared economic goals was already an ideal in retreat by the early eighteenth century, but the tendency among a good many modern scholars has been to extend the more bucolic parts of her vision through at least the late eighteenth century, particularly in regard to trading, artisanal, and proletarian families. Thus, Louise Tilly and Joan Scott's influential *Women, Work and the Family* (1978) emphasizes the way allocations of labor within the preindustrial family economy were "made in the interests of the group, not the individual." In addition, while they acknowledge that women were subordinate to men in some respects, they argue that this was less problematic than it might have been because, in the end, "the family's joint economic activity was the first priority for everyone." [18] Similarly, Bridget Hill's *Women, Work and Sexual Politics in Eighteenth-Century England* (1989), while it does not shrink from exposing the abusive underside of some marriages, concludes that "the relationship between husbands and wives [before industrialization] must have come nearer to achieving real equality" than was the case once industrial capitalism came to prevail. [19] Approaches like these do, rightly, remind us of the perils of assuming that modern notions of individualism are transhistorical and unchanging. But they also run the risk of obscuring just how many of the decisions made in early modern families resulted in differential benefits to males (both heads of household and dependents) in terms of freedom of movement, access to education, and access to capital and work opportunities.

There has long been a strain within the historiography that has emphasized the obstacles that deterred women from becoming independent traders. We now know a good deal about the exclusion of women from many trades from at least the thirteenth century, the highly disadvantaged position of single women and most, if not all, widows, the crippling effects of misogynist ideologies on female aspirations, and the ways in which the growth of state and municipal institutions further hindered women's access to lucrative work. This is important research, and it has told us much about both the opportunities available to women and the limits placed on them. However, what these writers have, for the most part, failed to examine closely (admittedly due to the paucity of detail in many of the surviving sources) is the way in which the family itself (or more properly, male domination within the family) might have worked to constrain women. Many of these scholars have continued implicitly to assume a fairly high level of cooperation *within* individual families around work, access to capital, and access to skills, even as efforts were being made by trade guilds, municipalities, and professional groups to exclude masters' wives and daughters from working alongside journeymen, suppress unlicensed female brewers and alehousekeepers, or attack female healers.[20]

In part this is a function of lack of evidence. Few records of private families in trade prior to the seventeenth century have survived, while good amounts of data on municipalities and guilds are available: historians have, naturally, gone where the sources are. But certain long-standing assumptions about women have also dogged, and hindered, research. One is the view, common to much writing on Protestant Europe especially, that heterosexual marriage and procreation was virtually universal, or at least universally desired, from the sixteenth century on. This is often linked to the argument, found in one form or another in a staggering number of social histories of the period, that women did not rise to positions of authority or hold the better jobs because they had to be at home endlessly bearing and rearing children.

The claim that occupational segregation by gender was based on "biological" or "functional" considerations depends upon some fallacious notions about what most eighteenth-century women's work lives were like. Women were *most* likely to have jobs outside the home during the prime childbearing years.[21] Women were heavily concentrated in occupations that were heavy and dangerous both for them and for their children (e.g., laundering and huckstering), that demanded that they spend a considerable amount of time away from home, and that left them little additional time for household tasks.

At first glance the functionalist model might seem to work better for those married women (including a number of middling women) who did not "have" to work outside the home. One might argue in effect that reproductive considerations came into their own as soon as the family could afford to have them do so. A closer look makes it clear how simplistic this view is, especially in the case of urban women. In the first place, infertility rates being what they were, tens of thousands of urban women bore no children, and many more had only one or two. A mother of two does not spend the bulk of her adult life incapacitated by pregnancy. Some women did bear considerably more children, but these women certainly did not represent the norm. Moreover, at a time when virtually all middling households (and many poorer ones) kept a servant and many had other unmarried female relatives living with them, childcare was a far less pressing problem than it is today.

The main thing that characterized almost all women's work, whether women were employed outside their homes as paid workers or inside them as unpaid cooks, cleaners, seamstresses, and overseers of servants, was not that it was easier to reconcile with reproductive needs, but that it tended to be intermittent and labor rather than capital intensive. What the prevailing division of labor was really aimed at was ensuring that the male household head would enjoy the lion's share of available capital, have a good deal of flexibility in terms of his ability to command the labor and the earning power of his dependents, and be largely exempt from boring and repetitive household tasks.[22]

Functionalist and biologistic assumptions about the nature of women's "role" have diverted attention from women who did not marry, as well as those married women who did not have children. It has also led historians to overlook the copious evidence existing for this period of women who sought to escape or modify the constraints of the nuclear family. Thus we have had few attempts to come to terms either with the massive migration of single women to the cities in the eighteenth century, or with the very substantial percentage of women who never married, a figure that went as high as 25 percent in late-seventeenth-century England.[23]

Prescriptive sources from the early modern period set out fairly clearly how middling women were supposed to behave in relation to the conduct of trade. The "ideal" woman scrupulously turned over all her capital (her inheritance or her portion) to the men of her family to invest in the family business. She was flexible and duly subordinate in her relations to her father, brothers, or husband. If she worked at a separate occupation (as many women did), all or most of what she earned went to family sustenance or to free capital for the "primary" family business—that is, the business run by the men. She had taste, but she was not extravagant; she was a credit to her family at a time when creditworthiness, in the financial sense, was heavily dependent upon an appearance of respectability.

As a widow, this woman administered her estate or trade so as to maximize the benefits for her children, especially her sons, and to facilitate their education, apprenticeship (if any), and eventual entry into business on their own account. So, for instance, she was portrayed as willingly giving up trade to her sons when they came of age. The ideal woman in trade personified the precarious balance between, on the one hand, male control of women and the monetary, labor, and reproductive resources that came with them, and, on the other, family continuity in the case of the death, disablement, or failure of the male head of household.

What did an ideal like this actually mean for women who sought to set up in trade? And did the vision of cross-gender solidarity (admittedly on male terms) that lay behind it have any objective basis? There is no doubt that it constituted what might be termed the "public face" of middling communities and households, and it seems likely that some people, including some women, did accept this particular formulation at some level. But the very frequency with which these and other "feminine" ideals were reiterated by moralists, as well as more ordinary folk, suggests that there were real difficulties putting them into practice. If one looks still further, into personal accounts and contemporary court records, women's experience with trade emerges as an extremely conflictual arena, not simply in "the world outside" but within the family itself. Within middling families men vied with their female kin for scarce resources, tensions simmered around women's labor contributions, and women's businesses frequently failed because of the depredations of their husbands. And yet, at the same time, there were loopholes through which some women could construct a livelihood and a way of life that was to some degree independent from men.

In 1690 Susannah Taylor of Suffolk, a prisoner for debt, wrote to a prison reformer named Moses Pitt with a doleful tale of marital betrayal. She was, as she described herself, "a poor Feme-Covert destitute of Money and Friends . . . under the over-ruling power of a Husband, and by him totally neglected and disregarded in . . . her distressed Condition."[24] Taylor, formerly a widow engaged in trade, was imprisoned after she remarried for debts incurred in the course of business. While she was in prison her husband, Samuel (who had obviously been an unwise marital choice), seized and sold all her trade goods, converted the money to his own use, and misappropriated some rents on tenements she held in trust for the bringing up of her children by a former marriage. She also charged that he refused to allow her money to pay for her upkeep in prison or to get her released. As a result, Susanna Taylor was forced to rely on charity, and she believed that her husband was in league with the gaoler and her major creditor ("A Concatenated Villany of Wicked Men, against whom I can . . . find no Remedy") to keep her in jail until she died of old age, disease, or starvation.[25]

The "Cruelties" of which Susanna Taylor complained were an unwholesome mix of legal, semilegal, and technically illegal (but in practice largely unpreventable) acts. Her husband was perfectly within his rights in selling off her goods and pocketing the money, and within the letter, if not the spirit, of the law in failing to get her released from prison. He was probably not within his rights in taking the income from her separate trust,[26] nor was it legal for him to refuse to pay for her upkeep while in prison. On the other hand, his wife's belief that he was engaged in a conspiracy with other men to keep her from gaining her freedom (whether or not it was true) reflects a quite reasonable fear on her part about the power of male combinations and male solidarity to keep her in a profoundly disadvantaged, even life-threatening position.

Historians have often pointed to the institution of the *feme sole* trader as indicative of the relative ease with which married women could trade on their own account. In many places, including London, borough customs were very early established that allowed certain married women to take apprentices, enter into contracts on their own account, and be liable for debts, thus making it easier and more convenient for them to enter trade.

But the *feme sole* trader was in an anomalous position, because while trading on her own account she was simultaneously expected, as all women were, both to run her household and to place her husband or male relatives' trading interests ahead of her own. Conversely, husbands were barred under the *feme sole* rules from helping their wives with their trades on pain of becoming liable for their debts, yet they continued, under common law, to have the right of disposition of their wives' profits. *Feme sole* rules ensured that husbands could realize maximum gain from their wives' trading activities without having to shoulder either the labor or the financial risk. But even when husbands refrained from taking their wives' profits (as some must have done), the expectation was that a woman's earnings would go to family expenses. A man, on the other hand, would have considerably more latitude to plough his profits back into his own business, use them for other outside investments, spend them on his own leisure pursuits or personal consumption, and otherwise withhold them from his wife and family.[27]

The manifold problems to which all this could give rise are well illustrated in the case of Thomas Brown and his wife Sarah, who lived in Stockport in the mid eighteenth century. As was common, the couple arranged their dwelling so as to accommodate not only themselves and their numerous progeny but two shops, one where he carried on his trade of waistcoat making and one where she carried on her trade as a grocer, selling cheese, butter, bacon, wheat, flour, potatoes, soap, sugar, and other goods. Thomas, it was said, fully consented to Sarah's keeping a shop but, in a pattern that one suspects was common, he insisted that the profits of her trade be used to support the household (including his own meals) while he contributed only two shillings a week from his profits to joint expenses.[28] Moreover, from time to time he unilaterally sold off items from her shop and pocketed the money. As a result, Sarah's business became increasingly starved for capital. Thomas would neither contribute to the household expenses at a level commensurate with his income nor supply her with money to buy goods, forcing her to use what stock she had to feed the family.[29] In desperation she resorted to borrowing money to supply both the shop and the family.

Some time in the early 1750s her main creditor pressed Thomas Brown for payment and this precipitated a quarrel between Thomas and Sarah that ended with him throwing her out of the house, selling her shop goods, and taking the proceeds for himself. He then refused to honor his wife's debts, arguing (the case is somewhat confused here) that they had not been authorized by him and that he had derived no benefit whatsoever from her trade.[30] Sarah's main creditor then brought suit in the Court of Exchequer, seeking to get Thomas Brown to admit that he and his household had benefited materially from his wife's business and that he was therefore liable for her debts. By this time Thomas and Sarah had reconciled and were refusing to disclose the details of their household finances.

The case shows clearly the confused and ambiguous nature of women's work and, particularly, women's trade. Was Sarah merely her husband's servant, so identified with her family that it was natural to demand that her profits go directly to household expenses rather than to keeping up a viable business, *or* was she an independent tradeswoman with her own shop and her own credit, making most of her own decisions, using her profits as she wished at least some of the time, and paying her own debts? The second, of course, is the *feme sole* trader model. Thomas sought to exploit the confusion, oscillating between treating her as his subordinate as long as he could use her shop income as a convenient source of funds and claiming she was independent when he did not wish to be liable for her debts. While maintaining this ambiguity may have been in Thomas's interests, it was hardly in Sarah's, and it is difficult to imagine that she gained in credit or reputation from this incident. In her case, like Susanna Taylor's, male power within the family, and male attempts to monopolize the money in the family (coupled here with a high degree of opportunism), were key destabilizing factors in her entrepreneurial life, and they probably rendered it difficult or impossible for her to set up shop again.

Thus far I have emphasized the internal dynamics of households. A case from the 1770s shows the way that forces external to the family, coupled with married women's contingent legal status, could destroy a woman's business and her credit. Mary Holl and Ann Turner set up as milliners in 1775 at the corner of Charles Court in the Strand. Mary Holl, a married woman, financed her entry into business with 250 guineas from her separate estate and £340 loaned to her by her husband, Joseph Holl. Mary soon bought out her partner, and she was doing well enough by the end of 1775 to claim sixty guineas in neat profit. Like most women traders, Mary ran her business as a *feme sole*, separate and distinct from her husband. In fact, Mary was so concerned about maintaining her credit that she actually went so far as to conceal her marital status from her wholesalers. As she later wrote, "many of my Cred[ito]rs did not even know I was a married woman, & it was upon my Industry & the punctuality of my payments, that my Credit was founded."[31]

But not for long. By 1777 Mary was having trouble meeting her bills, and around this time her husband Joseph went bankrupt (his trade is not known). Her wholesalers (who had, by this time, discovered her marital status) became restive and seized some of her stock as security for the money she owed them. In December of 1777, to set their minds at rest, Mary tendered a bill of sale for her stock in trade and effects to her principal creditor, one Mr. Clement, assuming she would be able to continue running the business. Unfortunately for her, Clement reached a separate accommodation with the assignees on Joseph Holl's bankruptcy commission, and he turned over the bill of sale to them. This in turn touched off a violent dispute between Mary's *other* creditors, who had not been included in the deal, and her husband's assignees. Her creditors pointed out that Mary Holl had financed the business out of her own separate estate, and they demanded that they be paid in full before Mr. Holl's creditors took their share. Joseph Holl's creditors, for their part, wished to recoup from Mary as much of the money owed to them by her husband as possible, and they were not inclined to honor her claim that she was running a separate trade.[32]

By March of 1778 the conflict had degenerated into a free-for-all, with the two groups of creditors vying to seize as much of Mary Holl's stock as they could. Meanwhile, Mary, literally caught in the middle, was petitioning her husband's assignees to allow her sufficient ready money to keep the shop open. Her business, although in its infancy, had been doing well. She was perfectly willing to have the bankruptcy commission oversee every transaction she made. Given that she was a *feme sole,* she should, in any case, only have been liable for the £340 originally put into the business by Mr. Holl; the assignees were not justified in demanding its whole value simply because she was Mr. Holl's wife. Moreover, one of her aims in keeping the business going was to assist her husband in the payment of his debts.

But the assignees rejected the petition unless Mary could come up with an impossibly large security, and they then seized a large consignment of her laces. Soon Mary was writing to the assignees that "My Business is quite ruined, for I have nothing to sell, & now no Credit or money to buy." She burst out in frustration at the commission's refusal to trust her abilities and her word:

> Alas, alas, why wou'd you not put some confidence in me, your not doing so has undone both you & myself, you, I fear, in the loss of your debt, or a great part of it, & me in an everlasting anguish of mind, in not fulfilling my engagements. . . . I never before, was worse than my word in my life, or gave a hope I did not fulfill, a disposition like that, you might have relied upon.[33]

Of course, that was precisely the point. The ambiguous position of women traders and, even more so, married women traders made them fundamentally unreliable, while the category of *feme sole,* in this, as in other cases, proved too weak and unstable to stand up to any real pressure. There was a way in which the whole conception of "profit" was gendered in the eighteenth century. Women's profits were complexly hedged and constrained by prior claims, something Mary Holl herself indicated her awareness of when she argued, implausibly, that her profits were really only intended to pay off her husband's debts. In contrast, men's profits moved relatively freely within a *laissez-faire* and possessive individualist universe of economic decision making. Middling men's money was already capital in the classic Marxian sense; middling women's was something for which we hardly have an adequate name and which fit only clumsily within liberal and Lockean conceptions of property, value, and profit.

Conflict and unhappiness tend to leave deeper traces in the historical record than harmony and contentment. But cases like the three outlined above do supply compelling evidence of the universe of worst-case scenarios within which women, and the people who did business with them, operated. To be successful in the world of eighteenth-century commerce required a very high degree of trust on the part of the people who supplied capital and extended credit. A married woman's business ventures would always be contingent, insecure, dependent at some level on another's will, and the last priority even in harmonious families. In inharmonious families the conflict could and often did have a direct bearing upon a woman's ability to conduct a trade, and it did so to a far greater degree than was the case for men. If a man and a woman fought frequently, it did little either for his reputation or hers, but it did not usually destroy his trade.[34] A woman's business was both extremely vulnerable and quite often her husband's first target of attack. Moreover, even if he did not attack it, his creditors had no such scruples. A good many married women continued to work and some proportion of them carried on independent trades, but these three cases, even though they represent extremes, tell us part of the reason why women so often hit a ceiling when it came to building up a large or successful business or a business outside the narrow range of enterprises deemed appropriate for, or traditional to, women.

REFUGEES FROM THE FAMILY ECONOMY?

The disadvantages, actual and potential, under which married women in trade labored suggest the need to look more closely at women who never married, who used their work to escape marriage, or who failed to remarry when their spouse died.[35] An earlier chapter discussed the girlhood and adolescence of the redoubtable Charlotte Charke, youngest daughter of Colley Cibber. The present discussion will focus on her work life.[36] The reader will recall that, while still in her teens, Charke set up as a herbal healer. For a time she was an actress, then an oil dealer and grocer, and then she took over the management of a puppet theater.[37] Charke had contracted an early and unsuccessful marriage, and she was determined to prevent her estranged husband from getting hold of her earnings, to which, of course, he was legally entitled. Accordingly she "gave and took all Receipts . . . in the Name of a Widow Gentlewoman, who boarded with me, and I sat quiet and snug with the pleasing Reflection of my Security."[38]

Around this time Charke adopted men's clothes and worked as a valet, a waiter, the manager of a traveling theater company, and, at one low point, an itinerant sausage seller. She also briefly owned a pub which proved a failure.[39] Charke lived in constant fear of being arrested for debt and, like much of the London population, lived between jobs by pawning articles of her clothing. Abandoned by her disapproving family, she was heavily dependent on the financial and emotional support of women friends, including one or more who were probably her lovers. To escape her creditors, she and one of these women went on the road as itinerant players, passing much of the time as husband and wife and calling themselves "Mr and Mrs. Brown."[40] Later the couple set up pastry shops in two different towns, financed, according to Charke, by another of her numerous female admirers. After the businesses failed they lived on a small legacy belonging to "Mrs. Brown," attempted to do theater benefits, and finally, after nine years' absence, returned to London, where Charke eked out an existence writing until she died at the comparatively early age of forty-seven.[41]

Talented, energetic, and possessed of considerable charm, if not, it seems, much of a head for business, Charlotte Charke did manage to extract more capital out of more people (although usually out of other women) than did most other women of her time. Her estrangement from her family and, especially, her famous father, her refreshing disregard for gender conventions, her probable lesbianism and antipathy to heterosexual marriage, which she referred to as "enslave[ment] . . . for life,"[42] her reliance on female support networks, and her association with the theater made for a more picturesque (and picaresque) career than most. They also condemned her to perpetual financial insecurity. Even taking into account her penchant for cross-dressing, most of Charlotte's jobs, including her ventures into trade, were well within the range of conventional women's work: irregular healing, itinerant sales, keeping a grocer's shop, and making and serving food.[43] It is questionable whether Charke would have had the discipline to succeed in business even had she had the advantages enjoyed by a good many men of her class. Still, the fact that she operated within the pinched economy of women and, for the most part, without male support or approval compounded her difficulties. She managed to escape the constraints of heterosexual marriage, but she was never able to lift herself out of poverty.

"Imagine an exchange-woman, shop-keeper, or the like, newly entring into Trade," an anonymous late-seventeenth-century woman opened an appeal to her middling sisters to take up bookkeeping.[44] Gertrude Rolles (d. 1699), was a real-life "exchange-woman," a widow who, with her two daughters, kept a milliner's stall in the Royal Exchange in the 1680s and 1690s.[45] She paid £50 a year rental for a stall with eight feet of frontage, drawers, cupboards, and additional storage, and a promise on the part of her landlord not to let the adjoining spaces to anyone else selling millinery. Hers was clearly a going concern, and in her will she flouted convention by giving £5 each to her two sons (a paltry sum given what her total income must have been) and the rest of her estate, including the stall lease, goods, chattels, some rental investments and money "equally and indifferently part and part alike" to her two daughters "for they have been industrious and diligent in the getting thereof." She also made them joint executrixes, "desireing and not doubting but they will be just loveing and kind to each other as sisters ought to doe." [46]

On occasion, women's joint trading endeavors supplied the basis for straying quite far from male expectations. Gertrude Rolles would have been expected to give control of the trade to one or both of her sons,[47] and her unconventional decision suggests the presence of a different kind of ideal, seldom expressed in writing, one encompassing themes of older women providing for the financial independence of women of the next generation, of work deserving financial recompense, even when women did it, and of enduring relationships between sisters.[48] One glimpses here the shadowy presence of a vision considerably at variance with dominant ideals.

Eleanor Coade (1733–1821) is one of the relatively few eighteenth-century English women in trade to retain some present-day reputation. A lifelong spinster, Coade set up in the 1760s as a manufacturer of a type of tastefully modeled artificial stone that came to be called coadestone, examples of which can still be seen today.[49] When Eleanor Coade died at almost ninety years of age she distributed her money among various charities and sixty-odd relatives and friends. Two-thirds of her bequests to individuals were to women, and more than half of these to spinsters or widows. Where she gave money to married women it was often in the form of trusts "for their separate use" so that their husbands could not appropriate the money. In one case she actually ordained that if the woman died intestate the money would go to her daughters, not her husband or sons, thus ensuring it would stay in the female line into the next generation. Her largest bequest was to her long-time female companion and housekeeper.[50]

It is easy to see the eighteenth century as something of a feminist wasteland—not least for women of the middling sort. There is absolutely no doubt that the dominant expectation within the trading class, one shared to a greater or lesser degree by women as well as men, was that women would place their labor power and the bulk of their capital, as well as their reproductive capacity, in the hands of men. It is also perfectly clear that strictures like these had a deleterious impact on many middling women. The assumption has tended to be that women were too passive or downtrodden to do much on their own behalf to rectify the situation. Yet when one looks at women who were self-possessed enough to write about themselves or to attempt to defend their interests in court, resistance to male abuse of power, ambivalence about male monopolizing of resources, and interest on the part of women in favoring other women at the expense of men all begin to surface. The feminist utterances that run through the whole period are too often represented by historians as cries in the wilderness; they were perhaps not so aberrant or out of touch with the sentiments of the generality of women as we used to think.

A RETREAT FROM TRADE?

Earlier it was suggested that, given the present state of the scholarship, we are not yet in a position to say whether middling women's work participation declined (or, for that matter, rose) over the course of the late seventeenth through the end of the eighteenth century. It may be useful to touch once more upon the changing environment of eighteenth-century trade and to look at a few of the trends that *may* have affected middling women's work lives. On the positive side, it seems very possible that some women benefited, in terms of trade opportunities, from the so-called consumer revolution of the eighteenth century. This is suggested at the beginning of the period by the admittedly temporary, yet still quite striking, rise of female newspaper publishers and distributors who capitalized on the explosion of literacy and interest in newspapers.[51] Something like this can be seen at the end of the period with the rising prevalence of pawnbrokers' shops, independent clothes-making establishments, china and earthenware and household furnishing shops, and girls' boarding schools, all owned and run by women. Some women, as well as some men, benefited from the breakdown of controls over certain trades. Mary Prior's article on women and work in Oxford contains a marvelous description of the spirited battle that went on in the eighteenth century between female milliners and mantua makers and old and established, but weakening, tailors' and mercers' companies.[52]

Other developments probably tended to inhibit women's entry into the more remunerative and prestigious sorts of paid work, especially ownership of a business. One was the growing cost of setting up. Attractive shop facilities, including glass windows, shop fixtures, and the like, were becoming more and more important. Consumers were coming to expect greater diversity in terms of stock, which meant large and costly inventories.[53] Meanwhile, the growth in the scale even of petty production and, from the 1760s, the rise of the highly capitalized factory with its expensive machines and substantial purpose-built plant meant that smaller manufacturers were increasingly squeezed out. In a society in which it was assumed that liquid capital would be controlled by men, rising costs probably made it harder for women to obtain the wherewithal to set up in trade or industry.

A development of central importance in the history of the middling, and in that of middling women, was the rise of relatively "safe" investments, the most important of which were the various stock and annuity schemes that flowed from the foundation of the Bank of England in 1694. The late seventeenth century was punctuated by complaints that investors were diverting money from trade, and this must have been true to some degree. A significant class of people who lived wholly or partially on their investments (and often on a combination of "paper" investments and rents on property) sprang up in the early eighteenth century, and although good statistical evidence is not yet available, much anecdotal evidence suggests that middling women, whether spinsters, married women, or widows, were extremely likely to number among this group.[54]

This trend had several consequences. First, it probably tipped the balance for some women who would otherwise have sought to become active traders but who now settled for living on their annuities or their company dividends. Second, it provided a relatively secure way for some women to avoid marriage or remarriage and live independently. And third, it meant that those women who were most able to be financially independent from men were also thoroughly implicated in some of the least palatable features of eighteenth- and nineteenth-century society. Complicity is a harsh word, but the evidence is hard to overlook. The larger milliners' shops depended for their profits on the starvation wages of much poorer women. Urban middling women's heavy reliance on rental income, often derived from tenements,[55] is unlikely to have proved a boon for the people who had to endure their crowded, squalid conditions. Finally, with government bonds and East India and related stocks the most highly favored investments throughout the period, middling women became tied to the political status quo, as well as to imperial expansion, in an extremely direct way.

Eighteenth-century women traders ran the same risks as did any businessperson, but they also encountered obstacles that were particular to their time and to their sex. Successful women entrepreneurs were not a rare species in this period, and one can point to numerous cases of creativity, industry, perseverance, and—that essential attribute of the successful small businessperson—sheer luck among women as well as men. Conversely, if we want to know why women's enterprises tended to be of small scale, to be less numerous than those of men, and to be concentrated in only a small number of occupations, one of the main places to look is the family. Future scholarship should examine in detail the ways in which "the family economy" fostered men's disproportionate access to resources; it should explore in greater depth why family conflict tended more to confirm than to undermine male dominance; and it should seek a better understanding of the linkages between hierarchical family structures and a larger polity that reproduced and extended male dominance even while much else was in flux.

CHAPTER SIX

The Bonds of Matrimony and the Spirit of Capitalism

They only who have felt it, know the Misery of being forc'd to marry where they do not love; of being yok'd for Life to a disagreeable Person and imperious Temper, where ignorance and Folly . . . tyrannizes over Wit and Sense: to be perpetually contradicted for Contradiction-sake, and bore down by Authority, not by Argument; to be denied one's most innocent Desires, for no other Reason but the absolute Will and Pleasure of a Lord and Master, whose Follies a Wife, with all her prudence, cannot hide, and whose commands she cannot but despise at the same Time that she obeys them.

MARY ASTELL, *REFLECTIONS UPON MARRIAGE*, 1706

O happy happy nuptial day
Whose morning Sun with splendour shone
Let ardent love each bosom sway
And heav'n with bliss our days will crown.

ZELOPHEAD VINCENT, HOT PRESSER AND SCHOOLTEACHER

Ambrose Barnes (1637–1710), merchant and alderman of Newcastle upon Tyne, married a Miss Mary Butler (said to be a great scholar of divinity) in 1655, and they had between them six children, four of whom lived to adulthood. Their household was a model of good order. No "smutty plays" were read there and "corrupt conversation was banisht from this family by law." The Barneses kept a frugal table, avoiding sauces and excessive numbers of side dishes, and Barnes himself rarely tasted the venison occasionally sent him by well-born acquaintances. These seeming fine points of cuisine are rich with meaning. Sauces ("pernicious sauces" as a later champion of the trading classes was to call them), like a superabundance of dishes, were markers of aristocratic profusion and addiction to things French; by ostentatiously failing to be impressed by gifts of venison Barnes was challenging a valued perquisite of high birth, the exclusive right to hunt game and make gifts of it to one's social inferiors. People who dined at the Barneses' came away replete with a simpler but perhaps headier fare: the satisfaction of having witnessed a series of small but telling blows against patronage, deference, and upper-class luxury.[1]

Barnes himself, although of the civic elite, could easily stand as a model for any would-be tradesman. He was, his biographer tells us, an early riser, going to bed at nine and getting up at four in the summer and five in the winter his whole life. Until a year or two before he died he would never have a fire in his chamber in the rainiest weather or the sharpest frost.[2] He was a man of charitable impulses, although on principle he never gave to those on parish relief. While in civic office he had regularized the size of bread and eased the relief rolls of vagrants and foreigners (this was typical seventeenth-century progressive Poor Law management).[3] A merciful employer, he refrained from attempting to convert his servants, seldom let anyone go, and looked upon purloining, cheating, and so on as "a crime . . . against God as the universal proprietor."[4]

Yet Barnes was no stranger to vicissitude. In the 1680s he sustained a major loss in a ship that foundered and sank on a voyage to Virginia. Soon after he met with a much greater loss in a colliery, and he "buried a good estate in lead mines." Finally the breaking of a son-in-law for whom he had stood surety is said to have swept away almost all he had in the world.[5] Barnes experienced that most emblematic of early modern commercial traumas, finding himself on or over the brink of failure, and, like the best of his class, he fought his way back. In sum, Ambrose Barnes was a seventeenth-century bourgeois paragon, who, as his biographer put it, was "every where imployed for God, whose count-book he kept as carefully as his own, and wherein, on one side of it he alwayes wrote himself Debtor et per contra Creditor."[6]

Barnes is said to have been a thoroughly home-centered man, one who entered intensely and self-consciously into family affairs. Although briefly attracted to cock-fighting in his youth, he repented, and in later life he avoided all such profitless pastimes. His leisure hours were divided between municipal affairs and his family, and he avoided taverns and coffeehouses. He displayed a highly responsible attitude toward parenting, carefully marking the aptitudes and dispositions of his children and taking great care what schools they attended. Meanwhile, Mistress Barnes was said to stay at home for the most part, except when she visited the sick and, presumably, attended church. Domestic to the core, Mary Barnes had no time for the

> ceremonious niceties of many haughty dames with their daughters, the custom of calling women ladies and mothers madams, being crept in . . . with the corruption of ancient manners.[7]

Ambrose and Mary Barnes made no attempt to marry off their daughters to "the Great," although one did marry a very considerable Newcastle merchant. Their sons went into the professions, law and the ministry, respectively; a son-in-law was an M.P. for Berwick on Tweed for twelve years, reputedly never making a penny's worth of profit for himself.[8]

Although Ambrose Barnes was a domestic man, his biographer leaves us in no doubt that he wielded supreme authority in his own home and was as accustomed to command there as he was in his counting house, at Burgesses' Hall, or at meetings of the Company of Merchant Adventurers. Seldom without some weighty remark on his lips, Barnes typified effective bourgeois patriarchalism. Indeed, his commanding presence was part and parcel of an intimate, tightly organized, and highly moral family order, notable precisely for the ways in which it differed from the pretentious, superficial, extravagant, and badly governed families allegedly characteristic of political elites.

Who can say at this remove whether Ambrose Barnes's family was really the model of concord his biographer claimed it was?[9] What interests us here is the performative quality of this man's life: its stagey manipulation of the symbols of rank, the ponderous moral set-speeches that punctuate the action, the distinct sense one gets of actions scripted from sermons and family advice books, the way it is proffered to the reader as a model of its kind. Not yet "middle-class" in the usual meaning of the term, these people were nonetheless fully capable of turning their outward lives into a sustained critique of aristocratic pretension. The account of Ambrose Barnes signaled what was already becoming a commonplace: the association of "privatized" family life with order, rationality, and usefulness, and "public" family life (that is, the family lives of political elites) with disorder, irrationality, and corruption.[10] Barnes himself missed none of the political implications of such stereotypes. Sympathetic to Oliver Cromwell (and later to the Duke of Monmouth) and deeply attracted to the ideas of the republican theorist James Harrington,[11] his conspicuous attachment to a particular vision of family life was as charged as any of these more familiar marks of radicalism and arguably was more long lasting in its effects.

This chapter is concerned more with those aspects of middling married life that turn up less often, either in the prescriptive literature or in family hagiographies. Here the focus is on less careful, less polished and less politicized performances: the leavings of people who were not as conscious of their public image, the odd letter attesting to one or another of the hidden complexities of marriage, the judicial reportage of family life gone terribly awry. The purpose here is not only to show how things were supposed to happen but also to look at why they often failed to turn out as planned. Success, it has often been said, erases the evidence of many failures, but failure often tells us far more about the workings of a system. From approximately 1700 on, a strong strain of thinking suggested that middling families were more harmonious, monogamous, well-ordered, and virtuous than were the families of other people. Modern theorists, by implying that the stresses and strains of the marketplace could somehow be left at the front door, distinct from family life, have done little to undermine this view.

In contrast, this chapter makes clear that at virtually every stage the middling family was thoroughly embedded in the marketplace, intimately connected to questions of money and power, and pregnant with the potential for serious familial conflict. We cannot, in the ultimate sense, ever fully grasp what impelled a man like Ambrose Barnes. We can, however, begin to get a sense of the abyss that he and people like him sought so strenuously to avoid.

COURTSHIP

The London physician Henry Sampson (1629–1700) had an interest in the phenomenon of upward social mobility, and in the 1690s he penned a list of "instances of men that have leapt into great estates from almost nothing." One of his categories, slightly startling if one is expecting a paean to industry, was made up of those who had risen by "marrying well."[12] In the early modern period, more explicitly than is the case today, who and how one married directly and decisively affected one's place in the social, cultural, and economic hierarchy. Consequently, the time when a person was searching for a mate was one in which anxieties about status and identity took an especially acute form. It was also an important time for the enforcement of social norms, with those who conformed often receiving the rewards and those who failed to conform tasting the bitter fruits of rejection.[13]

Samuel Marriott (fl. 1728), son of an ironmonger, found his attempts to marry frustrated because his father's patrimony turned out to be far less than he had been anticipating.[14] Marriott worked as a clerk at the London Guildhall, and despite his low salary, he lacked the self-confidence to give up his position for a more lucrative but potentially less secure place. Instead he tried other methods to increase his income, including investing in a salt meter office and embarking on a heroic plan of cost-cutting. None of his schemes met with much success. Some time earlier Marriott had refused to give up the woman he loved, even though to do so would have meant greater "Gain or Profit, or the Prospect of Preferment in the World." Now he found himself standing by impotently as she taxed him with the claim that what he made was not enough to maintain a family, assailed him for his want of resolve in not seeking a better position, and ultimately broke off the engagement.[15] This courtship had foundered on Marriott's misfortune with respect to his family's money and his failure to display a level of assertiveness that his fiancée thought essential for a man of his class.

Samuel Wright (1736–1797) was the orphaned son of a cabinetmaker and mill owner. The aunt who eventually inherited the task of rearing him failed to apprentice him to a suitable calling, and the want of early habituation to business (as Wright himself thought), plus insufficient capital resources meant that he had great difficulty establishing himself in trade. Initially this state of affairs caused him little concern; its full import became suddenly and gallingly clear when he began looking about for a wife some time in the 1750s:

> I began now to acquire a pretty large acquaintance among the fair sex, and to form some particular connections; but as I had made but little show in trade, having, indeed, but little spare money, I found myself objected to on this account.[16]

What he did next only aggravated his problems. Having fallen in love with a young woman of the neighborhood and eager, as he put it, "to remove the odium of following little or no trade out of the way of my being accepted as a husband," he imprudently borrowed money on his small estate to enter into a business about which he knew little with a partner who was quite willing to cheat a novice. Wright also sought to impress the young woman and her family with lavish gifts. Predictably, he dissipated his principal and ended up in a position worse than before. The courtship languished, an opportunity was lost, and in the end Wright had to settle for a far less desirable marriage, one that was to cause him no end of financial and emotional distress in later years.[17]

Courtship was a trying time not just for the principals but also for their families, who, if the suit was successful, stood to take on a whole range of new moral and financial obligations and vulnerabilities—as well as potential opportunities for profit. And so, when one Mr. Cooper pressed his suit with a female relation of the Doddridge family, letters began fanning out to their friends and coreligionists inquiring as to the young man's character and prospects. At least one of the replies must have given Mrs. Doddridge pause for thought. It concerned not Cooper himself, but "the person he is going to be connected with in Trade," who, the correspondent reports, "was partners with a Brother Blackwell-Hall Factor for a while and is now going into the Coal-Trade: I did hear before he came into Blackwell hall he once faild, but as to his present circumstance I am quite a stranger."[18] These were the uneasy rumblings produced by a system in which the risks of marriage involved more people than simply the couple taking the vows.

PORTIONS AND OTHER BENEFITS

Marriage was, for all ranks, the main means of transferring property, occupational status, personal contacts, money, tools, livestock, and women across generations and kin groups. Among the commercial classes one of the most important of these transfers came in the form of the portion or dowry. For many young men their wives' dowries would constitute the most important infusion of capital they would ever receive. As historians are fond of pointing out, a heavy emphasis on the size of portions did not mean that marriages were loveless, arranged against people's wills, or contracted without concern for psychological or sexual compatibility. Yet it is undeniably the case that immediate financial gain for the groom or the groom's family was a far more explicit criterion in choosing a wife than it would be today.[19]

Portions were also a feature of marriage among the elite, but there they were put to different uses. The landed tended to employ portions to buy more land, pay off mortgages, or finance jointures.[20] Trading families, on the other hand, were much more prone to plow portions back into the business. A typical case was that of John Fryer (1671–1726), pewterer and later Lord Mayor of London. Fryer came of trading, shopkeeper, and smallholder stock, and in 1693 he set up business with a loan of £300 at interest from his maternal uncle. Although he worked hard and kept a frugal household consisting only of himself and one maid, his business did not greatly increase. Accordingly, around 1696, he decided to take an apprentice and to get married to the daughter of a tanner. His new wife brought with her a portion of £500, "but sometime after her Father observing my industry & the increase of my business added to it, & made it up in all 1000 £[,] the same fortune he had before given his elder daughter."[21] For Fryer, as well as for his father-in-law, marriage was as much as anything else a business move, one rung on the ladder to success.

For the system to work harmoniously required a synchronicity between love and money and an ability to bend the passions in the direction of prudence and utility, a feat that was not always readily accomplished. The uncle of Jonathan Priestley (1633–1705), who came from a Yorkshire cloth factoring family, was, according to his nephew, "the strangliest inchanted and infatuated in his first marriage that I think ever any wise man was." He married a woman of ill extraction who had no portion and, according to his family at any rate, was profane and ignorant to boot—yet "all the counsels and projects of his friend could avail nothing to prevent it." After his first wife died the uncle somewhat redeemed himself by marrying the niece and heiress of Isabel Denton, a rich chandler of Halifax, but the diarist thought that his uncle's early marital misstep had haunted him to his grave.[22]

The job of negotiating and then actually raising a portion could be an arduous one.[23] Middling people seem generally to have taken their daughters' portions out of working capital. Few of them were in a position to finance portions with mortgages or land sales, which was the typical practice in landed families.[24] We may imagine that in some trading families this set up bitter competitions between daughters and sons over the disposition of scarce family capital. In London and some other towns, at least up to the early decades of the eighteenth century, law and custom dictated that one-third of a deceased man's estate be divided equally between his children without regard to gender, which meant that if a woman's father died solvent, she had a legal claim on some of the money.[25] Fathers could take a long time to die, however, and such equitable treatment could not always be relied on during their lifetimes; not a few of the daughters of middling families were destined to become the respectable but portionless, and therefore virtually unmarriageable, women of whom one hears so much in this period. There were other alternatives. Some middling families paid their daughters' portions by installment; some promised a portion, permitted the nuptials to take place, and then never paid up, thereby casting what could be a fatal pall over their daughter's marriage and their son-in-law's expectations—and sometimes tying themselves up in litigation as well.[26]

The portion was only the most visible of the benefits that flowed between affinal kin. When a man married he greatly expanded the pool of people who had some interest in, and responsibility for, his and his immediate family's welfare. A staggering range of real and symbolic benefits could be expected to come his way if he married well and cultivated his in-laws wisely. Sons-in-law were in a position to get additional business loans, job opportunities, introductions, and housing from their wife's kin. They got apprenticeships for their sons and places for their daughters. They gained privileged access to the investment funds of a new collection of relatives. They could, under some circumstances, expect to benefit from the free labor of an expanded pool of female relations, although sometimes they also had to take responsibility for them in their old age. If his fortunes declined, a son-in-law had a strong, although by no means absolute, moral claim on the charity of his in-laws: they might bail him out of jail, pay off his most pressing debts, or take in his wife and children for extended periods if he absconded. It is no exaggeration to say that a man's relationship to his wife's family could make or break him.

Wives played a significant mediating role in the endless negotiations that made up the fabric of eighteenth-century affinal kin relations. A wife often conveyed intelligence back and forth to her natal family as to the state of her husband's business or his treatment of her or her children— often the information upon which decisions about the distribution of resources would be made. In more straitened times a wife might adopt the traditional feminine role of supplicant. One often hears of women turning up on the doorstep of relatives with the requisite babe (or babes) in arms, to beg in stereotyped phrases that their portion be paid, a loan be extended, a debt be forgiven, or a husband be released from jail. As literacy increased, these appeals often came in written form, and they can be found in many seventeenth- and eighteenth-century letter collections.[27]

In theory, this system should have encouraged men to be attentive to their businesses and to refrain from maltreating their wives—a clear case of self-interest stimulating virtue. But for the formula to work, the wife's relatives actually had to come through at a level roughly commensurate with their son-in-law's expectations. If they did not, or could not, the wife stood in real danger of becoming a hostage to her husband's financial demands. If a woman's family was late with her dowry payment, seemed disinclined to furnish a loan, or was otherwise proving deaf to a son-in-law's demands, the husband (or his family) would, not infrequently, proceed to browbeat or physically abuse the wife, making sure that the news got back to her family. If the wife's relatives cared about her welfare, they would be forced to treat with the husband in the hope of moderating the treatment she was receiving.

Variants of this dreary tale turn up periodically in collections of family papers, besides being something of a commonplace in contemporary discussions of marriage. But it is in divorce court records that the unpleasant details of what was, no doubt, a more widespread problem can be most clearly seen. Any number of examples could be mentioned, but let us, somewhat arbitrarily, consider three cases from the London Consistory Court clerk's books for 1711 to 1713. In the first, Thomas Byfield, a prosperous pawnbroker, beat and kicked his wife while she was pregnant, dragged her about by the hair, locked her up and refused her food, threatened to turn her and her child out of the house, and "did continually and allmost day after day beat and abuse his said wife by kicking and striking her on the head, arms and leggs," because, among other things, "he never got a portion with her, though she was represented to him as a woman of considerable fortune."[28] In the second, Anthony Pitts, a butcher, locked his wife Hester up for two days, beat and kicked her in the presence of her mother, and threw her out in the street with her child because Hester's aunt had refused to stand surety for him for a loan. In the third, John Spinkes, a "practioner of physic," actually sent for Elizabeth Spinkes's sister on a pretext and when she arrived told her that "he had sent for [her] . . . for a witnesse & thereupon immediately with his fist doubled and with all his force struck [his wife] over the face by wch meanes her Nose & Eyes fell a bleeding & at the same time cursed & swore at her & gave her very opprobrious language." He too was trying to coerce his in-laws into advancing him money.[29]

This level of violence was clearly on the more extreme end of the spectrum, and there were, no doubt, families who managed all these complexities without resort to violence. Nevertheless, it seems likely that emotional coercion and both the threat and the reality of physical cruelty were in some sense endemic to this system. The cynic might even say that they oiled the system of intergenerational transfer. What is clear is that they were a logical corollary of a system that relied heavily on marriage and kinship as routes to capital formation while giving husbands considerable though not unlimited freedom to physically abuse their wives.

WOMEN, EXPENDITURES, AND FAMILY SOLIDARITY

Sixteenth- and seventeenth-century journalistic attacks on women, and especially on citizen's wives, had conventionally paid a good deal of attention to their alleged natural extravagance. As invidious comparisons between aristocratic luxury and middling frugality and prudence gained momentum in the latter part of the seventeenth century, this tendency to see women as the source of the problem came into conflict with the need to impress upon all middling people, including men, the importance of self-discipline and restraint.

Daniel Defoe's *Complete English Tradesman* contains a detailed prescription for the relationship that should, ideally, obtain between wife and husband; essentially it is one of mutual support in the interest of keeping down expenses. A tradesman is discernably unhappy, but refuses at first to disclose the problem to his wife because he is reluctant to burden her with his business affairs. Finally she succeeds in extracting from him the admission that he is in financial trouble, which puts her in mind of another husband who refused to let his wife know anything about his business affairs:

> *Wife.* Just so our old acquaintance G_____W_____did; his poor wife knew not one word of [his sorry financial state] nor so much as suspected it, but thought him in as flourishing circumstances as ever; 'till on a sudden he was arrested in an action for a great sum, so great that he could not find bail, and the next day an execution on another action was serv'd in the house, and swept away the very bed from under her; and the poor lady, that brought him 3000£ portion, was turn'd into the street with five small children to take care of.
>
> *Husb.* Her case was very sad indeed.
>
> *Wife.* But was not he a barbarous wretch to her, to let her know nothing of her circumstances? She was at the Ball but the day before, in her velvet suit, and with her jewels on, and they reproach her with it every day.[30]

The wife then lays out a sweeping program of cutting expenses, including dismissing most of the servants and ceasing to entertain, and forthrightly urges her husband to do the same:

> *Husb.* I know not where to begin
>
> *Wife.* Why you keep two horses and a groom, you keep _____ rich high company, and you sit long at the *Fleece* every evening. I need say no more, you know where to begin well enough.

Husb. It is very hard, I han't your spirit, *my Dear.*

Wife. I hope you are not more asham'd to retrench, than you would be to have your name in the *gazette* [i.e., as a bankrupt].[31]

Defoe, who generally had a high opinion of the capacities of women, does not present them as intrinsically more extravagant than men (at least not here). In fact, he seems to have regarded marriage among the trading classes as an alliance, not unmixed with affection, between two people with roughly comparable capacities who were jointly committed to business success.

Some people clearly took such advice to heart. Witness a real life correspondence from 1774 between a mother, Eleanora Hucks, and her daughter, Nelly, who was about to marry a businessman. Mrs. Hucks first advises her daughter to

do whatever will be most pleasing to your Husband & be frugal in the management of his fortune, as also in the management of your own time, for of that we must be accountable at a great and aweful Tribunal.[32]

Nelly is advised to avoid public places as much as possible, as they give little satisfaction to the mind and cause one to neglect one's family; if possible Nelly and her husband should avoid going to operas, plays, oratorios, and the like because they are ruinously expensive. Besides, Mrs. Hucks has heard of Mr. Ward that his

aim is Domestique happiness; nay he said in a letter he wrote to your Father, that he trusted he should see the absurdity of his former expensive way of Life, in the rational plan he was about pursuing with a Woman of Virtue and Sense, and with one that he chose merely for her self & just way of thinking.[33]

Mrs. Hucks hopes her daughter will not take the letter to indicate any suspicion of her conduct, "but as a provident General, I would most secure the place that is [in] the greatest Danger of an attack"—that is, the realm of expenditures. Nelly should endeavor to check her husband's generosity and can then expect him to esteem her the more for supplying restraint he may lack.[34]

Some women did throw themselves into home economies, often combining them with more direct labor or capital contributions to the family enterprises. But a nagging sense of specifically gendered insecurity often accompanied their more generalized anxieties. Commiserating with her mother in 1752 about two brothers they knew who had recently gone bankrupt, Miss Mercy Doddridge's usual compassion for the plight of married women was tinged with anger:

Broke for Sixty Thousand Pounds: I pitty their Families Extremely. How great must be their distress: who will feel and suffer so Much for what I fear must be call'd the imprudence of others. Perhaps of those too from whom she [*sic*] had the Highest Expectations.[35]

There was indeed an egalitarian strain to the notion of a family alliance in joint pursuit of financial solvency, but it was an extremely constrained egalitarianism. In most families the major business decisions were made by men, while law, custom, education, and the sanctions of patriarchal family life kept most women from intervening in any really significant way.

Some women, such as the Quaker convert Elizabeth Ashbridge, managed to pay off all their debts "principal and interest" in that heroic mode typical of the eighteenth century. But many women lacked the saleable skills, the credit, the contacts, and the support from extended family or coreligionists that would have permitted them to exercise this kind of initiative. The obstacles placed in the way of women "making Use of their ingenuity and industry to procure them a subsistance, when those who should provide it for them, refuse it, or are incapable of it" (as one eighteenth-century feminist writer put it) were very great.[36] This did not mean that women did not often find ways to scrape by, at least for a time. Women who ran small shops out of their homes or who kept lodgers were a familiar feature of eighteenth-century towns; many of them would have been the wives, widows, or spinster daughters of decayed businessmen. As a group they waged what must often have been a losing battle to retain some vestige of their former standard of living and to avoid total dependence upon relatives or the parish.

The public has rarely been able to resist the spectacle of innocence betrayed. Eighteenth-century people felt deeply for women and children caught in the clutches of financial crises they had little part in making and delighted in portraying them as even more helpless, passive, and persecuted than they actually were. It is doubtless true that such sentiments helped individual women convince others to assist them,[37] but the voyeuristic fascination with female victims of the market also had the effect of exaggerating feminine difference at the same time that it allowed people to be titillated by its painful effects. This occurred, moreover, at a time when aggressive pursuit of gain on the part of men was being celebrated and encouraged. It meant that the most resourceful and independent women operated in something of an ideological vacuum.

THE SEPARATE ESTATE

The wife's separate estate held an equivocal place in eighteenth-century family life, not least because as an institution it was hard to reconcile with the ideal of female financial dependence and passivity. Because it was explicitly exempt from coverture, the separate estate undeniably had the effect of empowering some women. In many other cases it proved impossible to keep the separate estate out of the hands of covetous or financially embattled husbands.

The separate estate (also called "separate settlement," "separate uses," or "separate maintenance") was a species of property awarded to the wife, generally in trust, that her husband and her husband's creditors were not supposed to be able to touch. The legal phraseology by which a separate estate was established generally went something like the following:

> [The sum of money or property in question] shall be for [the wife's] sole and separate use and benefit, independent and exclusive of her husband and without it being in anywise subject to his debts, control, interference or engagement.[38]

Provision for a separate estate was often made at the time of marriage as part of the prenuptial agreement (which was confusingly referred to in the eighteenth century as the marriage settlement).[39] A separate estate could originate in other ways, however. A post-nuptial arrangement might be worked out with a woman's husband that gave her formal legal rights over certain types of property. Alternatively, money or other assets could be bequeathed to a married woman with the stipulation that they be for her separate use. Although historians of women and the family have devoted much of their attention to separate estates arising from prenuptial agreements, testamentary bequests may well have been the most common mode by which middling women, at any rate, acquired separate estates in the eighteenth century.[40]

Eighteenth-century writers, most famously Sir Richard Steele, often called for eliminating the wife's separate estate altogether on the grounds that the device encouraged wifely disobedience and hence familial disharmony. But moralists' assaults on the wife's separate estate were in some respects misleading. Most of the critics of the separate estate directed their abuse at pin money, a device that comprised a kind of clothing allowance settled on a woman at marriage and that was mainly resorted to by the very rich. The effect of this fairly transparent rhetorical move was, first, to identify the separate estate *in general* with extremely rich women with luxurious tastes, and second, to trivialize the issue by implying that all that was at stake was a woman's ability to buy the latest Paris fashions. It is by no means clear how well this view of the separate estate accorded with actual practice even in elite families. It is certainly a very poor guide to what was going on among the commercial classes.[41]

We do not have a good sense of how many middling women possessed separate estates, although it is clear that such estates were not, as used to be thought, a largely upper-class phenomenon. Indications are that non-elites resorted to the use of separate estates in increasing numbers between the late seventeenth and the early nineteenth centuries. Amy Erickson has found that sample wordings for separate settlements were readily available in the standard legal handbooks, as well as in handbooks specifically directed at women, from the early eighteenth century on. On the other hand, actual resort to separate uses was still very little in evidence in a survey Erickson did of probate accounts in the courts of Lincoln, Chichester, Ely and Bath and Wells in the late sixteenth and early eighteenth centuries. Although marriage settlements were found in about 10 percent of the wills (most of these were arrangements for jointure), in only 10 percent of these, or 1 percent of the total sample, had provision been made for separate uses for the wife during her husband's lifetime. Either the sorts of records Erickson has examined are not conducive to finding evidence of separate uses or they were not yet all that common in practice, at least in the dioceses she studied.[42]

A very different picture emerges from Leonore Davidoff and Catherine Hall's examination of a sample of wills made in rural East Anglia and Birmingham between 1780 and 1850. Here a full one-third of the testators left property to women in trust for their separate use. The wills with trusts comprise 25 percent of what Davidoff and Hall term "lower middle class" wills, 55 percent of "upper middle class" wills, and 71 percent of wills of men of independent means.[43] The two samples are in many respects not comparable: Erickson's study examines separate uses originating in marriage settlements, while that of Davidoff and Hall looks at separate uses originating in testamentary bequests. Both studies, therefore, underestimate the incidence of the practice. Either way, the suggestion is strong that the wife's separate estate became "normalized" within middling groups over the course of the eighteenth century.

Among the middling the separate estate seems to have been an extremely flexible form. It could consist of real property, including, say, urban rental real estate (often a single house), but was just as likely to be in the form of paper investments, shop fittings, stock in trade, or cash. Whatever the original intent of the separate settlement, it had clearly evolved in such a way as to enable some married women to enjoy a degree of economic independence as well as partial control over some of the property they brought to their marriages.[44] Significantly, a goodly number of the middling separate estates surveyed in the course of this study were established by widows on the occasion of their remarriage or originated in bequests, often from female relatives. They were not negotiated on a young woman's behalf by her male relatives. Some wives clearly administered their separate estates themselves as part of an ongoing trade or program of investment. Others lent money to their husbands or to other male relatives. Still others, willingly in some cases, under duress in others, permitted their husbands to oversee the investments or use the proceeds of the separate estate for their own benefit.[45]

Let us look at one such woman. Judith DuBuc (b. 1678, fl. 1718–34), was of French Huguenot extraction, lived in London, and possessed a substantial separate estate. Among other things she used it to lend her husband £300 at 5 percent interest, apparently on a two-year term, in return for a note. This was a predictable move, although the seriousness with which both spouses approached the terms of the contract may not have been.[46] When her husband could not repay all the money by the stipulated date, the two of them contracted to mortgage some of his goods in lieu of immediate payment. DuBuc's separate estate, or, as she put it, assets "owned in my own right," included orders, lottery tickets, and South Sea stock, and the notations in her account book suggest that she administered her own funds.[47]

An extremely intricate case brought in 1761 in the Court of Exchequer reveals much about the ways a separate estate, combined with other stratagems, could be used to keep assets a woman considered to be hers away from a hostile or avaricious spouse. When Elinor Lally married William Fitzmaurice in 1735 he was a common soldier (or so it was later alleged) and she was a distiller possessed of a considerable personal estate including money, plate, jewels, and stock-in-trade. On marrying, she placed a good part of her property in trust "to prevent the same vesting in the said William Fitzmaurice and for the making of a provision for her as well during her coverture." Fitzmaurice managed to seize most of her assets anyway. He sold off her goods and fled to Ireland, forcing Elinor to move in with her son from a previous marriage who had established himself in stay making. After she separated from her husband, allegations were made that Elinor was concealing the existence of assets not covered by the separate settlement and that she had illegally transferred the title for some India Bonds to her son, all to keep Fitzmaurice from getting at them. Ultimately it appears that she used her remaining funds to set up again as a distiller, while continuing to live apart from her husband.[48]

Many husbands saw benefits in having a store of money in the family that could not easily be attached in an action for debt. But when a man was especially hard-pressed by his creditors, it was all too easy for him to develop his own designs on his wife's funds. Men were, after all, accustomed to believe that they had a "right" to the assets of female family members, and the notion that women as well as men could practice possessive individualism was not well advanced. It was also common for a husband to be the trustee of his wife's estate, which gave him an even greater sense of entitlement with respect to her money. In short, many a husband could be confident of his ability, as the saying went, to "kiss or kick" his wife into signing over her property.[49]

Kicking was more in evidence than kissing in the divorce courts, where disputes over separate estates look much like fights over unpaid portions. One of the physician John Spinkes's major grievances against his wife Elizabeth (apart from the issue of her portion) was that she refused to give him money from an estate in Wales that she owned in trust. Later in court Elizabeth alleged that John punched her in the face, beat her with a horsewhip, and locked her up first in her own home and then in Dr. Newton's lunatic asylum in an effort to get her to submit to his financial demands. After a time Elizabeth signed over the money "for the procuring of her peace and quiet . . . [and] in hopes and expectation of receiving a better usage than he had before treated her with."[50] In a similar case, Thomas Hull, a barber and peruke maker, is alleged to have beaten his wife Mary until she miscarried, threatened to confine her to a madhouse, encouraged his children from a previous marriage to abuse her, thrown her clothes in the fire, and tried to burn her. A major source of contention was her separate settlement, which she was "to keep in her own right and was to enjoy separate and distinct from her sd. husband." Thomas succeeded finally in terrorizing his wife into relinquishing the records of the estate.[51] In a third case, Gawen Hudson held a dagger against his wife Rebecca's neck and "threatened to cut her Neck off if she cryed out, stirred or spoke." At issue was whether she would consent to sell some of her own estate to pay his debts. It is not clear from the records whether she complied, but some time later he was threatening to confine her for life in a madhouse unless she released her jointure to him.[52]

The separate settlement lay athwart several conflicting middling concerns. One of these was the desire to fashion the family into an emotional and financial refuge from the vicissitudes of business, and the separate estate, because it could not in theory be taken by a husband's creditors, did partially do this. Another was the assumption, apparently more widely shared by men than by women, that the latter's resources should be given over to the control of their husbands or male relatives. And the third, which ventured onto more subversive terrain, was a notion held by some women, and occasionally confirmed by the courts, that women possessed something very close to a "right" to try to ensure their own independent survival, precisely because dependence was fraught with such risks.

The separate estate was a marker of the contested status of attempts to separate "the family" from the mercenary world of business. In fact, over time there is some suggestion that middling families sought stronger measures to safeguard women's separate estates by, for instance, placing at least some of the money in safe and relatively inflexible investments, such as irredeemable annuities, bank stock, or land. This had the effect of elevating the notion of the family as refuge over that of the woman who was first and foremost a conduit for investment funds. It also left both middle- and upper-class women with diminished freedom of action with respect to "their" money.[53]

In *The Mysteries of Conjugal Love Reveal'd,* which appeared in London in 1712 in English translation, Nicholas de Venette claimed that tradesmen were blessed with uncommonly robust children for the simple reason that they rationally scheduled their lovemaking to take place early in the morning:

> For being tired with the fatigue of the preceding day, they wait for the Morning to embrace their Wives, and avoid . . . in so doing, the Inconveniences other Men are subject to, who running headlong without any manner of reflection, abandon themselves to the violence of the Passion.[54]

Having sexual relations at times of peak energy made for more potent sperm and hence healthier children (along with more male births). This argument dove-tailed well with the centuries–old belief that the expending of semen during coitus (or indeed at any other time) depleted men's physical and mental powers. Appropriately, for a passage praising the erotic circumspection of commercial men, de Venette (or his English translator) articulated this latter doctrine using imagery drawn from accountancy: "[I]f we kiss after Supper we have nothing but the Night's rest to reimburse us of what we are out of pocket."[55] But it is not, alas, very likely that de Venette ever actually conducted a systematic poll of tradesmen's sexual habits. His assertions are interesting primarily because they exemplify the commonplace identification between "excessive" sexual activity and extravagance of other kinds, as well as the widely held belief that commercial folk were better at managing their time and conserving their substance than other people.

Unquestionably, what was really at issue was serious sins like fornication and adultery, not at what time of the day married people chose to have sexual relations. The persistent linguistic overlap in this period between words that referred to loss of sexual innocence and those that referred to business failure (such as the terms "ruined" and "undone") signal a quite thorough conflation of illicit sex and runaway consumption that is ubiquitous in late seventeenth-century urban culture. De Venette's analogy between coming and spending said it all.

It was no illusion to think that fornication could be costly in terms of both money and reputation, and adultery was almost guaranteed to impede good relations between husband and wife, which could easily lead to antagonizing one's in-laws and obstructing the flow of resources and favors upon which many sons-in-law depended.[56] In the early modern period, nonmarital or extramarital sex really could have devastating financial consequences. As we saw in an earlier chapter, a convenient locus for emphasizing the inseparability of illicit sex and excessive expenditures was the prostitute. Late-seventeenth- and eighteenth-century city dwellers were obsessed with whores, their out-of-control sexuality, and their alleged depredations against "innocent" householders.[57] In the seventeenth century one popular vehicle for expressing this concern was salacious "cautionary" tales about prostitutes. Mostly these circulated orally, but luckily for us, representative ones occasionally surface in print. In 1705 several of them were collected together in a semipornographic pastiche titled *The London Bawd: With her Character and Life: Discovering the Various and Subtle Intrigues of Lewd Women*. In one typical story a tradesman has taken up with a whore and begins neglecting his business in order to maintain her. He falls into debt and finally is "so haunted by Bailiffs and Sergeants" that he is forced to flee to the Netherlands. His friends advise him to abandon his wicked courses before he is ruined, and his blameless wife implores him to reform and warns him that he is sacrificing his "Credit and Repute." His whore then retaliates by counseling him to "beat [his wife's] Teeth into her throat" to stop her complaining, thereby confirming the deep-seated, destructive hatred of "respectable" women and conventional family life that all whores were alleged to possess. At the end of the story the man's wife dies, his estate is mortgaged twice over, he starves, and repentant, he too expires, presumably from the pox.[58]

It was typical of these cautionary tales, whether they were contained in sermons or in titillating little tracts like the *London Bawd,* to lay the bulk of the moral blame upon female sexual profligates, against whose blandishments men were thought to be largely helpless. As a counterweight they emphasized (although not always with much conviction) the importance of female chastity and the vast gulf said to separate the virtuous matron from the polluted whore.[59] The man who could withstand the latter's temptations was seldom described in much detail, since these narratives sought to convince their readers, in typically alarmist fashion, that the problem was far too great for any one individual to combat. But clearly such a man was thoroughly attentive to the vulnerability of the family unit under his care, and accustomed, in the interests of preserving it, to limiting his sexual appetites in much the same way that he did his expenditures.

Did the attacks on vice and the trumpeting of the virtues of monogamous private families succeed in "saving" the middling from sexual sin, or, for that matter, from insolvency? Clearly they did not. Among the middling, one of the commonest grounds for legal as well as informal separation in the eighteenth century was adultery. It was also fairly common to hear appeals for relief or redress from women who contracted venereal disease from their husbands (also a common theme of moral literature).

From the husbands' side there were persistent complaints that their wives refused to sleep with them, made a point of emphasizing their physical unattractiveness, spread gossip about their lack of sexual prowess, and were too familiar with other men.[60]

In short, there is absolutely no evidence that middling families were any less prone to sexual incompatibility or sexual peccadilloes than any other group. There are few groups, however, who have made more inflated claims for the moral superiority of their own brand of marriage and the lewdness and disorder of other people's marriages (or sex lives more generally). This tendency to stake their identity on having more successful home lives than other people left the middling anxiously poised between a stronger-than-usual impulse to police their own and others' sexual behavior (evident as early as the 1690s in the Reformation of Manners campaigns against prostitution) and a visceral reluctance to air their dirty linen in public (one of the factors that militated in favor of making middle-class families more "private"). This unlovely combination of prudery and hypocrisy was bequeathed wholesale to the nineteenth century, where a new generation of critics, less than sympathetic to the world of anxious striving that had spawned it, would hasten to label it "bourgeois morality."

WIDOWHOOD

In societies characterized by fairly overt forms of male domination, women are often quite clear-eyed about the realities of gender inequality. They do not, however, necessarily translate this "consciousness" into political action in the modern understandings of that term. Not too surprisingly, many eighteenth-century women were deeply ambivalent about marriage, and widowhood was sometimes positively welcomed. The author and vicar's wife, Catharine Cockburn, née Trotter, was only repeating standard women's wisdom when she wrote to a recently bereaved kinswoman in 1741 that "to have a good Husband early snatched from us is indeed a grievous affliction, but to live long with a very bad one might be much worse, wch is the lot of many & numberless [women]."[61] Although widowhood often meant poverty, dependence, and lovelessness, it *could* mean a more-or-less comfortable jointure, life insurance payments, and a welcome release from a husband's despotic authority.

In cash terms, marriage primarily benefited the groom or his natal family, but there were real benefits that accrued to the wife as well. One important function of marriage was to offer some minimal level of financial security for women and children during the husband's lifetime and, ideally, after it as well. In England measures had long before been instituted to encourage men to provide at least minimally for their wives and children: both the rule that a man was required to support his wife and the right of dower (the widow's right to a third of the deceased man's estate once his other debts had been paid) were intended to further this aim.

In practice, provision for women (and children) after the death of a husband could be a hit-or-miss affair among the middling. There were several reasons for this. Jointures were probably less common among these groups than among the landed—Earle suggests that this was because capital could not be tied up in land—but the right of dower was often meaningless because so many men left estates heavily encumbered by debt.[62] This left a woman with a choice of moving in with relatives or attempting to organize, if she had not done so already, some sort of income-producing activity. Neither could necessarily be depended on. It may well have been that middling families were less willing to take in widows and children than were their social superiors. Their houses were smaller, they had fewer servants, their incomes were more variable, and they were not, on the whole, champions of large households.[63] However, if a woman sought to retain her independence through trade, by waged labor, or by providing some service (such as taking in lodgers), she ran into the same disincentives—dearth of capital, low pay, labor intensive work, few options—that generally accrued to women's work.

The plight of widows seems to have inspired somewhat more constructive solutions than did some of the other glaring problems of middling family life, probably because attempts at relieving the problem involved little encroachment upon the prerogatives of male household heads during their lifetimes. Charities for widows were not, perhaps, the most fashionable form of eighteenth-century philanthropy, but they had an established place in the hearts and minds of urban donors. Guilds and other occupational groups (particularly those with a strong *esprit de corps,* such as sea captains or lawyers) had long had a tradition of providing pensions or lump sum payments for their widows and orphans. Increasingly in the eighteenth century these were supplemented by other sorts of arrangements, among them annuities and life insurance. Also catering primarily to a middling clientele were some new collective enterprises, such as pension and other payment schemes organized by masonic lodges on behalf of the widows of brothers and charities benefiting the widows and orphans of members of the clergy.

One of the latter was the Corporation of the Sons of the Clergy, chartered in 1678 to help alleviate the distress of Church of England clergymen persecuted during the Interregnum. By the eighteenth century most of the Corporation's beneficiaries were widows and "maiden daughters" (spinsters) and as such its records provide a window on the tactics such women used to survive. It was possible to live on the CSC pension, but only at a rather minimal level. Surviving records of the Corporation are full of heart-rending appeals from women well-versed in the rhetoric of helpless feminine virtue. These mingle with numerous reports of double dipping, the use of false certificates, underreporting of other income, and the like—tokens of a very different conception of femininity. The whole question of how widows, spinsters, and deserted wives supplied themselves in the inhospitable (at least for women) economic and cultural environment of eighteenth-century Britain remains virtually unstudied, but the petty criminality of at least some of the CSC pensioners suggests parallels with Olwen Hufton's work on eighteenth-century women salt smugglers in France, among other groups.[64] In the CSC, at any rate, women were also prominent in a different capacity. A substantial number of the people making donations to the widows' and spinsters' funds were themselves women.

Once again the evidence accords poorly with the received picture of the eighteenth century as a kind of feminist wasteland. What motivated these female donors to give, often extremely generously, to a charity of this kind?[65] We cannot know precisely, but it is not unreasonable to think that donations of this sort derived partly from a sense of unease on the part of middling women about their own position within the marketplace. Miss Mercy Doddridge's resentment on behalf of "[those] who will feel and suffer so Much for what I fear must be call'd the imprudence of others" came out of a keen sense of the gender injustice that lay at the heart of middling family life. In good times middling women might prosper, but any woman was only a man away from being seriously de-classed, and the system offered her few opportunities to regain her former status. The ambiguous position of middling (and later middle-class) women, the most precariously situated of all in a class that already felt financially insecure, was to resonate powerfully through bourgeois feminism all the way to the modern period.

ONE MIDDLING MARRIAGE

This chapter has sought to uncover those less than ideal aspects of eighteenth-century married life so often papered over by contemporaries and historians alike. There is another side to eighteenth-century middling marriage, one that recalls the sober, morally superior seventeenth-century burgher Ambrose Barnes, who opened this chapter. It is only fair to conclude this chapter with an apparently quite harmonious middling couple from York, Faith Gray and her solicitor husband, William Gray. With these two, the fragments of "middling culture"—the anxieties, the fear, the ambition—seem finally to have converged into something that, in its moral self-confidence and its aggressively outward-looking stance, feels "middle class." It has been suggested that the Evangelical movement represented a watershed in the development of middle-class culture, and the Grays seem a sterling example of what that movement could do for "bourgeois" self-confidence. Yet it is also clear that the Grays' interests, as well as their cares, are fully continuous with those of middling people much earlier in the century.[66]

Faith Gray's father, as she proudly tells us in her autobiography, had been an Anglican, "particularly attached to Cathedral Worship." He was apprenticed to a Mr. Atkenson, a prosperous hatter, hosier, and glover of York, and later worked in that trade in a somewhat strained partnership with his brother. Faith describes her father as having had "the greatest enjoyment in his family circle of any man I ever saw." Both her parents were "careful in guarding me against what might be hurtful to me in morals or general habits" and she was taught to keep yearly received/disbursed accounts from the age of fourteen, a habit she retained throughout her married life. William Gray also came from a trading background, being the son of a weaver, but he was articled to a solicitor, and some time after concluding his apprenticeship he became a partner in a firm in York. His wife makes a point of the fact that he too kept very accurate and particular accounts. Both the Grays were extremely hardworking and time-conscious. William Gray frequently remained in his office until eleven at night or later, "ever careful to comply with the [scriptural] exhortation 'diligent in business.' "[67]

The Grays were no strangers to hardship. In the late 1770s or early '80s the favorite nephew of William Gray's partner entangled his uncle in debt through extravagance and misconduct, and for three or four years the business, and hence the entire Gray family, was balanced on the brink of bankruptcy. In 1782 the sorry youth finally absconded, causing the partner to become insolvent, and the credit of the office was only preserved because Gray and several others laid out substantial sums from their own funds to save it. The partner was apparently prostrated from shock, and, for some time after, Gray worked until one, two, and three o'clock in the morning trying to sort things out and make up the shortfall. This experience shattered his nerves, and, as his wife delicately put it, made him irritable of temper, "which has given pain to his friends." Still, William Gray had joined a noble band: from the beginning until the end of this period the businessman (or professional) of truly superior virtue was one who had suffered in the marketplace and who, by dint of almost superhuman feats of fortitude and self-discipline, had managed to emerge spiritually and materially triumphant, although not unscarred.[68]

Both the Grays were deeply committed to charitable endeavors. William Gray was a founder of Sunday schools in York ("To promote among the lower classes the knowledge and practice of religious and moral duties, a regular attendance upon the ordinances in the Church of England, and principles of loyalty and subordination"), president of the York Auxiliary of the Church Missionary Society, and associated with the Bible Society, the York Dispensary, and the York County Hospital. Later, in 1816, he became a founding member of the York Savings Bank. He was a good friend to William Wilberforce, whose religious views he is said to have shared, and at one point he served as almoner to Wilberforce's Anti-Slavery Campaign. One of Gray's partners, Anthony Thorpe, was a founder of the York Philosophical Society, and the Grays were proud of this connection to the cause of science. Relatively muted in his political beliefs, at least as portrayed in this diary, Gray's whole career is a reproach to the leisured, the negligent, and the easily corruptible. For example, at one time he held an office charged with the distribution of stamps, one of those lucrative semi-sinecures so endemic to early modern European government. Not only was Gray conscientious about fulfilling his duties, but having decided that the emolument was excessive given the nature of the job, he formally requested that it be lowered and the surplus returned to the treasury. This ethos, efficient, utilitarian, self-consciously high-minded, and contemptuous of entrenched interests, was to epitomize the spirit of reform for generations to come.[69]

It is unclear whether Faith Gray assisted her husband in his business, although she certainly oversaw a constant round of entertaining of his business and reform-minded associates. Interestingly, she boasts of how *her* mother went out to work to provide additional cash when her father was on the verge of failing and also of her mother's very substantial labor contributions to her husband's business.[70] Certainly Faith raised her children to be as self-disciplined and time-conscious as herself, and presumably as adept at keeping accounts.[71]

Like her husband, she was heavily involved in charitable pursuits—in fact her interests are quite revealing of the concerns of urban middling women by the late eighteenth century. Charitable work had for centuries been a part of the virtuous woman's repertoire. But here it was becoming systematized and rationalized, incorporating, among other things, enlightened critiques of indiscriminate or ill-planned charity.[72] Faith Gray's forays into organized charity were neither indiscriminate nor ill-planned. One of them involved an arrangement with a Mr. Hooker, a local hemp manufacturer, for the "children and girls" who worked for him to learn reading at night and to accompany a middle-class woman to church on Sundays. It seemed, however, that a true "reformation of manners" was not being effectually achieved by such methods. In 1782, therefore, with the help of women friends, Faith Gray started a spinning school designed

> to excite a spirit of virtuous industry among the children of the poor, for . . . idleness and want of principle are the greatest forces of their poverty and wretchedness.[73]

The spinning school was entirely directed and run by middle-class women who did the accounts, the teaching, and the "Sunday visiting" to the homes of the poor. The idea was that poor girls would spin hanks of thread in return for clothes; a major aim of the project was to attempt to overcome the bad influence of lower-class parents, "the greater part of whom . . . are extremely ignorant and without any habits of self government." Soon the founders of the spinning school were able to extend their influence further. In 1785 they were approached for advice on the reform of the local charity school for girls. They submitted a comprehensive plan to "eliminate caprice" in the administration of the school and to stop inmates "being affected by the interests of the mistress." By the end of 1786 Faith Gray and her circle had fully taken over the direction and day-to-day administration of the school. The women instituted sweeping reforms that included abolishing the apprenticeship system for girls, dismissing the old Master as "unfit for the trust reposed in him," and providing "rewards" for work well done. The reformed charity school was as breathtakingly efficient and authoritarian as any of the new factories, and indeed it resembled them in a number of particulars. Accounts were figured closely and often, and there was a heavy emphasis on the inculcating of time-discipline and work-efficiency. In a short time economies in the diet of the children (they were not allowed tea, sugar, butter, eggs, or beer), and the sale of what these same children produced each day at the spinning wheel or stocking frame, resulted in very substantial savings.[74]

Faith Gray's life was full of small challenges to what she and her circle presumed to be aristocratic mores. She made special note of "a very excellent and striking sermon" dealing with "the contempt poured on the ministry of the Gospel by the highest and lowest classes of people" and was proud of her mother's refusal to assume on her relationship with a step-sister who had married up into the gentry. But these mild expressions of class consciousness pale beside the self-conscious sense of superiority that both Faith and William Gray derived from their highly domestic yet career-oriented marriage, a union typified as much by their common grasp of their accounts, their highly conscious attitude toward time, and their indomitable fight to maintain the credit of the firm as by their shared piety, their civic and philanthropic involvements, and their commitment to their children.[75] When this respectable wife of a solicitor turned her attention to issues beyond her immediate family, her assumptions about virtue, efficiency, and the role of the laboring classes were indistinguishable from those of Mr. Hooker, the hemp manufacturer with whom she was happy to collaborate. Her capacity, wife and mother that she was, to conceive and execute a rational plan of cost accountability and profit maximization matched that of any successful factory owner.

One of the most striking things about Faith Gray's married life is how poorly it harmonizes with any notion of a separate sphere for women. Instead, her story suggests powerfully the extent to which middling men and middling women shared in a common culture. Earlier in the century this might have simply been a joint commitment to bookkeeping, better time management, or cutting expenditures. By the 1780s, in this family at any rate, these obligations, which both of them imbibed from their parents, had been augmented by a range of other shared concerns, from evangelicalism and political reform to "scientific" philanthropy.

If middling married life was often more unified culturally than the notion of separate spheres would lead us to assume, it was probably also more conflictual. Faith Gray's autobiography is a meticulously constructed representation of family life. She is well-versed at concealing anything that might seem inconsistent with a picture of fervent commitment to prudential values, upright morals, and, above all, family solidarity. Hovering in the background, it is true, were the threats of insolvency, corruption in the ruling classes, dangerous emulation among youth, and the feckless and undisciplined poor. Still further back, already almost impossible to address, were all the other possible sources of conflict within families: the children who went wrong, the husbands who strayed, the in-laws who refused to help, the painful differences that could arise between husband and wife. But the Grays' own "rational plan" of "Domestick happiness," really had succeeded in marrying emotional fulfillment to particularist economic goals, and they were fully aware of and duly gratified by their achievement.

CONCLUSION

This chapter has explored the paradoxes and complexities that attend any attempt to translate an idealized schema into social practice. The surviving sources on eighteenth-century middling married life represent blurred traces of a rich, complicated, conflictual culture that never fully succumbed to contemporaries' efforts to make it into something cleaner, more presentable, and above all, more "rational." Middling marriage was filled with pitfalls, inequality, and potential for unhappiness, but it was also one of the central institutions of middling life. A good many people in this period, including a small but significant percentage of women, chose to forego marriage. Others, men and women, would have liked to marry but lacked the wherewithall or the nerve to accomplish it. At times these people came up with quite creative alternatives, at least some of which were emotionally and sexually fulfilling as well as economically viable. But, far more explicitly than is the case today, eighteenth-century marriage served as the springboard for married couples and, especially, married men to claim a lion's share of the available labor, capital, and reproductive and political resources. Those who did not marry may have had, in some cases, an easier time of it; perhaps they merely took on a new set of problems. There is no doubt that they shared a smaller piece of the pie. It was because the stakes involved in marriage among the middling classes were so high that it proved such a fertile ground for middling conflict and middling dreams.

CHAPTER SEVEN

Print Culture and the Middling Classes: Mapping the World of Commerce

[If we looked to our] Book of Accounts with God, we should find that wee are indebted to him, and not he to us.

JOHN WARNER, *THE GAYNE OF LOSSE, OR TEMPORALL LOSSES SPIRITUALLY IMPROVED*, 1645

This day is published . . . the completest Memorandum book, and by much the most generally approved, as any Thing of the kind ever publish'd . . . so contrived as to answer every Man's Purpose, and to enable him with the greatest Ease, to keep a regular and exact Account of all Monies received, paid, lent, or expended; where, of, and to whom, every Day of the Week throughout the Year; with a blank Space opposite each Day for all Appointments or Engagements, and a distinct Weekly Column for miscellaneous Memorandums and Observations.

PUBLIC ADVERTISER, NO. 6609, 2 JANUARY 1756

For Adam Smith "the propensity to truck, barter, and exchange one thing for another" was a relatively uncomplicated desire shared by all human beings. It was either a fundamental characteristic of the species or, what amounted to virtually the same thing, a consequence of the ability, such as even children possess, to speak and reason.[1] The basic instinct may have been simple, but by the eighteenth century the exchange economy had achieved such complexity that it seemed to many to have displaced individual volition. The elaborate calculations into which businessmen entered, the growing body of specialist knowledge they had to have, and the contacts they had to cultivate in order to operate successfully on a moderate to large scale made the sphere of commerce and business seem cognitively as well as financially inaccessible to all but a few. The "natural man" (or woman), howsoever ingrained his or her appetite for truck and barter, could find no place there. Thus we come up once more against the problem of how eighteenth-century people developed the capability and confidence to venture their money and reputation in commercial schemes.

This chapter examines one influence among many that helped form eighteenth-century commercial culture: that of the printing press. I argue that printed books and periodicals worked to educate and motivate early modern investors and justify the ways of commercial folk to the rest of the society. I also suggest some of the subtler and more coercive ways that commercial processes encroached on daily life through the medium of print. Lastly I examine some of the ways that print helped order and define eighteenth-century literate peoples' view of the world and England's place in it, to integrate commercial sensibilities and concerns into a national identity.

No attempt is made in this chapter to provide a comprehensive overview of print media in the eighteenth century. Indeed, one of the best-known print genres, the novel, is not dealt with at all. The purpose rather is to look at material that takes commerce as its explicit theme, either works about business or economics (or both) or the ephemeral by-products of business processes, from advertising bulletins, lottery tickets, or printed contracts to trade directories.

Over the course of the eighteenth and nineteenth centuries, economists, like natural philosophers, largely replaced religious explanations for "why things were" with secular ones. But most middling people, in the seventeenth century at any rate, first encountered commercial thinking under conditions that suggested that good business practice and true religion were very hard to separate.[2] In fact, in the late seventeenth century, trade and the characteristic preoccupations of traders had a quite prominent place in sermons and devotional literature. This seems particularly to have been true within the whig wing of the established church and among dissenters, and it was most conspicuous among divines in urban churches and chapels who catered to businessmen's spiritual needs, whatever their denomination.

The prominence of economic issues in late-seventeenth-century English religious writing was noted by R. H. Tawney in his classic study *Religion and the Rise of Capitalism* (1926), and it was treated in much greater detail by Richard Schlatter in *The Social Ideas of Religious Leaders* (1940). Both were struck by the ubiquity of mercantile metaphors in the religious language of the seventeenth century and by the heavy involvement of clerics in debates about the taking of interest, discretion in almsgiving, the morality of devoting oneself to increasing one's wealth, and the like.[3] As Tawney and Schlatter and before them Max Weber have pointed out, religious men, in the main, cooperated with commercial people in laying to rest residual religious scruples about usury, free trade, and refusal to give alms. It is worth asking what other consequences might have followed from this influx of commercial debates and commercial language—often language of the most prosaic sort—into the sphere of the sacred at a time when the most common form of reading was almost certainly devotional.

Take, for instance, a tract of 1679, Bartholemew Ashwood's *The Heavenly Trade or the Best Merchandizing: The Only Way to Live Well in Impoverishing Times*. The book turns on the notion that one's spiritual life ("heavenly trade") is, in virtually all respects, comparable to a private business. Thus, entering upon heavenly trade without sufficient stock to, as it were, set up business and without the skill or diligence to manage it will quickly lead to "great and frequent losses in thy spiritual interests." Like an earthly trade, one's heavenly trade often suffers from "great wastes and needless expenses." And, as in more secular enterprises, those who do not take care will find that the godly will begin to avoid them. After all, "who cares to deal with broken Merchants; or keep company with spendthrifts, that have wasted their estates and are come to nothing? no more do gracious souls care for converse with backsliders."[4]

The level of specificity of these metaphors of debt and credit is striking: at times we could be reading a practical handbook for traders, such as Daniel Defoe's much later book *The Complete English Tradesman* (1727), which is similarly full of portents of, in this case, secular failure. Ashwood's project is, however, a more exalted one. "We trade on God's stock," he asserts, and soon we will find ourselves having to compound with Him for our debts:

> Great debts are breaking, and will cast men back in Wisdom's Merchandise; when men owe more than they are worth, and know not how to pay it; run further on book every day, till their credit will pass no longer; they have often promised payment, but still fail'd, and now their word will not pass, they can get no more Goods, Creditours will not trust them, but begin to suspect them, and threaten to take them up [i.e., arrest them], then men shut up shop and break. This also is pernicious to Heavenly Traders, when [they] . . . are deep in debt to God for divine goodness.[5]

In Ashwood's tract the trauma of the shopkeeper who sinks more and more into debt until he loses everything becomes that of Everyman, immersed ever more deeply in the morass of sin and in real danger of forfeiting his immortal soul.

The Heavenly Trade represents an especially thorough working out of a formula common in the writings of clergy and laity alike in the late seventeenth and early eighteenth centuries. The relationship of God to human beings is as creditor to debtor. One should cast up one's spiritual accounts in the same way a shopkeeper does his earthly goods. The true Christian lays out all he has for the advancement of the spirit, just as a tradesman makes all things bend to the demands of business. Heaven operates like a cosmic account book wherein people's virtues and vices are continually being recorded. Judgment day is no longer the ancient apocalyptic drama of Jesus and the apostles sitting in solemn judgment over the saved and the damned; instead it has come to resemble a general audit.[6]

The popularity of metaphors of debt and credit (such as the notion that one "saved up" points in the bank of heaven) coincided with, and may have contributed to, the general shift toward more Arminian, as opposed to predestinarian, conceptions of salvation within a number of the dissenting sects and in mainstream Anglicanism.[7] What is clear is that the mixing of the language of salvation with more temporal anxieties helped confer new dignity and prestige upon trade, and because Christianity makes the claim to being a faith for all people, these kinds of parallels helped recast the private sorrow of the businessman into a much more universal drama. Finally, the ubiquitous talk of account books focused renewed attention on the superior efficacy and rationality of business methods (and those who comprehended their mysteries) not simply for making sense of cash flows and credit networks, but for attending to the most profound questions of all.

Such explicit attention to the relationship between trade and religion both at the rhetorical and the philosophical level did not last. Always more closely associated with dissent, the language of debtors and creditors in grace, of the bank of heaven, and of casting up one's spiritual accounts grated upon the sensibilities of some of the Anglican faithful, as well as the better class of dissenters. To their critics, such metaphors seemed to debase the grandeur of the Godhead and to subvert the spiritual and temporal majesty of the clergy. In any event, it was not long before this sort of language gave way, at least among Anglicans, Presbyterians, and Congregationalists, to more elevated tropes of the sort one associates with Joseph Addison and (most of the time) Isaac Watts and with the loftier sections of the King James Bible; in short with the expressive repertoire of mainstream Anglo-American Protestantism to this day.[8]

Commercial visions were in the air, however: only shortly after mercantile metaphors reached the height of their popularity within the devotional genre, some of the earliest efforts to popularize a more comprehensive and, this time, fully secular vision of a commercial nation appeared. One of the most interesting of these is a serial publication that appeared between 1692 and 1703, titled *Collection for Improvement of Husbandry and Trade*.[9] Its author, John Houghton, was a projector, sometime apothecary, and lesser known Fellow of the Royal Society, and he began the *Collection* on a grandiose note, proclaiming in one of the earliest issues that "the whole *Kingdom* made as one *Trading City* is the design of these my *Papers*."[10] First published on two sides of a single sheet for easy and cheap distribution, Houghton's journal represents an early attempt at a comprehensive compilation of useful data relating to commerce and agriculture. Houghton himself is remembered today mainly because some of his economic arguments were later picked up by Adam Smith, but his *Collection for Improvement of Husbandry and Trade* is a striking example of a new kind of mental surveying of the boundaries of trade and agriculture as well as a revealing testimonial to the projector's ambition.[11]

Houghton's goal was a comprehensive account of the possibilities presented by trade, both foreign and domestic. How joint stock companies worked, how and where to set up profitable salt works, how farmers could use entry data from customs houses to decide whether to export their corn, how the English might compete with the Dutch in trade, the virtues of enclosure ("it cannot depopulate, neither does it hinder production of corn"), the chemistry of glass making, the economics of the slave trade—these are only a few of the hundreds of "useful" topics dispassionately discussed in Houghton's work.[12]

The aim of this encyclopedic inventory was precisely to make the English reader look at the world afresh, to encourage the capacity to view, in terms of their profit potential, a whole range of things, people, and relationships that had not been seen in that way previously, or at least not to that degree. Houghton was one of what we might call the "commercial *virtuosi*," men who were inspired by the same Baconian thirst for knowledge that drove the scientists but were possessed of a much more concentrated commercial and entrepreneurial bent.[13] Most of them, unlike the majority of the experimental scientists, were, for part or all of their lives, active businessmen. They included men like William Petty, who worked as a clothier before he entered the surveying business and made a fortune in the Irish land grabs, Josiah Child of the East India Company, John Pollexfen, an India merchant, Nicholas Barbon, son of a leather-seller and himself an insurance and real-estate speculator, and Dudley North, a sometime Turkey merchant and son of a lord. These were among the first people to map out systematically the contours of economic inquiry, pioneering the genre that would culminate three-quarters of a century later in Adam Smith's *Wealth of Nations*.

Houghton's *Collection* proposes an energetic and newly systematized approach to the land and its fruits, to the realm of the "natural," and, inevitably, to human beings. It involves a charting of relationships: between rivers and peoples' ability to transport goods upon them; between the farmer, the middleman, and his city customers; between established shops on the better streets and the less respectable body of hawkers and stall holders who plied their trades outside; between manufacturers or plantation owners and the workers and slaves who labored on their behalf. Houghton's often seemingly random compilations of lists, statistics, visionary projects, and "useful knowledge" were meant to suggest a new way of conceiving of the world that was scientific, internationalist, deeply secular, thoroughly convinced of the virtues of commerce, and, judging from the discussions of labor and slavery, not overly humanitarian in outlook.[14]

John Houghton was only one of many who championed trade and finance at the close of the seventeenth century: the range of issues that caught the attention of these budding economists, and the enthusiasm with which they thrust their often bizarre schemes into the public eye, speaks volumes about the delusions as well as the sheer exhilaration of early English capitalism. Still, to read tracts like these in isolation is almost certainly to exaggerate the significance literate elites assigned to business endeavor. The English polity—and national self-understanding—was still, in most respects, a traditional one, in which long-established notions of history and historical agency still held sway. Sixteenth- and seventeenth-century histories, some of them not far removed from chronicles, virtually ignored trade, commerce, and finance, and focused instead upon the personalities of monarchs and the doings of a small class of aristocrats. When historians found themselves, through sheer force of circumstance, having to deal with other social groups and thus implicitly with other models of historical causality, they sometimes did so with bad grace: Clarendon complained in the *History of the Rebellion* that bankers "were a tribe that had risen and grown up in Cromwell's time, and never were heard of before the late troubles."[15] This was a trifle disingenuous, even coming from a lord, but it reflected notions shared by many of Clarendon's contemporaries about who "counted" in historical terms.

The writing of history demands assessments about the value of things in the present as well as the past. Which present is the one whose antecedents are deemed worthy of excavating? Which lives transcend their own time and place and which get consigned anonymously to the charnel pits of history? Who can actually be said to "make" change whether in the past or the present? The period from about 1680 to 1730 saw prospects widen, as more commercial processes and commercial people were admitted symbolically into the fold of historical significance. This trend is very evident in Addison and Steele's *Spectator:* it is not simply that *The Spectator* envisages an alliance between traditional ruling elites and people at the upper rungs of commerce—a point that has been often made—but that, as Addison's famous Royal Exchange essay and numerous others show, it views commerce and banking as having world significance.[16]

We can see something similar happening in one of the most popular history books of the period, Gilbert Burnet's *History of His Own Time* (1724). Burnet shared to some degree Houghton's respect for the schemes and projects of commercial men within their appointed sphere. But he also went beyond Houghton's and Addison and Steele's at times rather presentist perspective to award men of business a legitimate place within a larger politico-historical narrative.[17] *A History of My Own Time* still focuses largely upon the traditional *dramatis personae* and themes of political history: the character of individual monarchs, the conduct of war and diplomacy, and events in parliament and at court. Included in the mix, however, is an unusual degree of coverage of events and people more commonly discussed today in the context of economic history.

Burnet's book contains pithy discussions of the Bank of England and the East India Company along with descriptions of the Council of Trade, the coinage crisis, and the voting of the South Sea fund. It features character sketches of men like Sir Josiah Child, merchant, sometime governor of the East India Company, and writer on trade, and Thomas Firmin, mercer and projector of philanthropic schemes, thus placing upon the map of history men whose claim to fame was primarily mercantile. While the bulk of Burnet's attention was still directed toward traditional elites, he was not insensible of the importance of more socially heterogeneous movements such as the Movement for Reformation of Manners, of which, like many Whig churchmen, he thoroughly approved.[18] Burnet in a small way re-made the frame of history, altering ideas of who and what were important, revising notions of causality, and awarding a place within the historical continuum for trade, finance, and the people whose preoccupation they were.

READERS AND PRINT MEDIA

The English had long felt a special relationship to the Good Book, but by the early eighteenth century their country had become, in a new way, a nation of books—thousands upon thousands of them, on almost every conceivable topic, pored over, swapped, stolen, and cherished by people at every level of society from members of parliament to plowmen. Although non-elite people had certainly owned and read books considerably prior to 1700,[19] it is only around this time that we begin to see them, in significant numbers, using books (along with news-sheets and periodicals) to make sense of commerce and the economy.

Literacy, at least among urban middling people, almost certainly increased in the late seventeenth and early eighteenth centuries,[20] but we possess few details about what this actually meant in people's lives. We tend, with a few exceptions, to have only a broad sense of what non-elites read, and we have still less sense of whether, and to what extent, what they read affected their outlook or behavior. This section discusses two commercial readers, contemporaries of Bishop Burnet, for whom we have more than the usual amount of evidence on precisely these points. The purpose here is not to claim that these two men were "typical"; we do not currently have enough evidence about the reading habits of other men of commerce to be able to say. Rather, I want to suggest some of the ways books *could,* in the right hands, contribute to a greater comprehension of commercial culture and an enhanced ability to operate within it.

Samuel Jeake (1652–1699) was a merchant and moneylender from Rye in Sussex. He is interesting on a number of counts, not least by virtue of having been an early investor in the Bank of England. According to Michael Hunter and Annabel Gregory, who have recently produced a superb edition of his diary, his is "the only known journal of the Financial Revolution ... written from the point of view of one of the hundreds of small investors who helped to make it possible."[21] Jeake had inherited a fine library from his father, a nonconformist minister who educated the young man himself. Despite the fact that he grew up to become a merchant, Jeake's early reading was even more than usually focused on religion, although he also dipped into books on voyages and travel.[22] The somewhat unworldly education he received seems, if nothing else, to have fitted him extraordinarily well for a lifelong reliance upon the information to be found in books. When Jeake's interests began to branch out in his early to mid teens he could be found reading the great early-seventeenth-century economist Gerald de Malynes' *Lex Mercatoria* (1622) and embarking upon learning the art of memory, almost certainly from one of the numerous books on mnemonics then available. During this period Jeake also began applying himself closely to the study of astrology.[23]

When Jeake reached his twenties his time became fully occupied with trade, thanks, initially, to the usual small gifts of trading capital from his father, and for a few years he apparently ceased to have much time for leisure reading. Books and other printed matter did not disappear from his life though; in fact, they played a more important role than ever. On 1 January 1680 Jeake notes: "I began [on this date] to keep my Accompts in a Liedger [sic] after the method set down in Chamberlain's Accomptants' Guide; which course I alwaies continued henceforward."[24] And he drew up numerous horoscopes, using celestial tables from William Lilly's *Merlini Anglici Ephemeris* and the improved printed ephemerides of Henry Coley and George Parker.[25]

In the 1690s Jeake began investing heavily in the London money market. Initially he had some religious scruples about this, but he laid them to rest in characteristic fashion: by resort to a book. The sequence of events that led to this change of mind went as follows: Jeake traveled to London in April of 1694 in order to have a will proved, and he unexpectedly found himself caught up in lottery fever. The Million Lottery was an annuity and prize scheme passed in that year by Parliament to help pay for the Nine Years War. There had been a long-standing opposition to lotteries by many of the pious on the grounds that they sought to speculate on acts of God while at the same time discouraging true industry. But the terms of the Million Lottery were extremely advantageous, and Jeake had been losing on some of his other investments. He was torn: "I always was & still am an utter Enemy to the practice of all Lusory Lots; & all those Sales of goods by Lot & money Lotteries." After much soul-searching, Jeake decided that the Million Lottery was defensible because it was no mere "lusory" or sporting lottery, bereft of any other redeeming purpose, but a "Civil Lot," a patriotic measure, intended to assist a beleaguered nation in wartime.[26]

Having resolved to put £100 into the venture, Jeake also took the opportunity to buy Thomas Gataker's *Of the Nature and Use of Lots* (1619), a theological defense of lotteries, "which I carefully read over & considered after I came home," concluding however that Gataker's "Allegations for the lawfulness of Lusorious & needless Lots did not at all alter my Judgment."[27] In his own mind, Jeake had neatly separated his own investing activities from the sphere of "lusory lots," so the point was academic. It is interesting that it was at precisely this point that his involvement in the London money market really took off, soon extending to Bank and East India Stock and even some shadier ventures like the Lustring Company.[28]

The last two decades of the seventeenth century were the crucial period for the development of newspapers and periodicals, including the first dailies. Beginning in the 1680s, when Jeake turned to active trading, the post and news dispatches quite suddenly took on a new significance for him, and this grew with his entry into finance. Fluctuations in the value of money, parliamentary decisions on clipped coins, the onset of war—all had an immediate impact on his business ventures, which at this time included dealing in agricultural products of various sorts, cloth imports, and money lending. A typical entry, dated 18 July 1687, reads "news per post of the Proclamation concerning Wooll, whence it was concluded that the price would fall; at which [I was] concern'd having bought a great quantity dear."[29] When Jeake began investing in Bank of England and East India stock in the mid 1690s his response to the news became even more finely calibrated. An entry for 24 April 1699 reads: "Around 11h a.m. news of the French having an army at Dunkirk in transport ships, on which bank stock fell from 105 to 104, but next day by evening rose up to 105 again."[30] A long distance trader and active speculator simply could not afford to be provincial in his outlook.

Jeake's use of astrology to explain, if less often to seek to predict, business peaks and troughs seems at first blush to be inconsistent with the discernibly modern style with which he invested his money. But Michael Hunter and Annabel Gregory are entirely right to emphasize the systematic and "scientific" ethos of late-seventeenth-century astrology: for Jeake and other devotees it offered a seemingly highly rational approach to the barely comprehensible universe of business. For our purposes it is also useful to stress the astrologer's reliance on reference books, for Jeake kept his astrological reference tables as close to his side as his father's generation did their bibles.[31] Certainly astrology offered greater precision than the rather hit-or-miss biblical prognostications that were still popular. It also fit more readily into the increasingly providentialist and secular framework that Jeake's more liberal countrymen were beginning to adopt.[32]

Samuel Jeake was a man fully assimilated into the world of print and one accustomed to turn to books and periodicals for authoritative information on topics that ranged from casting a horoscope and the proper means of keeping accounts to moral justification for investing in lotteries. Just as telling is the fact that there was already a body of printed matter available that was precisely calibrated to the tastes and concerns of men like him, men who were literate—indeed quite well-educated—relatively cosmopolitan and growing increasingly so, secular and pragmatic in outlook, and accustomed to devoting the bulk of their time to commerce and investment.

Thomas Bowrey, a ship's captain and merchant of London, displayed this pragmatic, empirical, and commercial disposition to an even greater degree. In his case, unlike that of Jeake, we lack detailed evidence about his actual *use* of books, but the bent of his collection, a rough catalog of which survives in his private papers, is indisputable. Like most literate people of the time, Bowrey owned religious books, a predictable collection that included works by Tillotson, Hale, and Baxter, as well as some annotations on the Bible. But most of the hundred or so volumes he cataloged in 1711 are more secular in tone. Although the collection contained a few plays and some books on history, the most prominent category was practical how-to books, including treatises on agriculture, navigation, geography, and brewing. Bowrey also possessed Dutch and Malay dictionaries, Joseph Moxon's *Mechanick Exercises,* a book titled *Of Commerce,* Josiah Child's *Brief Observations Concerning Trade and Interest of Money,* Charles Lockyer's *Account of the Trade in India,* a selection of books on natural philosophy, including Harvey on the circulation of blood, books on Guinea and the East Indies, and a series of printed acts of Parliament relating to the excise, overseas trade, bankruptcy, the suppression of piracy, the coal trade, lighthouse systems, and fisheries.[33] This was a thoroughly utilitarian collection, intended to better comprehend the world of commerce at both the micro and macro levels.

Bowrey's view of things can be glimpsed with even greater clarity in an early production of his, a diary he kept of a six-week tour of Flanders and Holland in 1698. Passing through Calais at the very outset of the voyage, he drew up a rough plan of the harbor and added it to his travel diary. This innocuous act was thoroughly representative of what was to follow, namely a thoroughgoing mapping, in Bowrey's rather workaday prose, of the commercial institutions and relevant geographical features of the lands through which he was passing. Bowrey's account includes commentaries on the Amsterdam Bourse, municipal charities, distances between towns and the price of water carriage, the location of customs offices and storehouses, and the accounting procedures utilized most commonly in Dutch towns.[34]

It is true that some of this was rather conventional stuff for people traveling to the Low Countries. If Paris was the preferred destination of the social elite, Amsterdam was *de rigueur* for better-off travelers of the trading classes, precisely because of Holland's fabled success in trade, its staunch protestantism, and its uniquely commercial ambience. In fact, even gentle travelers to Amsterdam found themselves exclaiming over the Amsterdam Stock Exchange and the way, for better or worse, that merchants seemed to set the social tone.[35] But Bowrey's account, because it is so detailed and so functional in its orientation, powerfully recalls the injunctions of his contemporary, John Houghton, to his readers to learn to see the world and its people in new, more profit-oriented ways. Late-seventeenth-century economic writers were not speaking only to one another. They were part of an already highly developed culture of active traders, beset with everyday commercial cares and anxious to understand their world better so as to profit from it more abundantly.

Common both to Jeake and Bowrey was a demonstrated interest in books that sought to teach some new skill or body of knowledge. One finds a similar pattern among middling readers later on in the eighteenth century. The bulk of how-to literature had to do with teaching people to write with a better hand or to keep accounts, teaching them a specific (and sometimes saleable) skill, such as surveying or excise valuations, or familiarizing them with foreign countries and foreign languages, often explicitly with a view toward trade opportunities. Elites, too, we must hasten to acknowledge, read how-to books, including books on account-keeping, along with treatises on architecture, landscape gardening, mining, and the like.[36] But how-to books had a different meaning for the middling: they flattered their intelligence, encouraged their ambition, and promised, even if they did not always deliver, real techniques for improving their income and social standing. Middling reading reflected the growing sophistication of society, government, and the economy and taught the middling new ways to situate themselves within it, both at home and abroad. Samuel Jeake and Thomas Bowrey stood near the beginning of an illustrious bourgeois tradition.[37]

COMMERCIAL EPHEMERA

Historians tend to be fairly optimistic about the impact of printed matter in the early modern period. Books and periodicals democratized access to specialized knowledge, they encouraged literacy, and they may actually have encouraged new kinds of inquiry. Most of us are a good deal less accustomed to talking about the coercive, moralistic side of print media. The next section addresses this latter question, drawing its examples from what is, by comparison with the book or the periodical, an understudied body of material: commercial printed ephemera from the period just prior to the onset of the Industrial Revolution.

Middling reading has thus far been discussed as metatheory ("The whole Kingdom made as one Trading City"), or as genre (how-to books and other productions designed to help readers to better accept or better understand the knowledge systems of trade). As one moves on into the eighteenth century more ephemeral sorts of printed matter, generally quite specifically related to the day-to-day conduct of commerce, come into their own. Commercial ephemera included such items as printed rates of exchange, tax tables, model letters, dummy contracts, trade directories, appointment calendars, printed insurance policies, lottery tickets, newspaper advertisements, auction lists, charts of the prices of stock,[38] sample catalogs, and business stationery. This was the prosaic collective output of business people going about their daily round of activity, printed matter so commonplace that few thought to save it once its immediate purpose had been fulfilled.

The most obvious reason for printing something that might previously have been written out by hand is to ensure a wider distribution, presumably in response to a perception of growing demand for some kind of service, commodity, or body of information. But if the initial act of multiplying copies was, in an obvious sense, expansive, the end result could be more restrictive than we might at first imagine. Hand-written contracts for shipments of wool cloth or face-to-face business transactions with a traveling chapman were unique commercial acts in which personal considerations were often given extensive free play. In contrast, sample catalogs of the sort that came into use from about the 1750s implied a fairly large body of potential buyers, perhaps quite far apart from one another, all operating in relation to a predetermined set of choices. Hand-written letters of credit were consistent with fairly "customized" arrangements with one's payee, whereas printed ones suggested that a rigid series of formulas and procedures had come into being into which individuals had to fit themselves. When a government in need of funds resorted to the services of one or a few financiers, one could expect face-to-face transactions and personal relationships that might be of considerable psychological as well as fiscal complexity. Conversely, state lotteries, with thousands of subscribers and printed tickets, created multiple, largely anonymous transactions that were close to identical in kind.[39]

Printed contracts, covenants, and bonds compelled particular modes of doing business. They literally taught people how to operate in new ways in the market at the same time that they invited them to take the plunge (and a plunge, sadly, it often was). John Houghton was quite explicit about this. In his *Collection*, after invoking René Descartes to clear men's minds of prejudices against trading in stocks, he traced the history of joint stock companies, including a thumbnail description of how a committee votes. He then supplied dummy contracts for "refuse of shares," that is, the right to buy stock on some future date at a prearranged price (essentially futures trading) and other stock-related transactions. Later on, also in the spirit of openness, he provided tips about making small stocks rise "by the contrivances of a few men in confederacy." Evidently this techniqu · ɔs well known long before the South Sea Bubble of 1720, when just such ᴜ ᴅody of "men in confederacy" almost brought down the British financial system.[40] Houghton's novel form of "mass marketing" was intended to rationalize and democratize access to certain sectors of the market, just at a time when it was crucial to encourage investment.

Printed forms and commercial instruments of all sorts also supplied a means to patrol the boundaries of commerce. One of their main aims was to discourage forgery and counterfeiting. These crimes against the ideal of an ordered market terrified contemporaries, as the savage penalties meted out upon white collar criminals amply testify. But a more all-encompassing purpose was to standardize procedure in the face of extremely variable degrees of literacy, numeracy, and procedural sophistication, both on the part of potential investors and on the part of the growing company of clerks and petty bureaucrats who presided over the swelling paper stream. The intent was to direct and instruct, but also to minimize the impact and limit the agency of people whose skills were not up to par.

The moral content of commercial ephemera was often quite explicit. Take, for instance, the humble memorandum book. *The Public Advertiser* for 2 January 1756 offered to readers "the completest Memorandum book, and by much the most generally approved, of any Thing of this kind ever published." It was elegantly printed on fine paper, neatly bound with pockets for notes or letters, and was just the size to contain either Baldwin's Daily Journal or the Gentleman's and Tradesman's Complete Annual Accompt-Book (these were two widely available printed daily accounts ledgers). It contained an index to the year 1756 that would enable its users "to keep a regular and exact Account of all monies received, paid, lent, or expended; where, of, and to whom, every Day of the week throughout the Year." There was also "a blank Space opposite each Day for all Appointments or Engagements" and a separate weekly column for miscellaneous memoranda and observations. At the end was a list of useful facts, as material, the publishers claimed, for the gentleman and divine as for the lawyer and tradesman.[41] The memorandum book was, and still is, concerned with encouraging better management of one's time and closer control over one's money. At a deeper level it spoke to the utopian notion that these elusive assets could be fully managed while complimenting the energetic idealism of that class of persons who bought the fantasy most fully.

Much ephemeral printed material was intended for promotional purposes. Printed advertising had begun centuries earlier when publishers began publishing their book inventories. But practices like these took a big leap forward in the late seventeenth century, so that by 1750 or so there had come into being a wide assortment of printed stock lists, auction catalogs, schedules of boat, coach, and wagon arrivals and departures, handbills, engraved company stationery, and the like. One important contributing factor here was the proliferation of newspapers, especially from the 1680s on. The publisher-booksellers who distributed these papers were among the first to exploit them for advertising, but other industries soon followed suit. Important as a means to promote goods and services, newspapers may have been just as significant in terms of convincing businesspeople to resort to print for short-term promotional purposes. The late seventeenth and eighteenth centuries often saw cross-fertilization between newspapers and other dated ephemeral material. Thus even very early periodicals, such as Houghton's *Collection,* reprinted or mimicked the already existing lists of stock prices, transport schedules, currency exchange rates and other useful commercial information that circulated in print and in manuscript around the Royal Exchange and coffeehouses in the 1690s. Eighteenth-century newspapers and the somewhat later town directories were to do the same.

By mid century a significant proportion of the printed matter that passed through the hands of literate middling people, and, for that matter, their social superiors, must have been either overtly promotional (newspaper advertisements, handbills, tradesmen's cards) or in some way connected to the conduct of business (preprinted ledgers, decorated stationery, various kinds of bills, tickets, standardized contracts, and the like). In the towns, especially, these kinds of materials were a ubiquitous reminder of the centrality of commerce, with its distinctive modes of organizing people, information, and social transactions—in short, its own cultural style.

THE TOWN DIRECTORY

One of the most significant of the eighteenth-century experiments in the ordering of commercial information was the town directory. The age of directories really began in the 1730s, although a directory of London merchants had been compiled as early as 1677,[42] and by the last quarter of the eighteenth century they had become an established feature of urban life. Town directories are one of the most comprehensive and accessible sources we have for charting the growth of transport, the specialization of production, the founding of financial institutions, the proliferation of shops, and the rise of municipal institutions such as infirmaries and asylums.[43] From our present perspective, the other interesting feature of the directories is the way they helped promote a common municipal identity organized around a rationalized and idealized vision of commerce, industry, government, and cross-class cooperation.

What were the contours of the semifictional world of the town directory? The first directories were diverse in form, but by the 1770s a fairly uniform structure seems to have been tacitly agreed upon. Typically the directory consisted of an alphabetical list of *some*—by no means all—of the tradespeople of a given town, along with their place of business and trade. Other prominent persons (such as professionals and local gentry) were generally absorbed without fanfare into the main list, where they can be seen figuratively rubbing shoulders with their vastly more numerous commercial brethren. The body of the directory was frequently followed by a sort of chart or gazette of significant private, municipal, or religious institutions and organs of the central government, supplemented by listings of useful commercial information. Thus the gazette section of Elizabeth Raffald's *Manchester Directory* of 1772 listed:

Country Tradesmen with Warehouses in Manchester
Officers of the Infirmary and Lunatic Hospital
Officers of the Excise
Crofters or Whitsters [i.e., cloth bleachers]
Stage Coaches, Waggons etc.
Vessels to and from Liverpool
Bank and Insurance Office
Justices of the Peace
Committee for the Detection and Prosecution of Felons[44]

This rather pared-down list reflected the anomalous political status of pre-reform Manchester. It contrasted powerfully with the listings for some older and more established towns. The appendix to the *Norwich Directory* of 1783, as befitted an ancient corporation and cathedral town with a strong complement of local gentry, included:

Boarding Schools for Young Ladies
Lodging and Boarding Houses
Inns
London Traders
Freemasonic Lodges
Court of Aldermen
Offices of Court
Common Council
M.P.
Incumbents of Parishes
Corporation Committees

Corporation of Guardians of the Poor
Governors of Bethel
Treasurers of Hospitals
City Surgeon
Court of Requests
Excise Office
Assurance Office (Sun, Royal Exchange, New London)
Post Office
Dean and Prebendaries
List of Officers under Government (e.g., Receivers of Tax)
Surveyors of Duties
List of Carriers (wagons, coaches, etc.) [45]

As these brave lists suggest, town directories derived a not inconsiderable part of their *raison d'être* from simple municipal zeal, combined with the desire to rival other towns. The compilers gloried in the remarkable expansion in transport opportunities that had taken place over previous decades, in the sheer numbers of entrepreneurs engaged in local industry, in the number of churches and chapels each town supported, in its philanthropic endeavors, its masonic lodges, its libraries and schools, its banks and insurance offices, its local gentry, and its parliamentary representation. The directories are a marvelous window into at least some middling people's notion of what it was to be modern.

One of the more striking aspects of the directories is the idealized picture they project of town life. Here the stress was on smooth, rational cooperation between local and national government, church and chapel, commercial endeavor and private philanthropy, and the commercial, professional, and gentry classes. The tensions and uncertainties of eighteenth-century life and enterprise were barely evident: one could infer their existence only from the listing for the Court of Requests in Norwich (the main court for adjudicating claims for small debts) and the Committee for the Detection and Prosecution of Felons in Manchester.

These directories were as significant for what they left out as for what they put in. Absent was any mention of that large swath of the population starting with the laboring or, as the case might be, "idle" poor and running up through traders without a fixed place of business (stall holders, hawkers, milk sellers, and the like) and any number of other less respectable occupations. Largely absent too (although they made up large parts of the working-class populations of some towns) were the Irish, the Jews, the non-English born, and, as a previous chapter showed, women. The only hint of greater social complexity is found in the listings of charitable institutions, such as local hospitals, or of overseers of the poor. The directories amply confirm a rigid—some would say hardening—sense of difference that segregated the middling and elites from the "have-nots," many of whom would not have shared in a literate culture and few of whom could have legitimately approached philanthropic institutions as other than suppli-cants.[46]

The social cutoff point for inclusion in these directories varied from place to place, suggesting the difficulty, even for contemporaries, of agree-ing on what "respectability" was. It must also be said that the directories were a great deal wider in their social purview than another species of contemporary "directory," the peerages or heraldic dictionaries that had first assumed their modern form with Sir William Dugdale's *Baronage of England* of 1675.[47] The vision of society that emerges from the town direc-tories could not be more different from that of the peerages: it is of a contented commercial and professional community, thoroughly masculine but also (in comparative terms) fairly egalitarian, firmly in command of the infrastructure of business and philanthropy, and not too far removed from the reins of government.[48]

Finally, the town directories, although fundamentally middling enter-prises, testify to the strength within those groups of the ideal of coopera-tion between commerce and the genteel classes. Appeals to unity and co-operation, like appeals to tradition, could be powerful political tools, and they did not necessarily bespeak a retreat into deference on the part of men of commerce: elites, the directories implied, were approachable, mixed on a relatively equal plane with men of trade, and were as commit-ted to town improvement and the progress of commerce as any merchant. As is the case with a good deal of the printed matter that developed out of trading communities, the directory should be understood as an effort by middling people to educate not only their own cohort but also their betters on the new expectations obtaining in the culture of trade.

TRAVEL LITERATURE

The counterweight to the town directory was a less ephemeral form, the travel narrative.[49] Throughout much of the early modern period, travel accounts were among the most widely read of nonreligious books. In fact, by the last third of the eighteenth century there is evidence that in some places travel books rivaled or exceeded devotional reading matter in popu-larity.[50] Against the town directory's idealized vision of urban cooperation and commercial order, the travel narrative opposed a vivid, dystopian pic-ture of what the English, thankfully, were not. The town directory de-pended upon the elision or exclusion of ethnic, national, and socioeco-nomic difference. The travel narrative, by contrast, stressed difference, especially cultural difference, which was endlessly joked about, sensational-ized, exaggerated, or simply fabricated. Groups that were silent in more domestic genres sprang clamorously to life in the travel narrative and spawned legions of outlandish allies.

Travel has always inspired comparative thinking, and a central feature of all travel writing of the period was the drawing of comparisons between foreigners and English people. For the most part these were at the expense of foreigners, although there were a few exceptions: the Dutch were envied for their sturdy virtue and no-nonsense commercialism, and writers used the alleged innocence and presumed simplicity of so-called primitives, such as American Indians or South Pacific Islanders, to point up the decadence of "modern" values. Most other groups fell under a relentless barrage of criticism. The French were steeped in luxury, promiscuous, and in the thrall of priests. Africans were intellectually inferior, went about naked, and were cannibalistic and oversexed. The Irish were intellectually inferior, went about naked (or at least their children did), and were alcoholic and superstitious. American Indians were lazy, cruel, and incapable of complex political thinking. Italians were lazy, dirty, debased, and sodomitical. And so on. "Middling" moral concerns were not entirely absent from these early efforts at racial and national categorization, but it would be a mistake to see them as an exclusively middling project. Objectification of difference within travel narratives and in other kinds of eighteenth-century English writing was so widely diffused that it is more appropriately viewed as part of a larger project of national self-definition that transcended any one class.[51]

But travel writing *could* be explicitly commercial, especially as the number and proportion of mercantile travelers grew. As we have seen, Captain Thomas Bowrey's 1698 diary of a six weeks' tour of Flanders and Holland showed clearly the way business concerns could affect one's travel experience; Defoe's *Tour through England and Wales* (1724–1726) is much concerned with agriculture, commerce (especially shipping), and manufacture.[52] By 1758 at least one writer had set out to teach travelers how to cultivate a more sophisticated commercial eye. Josiah Tucker, one of the most important British economic theorists before Adam Smith, came out in that year with a book called *Instructions for Travellers* that urged travelers to gather systematic data on local soil conditions, taxation systems, climate, demography, the cost of labor, and such "singular Inventions of the inhabitants" as might be ripe for exploitation. Tucker's model traveler accustomed himself to asking questions like the following: "What improvements might be made in Water carriage?" "What new markets are opened for vending?" "Do Journey-men and Journey-women work by the Day or by the Great [i.e., piece]?" "What Machines are used to abridge the process of a Manufacture, so that one Person can do the work of many?" and "What Checks are invented to guard against Impositions of bad Work or embezzling the Materials, or idling away Time?" This was a thoroughly modern commercial sensibility that not only had absorbed the curiosity and the comparativist ethos of the traveler but also had turned them in a different direction and given them a new aim.[53]

THE WEALTH OF NATIONS

Alexander Carlyle's incomparable *Anecdotes and Characters of the Time* contains a brief but suggestive description of commercial society in Glasgow in the 1740s. Trade in those days was still in an undeveloped state, yet these Scots merchants

> [h]ad Industry, and Stock and the Habits of Business; and were Ready to Sieze with Eagerness and prosecute with vigour, every new object in Commerce or Manufactures that promis'd Success.

These men were not "learned" by the conventions of the day, which is to say that few of them had enjoyed a classical education. Yet a group of them met weekly, for well over two decades, in a society

> in which their Express Design was to Enquire into the Nature and principles of Trade in all its Branches, and to Communicate their Knowledge and Views on that Subject to each other.[54]

The Glasgow society was apparently one of a number of contemporary attempts to join the disseminating of commercial knowledge to male sociability. And this particular society would almost certainly have languished in historical obscurity were it not for the fact that one of its members was Adam Smith.

Adam Smith was a famously sociable man; he was also a notable reader. Not only was he well acquainted with the writings of earlier toilers in the vineyard of economic theory, including John Houghton, Josiah Tucker, and others, he also had in his personal library almost every major piece of published travel writing by a French or English writer of the seventeenth and eighteenth centuries. He was to cite more than twenty of these by name in *The Wealth of Nations*, his most famous work.[55] Smith's great synthesis is breathtakingly comprehensive as well as truly global in scope; it also sums up many of the themes of this chapter. Smith was respectful of commercial men, if somewhat less sanguine about their commitment to the common good than some earlier writers had been. He had no doubt that commerce and economic processes more generally had played a central role in the history of the human species. He was thoroughly familiar with commercial ephemera, and used a good deal of it—printed exchange rates, agricultural price lists, and so on—as the raw data from which he derived his formulas. Finally, he was a consummate armchair commercial traveler. *The Wealth of Nations* discusses demography and the price and conditions of labor, transport of goods, labor-saving devices, the quality and availability of land, the changing price of commodities, and the influence of geography in Scotland, Ireland, England, Holland, France, the East Indies, the Cape Colony, West Africa, China, Java, Mexico, Brazil, the West Indies, the North American Colonies, Japan, Imperial Rome and Republican Athens.

This chapter has treated the interplay between economic knowledge and commercial procedures and sensibilities and the mass-produced printed word. Real commercial people must perforce have played a central role here, although it is not always easy to recreate exactly what it was. What we do know is that by the early eighteenth century there were already economic autodidacts circulating in the coffeehouses in English and Scottish cities, men who delighted in impressing others with their command of the *minutiae* of trade and manufacture. Dudley Ryder mentions meeting a man "well-versed in the manufactures of England" in his London club in 1715. This man argued that all holidays should be banned, since each one cost the nation some £100,000 in lost labor; he also thought that a greater division of labor would improve productivity and advised his listeners that Customs House entry statistics were often inaccurate. Ryder and his friends, would-be lawyers, were powerfully impressed, and not a little intimidated.[56]

Like the early scientific lecturers, about whom rather more has been written, some of these commercial virtuosi and polyglot collectors of useful knowledge gathered circles of disciples around them. In the process they became active agents in the dissemination of new world views. One such was Andrew Cochrane (1693–1773), the leading light of the Glasgow group. Carlyle writes that

> the Junior Merchants who have flourish'd since [Cochrane's] time and extended their Commerce far beyond what was then Dream't of, Confess with Respectful Remembrance, that it was Andrew Cochrane who first open'd and enlarg'd their Views.[57]

And Adam Smith himself later acknowledged his obligation to him. This was a cycle that must have played itself out in smaller ways countless times across the century.

CONCLUSION

"[T]he whole *kingdom* made as one *trading city*" wrote John Houghton, another writer intent upon opening and enlarging others' views. Seventeenth- and eighteenth-century books and periodicals that dealt with commercial themes improved the spiritual and temporal status of commercial people and commercial modes of reasoning while also disseminating new skills and new bodies of information. Mass production of commercial ephemera helped to discipline and render more homogeneous a disparate range of market acts, from participating in a lottery to writing a business contract. Town directories sought to bind urban traders and elites into an informed and harmonious commercial culture. And travel books gave literate English people a newly sophisticated (if deeply problematic) body of knowledge about other "races," nationalities, and classes, and at the same time educated the alert reader to the profit potential these differences might contain.

CHAPTER EIGHT

Private Order and Political Virtue: Domesticity and the Ruling Class

[The Gentry have] extravagantly wasted their Substance in polluted Amours in the City.

THE LEVELLERS: DIALOGUE BETWEEN TWO YOUNG LADIES
CONCERNING MATRIMONY, 1703

The Happiness of Society in general, greatly depends on the proper behaviour of individuals in social and domestic life.

A DIALOGUE CONCERNING THE SUBJECTION OF WOMEN
TO THEIR HUSBANDS, 1765

The middling pursuit of "domestick order" and prudential morality was, at times, insular and individualistic, confined purely to the sphere of the family or personal behavior. But it could also be expansive, forming the basis for efforts to reinterpret political virtue as well as attempts to mould and influence those groups at the top of the eighteenth-century social pyramid. Theoretical and practical analogies between government and family life date from classical times. Historians of political thought, however, have tended to view these with a certain amount of discomfort. We find a dramatic illustration of this in the much-studied debate between Robert Filmer and John Locke over whether fatherhood was analogous to kingship. Until recently scholars have tended to side with Locke when he argues that the "rules" of politics are distinctly different from those that govern families, and hence, that fathers are not at all like kings. Indeed, Locke's not entirely successful attempt in the *Two Treatises of Government* to sunder analytically the realms of politics and the family is widely viewed as part of a pivotal shift in the early modern period from "organic" conceptions of governance to more abstract and secular notions that construct the "sphere of politics" as a largely autonomous and hence highly specialized moral realm.[1]

Few of us are so naive as to think that once a well-known theorist provides one solution to some persistent philosophical problem, the rest of the population simply falls into line behind it. Yet, however much we might deplore such simplicity in the abstract, it is thoroughly conventional to

193

divorce discussions of eighteenth-century politics from contemporary theories about the family. Practically speaking, historians assume that Locke's
prescriptions for how politics should be understood actually reflect the
ways late-seventeenth- and eighteenth-century people thought, wrote,
spoke, or acted politically, and they tend to ignore or downplay evidence
that points in the opposite direction. This chapter shows some of the ways
that family ideology and political ideology continued to overlap throughout the eighteenth century. I contend that it was *because* of this overlap that
certain shifts in conceptions of virtue and political agency were able to
take place, shifts that, over the long run, occurred at the expense of the
moral authority of elites. To treat politics and moral (or family) discourse
as separate systems is to miss one of the main avenues through which politics became an at least partially middle-class province.

Let us begin by recalling, once again, one of Locke's lesser-known contemporaries, Ambrose Barnes, merchant of Newcastle upon Tyne, whose
exemplary home life was discussed in a previous chapter.[2] How did
Barnes's deep moral convictions, his emphasis on plain food and plain
speaking, productive work, early rising, and conspicuous family order intersect with modes of thought more usually termed "political?" Is Barnes a
model for the way that "trading morality," under the right circumstances,
might be transformed into a political program?

In the 1650s Barnes, then an alderman in Newcastle upon Tyne, attempted to enforce moral statutes irrespective of the rank or birth of the
offenders, to clean up corruption in municipal government, and to suppress dueling. After 1660 he suffered periodic harassment and found it
politic on at least one occasion to resign from municipal office. Still later
he was to express his keen disappointment with the revolutionaries of
1688–89 on account of their failure to punish "the zealots of Charles II's
odious reign."[3] But despite these travails Barnes remained active in trade,
and he entertained himself, in the political purgatory to which he and
men like him had been consigned, by devising visionary programs of
moral, political, and commercial reform. These he apparently would air
for the benefit of his fellows in the Company of Merchant Adventurers, at
the meetings of which it is said "his discourses were alwayes heard with
great attention."[4]

Barnes was an intensely political man, but he was also an active trader,
and he often articulated commercial concerns in the familiar language of
Commonwealth thought.[5] Great trading towns even more than other
towns needed to be kept free from "mercenary militia"; their presence
discouraged trade as surely as did arbitrary tolls on merchandise. In general, "conquest and despotic power obstructs trade, which evermore decays
as freedom does."[6] Like other commonwealth theorists Barnes felt a strong

distaste for financiers, but for him the problem was less their potential for wielding undue influence as that state lotteries and "the pernicious practices of brokers and stockjobbers . . . would find men a new way to imploy their money, to the neglect of trade, which would bring a terrible shake to public credit some time or other."[7] Taken individually, none of these positions was very novel or astounding; Barnes's originality lay in the way he used his own trading experiences in the German states to buttress his arguments and in the way urban values and commercial vitality displaced landed virtue in his thought. *Pace*J. G. A. Pocock, this was a man who experienced no difficulty marrying commonwealth ideas to capitalism.[8]

Barnes was entirely comfortable with the more radical side of commonwealth thought. An unpublished political tract by Barnes, only fragments of which have survived, is heavily indebted to the writings of James Harrington, the great mid century theorist of republicanism. According to Barnes, commerce and liberty were alike threatened by the "depraved desire of rule, which yet issueth from a noble root."[9] His brand of republicanism, however, relied as much upon puritan and prudential morality as it did on classical *virtus* (or, for that matter, Renaissance *virtù*). And so, when Barnes (or his biographer) wrote "the people have never been more fond of kings than their manners have been corrupted to the heights, nor have ever more distasted them than when their spirits were bravest and most refined," the kinds of corruption this inveterate enemy of personal vice seems to have had in mind were sabbath violations, public drunkenness, oaths, unclean language, sloth, and disorderly families. Older conceptions of republican virtue—independence, battlefield bravery, leadership, political integrity, "manhood"—had receded into the background.[10]

When Barnes put all this together into a political program the result was, to say the least, startling. After the defeat of the Commonwealth, Barnes seems to have consoled himself with visions of an England composed of small self-governing commercial republics ("Every country and every corporation might easily become a free commonwealth"), with Newcastle upon Tyne preeminent among them.[11] Barnes's thought, eccentric though it was, illuminates one of the intellectual routes from the preoccupations of the more radical side of the interregnum to those of an increasingly commercial society. Clearly, for him independence was political, quaintly reflected in an England made up of numerous small Genevan-inspired republics, but it was also economic and social. Independence informed his passionate espousal of free trade principles, and it was likewise independence that lay behind his personal distaste for the mores, and particularly the immunity from censure or prosecution, of the well born.

Perhaps it was not so strange after all for an old trader and corporation

politician to have visions of an England dotted with tiny independent republics. Many of the most famous trading and banking *entrepôts* of medieval times and of the early modern period were oligarchically organized
city states, and trading cities like Geneva and Venice retained their *cachet*
well into the eighteenth century. Even more to the point, England's chief
commercial rival in the seventeenth century was a republic—or rather a
confederation of republics—the United Provinces of the Netherlands, and
stories were legion about alleged Dutch preeminence in everything from
keeping down interest rates and having more humane bankruptcy laws to
teaching the dissolute sons of the rich to respect thrift and hard work.[12]

Did Barnes sense a certain commonality of interest with a nation in
which antimonarchical sentiments were often expressed as attacks on the
personal morality of the high born? William Mountague, who made one of
the requisite trips to the Netherlands in the 1690s, was fascinated by the
"wanton republican expressions" of the merchants on the floor of the Amsterdam stock exchange; apparently the brokers were well known for inter-
larding the stock prices with shouted commentary on the sexual proclivities
and incapacity to govern of contemporary European monarchs.[13] Barnes
may have heard of such things; perhaps he had even witnessed them.

Barnes was a man who outlived his time. Historical associations notwithstanding, eighteenth-century English men and women of commerce did
not become a republican fifth column. The commonwealth rhetoric itself
was assimilated into mainstream British political thought shorn, in most
cases, of its republicanism. Yet some of its elements, the stress on high-
minded virtue, the emphasis on the corrupting power of dependence, the
distrust of luxury, the penchant for self-discipline, were taken up enthusiastically by middling people, who often, in the process, altered them to fit
their own particular preoccupations and situations in life. Non-elite critics
of dependence might begin with conventional attacks on placemen and
corrupt government patronage, but, like Barnes, they soon expanded their
purview to include attacks upon patronage and deference more generally—those vertical social ties that were, it is so often argued, the social
cement of pre-reform England.[14] They were especially likely to worry over
problems of *cultural* dependence, or what historians now like to call emulation. French sauces, fashion, gaming, irreligion, libertinism, slothfulness—
all the things that preoccupied Ambrose Barnes—lay at the very center of
middling social and political "theory" in the eighteenth century.

For the middling, as we have seen, true independence of mind was
much more likely to lie in a course of diligence, thrift, chastity, domesticity,
respect for contracts, and rationality in the face of strong pressure to submit slavishly to "fashion." In some sense this did represent a shift of emphasis away from that side of the commonwealth tradition that was concerned
primarily with active citizenship,[15] but it would be a mistake to construe it

as an endorsement of middling political noninvolvement. Instead it opened up a range of opportunities for middling activism. It gave ammunition to generations of middling projectors and builders of philanthropic institutions and societies. It provided numerous opportunities for high-minded criticisms of the social and political elite and for self-congratulation on the part of the middling themselves. In later years it was to lend ethical backbone and rhetorical power to the middling wing of the evangelical movement, to civil service reform, and to campaigns to extend the franchise.

An older scholarship has tended to present the middling as politically quiescent: this position can no longer be sustained. We now know a great deal about municipal corporations and municipal philanthropy, Toryism (and also Jacobitism) among the middling, the involvement of the commercial classes in parliamentary lobbying particularly on social and economic questions, non-elite participation in agitation for parliamentary reform, and middling patriotic endeavors. Historians are gradually charting the outlines of an urban middling political culture. The aim of the rest of this chapter is, however, more modest: to suggest a few of the ways in which middling preoccupations with prudential morality and with family life might provide an intellectual backdrop both for middling efforts to "reform" the ruling class and for middling activism more generally. This enquiry is necessarily preliminary and designed to be suggestive rather than in any sense definitive. I make no pretense to discuss the ways rhetoric was, or was not, translated into concrete political programs. The discussion begins with one of the oldest tropes of Western political thought, the putative correspondence between the family and political governance.

PRIVATE ORDER AND PUBLIC DISORDER

Sir Josiah Child (1630–1699), sometime governor of the East India Company, once referred to the laws of his native land as

> an Heap of Nonsense, compiled by a few ignorant Country Gentlemen, who hardly knew how to make laws for the good Government of their own private Families, much less for the Regulating of Companies and foreign Commerce.[16]

Sir Josiah, a man of absolutist tendencies, wanted his personal directives, not the laws of England, to be the rule by which his employees abroad acquitted themselves. He expressed himself in terms of the alleged inability of the traditional gentry to order their private households because he was well aware that this charge had contemporary resonance.

The juxtaposing of issues of private or family governance with competence in leadership also turns up in a manuscript account by Sir Francis

Child of a trip he made to Holland in 1697. Here the purpose was to commend an unusually meritorious aristocrat, the Earl of Pembroke and First Plenipotentiary in the Hague:

> He was well beloved by all this country, for his learning, sweet-temper and easiness of accesse, by all the inhabitants of this place, for by paying all accounts of[f] weekly, he never owed them much, he always made his household come to prayers, and by his example taught them to be good[.] He never suffered any drinking to excesse in his house, and govern'd his family with that discipline that tho a numerous, yet it seem'd as quiet as any private family.[17]

The Earl of Pembroke was what one might call a domesticated aristocrat. He was approachable, he paid off his debts promptly, and he kept his household to a standard of moral discipline and efficiency more reminiscent of a man of trade than of a peer of the realm. It is hardly necessary to point out that, had the Earl of Pembroke been more typical of his class, eighteenth-century moralists would have had a great deal less to complain about.

It was no new thing to link private morals to questions of political competence; however, the late seventeenth and eighteenth centuries do seem to have coincided with an upsurge of interest in such matters. The fairly open discussion of the morals of elites that obtained through much of the eighteenth century owed a great deal to the challenge administered to strict notions of patriarchal kingship by the Revolution of 1688–89. Whatever else they might have been, the reigns of Charles II and James II presented clear cases of private immorality, family disorder, and political incompetence at the highest level. The Glorious Revolution saved the institution of monarchy but dealt a severe blow to the belief that kings were above moral reproach and beyond earthly sanctions. Inevitably it also detracted from the luster of peers, and it did away, to a surprising extent, with any residual immunity from open moral censure they might once have enjoyed. In fact, the hallmark of middling critiques of the high born was an exceptionally powerful emphasis upon the private family as *the* optimum location for the formation of good morals, social usefulness, and political virtue. This lent a peculiar note of self-congratulation to middling attacks upon the well born, while at the same time it tended, *pace* Locke, to scramble "political" and "moral" (or family) discourse to an almost irrevocable degree.

PROSTITUTION AND POLITICAL INDEPENDENCE

In 1715, in the midst of the Reformation of Manners furor, Samuel Wright, a prominent Presbyterian, preached an inflammatory sermon at Salters

Hall in which he charged that the vicious included "Men of the highest Condition and Fashion in the World, supporting and encouraging them [the vicious], by living in the same Vices."[18] As has already been noted, mainstream Reformation of Manners campaigners generally responded cautiously to claims about the prevalence of upper-class vice,[19] but that did not stop more independent-minded moralists from taking up the topics that others shrank from addressing. One of these was a critique of elite sexual mores and elite family life more generally. Moralists, most famously Daniel Defoe, took up the standard Reformation of Manners attack on public lewdness but endeavored to shift readers' attention away from London's meaner streets and seamier stews to the sumptuous residences on the more fashionable side of town. Defoe's suggestively titled *Conjugal Lewdness; or, Matrimonial Whoredom* (1727) is not an attack upon elite marriage pure and simple: some of the "whorish" unions with which the book abounds come from other ranks. Still, in essence, Defoe is arguing that women who exploit their sexuality (or men, their masculine prerogatives) for political, mercenary, title-seeking, or frivolous ends, instead of placing it in the service of a serious vision of domesticity and social usefulness, are little better than prostitutes. "Real" prostitutes have retreated in favor of women who are no better than prostitutes, and Defoe leaves little doubt that such women are to be found in the greatest numbers among the high born and those who would emulate them.[20]

Conjugal Lewdness has been called an old man's book,[21] but in some respects it marked the beginning of a tradition. Hogarth's *A Harlot's Progress* and *A Rake's Progress*, discussed in an earlier chapter, appeared only a few years later.[22] As we saw, both series deal frontally with the connections between emulation and illicit sexuality. George Lillo's very popular tragedy, *The London Merchant, or the History of George Barnwell*, about a middling family destroyed by sexual lust, opened in 1731. Nine years after that, in 1740, the eponymous heroine of Samuel Richardson's *Pamela* won fortune and honor precisely because of her ability to withstand the same temptation. It is true that these works barely touch on the whorish tendencies of elite women; indeed, *A Harlot's Progress* tends to reinstate the conventional picture of a prostitute as an unmarried woman down on her luck. However, all adopted an extremely moralistic notion of family life, and all assumed that criminal lust, that ravager of average families, stemmed either from the upper classes themselves or from efforts to emulate them. By 1740 these were clearly well-established elements of middling moral discourse.

But did they have political implications? No distinctly "middling" political theory has yet emerged from scholarship on the eighteenth century, nor is it likely to do so. The commercial and professional classes were far too variegated; the tendency to see politics as at best a matter of temporary alliances between diverse groups, and at worst someone else's province en-

tirely, was far too well entrenched. But this does not mean that characteristi-
cally middling preoccupations had no effect upon political thinking. The
later history of the application of metaphors of prostitution or sexual excess
to elites affords one example. Let us look, for purposes of illustration, at a
didactic tract of 1745, David Fordyce's *Dialogues Concerning Education.*

David Fordyce was the elder brother of James Fordyce, a well-known
London divine and writer of moral tracts, and Alexander Fordyce, the fi-
nancier whose machinations were to touch off the credit panic of 1772.[23]
Like his brother James after him, David Fordyce wished to encourage a
kind of alliance of men and women of reason against courtly levity, luxury,
and libertinism. The Fordyce brothers were part of an alternative strain in
eighteenth-century moral thinking that stressed the virtues of mixed male-
female sociability *as a supplement to,* generally not as a replacement for, the
all-male milieu of the men's club, the male academy, or the religious society. Originally from Aberdeen, the Fordyces also shared a somewhat exaggerated faith, even stronger among the Scots than among the English, in
the benefits of sociability.

Dialogues Concerning Education sought to open up at least a portion of
male sociability to women so as to provide a virtuous and highly platonized
alternative to the shallow and promiscuous gatherings of the fashionable.
David Fordyce criticized emulation, but he also leveled a more direct attack
upon upper-class moral corruption than even Defoe had done, going so
far as to flirt with republicanism.[24] Among the social elite, according to
Fordyce, women are made into pets or playthings "on the same footing
with Hawks and Hounds." By contrast, the woman of virtue will cut
through the conceits of fashionable male-female relations and insist upon
honesty and plainspokenness. "I am not used to the pretty Prattle with
which your fine Ladies are commonly entertained. We shall converse more
freely if we do it on equal Terms," says one of his female characters, the
beautiful and philosophically inclined Cleora, to an overeffusive youth
who is attending Fordyce's fictional male academy.[25] Virtuous women
helped create an atmosphere of affability and complaisance which lessened distinctions based on any factors other than merit. They possessed
a depth of character that contrasted strongly with the superficiality of the
lady of quality, and they promoted a form of socializing that was moral
and rational, yet at the same time entertaining. Finally they shielded their
brethren from the evil influence of those silly, debased, coquettish women
who spiritually prostituted themselves before fashionable society and contributed largely to the hypocrisy and corruption of the age.[26]

Fordyce's criticisms of aristocratic society were couched in Country
terms, but they were enriched with a more than usually generous infusion
of Reformation of Manners–inspired loathing for public lewdness. The result was a lavish series of analogies between mercenary sex and mercenary

politics that had the effect of throwing the relations between the sexes into the center of both social and political discourse. Wanton flattery of women (damned by Fordyce as the "low and promiscuous Prostitution of Praise") was inseparable from the toadying of corrupt courtiers. The same people indulged in it, the same contravening of decent virtues was involved, and the same kinds of corruption ensued. The courtesan was the necessary counterpart of the courtier. Their relations, overlain with hypocrisy, luxury, and mercenary aims, constituted the sensual equivalent of political servility.[27]

What, however, were the alternatives? Let us turn to a less public genre, represented by a series of love letters written at almost exactly the same time (1744–1747) by a young surgeon from Exeter named George Abraham Gibbs to his betrothed, one Anne Vicary. George Gibbs had two great aims in life: a harmonious marriage and the successful pursuit of his professional career. In fact, he was eventually to become chief surgeon at the Exeter hospital, although he also endured bankruptcy toward the end of his life apparently as a result of some ill-advised merchant ventures. George Gibbs's notion of marriage joined the valorization of careerism to a vision of privatized and dependent femininity worthy of any Victorian. Fordyce's courtesan (like all corrupt, upper-class women) had moved within the public and highly politicized world of the Court as an independent and decidedly malign agent. By constrast, Gibb's wife-to-be, in theory at least, lived to be supported. As he wrote to Anne Vicary,

> you know how necessary it is for me to preserve a close attention to the Business of my Profession; every neglect of this I consider as an injury done to you; who I must forever think have a right to all my Diligence & Industry in order to make your Life as easy & agreeable as I can.[28]

In spite of Gibbs's obvious commitment to feminine economic dependence, he was not positing a separation between the "public" and the "private" along gender lines. Letters written later in his life show that George Gibbs, like the middling moralists, considered a taste for home pleasures to be a *sine qua non* not just of feminine respectability but of the mature male character as well, and the foundation upon which all other virtues were to be erected.[29]

In the mid 1740s George Gibbs was more absorbed with making unfavorable comparisons between the affectations so prevalent among "the fashionable" (by which he meant social elites and those who emulated them) and the rational affection he felt for Anne Vicary. The men, says Gibbs, make ladies into "Angels and goddesses" by means of their extravagant flattery, to which the ladies respond by coolness and diffidence. The real absurdity is that all this is acted "between those who design one day or other to live together upon some Terms of Equality." Gibbs's love, by contrast, is "a reasonable & undissembled Passion" for a "sensible & deserving woman"—a rational yet deep affection that avoids artifice and dissimulation and supports "the Cause of Truth."[30]

What chiefly characterized "the fashionable" was a slavish attachment to purely sensual forms of gratification. Gibbs says repeatedly that his way of thinking is "unfashionable" and "plain," but he is also certain that it is morally superior to other ways of thinking, as well as more conducive to real happiness. He is sure that "the fashionable folk" would laugh at the endearments he and Anne exchange. But:

> Let 'em enjoy their Jest; they pay dear enough for it in giving up the Pleasures of an honest & disinterested affection. I hope we shall never be so slavishly dependent, as to rate our Enjoyments, by the Opinions that other people are pleased to intertain of them.[31]

True happiness came, in Gibbs's view, to the independent of mind—men and women who perceived the emptiness and artificiality of the Great and their camp followers and who devoted their lives instead to the wholehearted pursuit of rational and high-minded goals.

Gibbs's notion of virtuous independence resembled the classic "commonwealth" picture of landed virtue no more than Ambrose Barnes's had done. For Gibbs, true independence had shifted its locus from the traditional political classes to "private men" and "private families," urban and urbane and situated firmly, as was Gibbs himself, in the world of trade, the professions, and rational domesticity. Independence had also changed its focus, so as to encompass that most private matter of all, the individual's capacity, increasingly rare in a corrupt world, to feel authentic, undissimulated happiness. This very modern-seeming conception of identity emphasized personal fulfillment achieved through erotic restraint, careerism, and an idealized conception of private domesticity, and it measured itself explicitly against other, more disorderly notions of identity and family.

Neither David Fordyce nor George Gibbs was swimming against the tide by the mid 1740s. Moral high-mindedness had itself come into fashion, and a new mood of disgust at upper-class artificiality and moral and political corruption was sweeping across England and Scotland, indeed, across much of Europe, not least among the upper classes themselves.[32] More worthy of comment is the way Fordyce and Gibbs combined middling moralism and Country thought and in so doing uncoupled or weakened the link between virtue and landed independence. The other striking element here is the centrality of women and issues of sexuality to middling notions of corruption. Aristocratic women, as will be seen, were to prove an especially tempting target for reformers of all stripes.

A FEW VIRTUOUS NOBLES

Well before Wilberforce and his colleagues embarked on their programs of evangelical renewal and moral reformation in the last quarter of the eighteenth century, moralists had shown an interest in mending the morals of the high born. Emulation may not have been the crudely imitative phenomenon some historians have suggested, but neither is it simply a figment of the twentieth-century imagination. The nobility's reputation, not always deserved, for sexual libertinism, conspicuous consumption, disdain for honest work, and negligent business habits clearly made it more difficult for their social inferiors to argue that sexual restraint, thrift, diligence, and careful accounting for both one's time and one's money were good or fashionable rules by which to live. In the eighteenth century a new view of the "social fabric" gradually began to emerge, one that reflected the realities of an economy in which virtually everybody lived by exchange and by contract. The problem, of course, was that the gentry and aristocracy participated extensively in this economy, yet some number of them conspicuously refused to play by the rules, and what was more galling, they succeeded much of the time in getting away with it.

Criticism of the nobility for their failure to honor contracts and their negligence in paying bills was no new thing. An apparently fairly typical satire on debtors from 1619 relates the author's meeting on the street with one of his gentleman debtors: "[He] imagines he doth me exceeding grace / If when I meete him, he bestowes a nod"; it concludes with the couplet "One Part of Gentry he will ne're forget / And that is, that he ne're will pay his dett." [33] The same basic problem is expressed less directly in an anonymous comment concerning the Royal African Company in the mid 1670s: "[It] now consisteth of most merchants [as opposed to courtiers], that conduct the company businesse better and will most certainly comply with any contract they make." [34]

The patronage of persons of quality was desired, indeed eagerly sought, by the middling, not least because it attracted other business. On the other hand, actually dealing with the upper ranks could induce anxiety. In 1789 Elizabeth Cornish, a struggling Richmond shopkeeper, wrote to her brother Richard Haynes in Bristol in some excitement: the Duke of Clarence had bought a bulk order of ribbon from her and her husband to make favors for a cricket game. "He had of us as much Ribbon as came to Seventeen Pounds & sixpence," she reported, but she was careful to add, "what is still better he pays his Tradesmen's Bills every Monday." Prompt settlement of debts was not something that could be depended on with this class of customer, and the issue was all the more pressing because the Cornishes were chronically in debt and in danger of having to close their shop. [35]

The majority of traders and shopkeepers of England were not in the practice of making contracts with the gentry and aristocracy, nor, in most cases, did they rely heavily upon their custom. Most of the debts on the typical tradesman's books were contracted by people with no claim to gentility of any kind. In fact, unless one were engaged solely in providing very high-priced luxuries, gentlemanly nonpayment of bills was probably more of a symbolic irritant that a direct one. It is easy to see, however, why the issue should have been such an emotive one, for it illustrated all the contradictions of a society in which political security still rested on the assigning of special privileges according to birth, but in which economic security seemed to demand more universalist codes of conduct.

The result was that attacks upon the mores of the nobility became rather a commonplace. The countless sly attacks upon the sex lives of the aristocracy and gentry, as we have seen, were closely connected in the popular canon to extravagance and indiscipline. The melodrama, with its obligatory aristocratic rake, had already come into its own; similar themes were making their way into popular prints, broadsides, and, with Samuel Richardson, the novel. Contemporary advice books carped *ad nauseam* on aristocratic eating habits. They also denounced the vicious habits prevalent in the schools to which elites sent their children and censured the nobility's alleged habit of overindulging their children.[36] Elites sometimes cooperated by conducting their own campaigns of self-reproach.

But negative campaigns have a limited appeal, as eighteenth-century people well knew, and so one popular genre of contemporary criticism took a different route. It set out to discover and celebrate the "virtuous aristocrat," that man or woman who stood out from the dissolute throng to embody all the moral qualities that commercial people, especially, most admired or sought in themselves, in their children, and in those with whom they transacted business. Aristocratic women lent themselves particularly well to such treatment, and celebrations of conventional feminine virtue among high-born women (often coupled with commentary as to its extreme rarity) were centuries old. *The Spectator,* that marvelous hybrid of genteel and commercial views, contains numerous portraits of dissolute, undomestic, or merely silly high-born women. But the women who truly stand out are the virtuous ones, such as the lovely Aurelia, who

> tho' a Woman of Great Quality, delights in the Privacy of a Country life, and passes away a great part of her Time in her Own Walks and Gardens. Her Husband, who is her Bosom Friend, and Companion in her Solitudes, has been in Love with her ever since he knew her. They both abound with good Sense, consummate Virtue, and a mutual esteem; and are a perpetual Entertainment to one another. Their Family is under so regular an Oeconomy, in its Hours of Devotions and Repast, Employment and Diversion, that it looks like a little Common-Wealth within it self.[37]

The force of the passage derives from the way it flies in the face of what everyone "knew" to be true, namely that aristocratic women were less chaste, less domestically inclined, less careful in the management of their time, more addicted to luxury, and more prone to interfere in matters of state than were women of other classes. Aurelia and her household are models of good order, something that is as evident in her leisure pursuits as in the way this family schedules its daily round of activities. She is the exception that proves the rule. And yes, this household *might* bring to mind a "little Common-Wealth" (to Addison, too, the analogy was as natural as breathing), but it would be a much more rationalized and—dare one say it?—bourgeois nation than that of which most English people in 1711 were conscious of being a part.

It is not always worthwhile to separate middling criticisms from more generalized attacks on elite women. Still, one topic that does seem to have especially interested middling commentators was that of noblewomen breastfeeding their own children.[38] Apart from the erotic appeal the subject contained for men who were not, in real life, likely to view that area of a noblewoman's anatomy at close hand, breastfeeding was a potent symbol of domesticity, interventionist childrearing, and serious commitment to one's calling. The breastfeeding mother mirrored the attitude with which everyone in society, male or female, high born or low, was supposed to approach his or her appointed duties. Like other middling moralists of the period, the lobbyists for breastfeeding were working as hard to restrain people of their own class as they were to reform the aristocracy; thus they seldom passed up the opportunity to attack non-elite women who copied those in high life by putting out their children to nurse.[39]

Here too one sees efforts to find and then celebrate ostensibly "real" aristocrats who were already taking the moralists' advice. James Nelson's extremely popular *Essay on the Government of Children, Under Three General Heads, viz. Health, Manners and Education*, first published in 1758, was advertised as an attempt to apply what Nelson calls "natural and rational" methods to childrearing. Nelson was an apothecary by trade, and, like Defoe before him, he lauded the way intermarriage with the nobility civilized the trading ranks. In fact, Nelson's vision of the civilizing process was a good deal more complicated. Civility and good morals tended to seep up from the truly virtuous and independently rational among the middle ranks to the virtuous among their social superiors (sparse in number though they were) and then trickle back down to those still inclined to emulate their betters. The book starts off, therefore, with another idealized aristocratic woman, the "Countess of _____," a paragon of feminine virtue who has foregone the "Assemblies of the Great" and "the Splendor of the Court" to yield to "the stronger Attractions of Parental Affection." Nelson went into voyeuristic flight at the emulative possibilities the Countess presented: when the world saw her taking on the "Office of a tender Mother, by cherishing, watching over, and instructing [her] Offspring," it would be "powerfully animated to pursue the same measures; which alone can procure that solid Happiness all seek, or seem to seek, yet so few find."[40] Nelson, too, saw a close connection between domesticity, sincere emotions, and "solid Happiness," the converse of which included addiction to fashion and public life, superficiality, and an inability to experience true happiness. He was anxious to establish his own model of family order as a universally applicable one that would replace narrower, more class-specific systems.[41]

The virtuous nobleman was also given his due. Sir Francis Child's account of the Earl of Pembroke and his household, mentioned above, is an idealized example from real life. In David and James Fordyce's *The Temple of Virtue* (1759), one of the virtuous mortals honored by the Gods was a man in a "place of highest trust and authority under his *sovereign*," whose house was nevertheless "the dwelling-place of *Order, Contentment,* and *Domestic Bliss*," who was revered and confided in by his children and adored by his wife, and who preferred, when the duties of his high office permitted, to entertain unostentatiously at home among intimate gatherings of "kindred minds."[42] Here, as elsewhere in the Fordyce brothers' writings, domestic order was closely linked to disinterested public service: they made explicit what some other middling people preferred to leave unsaid.

A still more comprehensive treatment of all these themes is to be found in the Reverend Philip Doddridge's carefully contrived hagiography, *Some Remarkable Passages in the Life of the Honourable Col. James Gardiner* (1747). It is today little read, but in his own time it was probably Doddridge's most popular work.[43] Like many of his writings, this book was especially aimed at "young listeners," to whom he wished to give the opportunity

> [to] survey a Character of such eminent and various Goodness, as might demand Veneration, and inspire him with a Desire to imitate it too, had it appeared in the Obscurest Rank.[44]

Colonel Gardiner represented a particularly exciting variant of the virtuous gentleman, one who had reformed after a profligate youth, which in his case had included dueling, "criminal amours," and hanging about the dissolute court of the French regent, the Duc d'Orléans. As Doddridge tells it, Gardiner, in the midst of these diversions, had a miraculous vision of Jesus Christ and thenceforward embarked on a "methodical *Manner of Living*," which included rising at four A.M. or earlier to spend several hours in prayer, eating little, and pursuing "rational habits of self-denial."[45]

Surrounded by debauchees, Gardiner nevertheless managed to contract a loving marriage to Lady Frances Erskine, the daughter of the Earl of

Buchan, and together they had thirteen children. Gardiner ran a well-ordered but frugal household, being "contented with a very decent Appearance in his Family" without affecting an air of grandeur. Both Colonel Gardiner and Lady Frances were devoted to their children but, unlike other high-born parents, were careful not to indulge them.[46]

Colonel Gardiner believed in careful application to business and had a special gift for fair-minded leadership, always distributing preferment according to merit and making no distinctions of rank with regard to cursing, dueling (which he had come to abhor), Sabbath breaking, and the like. To his servants he was always courteous and correct, displaying no "indecent sallies of ungoverned anger . . . (by which some in High-Life do strangely debase themselves, and lose much of their Authority),"[47] and he maintained sincere, egalitarian friendships with men of merit such as Doddridge himself. "[H]e considered," wrote Doddridge, "*all the Children of Adam* as standing upon a Level before their great Creator."[48] Finally, this model of rectitude was a man of conspicuous bravery, dying usefully on the battlefield at Prestonpans in 1745. Military heroism, almost the only aristocratic impulse still alive in Colonel Gardiner's thoroughly bourgeois soul, finally proved his undoing. This was a man whom middling youths, presumably in less life-threatening callings, might safely take as a moral exemplar, and he was a standing indictment to the morally and politically corrupt of his own class.

WAS THE NOBILITY REALLY SO DIFFERENT?

Persons of quality were simplistically linked in the minds of their contemporaries to practices and habits of mind very different from the ones deemed requisite for individual trading success. Not surprisingly, what we know of the behavior of real nobles suggests a more diverse picture. The more interesting problem, however, is a cultural one. England in the late seventeenth and eighteenth centuries was changing very quickly, in ways that affected almost everyone. How did the gentry and aristocracy respond to these shifts? Did they inhabit a moral universe entirely distinct from that of middling people, or did the two groups draw, at least to some extent, upon a common reservoir of cultural values? Let us look once again at bookkeeping, this time in the context of aristocratic allegiance both to estate consolidation and to the ideal of leisure independence.

Contemporary protestations of difference notwithstanding, many of the things that most preoccupied middling people—reading, accounting, domestic virtue, and the like—also struck a chord in members of the elite, although, as will be seen, not always for precisely the same reasons.[49] Elites too wished to see their children (especially their sons) learn to read and write at a very high level, because one could not exercise much agency or authority in eighteenth-century politics or fashionable society without these skills. And elites shared with the middling a tendency to equate literacy with godliness and Protestantism, and hence, with "Englishness."

But a common culture can be inflected in more than one way, and skills such as reading and writing resonated differently for the middling than they did for elites. For the former the ability to read and write at a high level was a skill of relatively recent vintage, and, as earlier chapters have shown, it could mean the difference between achieving a respectable position or sinking down into the rank of journeyman or worse. The middling were hungrier and more anxious in the pursuit of literacy than were their betters, as well as more prone to focus on its day-to-day functionality (the writing of business letters, for example, or the acquisition of a clear hand). On the other side, elites (or at least elite males), who were jockeying for power in a very different milieu, could afford to devote more time to the classics and *belles lettres*, that is to say, to "insider" languages and aesthetic systems that symbolized both their membership in a highly select group and their transcendent claim to social and political leadership.[50]

When bookkeeping began to spread more widely in the seventeenth century, people of commerce adopted it first, and probably in the largest numbers. But quite a few elites learned accounting too, or at least sought to have it taught to their children. For what it is worth, this was clearly a case where the direction of cultural influence was upward, as one of the commoner seventeenth-century terms for double-entry bookkeeping, "merchant's accounts," demonstrates. But origins aside, the belief that reducing phenomena to numbers was an intrinsically "rational" and therefore desirable undertaking was common to a wide spectrum of literate opinion, both elite and non-elite, in England and elsewhere in the eighteenth century. At a more functional level, accounting appealed to what must have been a rather widespread interest in keeping track of one's income and expenditures at a time when the gentry and aristocracy faced rising costs and strong temptations to invest their money in new, more "modern" ways.

Yet, once again, differences between the two groups influenced the way they viewed accounting. The claim to distinctiveness of the gentry and aristocracy was based first and foremost upon their ability to sustain a life of leisure, or at least the appearance of it. G. E. Mingay writes of the gentry that they were

> basically a class whose superior incomes made possible a certain kind of education, a standard of comfort, and degree of leisure and a common interest in ways of spending it, which marked them off from those whose incomes, perhaps as great or greater in money terms, could only be obtained by constant attention to some form of business.[51]

Gentry status was also linked to the ownership of land sufficient to ensure financial independence for the eldest son of each generation. In practice, a good many gentry families and even a few aristocrats in the late seventeenth and eighteenth centuries had difficulty sustaining themselves in style through rents. Costs were rising, owing to inflation and changing standards of consumption, and agricultural prices, and hence landed incomes, were depressed throughout much of the seventeenth and eighteenth centuries.[52] In response, gentry families sent representatives into the professions, government sinecures, and, occasionally, trade. They looked to new kinds of investments. They sought lucrative marriages and made heavy demands upon the generosity of well-placed relatives. And of course they learned accounting, drawn, as were their social inferiors, by the appealing belief that if they could keep track of their money, great riches would result. But their group identity continued to be tied up symbolically with land and independence from most kinds of work.

Conversely, as a social category the middling stood for the buying and selling of goods and services, and if particular individuals did not themselves buy and sell, their grandparents, parents, siblings, or cousins almost certainly did. Their very identities as independent persons were bound up with the translating of work—their own and others'—into money. Risky, ill-secured enterprises were their daily bread.[53] Such "independence" as they possessed derived from financial solvency and (at least in the case of men) from being masters rather than journeymen, proposers rather than simply disposers, shop owners rather than people who stood behind the counter at another's behest. Within this milieu accounting was more than just another useful skill. It was a powerful symbol of social worth, with far greater cultural significance that it ever had for the landed classes.

Commerce was not the sole monopoly of "the commercial classes," but when aristocrats or the landed gentry entered the world of filthy lucre they tended to favor precisely those activities that would provide lasting monuments to them (canals, the better class of real-estate projects), would be in some sense identifiable with farming (e.g., mining and mineral extraction), and would involve them minimally in commercial culture. There were exceptions, but not many.[54] The ideal aristocratic trading venture was a relatively passive investment, a case of supplying capital for a return or collecting a "safe" income on the funds. It was *not* running down to the docks, overseeing a counting house, overtly buying and selling, rubbing shoulders daily with other traders, building a factory or warehouse across the street from one's own home, storing goods for sale on the premises, or organizing transport, day after day, week after week, year after year.[55] Few elites, in any time or place, are averse to making money. The more provident and profit-minded among the gentry were by this time seeking to diversify and improve and keeping a close eye on their estate accounts;

they were perfectly willing to take lessons from merchants on how to make money more efficiently. But most English elites, like their Continental counterparts, still preferred to do these things in ways that were as remote as possible from the workaday world of commerce. They were, moreover, unlikely to measure a person's worth—at least a person of their own rank— by his or her ability to keep accounts, a kind of judgment that middling people found reasonable and, increasingly, essential.

MORAL UNCERTAINTY AT THE TOP

The Norths of Suffolk and Cambridgeshire were a family of distinguished lineage but diminished estate. Accordingly, all the sons except the eldest were "destined to imployments" (namely the law, trade, and a university fellowship), and the parents encouraged their younger sons, especially, to shun the wild, extravagant, and idle habits they viewed as all too typical of people of their rank. Roger North writes of his upbringing that "Wee were not deluded by a vaine pompous way of living, which in strait circumstances accelerates Ruin, or taught accomplishments proper for such a way of living." The Norths' childrearing practices derived from stoic, puritan, and Country roots, but they were also seasoned with a strong dash of realism and a willingness to look to the example of traders.[56]

Despite these leanings toward bourgeois respectability, the Norths' primary allegiance was to landed values, and their eldest son was more gently bred—which, in later years, did little to promote good relations with his younger siblings. These parents chose from a range of alternative rearing strategies with a keen eye to their children's divergent futures. The intense moralism and emphasis on self-discipline to which the younger sons, Roger and Dudley North, were exposed from an early age was an offshoot of a larger moral and intellectual inheritance at least theoretically available to (if not always utilized by) both commercial and political elites. Elite parents knew, or could easily discover, the formula for rearing sons to trade, but the elder Norths' ready knowledge of what it meant to be "bred to imployments" was accompanied by a distinct nervousness about more conventional elite behavior patterns.

Early modern English people often voiced doubts about the wisdom and long-term benefits to the nation of a political class addicted to sloth and luxury. This was, indeed, a very ancient theme. The inflection of such concerns changed in the seventeenth century with the expansion of trade and the fact that commercial competition had become a centerpiece of international affairs. Elites were often ambivalent about engaging in trade themselves, but this did not stop a good many of them from identifying English (and British) interests with the health of commerce. Here the wars with Louis XIV played a key role. In England and Holland they generated a flood of jingoistic literature that presented the conflict as one not merely of nations but of incompatible world views. In these writings, rational tolerant Protestantism was pitted against superstitious intolerant Catholicism. Honest trading nations (England and the Netherlands) vied with a nation most famous for its luxury exports. Sturdy, no-nonsense country squires allied with thrifty Dutch merchants in a battle to the death against decadent and effeminate French aristocrats or their lackeys. As often as not, homegrown sexual virtue and monogamy stood bravely against courtly libertinism.[57] Spells of this sort of thinking were to recur throughout the eighteenth century, generally reaching a peak in wartime and receding in times of peace, and their importance should not be exaggerated. Still, they did imply a certain vulnerability to criticism on the part of elites who failed to live up to the patriotic rhetoric. An assault upon the luxurious tastes of the Continental aristocracy could too readily grow to include that class of English people who insisted upon retaining French cooks, wearing Paris fashions, and keeping a mistress on the side.

The fact is that few people are entirely immune to criticisms aimed at their personal lives and character. Elites measured status and merit among themselves by considerations that included how one ordered one's household, and how well one was served, and analogies between family governance and national governance were natural ones for them too. And at least some thought they discerned a lack of vocation among the nobility. As Lord Balcarres wrote in 1762, after attacking what he argued was the vain desire of perpetuating ancient families, "scarce anyone born to [high life] ever becomes eminent, either in science or station; it's only want that sharpens the mind of men."[58]

Elite men were especially susceptible to the suggestion that they could not control their wives, which explains part of their willingness to join with moralists in condemning the political involvements and alleged sexual immorality of women of their own class. We know less about the impact upon upper-class self-perception of a related strain of thinking that, by identifying libertinism, luxury, and francophilia with effeminacy,[59] highlighted the uncertain masculinity (and hence doubtful capacity to govern) of political elites. Terry Eagleton has suggested that in the eighteenth century the "middle class" defined itself as feminine as against the predatory masculinism of the top ranks of society.[60] But if this is the case (and archetypal productions like Richardson's *Pamela* might indeed suggest such a conclusion), the opposite view, that too many elite men were mired in effeminacy, was at least as prevalent. Thus, *The Levellers: A Dialogue Between Two Young Ladies, Concerning Matrimony* (1703) easily linked the gentry to "polluted amours" and luxury, remarking that the men had "grown as effeminate as

Women" and "understood Ribbons and Silk as well as a Milliner or Mercer."[61] And Edmund Curll's pornographic *Cases of Divorce for Several Causes*, published a little more than a decade later, featured one Robert Feilding, Esq., a man softened by women and love. "Nor can I find from all the Information that I can procure, that our Hero's Education was ever masculine," writes Curll, noting that Feilding never studied classical languages but excelled at French.[62]

A half-century later moralists were singing much the same tune. *A Dialogue Concerning the Subjection of Women to their Husbands* (1765) combines the themes of upper-class effeminacy and lack of control over wives with the belief that the manliness resides in the bourgeoisie. On one side of the debate is a commoner named "Freeman." Blunt, plain and masculine in his speech and manner, he is appalled at the way originally aristocratic practices, such as giving ladies preference at table, have spread across society, with the result that "we have refined ourselves into a ridiculous degree of effeminacy." As a consequence of this and other fopperies, men are losing power in marriage, which manifestly thwarts the intention of nature. On the other side is an unmanly and frenchified aristocratic character, aptly named "Beaumont," who proffers feeble assertions about the charms of feminine company and expresses his willingness, in the name of civility, to be ruled by women, but soon concedes the argument to his more vigorously rational colleague.[63]

None of this is to suggest that there is clear evidence one way or another for a greater "crisis of masculinity" among the upper classes than among any other group in eighteenth-century society.[64] Masculinity is a delicate flower at the best of times, and moralists and politicians were accustomed to fretting over its decline or charging (and being charged by) their opponents with a want of it. Rather, masculinity fears played into the larger sense of unease afflicting some elites in this period and had a particular resonance in relation to the choice between monogamous domesticity and its less estimable alternatives.

THE ARISTOCRACY AND THE DOMESTIC IDEAL

The last few decades of work on English family history have shown clearly that the eighteenth-century aristocracy, too, was drawn to the ideal of domesticity and that, moreover, the appeal was often thoroughly pragmatic. Among elite families personal preference with respect to a marriage partner was traditionally subordinated to the demands of lineage, money, and power politics. The ambivalence toward marriage displayed by seventeenth-century libertine writers had a real social basis;[65] the situation was even worse for aristocratic women, who routinely found themselves trapped in loveless marriages but who, because of the sexual double standard, had significantly less access to extracurricular sexual and romantic involvements than did their husbands. It is understandable that some of the earliest elite champions of domesticity would have been women,[66] and it is hardly surprising that, in the long run, an ideal that linked marriage for love to well-ordered families should have proved attractive to growing numbers of elite males as well. Domesticity and privacy meant something different among the landed than it did in most middling families, and the reasons for adopting these ideals were probably quite dissimilar. Nevertheless, in the eighteenth century both came to have an allure that transcended any one social group.

The fact is that although marital warmth may not have been so central to the value systems of the upper class as it was to those of their inferiors, it was esteemed where it appeared, a point that is evidenced in upper-class memorials. The monument in St. Mary's parish church, Walthamstow, to Edmond Clarke Esq. and Elizabeth his wife (d. 1721 and 1719, respectively), which depicts them as "Great Examples of a True Uninterrupted Conjugal Affection," is not untypical. The close reader may detect a hint of defensiveness to this and some other inscriptions. Still, they suggest a reverence among some elites for companionate marriage that belies bourgeois moralists' charges.[67]

There seems little doubt that eighteenth-century elites took a greater interest in the habits and mores of people of commerce than previous generations had done—especially when they felt they could turn them relatively painlessly to their own profit. Emulation can work in both directions. This study has focused on a culture that was, at points, self-consciously distinct from the public culture of landed elites and from the values, both positive and negative, for which the latter were best known. But it would have been strange indeed if commercial values and commercial anxieties had had no relevance beyond the commercial classes. One of the other stories about the eighteenth (and, even more, the nineteenth) century concerns the way in which a good many "trading virtues" came over time to be English, and even British, virtues, in the process partially, if never wholly, displacing older, more "classical" notions of virtue, even among the political elite.

CONCLUSION

"[T]here was another kind of *Harmony* which was still more pleasing," wrote one S. Clark to Philip Doddridge's widow in 1762 of the household of some mutual friends. "I mean the regularity & order w*ch* reigns in the Family, & w*ch* affords so agreeable a prospect of their future usefulness."[68]

A decade after his death the Reverend Doddridge's family and friends were still self-consciously promoting the "family values" he had so assiduously championed in his sermons and his published work. It is hard to resist the comparison with an almost exactly contemporary enunciation of family values from higher on the social scale. This one comes in the form of a monument from 1765, enshrined in Bath Abbey. It commemorates "C. M. One of the most valuable Women that ever lived; Whose principal Happiness consisted (*altho' she was of some rank,*) in a real & unbounded Affection and Tenderness for her Husband & Children." [69] One could easily see the Doddridge letter as a testimony to the close relationship between domestic prescription and lived reality among the middling. Conversely, the inscription in Bath Abbey might be read as indicating a failure of nerve on the part of the upper classes about their private values.

In fact, the Doddridges were rather too deliberately a "model" family to stand in for all or even most middling families. They saw themselves as embodying the superiority of dissenting values as well as of non-elite sensibilities. Nor was it ever the case that dissenters maintained a monopoly on conspicuous outward virtue. Faith and William Gray, the middling evangelical couple from York discussed in the previous chapter, espoused almost identical values. [70] But dissenters and Anglican evangelicals were precisely those groups in which consciously pursued moralism was especially likely to develop into a social and political program. Similarly, "C. M. One of the most valuable Women that ever lived" may have felt some slight insecurity about her relationship to domesticity (or her family did): noblewomen were, after all, encouraged to feel anxiety on that score. There is little indication that her male relatives felt inclined to relinquish the reins of power as a result.

Clearly political assumptions *do* alter, if slowly, in the face of new social, economic, and cultural realities. Virtuous private families and vicious aristocrats were cultural clichés. But the clichés developed color and complexity over the course of the eighteenth century, and as they did so, notions of what was politically feasible also began to change. The process was slow. Republicanism and other radical creeds had their isolated representatives, but they never gained a real foothold in eighteenth-century England. In most cases we are talking about a series of discussions whose tangible results came later. Evangelicalism, parliamentary reform, utilitarianism, the campaign to abolish imprisonment for debt, marriage reform, and nineteenth-century radical activism all owed some part of their popularity to accumulated suspicions about whether traditional elites could act morally within a commercial society, either as heads of families or in a "political" capacity—suspicions that some of these same elites came to share. In the eighteenth century the story is a more inchoate one. It traces the continued currency of analogies between the family and government well after they are supposed to have been laid to rest and treads once more the circuitous routes by which conceptions of virtue linked to the Court, the battlefield, and ideals of landed independence began to be replaced by moral preoccupations deriving from the market, moveable wealth, and forms of domestic life conventionally associated with traders rather than with lords.

Conclusion

This study has attempted to move beyond what K. Davies once called "the mess of the middle class"[1] to focus on flesh and blood individuals, people who confronted daily the immense potentialities as well as the inadequacies of early modern English commercial society. It was sometimes argued in this period that the market was a leveler of social difference. A broadside circulating in London in the 1690s claimed, in uneven scansion, that

> *Grocers-Hall* brings all to Par
> Here first and last all equal are
> *Grocers-Hall* is a Level
> Where little C____per will sell as well
> As tall and trusty Sir J__n E____well.[2]

Actually, those people who dealt in the market every day felt its pressures more directly and in more intimate ways than their superiors ever did. Late-seventeenth- and eighteenth-century trade was volatile, confusing, and extremely hard on legions of people, from the foolish and feckless to the merely unlucky. It is hardly surprising that a sense of vulnerability on the part of both individuals and families to insolvency, business failure, and imprisonment for debt loomed large when middling people attempted to fashion a metaphorical language to describe the most fundamental experiences of their lives. It is one of the contentions of this study that fears like these also contributed to new and original ways of organizing work, the family, group morality, and civic life.

Much lay ahead. Evangelicalism would soon bring moral and family issues, and especially the problem of immoral nobles, further into the public eye than ever before. The factory system would transform consumption patterns throughout the length and breadth of England. Cities would grow even larger, and the characteristic concerns of middling town dwellers—

philanthropic activities, men's societies, law and order, the building and promoting of new municipal institutions—would carry over unabated into the nineteenth century. Banks, more sophisticated forms of insurance, more efficient mechanisms for determining credit, limitations on liability, and ultimately the abolition of imprisonment for business debts (imprisonment for small consumer debts, the scourge of the poor, was to remain in place into the twentieth century) [3] would alleviate at least some of the insecurity associated with middle-class entrepreneurship. Middling (by now middle-class) politics would come into its own, not just in the form of agitation over the corn laws and the expansion of the franchise, but in the campaign to abolish the slave trade and in feminist efforts to improve women's education and ensure more property rights for wives.

In any society there is a wide gulf between prescription and practice. Seventeenth- and eighteenth-century middling family life was fraught with internal tension. Women had grave reservations about subordination and dependence, and these were only reinforced by the highly unstable setting in which early modern business endeavors took place. Young people often rebelled against the strict regimen that was being imposed upon them and embraced the very opposite of the prudential values with all the passion that their more virtuous contemporaries brought to thrift, chastity, sobriety, diligence, and good time management. Middling family life was full of conflicts deriving in part or in whole from the strains of the market: conflicts between men and women, between the interests of small family groupings and those of more extended kin, between the "moral" and those who, patently, were not. Eighteenth-century middling culture, as this study has tried to make clear, was as much about a failure to live up to widely accepted moral norms as about their adoption.

In the late seventeenth and eighteenth centuries more English people than ever before confronted the world of commerce. What they saw bore only a passing resemblance to what one sees among the middle classes today. If these middling people's responses often seem extreme, it is precisely because their society demanded an almost inhuman level of self-discipline from those who would profit from it—while offering no sure formula for success. In subsequent generations the mores that early modern middling folk pioneered became second nature. For the comfortable classes they were buttressed by a wide range of practices and institutions that helped to spread out and minimize, if never entirely eliminate, capitalist risk. The original moral vision became vaguer, its original rationale obscured by time and other concerns. Privilege is a powerful solvent, and the more rigorous, hard-edged, painful, and, for many, simply unattainable moralities are now less often found among the middle classes. Yet neither have they died out. Recognizable variants are still to be found in those communities where money is scarce, the infrastructural supports to enterprise are few, and the price of failure or moral nonconformity is prison or the bread lines.

The people whose lives have been described here were, many of them, both insular and self-interested. The world they were intent on creating was not ideal from the perspective of anyone but themselves. A rather large part of their self-presentation was designed to paper over the fissures, inconsistencies, gender conflict, and, often, sheer exploitation that lay just beneath the surface of the much-vaunted "well-ordered family." The standards they set for themselves and attempted to impose on others, sometimes to devastating effect, could be inhuman and life-denying. Yet, on another level, we can view with some sympathy middling people's resourcefulness and individuality, their struggles with illiteracy and profit margins, their willingness to remake the rules and their alacrity in breaking them, their alien and yet familiar family problems, their forays into social activism, their humanity, and lack of it, even, for better or worse, their social vision. These aspects of middling life speak to us, who live with a system that often seems bloated and sclerotic, about a time when the marketplace still seemed new, young, and full of promise, if not remote from care.

ABBREVIATIONS USED IN THE NOTES

BL	British Library
Bodleian	Bodleian Library, Oxford
BRL	Bristol Reference Library
BRO	Bristol Record Office
CLRO	Corporation of London Record Office
DNB	Dictionary of National Biography
Dr. Williams's Library	Dr. Williams's Library, London
Friends' Library	Friends' Library, London
GLRO	Greater London Record Office
Guildhall	Guildhall Library, London
PRO	Public Record Office, London
RO	Record Office (e.g., East Sussex R.O.)

NOTES

INTRODUCTION

1. Samuel Johnson, *The Idler,* no. 18 (Saturday, 12 Aug. 1758) (reprinted London: Jones & Company, 1826), 17–18.

2. Harold J. Perkin, *The Origins of Modern English Society, 1780–1880* (London: Routledge & Kegan Paul, 1969), 37, 47–51, 92–97 et passim.

3. J. H. Plumb, *The Commercialisation of Leisure in Eighteenth-Century England,* The Stenton Lecture, 1972 (Reading: University of Reading, 1973), 19; Neil McKendrick, "Home Demand and Economic Growth: A New View of the Role of Women and Children in the Industrial Revolution," in Neil McKendrick, ed., *Historical Perspectives: Studies in English Thought and Society in Honour of J. H. Plumb* (London: Europa, 1974), 152–210; Neil McKendrick, John Brewer, and J. H. Plumb, *The Birth of a Consumer Society: The Commercialization of Eighteenth-Century England* (London: Hutchinson, 1983), 11–15, 18, 20–22 et passim; David Cannadine, *Lords and Landlords: The Aristocracy and the Towns, 1774–1967* (Leicester: Leicester University Press, 1980), 36–39; J. C. D. Clark, *English Society 1688–1832: Ideology, Social Structure and Political Practice During the Ancien Regime* (Cambridge: Cambridge University Press, 1985), 70–73; and Peter Borsay, *The English Urban Renaissance: Culture and Society in the Provincial Town, 1660–1770* (Oxford: Clarendon Press, 1989), 225–226.

4. Nicholas Rogers, "Money, Land and Lineage: The Big Bourgeoisie of Hanoverian London," *Social History* 4 (1979):437–454, especially 447. The representativeness of Rogers's sample has come under criticism. See Donna T. Andrew, "Aldermen and the Big Bourgeoisie of London Reconsidered," *Social History* 6 (1981):356–364; and, in the same issue, Nicholas Rogers, "A Reply to Donna Andrew," 365–369.

5. Lawrence Stone and Jeanne C. Fawtier Stone, *An Open Elite? England 1540–1880* (Oxford: Clarendon Press, 1984), 201–221, 403–405 et passim. See also John Cannon, *Aristocratic Century: The Peerage of Eighteenth-Century England* (Cambridge: Cambridge University Press, 1984), 19–20.

6. Henry Horwitz, " 'The Mess of the Middle Class' Revisited: The Case of the

'Big Bourgeoisie' of Augustan London," *Continuity and Change* 2 (1987):263–296, especially 273 and 282.

7. Ibid., 272, 277.

8. Ralph Davis, *Aleppo and Devonshire Square: English Traders in the Levant in the Eighteenth Century* (London: Macmillan, 1967), 9, 15–16.

9. Dudley Ryder, *The Diary of Dudley Ryder, 1715–1716*, ed. William Matthews (London: Methuen & Co., 1939). There are few more revealing sources on the complexity of emulation than this one. Ryder was the son of a Cheapside linen draper, and virtually all the male members of his immediate and extended family were active traders. For Ryder's brother see 82–84, 151, 164, 184, 205, 254–255, 259, 273–274, 277. Ryder himself had to endure taunts from his grandmother, who thought he went "too fine" for the son of a tradesman (18). For Ryder's views on country life see 90, 99, 228. For other indications of his distaste for "gentry" values, at least when they conflicted with principles of thrift or with solid application to work, see 33–34, 43–44, 58, 74, 78 et passim. On the other hand, he sought preferment by attending upon influential noblemen and jurists, he worked assiduously to polish his general deportment, and, although raised a dissenter, he later conformed. And he was no puritan in sexual matters. In later life Ryder became a Member of Parliament and served as Attorney General (see William Matthews, "Introduction," in Ryder, *Diary of Dudley Ryder*, 20–25).

10. Quoted in Patricia James, *Population Malthus, His Life and Times* (London: Routledge & Kegan Paul, 1979), 36.

11. R. J. Morris, "The Middle Class and the Property Cycle During the Industrial Revolution," in T. C. Smout, *The Search for Wealth and Stability: Essays in Economic and Social History Presented to M. W. Flinn* (London: Macmillan, 1979), 91–113. Morris looks closely at three exemplary "middle-class" men of the late eighteenth and early nineteenth century and shows them beginning to invest their capital in loans and mortgages, public utilities, and, to some degree, rentier activity as they got into their fifties. This way they "gained an income which fluctuated less and . . . required less effort to maintain." One of the few known, active women in long-distance trade, Esther Prager, who was from a well-known Jewish family with interests in diamonds and medicinals, wound up business in the 1790s because none of her sons or grandsons was deemed capable of taking over its management. See Gedalia Yogev, *Diamonds and Coral: Anglo-Dutch Jews and Eighteenth-Century Trade* (New York: Leicester University Press, 1978); and Deborah Baumgarten, *The Fruit of Her Hands: Esther Prager, an Anglo-Jewish Woman in Eighteenth-Century Trade*, senior thesis, Amherst College, 1992. A decade earlier Eleanora Hucks wrote to her daughter Dorothea of one Mr. Beckwith who was "declining business, and their two sons have turn'd out so bad that they are not thought worthy or proper to succeed them, so they are selling all their Stock off" (Guildhall MS 11021/1, E. Hucks to Dorothea [née Hucks], 22 Oct. 1780).

12. BRO Acc. No. 26226, Samuel Lowder in Bristol to William Prattinton in Bewdley, Worcestershire, dtd. 4 June 1775. One of the recurrent themes of Lowder's correspondence in the 1770s (when he himself was beginning to feel the effects of advancing age and ill health) concerned who among his friends and relatives could continue in business: "Mr. Jones has had a stroke, and being so far

advanced in Years, tis thought he can never more attend to Business" (Lowder to Prattinton, dtd. 11 July 1775).

13. Dr. Williams's Library MS 24.157, fol. 274, Samuel Kenrick to James Wodrow, Bewdley, 27 June 1809.

14. Peter Earle, *The Making of the English Middle Class: Business, Society and Family Life in London, 1660–1730* (Berkeley and Los Angeles: University of California Press, 1989); Leonore Davidoff and Catherine Hall, *Family Fortunes: Men and Women of the English Middle Class, 1750–1850* (Chicago: University of Chicago Press, 1987).

15. John Smail, *The Origins of Middle-Class Culture: Halifax, Yorkshire, 1660–1780* (Ithaca and London: Cornell University Press, 1994). Smail's definition of "the middling sort" differs from mine. See pp. 15–16.

16. See, inter alia, D. C. Coleman, *The Economy of England, 1450–1750* (London and New York: Oxford University Press, 1977); P. G. M. Dickson, *The Financial Revolution in England: A Study of the Development of Public Credit 1688–1756* (London and New York: Macmillan and St. Martin's Press, 1967); M. W. Flinn, *Men of Iron: The Crowleys in the Early Iron Industry* (Edinburgh: Edinburgh University Press, 1962); Julian Hoppit, *Risk and Failure in English Business, 1700–1800* (Cambridge: Cambridge University Press, 1987); Hoh-Cheung Mui and Lorna H. Mui, *Shops and Shopkeeping in Eighteenth-Century England* (Kingston, Ont.: McGill-Queen's University Press, 1989); Jacob M. Price, *Capital and Credit in British Overseas Trade: The View from the Chesapeake, 1700–1776* (Cambridge, Mass.: Harvard University Press, 1980); Marie B. Rowlands, *Masters and Men in the West Midland Metalware Trades Before the Industrial Revolution* (Manchester: Manchester University Press, 1975); Barry Supple, *The Royal Exchange Assurance: A History of British Insurance 1720–1970* (Cambridge: Cambridge University Press, 1970). For important revisionist views see Maxine Berg, "What Difference Did Women's Work Make to the Industrial Revolution?" *History Workshop Journal* 35 (1993):22–44; L. D. Schwarz, *London in the Age of Industrialisation: Entrepreneurs, Labour Force and Living Conditions, 1700–1850*, Cambridge Studies in Population, Economy and Society in Past Time, 19 (Cambridge: Cambridge University Press, 1992); and Smail, *Origins of Middle-Class Culture.*

17. See E. P. Thompson, *The Making of the English Working Class* (London: Gollancz, 1963); John Brewer, *Party Ideology and Popular Politics at the Accession of George III* (Cambridge and New York: Cambridge University Press, 1976) and *The Sinews of Power: War, Money and the English State 1688–1783* (New York: Alfred A. Knopf, 1989); Gary DeKrey, *A Fractured Society: The Politics of London in the First Age of Party, 1688–1715* (Oxford: Clarendon Press, 1985); Cannadine, *Lords and Landlords;* Nicholas Rogers, *Whigs and Cities: Popular Politics in the Age of Walpole and Pitt* (Oxford: Clarendon Press, 1989); Donna T. Andrew, *Philanthropy and Police: London Charity in the Eighteenth Century* (Princeton, N.J.: Princeton University Press, 1989); Linda Colley, *In Defiance of Oligarchy: The Tory Party, 1714–60* (Cambridge: Cambridge University Press, 1982), and *Britons: Forging the Nation, 1707–1837* (New Haven and London: Yale University Press, 1992); Joanna Innes, "Parliament and the Shaping of Eighteenth-Century English Social Policy," *Transactions of the Royal History Society,* 5th ser., 40 (1990), 63–92, and "Politics and Morals: The

Reformation of Morals Movement in Later Eighteenth-Century England," in Eckhart Hellmuth, ed., *The Transformation of Political Culture: England and Germany in the Late Eighteenth Century* (Oxford and London: Oxford University Press and the German Historical Institute, 1990), 57–118; Kathleen Wilson, "Urban Culture and Political Activism in Hanoverian England: The Example of Voluntary Hospitals," in Hellmuth, *Transformation of Political Culture*, 165–184; and Kathleen Wilson, *The Sense of the People: Politics, Culture, and Imperialism in England, 1715–1785* (Cambridge and New York: Cambridge University Press, 1995). The excellent new collection edited by Lawrence Stone, *An Imperial State at War, Britain from 1689 to 1815* (London and New York: Routledge, 1994), also contains a great deal of material bearing on this issue.

18. McKendrick, Brewer, and Plumb, *Birth of a Consumer Society;* Borsay, *English Urban Renaissance;* Lorna Weatherill, *Consumer Behavior and Material Culture in Britain 1660–1760* (London: Routledge, 1988); John Brewer and Roy Porter, eds., *Consumption and the World of Goods* (London: Routledge, 1993). For a critique of emulation theory, including a discussion of its implicit gender politics, see Amanda Vickery, "Women and the World of Goods: A Lancashire Consumer and Her Possessions, 1751–81," in Brewer and Porter, *Consumption and the World of Goods,* 274–301, especially 275–278.

19. Joseph Melling and Jonathan Barry, "The Problem of Culture: An Introduction," in Joseph Melling and Jonathan Barry, eds., *Culture in History: Production, Consumption and Values in Historical Perspective* (Exeter: University of Exeter Press, 1992), 3–27 contains a provocative discussion of some of these issues.

20. Lawrence Stone, *The Family, Sex and Marriage in England, 1500–1800* (London: Weidenfeld & Nicolson, 1977) 221–404; Randolph Trumbach, *The Rise of the Egalitarian Family: Aristocratic Kinship and Domestic Relations in Eighteenth-Century England* (New York: Academic Press, 1978), 83–87, 97–124, 150–153, 165–166 et passim; Bridget Hill, *Women, Work and Sexual Politics in Eighteenth-Century England* (Oxford and New York: Blackwell, 1989), 44–46, 194–195, 198–201. Hill relies in part for her chronology upon K. D. M. Snell, *Annals of the Labouring Poor: Social Change and Agrarian England, 1660–1900* (Cambridge: Cambridge University Press, 1985).

21. Earle, *Making of the English Middle Class,* 198–209. Davidoff and Hall acknowledge this potential interpretive problem, noting that had they chosen less successful families or had access to court records they might have ended up with a more conflictual picture (*Family Fortunes,* 34).

22. Smail, *Origins of Middle-Class Culture,* 165–187.

23. Happily this is not true of all scholars of the period. See Maxine Berg, *The Age of Manufactures: Industry, Innovation and Work in Britain, 1700–1820* (London: Blackwell/Fontana, 1985), 129–158; Maxine Berg, "Women's Work, Mechanization and the Early Phases of Industrialization in England," in R. E. Pahl, ed., *On Work: Historical, Comparative and Theoretical Approaches* (Oxford: Basil Blackwell, 1988), 61–94; Peter Earle, "The Female Labour Market in London in the Late Seventeenth and Early Eighteenth Centuries," *Economic History Review,* 2d ser., 42 (1989):328–353; Catherine Hall, "Private Persons Versus Public Someones: Class, Gender and Politics in England, 1780–1850," in Carolyn Steedman, Cathy Urwin, and Valerie Walkerdine, eds., *Language, Gender and Childhood* (London and Boston:

Routledge & Kegan Paul, 1985), 10-33; Catherine Hall, "Gender Divisions and Class Formation in the Birmingham Middle Class, 1780-1850," in Raphael Samuel, ed., *People's History and Socialist Theory*, History Workshop Series (London and Boston: Routledge & Kegan Paul, 1981), 164-175; Catherine Hall, "The Early Formation of Victorian Domestic Ideology," in Sandra Burman, ed., *Fit Work for Women* (London: Croom Helm, in Association with Oxford University Women's Studies Committee, 1979), 15-32; Mary Prior, "Women and the Urban Economy: Oxford 1500-1800," in Mary Prior, ed., *Women in English Society 1500-1800* (London: Methuen, 1985), 93-117; and Schwarz, *London in the Age of Industrialisation*, 14-22, 45-50 et passim. Older works are Alice Clark, *Working Life of Women in the Seventeenth Century*, intro. Amy Louise Erickson (London and New York: Routledge, 1992); Ivy Pinchbeck, *Women Workers and the Industrial Revolution, 1750-1850* (London: Frank Cass, 1977), and M. Dorothy George, *London Life in the Eighteenth Century* (New York: Harper & Row, 1964).

24. Erickson, *Women and Property in Early Modern England;* Colley, *Britons;* Wilson, *The Sense of the People;* Schwarz, *London in the Age of Industrialisation;* Smail, *Origins of Middle-Class Culture.* All of these have appeared in the last four years.

25. Of the historians just mentioned, Erickson, Colley, and Wilson are quite skeptical of the theory of separate spheres (see Erickson, *Women and Property in Early Modern England,* 8-11; Colley, *Britons,* 237-281; Wilson, *Sense of the People,* 49n), while Schwarz skirts it entirely. Smail is the only one who still accepts it; see his *Origins of Middle-Class Culture,* 121-187, although also see his discussion of some of the methodological difficulties, 164-166.

26. One of those accounts, it is only fair to acknowledge, is my own doctoral dissertation. See Margaret Hunt, "English Urban Families in Trade, 1660-1800: The Culture of Early Modern Capitalism," Ph.D. diss., New York University, 1986, 180-217, 245-259. I would not at present make such claims either for the "reality" of separate spheres or its centrality to class formation. See also Davidoff and Hall, *Family Fortunes,* 149-192, 357-396; and Smail, *Origins of Middle-Class Culture,* 121-187. An important recent critique of the usefulness of separate spheres is Amanda Vickery, "Golden Age to Separate Spheres? A Review of the Categories and Chronology of English Women's History," *The Historical Journal* 36 (1993):383-414.

27. It is especially not my purpose to argue that *family life* remains static over time.

28. See Thomas Turner, *The Diary of Thomas Turner, 1754-1765,* ed. David Vaisey (Oxford: Oxford University Press, 1984); Samuel Jeake, *An Astrological Diary of the Seventeenth Century: Samuel Jeake of Rye, 1652-1699,* ed. Michael Hunter and Annabel Gregory (Oxford: Oxford University Press, 1988); Joshua Johnson, *Joshua Johnson's Letterbook 1771-1774: Letters from a Merchant in London to His Partners in Maryland,* ed. Jacob M. Price (London: London Record Society, 1979); Paul S. Seaver, *Wallington's World: A Puritan Artisan in Seventeenth-Century London* (Stanford, Calif., Stanford University Press, 1985); and James Oakes, *The Oakes Diaries: Business, Politics and the Family in Bury St. Edmunds 1778-1827,* Suffolk Records Society vols. 32 and 33, ed. Jane Fiske (Woodbridge: Boydell, 1990-1991). See also the older William Stout, *Autobiography of William Stout of Lancaster, 1665-1752,* ed. J. D. Marshall (Manchester and New York: Manchester University Press and Barnes & Noble, 1967); and T. S. Willan, *An Eighteenth-Century Shopkeeper: Abraham Dent of*

Kirkby Stephen (Manchester: Manchester University Press, 1970), a reconstruction of Dent's life and commercial involvements that often reads like a first-person account.

29. Civil and church court records have been surprisingly little used by social historians of the eighteenth century; divorce actions represent one recent exception. See Lawrence Stone, *Uncertain Unions: Marriage in England 1660–1753* (Oxford and New York: Oxford University Press, 1992), which zestfully narrates some few of the thousands of surviving marriage cases that came before the ecclesiastical courts in the eighteenth century. Some of the cases Stone selects concern middling people. See also Margaret Hunt, "Wife-Beating, Domesticity and Women's Independence in Eighteenth-Century London," *Gender and History* 4 (1992):10–33.

30. Matthews, "Introduction," in Ryder, *Diary of Dudley Ryder,* 1.

31. This is particularly the case in the late seventeenth century, when many of the surviving non-elite journals came from dissenters and especially from Quakers, a remarkable group but in no way a representative one.

32. This study has benefited especially from Jeremy Black, *The English Press in the Eighteenth Century* (London: Croom Helm, 1987); John Money, *Experience and Identity: Birmingham and the West Midlands, 1760–1800* (Manchester: Manchester University Press, 1977), 121–130; and Kathryn Shevelow, *Women and Print Culture: The Construction of Femininity in the Early Periodical* (London and New York: Routledge, 1989).

33. For a noteworthy recent account of popular politics see Wilson, *Sense of the People.*

34. Patty Seleski's forthcoming book on eighteenth-century domestic servants promises to fill a serious gap in the recent literature. Smail, *Origins of Middle-Class Culture,* contains a lengthy and valuable discussion of changing labor relations, as does Schwarz, *London in the Age of Industrialisation.* For slavery and racism see Peter Fryer, *Staying Power: Black People in Britain since 1504* (Atlantic Highlands, N.J.: Humanities Press, 1984); and Margaret Hunt, "Racism, Imperialism and the Traveler's Gaze in Eighteenth-Century England," *Journal of British Studies* 32 (1993):333–357.

35. For the early modern period see, variously, Christopher Hill, "A Bourgeois Revolution?" in J. G. A. Pocock, ed., *Three British Revolutions: 1641, 1688, 1776* (Princeton, N.J.: Princeton University Press, 1980), 109–139 (see especially 136n); E. P. Thompson, *The Poverty of Theory and Other Essays* (London: Merlin Press, 1978); and E. P. Thompson, "Argument: Eighteenth-Century English Society: Class Struggle Without Class?" *Social History* 3 (1978):133–165. Although it overstates the case, J. H. Hexter's "The Myth of the Middle Class in Tudor England," in his *Reappraisals in History* (London: Longman, 1961), 71–116, contains much that is relevant to the seventeenth and eighteenth centuries. I have also benefited much from reading Mary P. Ryan, *Cradle of the Middle Class: The Family in Oneida Country, New York, 1790–1863* (Cambridge: Cambridge University Press, 1981), one of the first serious efforts to combine the study of women with the study of the formation of the middle class.

36. Pierre Bourdieu, "Social Space and Symbolic Power," *Sociological Theory* 7 (1989):19. With respect to "oppositionality" among *sections* of the middling see especially Donna T. Andrew, "The Code of Honour and Its Critics: The Opposition

to Duelling in England, 1700–1850," *Social History* 5 (1980):409–434; Rogers, *Whigs and Cities,* 128–129; and Wilson, *Sense of the People.* See also Margaret R. Hunt, "Hawkers, Bawlers and Mercuries: Women and the London Press in the Early Enlightenment," in Margaret R. Hunt, Margaret Jacob, Phyllis Mack, and Ruth Perry, *Women and the Enlightenment, Women and History* no. 9 (New York: The Institute for Research in History and the Haworth Press, 1984), 41–68. This oppositionality was, however, inconsistent: It only seized sections of the middling classes, and it often garnered support from other elements in society (e.g., the laboring classes, artisans, decaying gentry, reformist aristocrats, and so on). See also R. J. Morris's wise little book, *Class and Class Consciousness in the Industrial Revolution 1780–1850* (London and Basingstoke, Macmillan, 1979).

37. In this vein see Anna Clark, *The Struggle for the Breeches: Gender and the Making of the British Working Class* (Berkeley: University of California Press, 1995).

38. The radical nominalism of postmodernist thought meshes well with a kind of history that is suspicious of the traditional categories of social analysis (including class), that sticks close to the textual evidence, that is relatively accepting of confusion and paradox, and that roves at will across the subdisciplines. At the same time, the residual egalitarianism of postmodernism, its historical links to liberation movements, and its indebtedness to theorists like Gramsci has the potential to keep the new empiricism from turning into blind support for the status quo. My views on postmodernism, and on cultural history more generally, have benefited especially from the following: Jackson Lears, "The Concept of Cultural Hegemony: Problems and Possibilities," *American Historical Review* 90 (1985):567–593; Joan Wallach Scott, *Gender and the Politics of History* (New York: Columbia University Press, 1988); Patrick Curry, "Towards a Post-Marxist Social History: Thompson, Clark and Beyond" in Adrian Wilson, ed., *Rethinking Social History: English Society 1570–1920 and Its Interpretation* (Manchester and New York: Manchester University Press, 1993), 158–200; and Vickery, "Golden Age to Separate Spheres?"

39. On Adam Smith's notion of class see Penelope Corfield, "Class by Name and Number in Eighteenth-Century Britain," *History* 72 (1987):59. Other recent discussions of eighteenth-century notions of class are Paul Langford, *A Polite and Commercial People: England 1727–1738* (Oxford and New York: Oxford University Press, 1992), 652–655; and Dror Wahrman, " 'Middle-Class' Domesticity Goes Public: Gender, Class, and Politics from Queen Caroline to Queen Victoria," *Journal of British Studies* 32 (1993):396–432.

40. I am conscious of the perils of claiming that any category is purely "heuristic." On this problem see especially Jacques Derrida, *Of Grammatology,* trans. Gayatri Chakravorty Spivak (Baltimore: Johns Hopkins University Press, 1976).

41. Smail, *Origins of Middle-Class Culture,* 14–17. I find Smail's book in many ways the most convincing study of class formation I have seen, in part because he refrains from broad generalizing outside of the Halifax context. At the same time, it could be argued that Smail has traced the emergence of a mercantile-industrial urban elite rather than a "middle class," even given the elastic meaning of that term.

42. For a discussion of eighteenth-century usages see Corfield, "Class by Name and Number," especially 38, 43, 48–54, 57, 59. I would include within the "middling" at least *some* of the people in John Smail's "middle class" along with a

substantial cadre of urban non-elites above the level of laborers. (This latter group, perforce, has only an ancillary role in Smail's narrative by the mid eighteenth century). See Smail, *Origins of Middle-Class Culture*, 26–27, 31–38, 42–43.

43. Earle, *Making of the English Middle Class*, 14–15, has a discussion of income and middling status. His estimates seem reasonable ones for the early eighteenth century; however, £50 bought less later in the century, and places like London were notoriously expensive. An £80–£100 figure is probably more appropriate for the later eighteenth century. (See Schwarz, *London in the Age of Industrialisation*, 51–73.)

44. J. V. Beckett, *The Aristocracy in England, 1660–1914* (Oxford: Basil Blackwell, 1986), 289.

45. George Chalmers, *An Estimate of the Comparative Strength of Great Britain*, Reprints of Economic Classics (New York: Augustus M. Kelley, 1969 [orig. 1794]), xiii.

46. On cities as centers of culture see Andrew, *Philanthropy and Police;* Borsay, *English Urban Renaissance;* Penelope Corfield, *The Impact of English Towns, 1700–1800* (Oxford: Oxford University Press, 1982); Earle, *Making of the English Middle Class;* Gail Malmgreen, *Silk Town: Industry and Culture in Macclesfield, 1750–1835* (Hull: The University of Hull Press, 1985); and Money, *Experience and Identity*.

47. L. D. Schwarz, "Income Distribution and Social Structure in London in the Late Eighteenth Century," *Economic History Review*, 2d ser., 32 (1979):258. The social composition of the "middling" group is explored in greater detail in L. D. Schwarz, "Social Class and Social Geography: The Middle Classes in London at the End of the Eighteenth Century," *Social History* 7 (1982):167–185; and Schwarz, *London in the Age of Industrialisation*.

48. Earle, *Making of the English Middle Class*, 80–81. The higher figure may be a trifle optimistic. On this see the suggestive work of D. V. Glass, "Socio-economic Status and Occupations in the City of London at the End of the Seventeenth Century," in A. E. J. Hollaender and William Kellaway, eds., *Studies in London History Presented to Philip Edmund Jones* (London: Hodder and Stoughton, 1969):373–389. Using poll tax statistics from 1692 and an enumeration of population from 1695 across forty London parishes, Glass estimates the average percentage of persons with incomes of £50 or more per annum or personal estates worth £600 or more was 16.6 percent. However some better-off parishes contained considerably higher percentages, up to 40 percent (see 575 and 584).

49. E. A. Wrigley and R. S. Schofield, *The Population History of England 1541–1871: A Reconstruction* (London: Edward Arnold, 1981), 208–209, table 7.8; Corfield, *Impact of English Towns*, 8. Corfield's base population figures (5.2 million for 1700 and 8.8 million for 1801) are higher than Wrigley and Schofield's figures because of her inclusion of Monmouth and Wales. One could, of course, settle a different interpretation on such figures. Compare Clark, *English Society*, 69–70.

50. E. A. Wrigley, "Urban Growth and Agricultural Change: England and the Continent in the Early Modern Period," in his *People, Cities and Wealth: The Transformation of Traditional Society* (Oxford: Basil Blackwell, 1987), 162, table 7.2.

51. Compare Patrick Colquhoun's more capacious estimates, based on the census returns of 1801: persons in shopkeeping and trade 372,500; lesser merchants: 91,000; liberal arts and sciences, 81,000; lesser clergymen, 50,000; persons of the

law, 55,000; lesser civil offices, 52,000. Reprinted in Roy Porter, *English Society in the Eighteenth Century* (London: Penguin-Allen Lane, 1982), 388. Colquhoun's figures (unlike those of this study) group together people in towns and rural areas.

52. Cannon, *Aristocratic Century*, 15.

53. G. E. Mingay, *The Gentry: The Rise and Fall of a Ruling Class* (London and New York: Longman, 1976), 13–14. I know of no estimates of the numbers of gentle*women.*

54. On this see especially Nicholas Crafts, *British Economic Growth During the Industrial Revolution* (Oxford: Clarendon Press, 1985).

55. Mui and Mui, *Shops and Shopkeeping*, 34–36. For a subtle discussion of retailing and retailers in London see Schwarz, *London in the Age of Industrialisation*, 52–56, 59–66.

56. There is a voluminous literature on these developments. I have especially benefited from the following: Joyce Appleby, *Economic Thought and Ideology in Seventeenth-Century England* (Princeton: Princeton University Press, 1978); Berg, *Age of Manufactures;* Maxine Berg, Pat Hudson, and Michael Sonenscher, eds., *Manufacture in Town and Country Before the Factory* (Cambridge: Cambridge University Press, 1983); Borsay, *The English Urban Renaissance;* Brewer, *Sinews of Power;* Coleman, *Economy of England, 1450–1750;* Corfield, *Impact of English Towns;* Ralph Davis, *Aleppo and Devonshire Square,* and his *The Rise of the English Shipping Industry in the Seventeenth and Eighteenth Centuries* (Newton Abbot: David and Charles, 1972); Dickson, *Financial Revolution;* Geoffrey Holmes, *Augustan England: Professions, State and Society, 1681–1730* (London: Allen and Unwin, 1982); Rowlands, *Masters and Men in the West Midland Metalware Trades;* McKendrick, Brewer, and Plumb, *Birth of a Consumer Society;* Mui and Mui, *Shops and Shopkeeping;* Margaret Spufford, *The Great Reclothing of Rural England: Petty Chapmen and Their Wares in the Seventeenth Century,* History Series No. 33 (Ronceverte, W.V.: The Hambledon Press, 1984; and Schwarz, *London in the Age of Industrialisation.*

57. Holmes, *Augustan England*, 268–287.

58. Holmes (ibid.); tends to focus on the cream of each profession, particularly those who bought country estates, rather than the littler people. His is still an extremely valuable account, and the contrasts between the upper and lower echelons of many of the professions seem as striking to today's reader as they must have to people 250 years ago. See 118, 120–135, 147–154, 157–160, 166–167, 219–222, 230–231. See also Edward Hughes, "The Professions in the Eighteenth Century," in Daniel A. Baugh, ed., *Aristocratic Government and Society in Eighteenth-Century England* (New York: New Viewpoints, 1975), 184–203, especially 184–185. Michael Birks, *Gentlemen of the Law* (London: Steven & Sons, Ltd., 1960), 188–205, contains some entertaining and informative accounts of eighteenth-century attorneys and their business deals.

59. On schools and schoolteaching see Holmes, *Augustan England,* 43–80; John Money, "Teaching in the Market-Place, or 'Caesar adsum jam forte Pompey aderat': The Retailing of Knowledge in Provincial England During the Eighteenth Century," in Brewer and Porter, eds., *Consumption and the World of Goods,* 335–377, 335–338, 343–346; and J. H. Plumb, "New World of Children in Eighteenth-Century England." For a typical small schoolteacher, in this case a scientific instrument maker who doubled as the keeper of a mathematics school, see BL, Add. MSS

15,627, Memoir of Thomas Wright, 1710s–1730s. For his problems with debt see fol. 6, Nov. 1732.

60. The range of middling occupations is by no means exhausted by the professions enumerated above. The period also saw the rise of a large number of new or renovated occupational categories linked to finance (accountants, brokers, bankers, insurers), infrastructural development (canal engineers, architects, lecturers in science), government (war contractors, naval engineers), and the arts (engravers, portrait painters, musicians, landscape gardeners).

61. Thus Dudley Ryder, would-be lawyer and son of a linen draper, struggled to expand his horizons through reading Latin and Greek authors, Locke and Berkeley, "Spectatorial" literature, and French comedies. He also devoted much thought to the problem of how best to display his intellectual accomplishments in polite society (Ryder, *Diary of Dudley Ryder*, 29, 31, 37–38, 40–41, 44–45, 56, 59, 65–66, 78, 91, 93–95 et passim). For a discussion of the mediatory role of the clergy in one provincial town see Shani d'Cruze, *Our Time in God's Hands: Religion and the Middling Sort in Eighteenth-Century Colchester* (Chelmsford: Essex Record Office and Local History Centre, University of Essex, 1991), 5–6, 8.

62. This reference is from Edward Gibbon, *The Autobiographies of Edward Gibbon*, ed. John Murray (London: John Murray, 1907), 294. I am indebted to Patricia Spacks for her discussion of Gibbon's pessimism. See Patricia Spacks, *Imagining a Self: Autobiography and Novel in Eighteenth-Century England* (Cambridge, Mass., and London: Harvard University Press, 1976), 95. Edward Gibbon's *maternal* grandfather was a London merchant who was ruined and absconded in 1748 when Gibbon was twelve years of age. See Gibbon, *Autobiographies*, 48–49.

CHAPTER 1: CAPITAL, CREDIT, AND THE FAMILY

1. See PRO C112/76, Chancery Masters' Exhibits, for the correspondence between Fisher and Franklin.

2. Eliot Howard, ed., *The Eliot Papers*, vol. I: *John Eliot of London, Merchant, 1735–1813* (Gloucester: Privately Printed by J. Bellows, 1893), 74.

3. Christopher Sutton, *Disce Mori: Learne to Die* (London, 1600), 19–20, quoted in Louis B. Wright, *Middle Class Culture in Elizabethan England* (Chapel Hill: University of North Carolina Press, 1935), 250.

4. In this period the term "friends" was more often used of family (including immediate family) and less often in the modern sense of intimates who were nonrelatives. On trade credit in eighteenth-century England see B. L. Anderson, "Money and the Structure of Credit in the Eighteenth Century," *Business History*, 12 (1970):85–101.

5. H. A. Shannon, "The Coming of General Limited Liability," in Eleanora Mary Carus-Wilson, ed., *Essays in Economic History* (London: Edward Arnold, 1954), vol. I, 358–379.

6. Historians are unanimous on the importance of kin in capital formation up through the early modern period. Two studies dealing with the beginning and the end of our period are D. W. Jones, "London Merchants and the Crisis of the

1690s," in Peter Clark and Paul Stack, eds., *Crisis and Order in English Towns 1500–1700: Essays in Urban History* (London: Routledge & Kegan Paul, 1972), see especially 327–331; and Perkin, *Origins of Modern English Society*, see especially 82–83. Studies of preindustrial capital formation on the American scene show the same pattern up through the first half of the nineteenth century. See Bernard Bailyn, *New England Merchants in the Seventeenth Century* (New York: Harper Torchbooks, 1964), 34–35; Bernard Faber, *Guardians of Virtue, Salem Families in 1800* (New York: Basic Books, 1972); and Michael B. Katz, Michael J. Doucet, and Mark J. Stern, *The Social Organization of Early Industrial Capitalism* (Cambridge, Mass.: Harvard University Press, 1982), 29–32.

7. Dickson, *Financial Revolution in England*, 54–55.

8. Ibid., 298. Even those M.P.s who invested in the funds tended to be mercantile men or office holders rather than from the ranks of the landed. Very small people also had new investment options available to them, although not necessarily very safe ones. For a recent account of some of the more unsavory private schemes generated in imitation of government lotteries see Lee Krim Davison, "Public Policy in an Age of Economic Expansion: The Search for Commercial Accountability in England, 1690–1750," Ph.D. diss., Harvard University, 1990, 17–90. Some of these schemes were deliberately geared to very small investors indeed.

9. Jeake, *Astrological Diary*. See especially the editors' introduction, 58–73. For more on Jeake see pp. 178–182.

10. For a closer look at middling investment, at least by Londoners (not, however, a necessarily representative group), see Earle, *Making of the English Middle Class*, 143–157. Earle found that people with a net worth under £2000 on their decease tended to invest for the most part in private loans and leases, while bigger people had diversified investments including government and company stock and shipping (147). On the other hand, over time Earle found a rising share of the latter type of investment across his sample, with poorer people especially favoring investments in the short-term debt and in government lotteries. For men who died after 1710, one in three held lottery tickets (150–151).

11. William Fleetwood, *The Relative Duties of Parents and Children, Husbands and Wives, Masters and Servants, Consider'd in Sixteen Sermons: with Three More upon the Case of Self-Murther* (London: C. Harper, 1705), 153.

12. Ibid., 149. The gender-specific usage ("child ... he," "Parent ... he") is Fleetwood's. I have reproduced it in my discussion of his ideas. For discussions of the legal grounds for disinheriting an heir see William Holdsworth, *A History of English Law* (London: Methuen & Co., Ltd., 1937), vol. 12, 542–560, vol. 13, 264–266, 376–378, and vol. 15, 97–100.

13. Fleetwood, *Relative Duties*, 151.

14. Ibid., 152.

15. Samuel Bury, *Account of the Life and Death of Elizabeth Bury Who Died May the 11th, 1720, Aged 76. Chiefly Collected Out of her Own Diary* (Bristol: J. Penn, 1721), 147 (diary entry for 27 March 1701).

16. Bernard Mandeville, *The Fable of the Bees*, ed. Phillip Harth (Harmondsworth: Penguin, 1970), 323, quoted in Simon Schaffer, "A Social History of Plausibility: County, City and Calculation in Augustan Britain," in Wilson, ed., *Rethinking*

Social History, 141. Mandeville added "An Essay on Charity and Charity Schools," from which this is taken, to the larger work in 1723, and it reflects some of the pessimism of the years immediately following the South Sea Bubble.

17. Bodleian MS Rawlinson D 114, "A Narrative (with the Continuation thereof); of Certain Particular Transactions and Events: (Together with Copies of Some Papers mentioned or referr'd to in the Same) Relating to the Transcriber of them, S[amuel] M[arriott] Anno Dni 1728," fols. 422, 205.

18. Marriott obviously spent some time delving into this knotty question. Among the tracts he cites are Ofspring Blackall's *Practical Discourses upon Our Saviour's Sermon on the Mount,* 8 vols. (London: Thomas Ward, 1718), which includes a discussion of all the possible ills one brother (meaning brother by blood) can do to another (e.g., "real damage in his Trade or Business"), quoted by Marriott, fol. 280; and Samuel Bradford, *Honest and Dishonest Ways of Getting Wealth* (London: Printed for John Wyat, 1720), cited by Marriott, fol. 419.

19. Rawlinson D 114, fol. 68.

20. Ibid., 26–27, 30, 67, 69–73.

21. Bodleian MS Rawlinson D 908, fol. 118, "Fragment of a preface to some tract exposing the conduct of one Capt. W.M., a prisoner in Newgate for a debt of £750 to a younger brother; written by that brother in the strongest terms of virulent abuse, shortly after the year 1724."

22. Ibid., fol. 118.

23. Ibid., fol. 119.

24. Ibid., fol. 118. Unfortunately the full account of the Mackenzie brothers' disaffection from each other has not survived; the "Fragment" only comprises the preface to what Mackenzie indicates is a much longer work. Rawlinson D 924, fol. 245, comprises a presentation of Rod. MacKenzie to the Quarter Sessions of the Peace for Middlesex, 18 Oct. 1725, saying his brother and his brother's council are slandering him. For another case in which one William Corbet arrested his brother (presumably his stepbrother or a brother-in-law) Isaac Wattington for £50, see Guildhall MS 205, Diaries of Stephen Monteage, fol. 254, entry for 11 Oct. 1733.

25. On medieval business culture see Sylvia Thrupp, *The Merchant Class of Medieval London, 1300–1500* (Ann Arbor: University of Michigan Press, 1962 [originally published 1948]); and M. M. Postan, "Credit in Medieval Trade," in Carus-Wilson, ed., *Essays in Economic History,* vol. 1, 61–87.

26. Coleman, *Economy of England,* 151–158. On rural England see especially Spufford, *Great Reclothing of Rural England.*

27. Coleman, *Economy of England,* 120–124, 134–137, 158–159.

28. Ibid., 120–121. The competitor for that honor was, of course, the Dutch Republic.

29. On European-wide liquidity problems and their implications see E. E. Rich and C. H. Wilson, eds., *The Cambridge Economic History of Europe* (Cambridge: Cambridge University Press, 1977), vol. 5, 300–301. For the ideological dimension of the liquidity problem up to about 1700 see Appleby, *Economic Thought and Ideology,* 119–216. For a discussion of the dimensions and implications of the lack of public confidence in coin see Anderson, "Money and the Structure of Credit," 86–91 et passim.

30. Andrew Federer, "Payment, Credit and the Organization of Work in Eigh-

teenth-century Westminster," unpublished paper given at the SSRC Conference on Manufacture in Town and Country before the Factory, Balliol College, Oxford, September, 1980. I am grateful to Andrew Federer for allowing me to cite his work in progress.

31. Ibid., 2–3.

32. Ibid., 18, table I. Percentage of assets able to be readily liquidated in proportion to book debts computed based on Federer's figures for cash balance in hand plus stock in trade for the years 1769 through 1785. Andrew Federer has pointed out to me that an equally revealing comparison might be between book debts due to the firm and total debts owed by them. Whereas in the early years business book debts due to the firm were at a ratio of about 1.1 to debts owed, sixteen years later the ratio was more than 2.2 to 1, with some £38,369 worth of debts outstanding.

33. Ibid., 7.

34. Federer points this out, ibid., 7.

35. Ibid., 8.

36. Stout, *Autobiography*, 119.

37. Ibid., 69–73, 89.

38. Ibid., 89, 96.

39. Ibid., 80, 90, 97–98, 102–103. Stout was convinced that working in a cold shop until 9:00 at night from a young age, and sometimes sleeping there as well, had made him hardy and had contributed to his general good health. This seems to have been a common belief in this period. Certainly it was not invented by John Locke, although he improves upon it by recommending that parents keep their children away from the fire even in winter and that they expose their heads and feet frequently to the cold and wet. John Locke, *John Locke on Education*, Classics in Education, no. 20, ed. Peter Gay (New York: Bureau of Publications, Teachers' College, Columbia University, 1964), 21, 26. For Stout on business failure see *Autobiography*, 99–100, 118–199, 121, 125, 135, 143 et passim.

40. On the rise of property (initially fire) insurance see P. G. M. Dickson, *The Sun Insurance Office, 1710–1960* (London: Oxford University Press, 1960); and Supple, *Royal Exchange Assurance*.

41. Stout, *Autobiography*, 67, 70–72, 75. One would not however wish to exaggerate the degree of security of the small landholder. As the best recent studies have shown, the position of small- to medium-sized landowners was extremely complex in the early modern period. People capable of marketing a substantial surplus, or those simply with cash in hand to lend, seem to have expanded quite successfully onto land previously owned by their smaller and less fortunate neighbors. For those with fewer resources and smaller land holdings, life could prove very precarious indeed. See especially Margaret Spufford, *Contrasting Communities: English Villages in the Sixteenth and Seventeenth Centuries* (Cambridge: Cambridge University Press, 1974), 58–167.

42. Stout, *Autobiography*, 99, 118–119.

43. Ibid., 29.

44. Ibid., 46.

45. Guildhall MS 11021/1, fol. 78a, C. DeLart to an unknown recipient, possibly George A. Gibbs, Sr., dtd. 16 Dec. 1763.

46. Decisions about access to credit cards, business or any long-term loans, and most mortgages are based on criteria such as income (and a relatively high one at that), job stability, evidence of higher education, occupation, income and occupation of parents or spouse, and home ownership, in addition to evidence of previous credit. So, for example, where the "comfortable classes" get credit cards, special checking accounts, and ready bank loans, more economically insecure groups rely upon pawnshops, "lay-away" plans, and installment buying backed by extremely easy arrangements for repossession by the retailer. One confounding feature of this system is the treatment of middle-class women, who tend to fare badly unless they are married to a middle-class man.

47. None of this is especially surprising. The institutions of a society tend naturally enough to mirror the prevailing values of that society and to reward individuals and families that do the same. Capitalist societies require that a substantial number of people pay their bills; consequently they do their best to limit the degree of credit permitted to people who do not possess commonly recognizable security. (The situation is somewhat more complicated than that, of course, for there are a number of other less evidently functionalist criteria that have traditionally played a role in the assigning of benefits—race and gender being the most obvious. That larger issue is outside the scope of the present discussion.)

48. Arguably, working-class entrepreneurs in the urban centers of Europe and America or the lower rungs of the business classes in many other parts of the world—those whose businesses are small-scale, generally unincorporated, lacking any but the most minimal infrastructural supports, heavily reliant on personal, familial, and neighborhood networks, and often semilegal or illegal—have more in common with eighteenth-century English middling people than does today's middle class. For an important study that touches on some of these issues see Carol Stack, *All Our Kin: Strategies for Survival in a Black Community* (New York: Harper & Row, 1974). For attempts to apply some of Stack's insights to the early modern English context see Miranda Chaytor, "Household and Kinship, Ryton in the Late Sixteenth and Early Seventeenth Centuries," *History Workshop Journal* 10 (1980):25–60. See also Miriam Slater, *Family Life in the Seventeenth Century: The Verneys of Claydon House* (London: Routledge & Kegan Paul, 1984).

49. The existence of widespread concern about insolvency is uncontrovertible; it is another matter to uncover what actual failure rates were at any given time or which sectors of the economy were likely to be affected. Data on, for example, bankruptcy in the eighteenth century are only now receiving systematic scrutiny and are, in any case, highly selective, representing only a fraction of all insolvent debtors. For this see Hoppit, *Risk and Failure in English Business*, 134–139. I am grateful to Julian Hoppit for explaining a number of the peculiarities of eighteenth-century business failure to me. For information on debt prior to 1732 see Francis J. J. Cadwallader, "In Pursuit of the Merchant Debtor and Bankrupt, 1066–1732," Ph.D. diss. (Laws), University of London, 1965. On the chronology of imprisonment for debt see Joanna Innes, "Parliament and the Shaping of Eighteenth-Century English Social Policy," *Transactions of the Royal Historical Society*, 5th ser., 40 (1990), 72–73. Innes shows, in fact, that there was a decline in the number of people imprisoned for debt after a series of reforms in the 1720s.

50. For an important discussion of the rights and responsibilities of extended

kin in the seventeenth century see David Cressy, *Coming Over: Migration and Communication Between England and New England in the Seventeenth Century* (Cambridge: Cambridge University Press, 1987), 263–291.See especially 275–276, where Cressy quotes one Robert Keayne, a Boston merchant, on the assistance he has rendered to a feckless brother-in-law:

> I have done very much for him in England divers times, in releasing him out of prisons, paying his debts for him, in furnishing him with stock to set up his trade when he had spent all his own, in taking up many quarrelsome businesses which he in his distempered fits had plunged into dangerous consequences; yet I compounded them for him and, at his sister my wife's entreaty, with some other friends of hers I sent him over into New England when his life was hazard. I paid his passage and some of his debts for him in England, and lent him money to furnish himself with clothes and other necessaries for the voyage. For many years I found him diet and clothes gratis.

The source is the Record Commissioners of Boston, *Tenth Report* (Boston, 1886), 25, "The last will and testament of me, Robert Keayne," although the events described here took place in the 1620s and 1630s.

51. Edward Stephens, *A Collection of Modern Relations of Matter of Fact, Concerning Witches and Witchcraft Upon the Persons of People To Which is Prefixed a Meditation . . . by the late Lord Chief Justice Hale Upon Occasion of a Tryal of Several Witches Before Him* (London, 1693); Jeake, *Astrological Diary*, 5–21, 73–75; Keith Thomas, *Religion and the Decline of Magic* (New York: Scribner's, 1971), 231, 241. Samuel Jeake, the writer of the astrological diary, is discussed in more detail in a later chapter of the present work.

52. Obviously, belief in magic hung on a great deal longer in some places. On this see Money, "Teaching in the Market-Place," 356–359.

53. Wright, *Middle Class Culture*, 160–169, 187–198.

54. William Scott, *An Essay of Drapery: Or, the Compleate Citizen. Trading Iustly. Pleasingly. Profitably*, Publication No. 9 of the Kress Library of Business and Economics, ed. Sylvia L. Thrupp (Boston: Baker Library, Harvard Graduate School of Business Administration, 1953 [orig. 1635]), 22.

55. Simonds D'Ewes, *The Autobiography and Correspondence of Sir Simonds D'Ewes*, ed. James Orchard Halliwell (London: R. Bentley, 1845), vol. 1, 209–210.

56. Seaver, *Wallington's World*, 54; Richard Baxter, *Faithful Souls shall be with Christ: The Certainty Proved and their Christianity Described and Exemplified in the Truly Christian Life and Death of that Excellent, Amiable Saint, Henry Ashurst, Esq., Citizen of London*, in his *Works* (London, 1681), vol. 18, 146–160, cited in Richard Schlatter, *The Social Ideas of Religious Leaders, 1660–1688* (Oxford and London: Oxford University Press and Humphrey Milford, 1940), 184–185.

57. But compare that with the apparently quite secular, if morally censorious, contemporary response to the collapse of Alexander Fordyce and the Ayr Bank in 1772, as described in Hoppit, *Risk and Failure in English Business*, 134–137.

58. Oliver Heywood, *The Rev. Oliver Heywood, B.A., 1630–1702, his Autobiography, Diaries, Anecdote and Event Books*, ed. J. Horsfall Turner (Brighouse: Printed for the Editor, 1881–1885), vol. 1, 21.

59. Ibid., 22–23.

60. For sixteenth-century articulations of these themes, already pitched toward the maintenance of good credit, see Wright, *Middle Class Culture*, 160–162,

186–187, 192–193, 195, 216–217, 265–266, 440. Nor was this moralism distinctively English. For some Continental examples see Steven Ozment, *When Fathers Ruled: Family Life in Reformation Europe* (Cambridge, Mass.: Harvard University Press, 1983), 148.

61. Quoted in Schlatter, *Social Ideas of Religious Leaders*, 45. The classic study of the process of secularization is Max Weber, *The Protestant Ethic and the Spirit of Capitalism*, trans. Talcott Parsons (New York: Charles Scribner's Sons, 1958 [originally published 1904–05]). See also Perry Miller, *The New England Mind: The Seventeenth Century* (Cambridge, Mass.: Harvard University Press, 1954).

62. David Spadafora, *The Idea of Progress in Eighteenth-Century Britain* (New Haven and London: Yale University Press, 1990). Spadafora only really sees English secularism hoving into view with William Godwin and the Lake Poets, and then irresolutely (389–392).

63. Ibid., 370.

64. When Spadafora discusses Scotland he spends more time on lay thinkers, and the resulting picture is of a more divided intellectual tradition (ibid., 309–320). Larry Stewart, in *The Rise of Public Science: Rhetoric, Technology, and Natural Philosophy in Newtonian Britain, 1660–1750* (Cambridge: Cambridge University Press, 1992), examines a different cohort than does Spadafora and uncovers a much more secular and utilitarian ethos as early as the late seventeenth century; see Stewart, 17, 32, 39, 45, 259–260, 385.

65. See Guildhall MS 10823/1, Commonplace Book of George Boddington, fol. 3, for his grandfather, and fols. 6 and 23, for his son-in-law who went spectacularly bankrupt around 1705 after having insured a fleet of Barbados and Jamaica ships that went down in a storm. This son-in-law subsequently forfeited his house and absconded. See also fol. 23, for George Boddington's brother James, for whom he put up bail in 1702 for debts totaling £374.

66. Appleby, *Economic Thought and Ideology*, 242–279.

67. William Fleetwood, *Two Sermons; the One Before the King on March the 2nd 1717 Being the First Sunday in Lent and Publish'd by His Majesty's Special Command. The Other Preach'd in the City on the Justice of Paying Debts* (London: Printed by W.C. for J. Wyat, 1718), 27.

68. Ibid., 28.

69. Ibid., 36.

70. Ibid., 36.

71. Ibid., 37.

72. Elsewhere Fleetwood was even more explicit on the benefits of enlightened self-interest. Appointed Boyle lecturer around 1700, he fell ill and was unable to appear. His lecture notes, however, which were later published, were on the theme of the working of enlightened self-interest. For Fleetwood and the Boyle lectures see Margaret C. Jacob, *The Newtonians and the English Revolution, 1689–1720* (Hassocks, Sussex: Harvester Press, 1976), 167. Fleetwood had also ventured into the field of economics, notably in his *Chronicon Preciosum: Or an Account of English Money, the Price of Corn, and other Commodities for the Last 600 Years* (London: C. Harper, 1707). Schlatter, *Social Ideas of Religious Leaders*, 202–203, has a discussion of the belief, common to a number of late seventeenth-century divines, that religious virtues were identical with those necessary to succeed in business. Thus, one

very highly placed latitudinarian churchman, Archbishop Tillotson, defended the proposition that Christian honesty is always the best policy in trading by arguing that "the unjust man will be found out, his credit fail and his trade shrivel" (quoted in Schlatter, 206).

73. PRO C106/65, Chancery Masters' Exhibits, William Jackson (the younger) in Retribution Hulk, Woolwich to William Jackson, Esq., Gloucester Place, London, dtd. 17 May 1813. The letter is transcribed in the elder Jackson's manuscript account of his son's misdeeds titled "The History of the Profligate Son," vol. II.

74. For "the poor as a productive resource" see the chapter of that name in Appleby, *Economic Thought and Ideology*, 129–157. On institutions for regulating the poor see Mary Gwladys Jones, *The Charity School Movement: A Study of Eighteenth-Century Puritanism in Action* (Cambridge: The University Press, 1938); Betsy Rodgers, *Cloak of Charity: Studies in Eighteenth-Century Philanthropy* (London: Methuen & Co., 1949); and Andrew, *Philanthropy and Police*.

75. Elizabeth Ashbridge was able to raise the not inconceivable sum of £80 because the income she could realize from both school teaching and fine needlework in Pennsylvania, where she then lived, was higher than would have been the case in England. Elizabeth Ashbridge, *Some Account of the Early Part of the Life of Elizabeth Ashbridge, Who Departed this Life in Truth's Service, in Ireland, the 16th of the 5th Month, 1755, Written by Herself* (Dublin: C. Bentham, 1820), 52.

76. (Mrs.) Edwin [Almyra] Gray, ed., *Papers and Diaries of a York Family, 1764–1839* (London: Sheldon Press, 1927), 34. For a similar account, this time by an Anglican minister of decayed gentry stock, see William Stukeley, *The Family Memoirs of the Rev. William Stukeley, M.D.*, Surtees Society Publications, vol. 73 (Durham: Andrews & Co., 1882), 26.

77. David Fordyce, with additional material by James Fordyce, *The Temple of Virtue: A Dream* (London: James Magee, 1759), 68. Ironically, one of the other Fordyce brothers, Alexander, a financial speculator, "broke" and helped precipitate a major financial panic in 1772 (Hoppit, *Risk and Failure in English Business*, 135–136). According to James Fordyce's wife Henrietta, who penned a melodramatic eyewitness account of Alexander's fall, the failure of the Ayr Bank swept away his brothers' fortunes as well. See Henrietta Fordyce, *Memoirs of the Late Mrs. Henrietta Fordyce, Relict of James Fordyce, D.D.; Containing Original Letters, Anecdotes and Pieces of Poetry. To Which is Added a Sketch of the Life of James Fordyce, D.D.* (London: Hurst, Robinson & Co., 1823), 53–56.

78. Mary Hays, *Letters and Essays, Moral and Miscellaneous* (London: T. Knott, 1793), 41–43. Loathe to abandon her theme, Hays actually makes poor Melville endure still another financial crisis (owing to "the bankruptcy of a house, which involved the greater part of [his] property") before she lets him marry his beloved Cecilia. After this further setback he settles his mercantile affairs yet again and prudently decides to retire from business altogether (62).

79. For debt in rural areas see Joan Thirsk, ed., *Agrarian History of England and Wales* (Cambridge: Cambridge University Press, 1984–1985), vol. 5(1); xxvii, 24–25, 45, 113, 166, 299; vol. 5(2); 145, 149–154, 172, 231–232; vol. 6, 587. See also Spufford, *Contrasting Communities*, 79–80, 141–142, 212–213.

80. See pp. 84–86 for a discussion of the distribution of literacy.

81. See for instance the case of Sir Richard Grosvenor, later created Earl

Grosvenor, detailed in J. V. Beckett, *The Aristocracy in England, 1660–1914* (Oxford: Basil Blackwell, 1986), 304–305.

82. One of the privileges of peers was that they could not be arrested or imprisoned for debt, and the same privilege extended to M.P.s while parliament was sitting. See Michael L. Bush, *The English Aristocracy: A Comparative Synthesis* (Manchester: Manchester University Press, 1984), 17, 20–21. We do know of some exceptions to this: Edward Hughes, *North Country Life in the Eighteenth Century* (London: Oxford University Press, 1952), vol. 1, 1, reproduces a statement by a Yorkshire baronet, Sir William Chaytor, in Fleet Prison for debt in 1700 owing to encumbrances on his estate. This was, presumably, a rare case. For a survey of aristocratic debt and sources of credit see Beckett, *Aristocracy in England,* 295–321.

83. Joanna Innes has informed me that she has encountered other "gentlemen" prisoners in her work on debtors' prisons. On the conditions under which gentry could be imprisoned see Cadwallader, "In Pursuit of the Merchant Debtor and Bankrupt," 427, 490–492.

84. William Fennor, *The Compter's Common-Wealth, or a Voiage made to an Infernall Iland long since Discovered by many Captaines, Seafaring-men, Gentlemen, Marchants, and other Tradesmen; But the Conditions, Natures, and Qualities of the People there Inhabiting, and those that Trafficke with them, were Never so Truly Expressed or Lively set foorth* (London, 1617, unpaginated preface, and 27–28. The description of debtor's prison as a "costive creature" is found on 9.

85. Francis Osborne, *Advice to a Son* (London, 1656), 179. Osborne's friend Thomas Hobbes had a strong influence both on his religious views and on his view of nobility and monarchy: "*Fresh Families . . .* cannot be denied to have ascended by the same steps, those did we stile Ancient" and "*All Government now extant, had their foundations laid in the dirt,* though time may have dried it up by oblivion, or flattering Historians lick't it off," 113.

86. Ibid., 32–33, 24–26.

CHAPTER 2: A GENERATION OF VIPERS

1. Guildhall MS 10823/1, Commonplace book of George Boddington, fol. 24.

2. Ibid., fols. 24–25.

3. Ibid., fol. 26.

4. Ibid., fols. 32–33.

5. Wright, *Middle Class Culture,* still one of the best sources on late sixteenth-century trading culture, leaves no doubt as to Elizabethan fears about youth. See 121–200 et passim. See also Susan Brigden, "Youth and the English Reformation," *Past & Present* 95 (1982):37–67.

6. This was not a new theme. See for example the 1616 model letter book by Thomas Gainsford, *The Secretaries Studie: Containing New Familiar Epistles or Directions for the Formall, Orderly, and Iudicious Inditing of Letters,* The English Experience, no. 658 (Amsterdam and Norwood, N.J.: Walter Johnson, Inc., and Theatrum Orbis Terrarum, Ltd., 1974 [orig. pub. 1616]), 55. This is a letter to a son which chides him for keeping bad company, profuse expenses, "intemperate abusing of the time," and getting into debt. The list already has a formulaic sound to it.

7. Trumbach, *Rise of the Egalitarian Family*, 254. Aristocratic parents did voice some concern about morals in the public schools (notably about the boys whoring and learning how to masturbate), however little or nothing was done to respond to these and other perceived problems until the nineteenth century, and at least 75 percent of noble parents continued to send their sons to these schools during this period (ibid., 257–265).

8. Stout, *Autobiography*, 69, 73, 83; Abraham de la Pryme, *The Diary of Abraham de la Pryme, The Yorkshire Antiquary*, Surtees Society Publications, vol. 54 (Durham: Surtees Society, 1870), 66–71.

9. John Fryer's mother was Anglican, whereas his father joined or flirted with the dissenters (Guildhall MS 12017, fol. 9). Both the second and third wives of the Manchester wigmaker, Edmund Harrold, were nonconformists. His second wife vacillated, bickering with Harrold about the frequency with which he took communion and, finally, on her death-bed, asking to be buried at the dissenting meeting house. Harrold prevailed on his third wife to conform. John Harland, ed., *Collectanea Relating to Manchester and its Neighbourhood in Various Periods*, Chetham Society Publications, vol. 68 (Manchester: Chetham Society, 1866), 190. There were many more such cases.

10. Guildhall MS 205, Diary of Stephen Monteage the younger for 1733, fols. 14, 18, 75, 82–83, 88, 150, 269. Other "seekers" include Roger Lowe, a shopkeeper, for whom see his *Diary of Roger Lowe of Ashton-in-Makerfield, Lancashire, 1663–74* (London: Longmans, Green and Co., 1938); Elizabeth Ashbridge, the Quaker schoolteacher and seamstress, for whom see her *Some Account of the Early Part of the Life of Elizabeth Ashbridge;* and Edward Baker, a mathematical instrument maker, whose letterbook for 1779 to 1782 is lodged in the Guildhall Library (Guildhall MS 16927).

11. Thrupp, *Merchant Class of Medieval London*, 164–169. On the introduction of double-entry bookkeeping see Basil Yamey, *Historical Accounting Literature: A Catalogue of the Collection of Early Works on Book-keeping and Accounting in the Library of the Institute of Chartered Accountants in England and Wales, Together with a Bibliography of Literature on the Subject Published Before 1750 and Not in the Institute Library* (London: Mansell, 1975).

12. Daniel Defoe, *The Complete English Tradesman in Familiar Letters, Directing him in all the Several Parts and Progressions of Trade*, 2d ed., 2 vols. (London: Printed for Charles Rivington, 1727, reprinted New York: Augustus M. Kelley, 1969 in facsimile), is much concerned with the dilemma presented by the need to save money and at the same time keep up appearances so that one's creditors will not panic and call in their debts. See for example, vol. 1, vii–viii, 109–126, 142.

13. Glückel, *The Memoirs of Glückel of Hameln*, trans. Marvin Lowenthal (New York: Schocken Books, 1977).

14. The foregoing discussion is based upon Cecil Roth's *Anglo-Jewish Letters (1158–1917)* (London: The Socino Press, 1938), 97–98. The letter is quoted in its entirety by Roth; the original is in the Lansdowne papers in the British Library.

15. For family credit networks and fear of indebtedness among Jewish traders see BL Egerton MSS 2227, Diary and Letterbook of David Mendez Da Costa, war contractor, especially fols. 86, 90–91, consisting of family correspondence from the

late 1750s. For Jewish charities for the relief of imprisoned debtors see Cecil Roth, *A History of the Jews in England* (Oxford: Oxford University Press, 1949), 199.

16. Guildhall MS 9941, Memoranda, Letters and Documents of the Mawhood Family, William Mawhood the elder to William Mawhood the younger (copy), dtd. Dec. 1778; and same to same (copy), dtd. 3 March 1779. The elder Mawhood was an extremely rich man, and the claim of poverty ("I am oblig'd to be as saving as possable"), given the context, should probably be understood either as rhetorical or as very relative.

17. Guildhall MS 9941, Wm. John Darby to William Mawhood the elder, dtd. New York, 7 March 1779.

18. William Mawhood the elder to William Mawhood the younger (copies), dtd. 7 March 1781 and 2 May 1781.

19. Memoranda of William Mawhood the elder dtd. 22 May 1782, 25 February 1783, 3 March 1783, 2 June 1784, 3 June 1784, 3 April 1785 ("Charles was from 3 to 4 in the Maids Room—Joseph [the Porter] was brushing his Cloaths & see this. Charles talked very slightingly of Religion"), 31 May 1785, and 18 Oct. 1788 ("M. _____ says Charles is for ever after common women").

20. Guildhall MS 9941, William Mawhood the elder, memoranda dtd. 3 March 1783, 3 June 1784, 31 May 1785, 2 June 1785, and 9 June 1785.

21. Guildhall MS 9941, William Mawhood the younger to William Mawhood the elder, dtd. St. Quentin, 25 Feb. 1791 (see also William Mawhood the younger to Mrs. Mawhood, dtd. Bruges, 6 Nov. 1790); Memorandum of William Mawhood the elder, dtd. 1796, and bill for lawyer's expenses of 20 Sept. 1796; Account of the examination by the Lunacy Commission, 1796. See also Guildhall MS 9939, consisting of 49 volumes of diaries written by William Mawhood the elder between 1764 and 1790. Selections from these papers have been published as William Mawhood, *The Mawhood Diary. Selections from the Diary Notebooks of William Mawhood, Woollen-Draper of London, for the Years 1764–1790,* Publications of the Catholic Record Society, vol. 50, ed. E. E. Reynolds (London: Privately Printed for the Society, 1956).

22. E. P. Thompson, "Time, Work-Discipline, and Industrial Capitalism," *Past & Present* 38 (1967):58–97, is the best-known of these. One scholar who attempts a broader view is David Landes, *Revolution in Time: Clocks and the Making of the Modern World* (Cambridge, Mass., and London: Belknap Press of Harvard University Press, 1983).

23. Wright, *Middle Class Culture,* 30.

24. Guildhall MS 10823/1, fols. 19, 21. Watches also enjoyed considerable popularity among the early modern aristocracy, both in Britain and on the Continent, but, again, we do not know how much influence the wearing of a watch actually had in altering the way people used their time.

25. Quoted in Seaver, *Wallington's World,* 126. Later Puritans tended to back away from such extreme otherworldliness. Moreover, the sacral, if not salvific, nature of a worldly calling properly pursued was an explicit feature of both Lutheranism and, more famously, Calvinism, almost from their earliest days.

26. Lowe, *Diary,* 1, 16, 35, 55, 58–59, 60, 62, 67, 104–106, 108.

27. Richard Steele, *The Trades-man's Calling Being a Discourse Concerning the Na-*

ture, Necessity, Choice &c. of a Calling in General. Directions for the Right Managing of the Tradesman's Calling in Particular (London, 1684), 72, 79.

28. Bodleian MS Rawlinson C 861, Diary of an anonymous wigmaker. See for example the notations for 11 Oct. and 18 Oct. 1707. This is a religious diary doubling as an account book.

29. For more on appointment calendars see below p. 184.

30. Dr. Williams's Library Henry MSS 90.4, Letterbook of Sarah Savage, fol. 8, Sarah Savage to Phil. Savage, dtd. 5 Aug. 1712. Sarah Savage was the daughter of the prominent dissenting minister, Matthew Henry.

31. Ibid., fol. 9, Sarah Savage to Phil. Savage, dtd. 15 Jan. 1713/14.

32. Ibid., fol. 11, Sarah Savage to Phil. Savage, dtd. Dec. 1714 [*sic.*, actually January 1714/15].

33. Ibid., fol. 12, Sarah Savage to Phil. Savage, dtd. 5 Oct. 1715 (the italics are not in the original).

34. Ibid., fol. 15, Sarah Savage to her daughter, Mrs. Wilton, undated, but written after 1714.

35. John Wesley was well known for his obsession with time discipline, and especially with early rising. For this see Henry Abelove, *Evangelist of Desire: John Wesley and the Methodists* (Stanford, Calif.: Stanford University Press, 1990), 96, 99–102. For time management later in the century see Henry Longden, *The Life of Henry Longden, Late of Sheffield, Compiled from his Own Memoirs* (Liverpool: Thomas Kaye, 1813). Mrs. Longden, Henry's mother, encouraged him to keep a diary from the age of nine (which would have been in the 1760s): "I wrote a faithful register of every hour . . . [and] found a pleasure in reflecting upon the hours of my improvement; and I reviewed with equal shame the hours spent in foolish plays and diversions" (3). Sarah Trimmer's *An Easy Introduction to the Knowledge of Nature, and Reading the Holy Scriptures. Adapted to the Capacities of Children* (London: T. Longman, 1793) tries to teach children respect for time by having a figure ostentatiously look at his watch and announce that it is time for breakfast (54). Bees are considered to be especially useful animals as "they do not saunter away their time, but take care of their families, and build houses" (82). Trimmer also includes a detailed description of how a watch is constructed (156–158). See also Gordon Rattray-Taylor, *The Angel Makers: A Study in the Psychological Origins of Historical Change, 1750–1850* (New York: E.P. Dutton & Co., 1974), 115–135.

36. See for example Dr. Williams's Library Doddridge Collection MS L/4, fol. 195, S. Clark to Philip Doddridge, Jr., undated but from around 1752, reproving him for "a growing negligence in the Improvement of yr Time, & Attention to yr Studies" and for not allowing himself "Time for Business" (i.e., studies) before breakfast. This is one of a number of letters from friends and relatives alluding to "Philly's" laxness in respect to time. The Doddridge family was, however, somewhat straitlaced.

37. For an effort to interest elite women in better time management see Joseph Addison and Richard Steele, *The Spectator,* no. 15 (17 March 1710/11), ed. Donald F. Bond, (Oxford: Clarendon Press, 1965), vol. 1, 66–68.

38. *Aris's Birmingham Gazette,* 7 Jan. 1760, quoted in Rowlands, *Masters and Men in the West Midland Metalware Trades,* 86.

39. Dr. Williams's Library Doddridge Collection MS L1/7, fol. 77, Richard

Maris to Mrs. Mercy Doddridge, dtd. Worcester, 23 July 1765. See also Guildhall MS 9941, William Mawhood the elder to William Mawhood the younger, dtd. London, 3 March 1779, in which Mawhood encourages his son to learn to write clearly and spell correctly.

40. BRO Acc. No. 26226, Samuel Lowder to William Prattinton, Bristol, dtd. 11 Feb. 1772.

41. Ibid., Samuel Lowder to William Prattinton 18 March 1775; and same to same, 30 April 1775.

42. Steele, *Trades-man's Calling*, 40.

43. For some speculations on the impact of literacy on worldviews see Carlo Ginzburg, *The Cheese and the Worms: The Cosmos of a Sixteenth-Century Miller*, trans. John and Anne Tedeschi (Baltimore: Johns Hopkins Press, 1980). See also Spufford, *Contrasting Communities*, 206–218, 318; and Elizabeth Eisenstein, *The Printing Press as an Agent of Change: Communications and Cultural Transformations in Early-Modern Europe*, 2 vols. (Cambridge and New York: Cambridge University Press, 1979). Others have been more skeptical about the cognitive and epistemological significance of reading. See especially the remarkable study by Sylvia Scribner and Michael Cole, *The Psychology of Literacy* (Cambridge, Mass.: Harvard University Press, 1981), 234–260, which suggests that how literacy is used is as crucial for changing patterns of thought as the simple fact of whether people can read and write. Scribner and Cole show that other variables that often, but not always, accompany literacy, such as the experience of living in an urban center or of attending school, are just as salient or more salient than literacy itself in determining research subjects' ability to perform certain specialized cognitive tasks. David Cressy, "Literacy in Context: Meaning and Measurement in Early Modern England," in Brewer and Porter, *Consumption and the World of Goods*, 305–319, reminds us how very many illiterate people functioned perfectly successfully in the seventeenth and eighteenth centuries.

44. Sidney Pollard, *The Genesis of Modern Management: A Study of the Industrial Revolution in Great Britain* (London: Edward Arnold, 1965), has a very full discussion of both middling and elite interest in bookkeeping; see 56, 112–116, 122–123, 129, 138, 209–249. For numeracy more generally see Patricia Cline Cohen, "Reckoning with Commerce: Numeracy in Eighteenth-Century America," in Brewer and Porter, *Consumption and the World of Goods*, 320–334.

45. *Advice to the Women and Maidens of London. Shewing, that Instead of their Usual Pastime; and Education in Needlework, Lace and Point-making, It were Far more Necessary and Profitable to Apply Themselves to the Right Understanding and Practice of the Method of Keeping Books of Account: Whereby, Either Single, or Married, They may Know their Estates, Carry on their Trades, and Avoid the Danger of a Helpless and Forlorn Condition, Incident to Widows . . . By One of that Sex* (London, 1678), 3.

46. Ibid., 2.

47. For magic and credit see pp. 34–35.

48. Josiah Child, *Brief Observations Concerning Trade and Interest of Money* (London, 1668), 4–5.

49. For an impressive series of single-entry estate accounts from the turn of the eighteenth century, kept by a gentry woman in her own hand, see B.L. Add. MSS 45,718, Diary of Elizabeth Freke. One among several books on accounting de-

signed for the gentry and aristocracy is Roger North, *The Gentleman Accomptant; An Essay to Unfold the Mystery of Accompts. By Way of Debtor or Creditor, Commonly Called Merchants Accompts, and Applying the Same to the Concerns of the Nobility and Gentry of England. Shewing I. The Great Advantages of Gentlemens Keeping their own Accompts, with Directions to Persons of Quality and Fortune. II. The Ruin that Attends Men of Estate by Neglect of Accompts. III. The Usefulness of the Knowledge of Accompts, to Such as are Any Way Employed in the Publick Affairs of the Nation. IV. Of Banks . . . V. Of Stocks and Stock-Jobbing . . . VI. A Short and Easy Vocabulary* (London: E. Curll, 1714).

50. *Advice to the Women and Maidens of London*, 3, 14. The author adds, "*Shee* that is so well versed in this as to keep the accounts of her Cash right and dayly entred in a book fair without blotting, will soon be fit for greater undertakings."

51. Guildhall MS 10823/1, fols. 19, 32.

52. BRO, Acc. No. 26226, Samuel Lowder to William Prattinton, dtd. Bristol 7 July 1771. See also same to same, dtd. Bristol, 30 Jan. 1772.

53. See Guildhall MS 10823/1, fol. 33, on a man in Aleppo in the late seventeenth century who "keept no books[,] owing much money." Accounts had for some time been admissable as evidence in some courts, as numerous Chancery cases show.

54. Charlotte Charke, *The Lover's Treat: Or Unnatural Hatred, Being a True Narrative as Deliver'd to the Author by One of the Family Who was Principally Concern'd in the Following Account* (London: Bailey's Printing Office, ca. 1758), 6. The "unnatural hatred" of the title is the enmity the hero's brother Anthony feels for his virtuous brother George, on account of the latter's "good Behaviour and Assiduity in Business." Anthony, for his part, makes "Pleasure his only study," lies, cheats, and consorts with whores.

55. Basil S. Yamey, H. C. Edey, and Hugh W. Thomson, *Accounting in England and Scotland: 1543–1800: Double Entry in Exposition and Practice* (London: Sweet & Maxwell, 1963).

56. Ibid., 3.

57. Defoe, *Complete English Tradesman*, vol. 1, Supplement (separately paginated), 31.

58. Ibid., vol. 1, Supplement, 34.

59. Samuel Pepys, *The Diary of Samuel Pepys*, ed. Robert Latham and William Matthews (London: Bell & Hyman, 1970–1983), vol. 3, 40 (entry for 3 March 1662). Pepys makes frequent reference to the keeping of personal accounts.

60. See especially Appleby, *Economic Thought and Ideology*, 80–83, on Mun, Petty, and others and their attempts to subject economic processes to "scientific" analysis.

61. Quoted in Geoffrey Howson, *A History of Mathematics Education in England* (Cambridge: Cambridge University Press, 1982), 5.

62. See for example John Crowne, *City Politiques. A Comedy* (London, 1683), 10. Sir Samuel Forecast in Charles Sedley's *The Mulberry Garden, a Comedy* (London, 1668) is a citizen turned gentleman who is unable to shed his obsessive need to look at everything in terms of future profit.

63. Philip Doddridge, *Sermons to Young Persons* (London: R. Hett, 1734), 37–38.

64. For a discussion of aristocrats as more concerned consumers of education see Trumbach, *Rise of the Egalitarian Family*, 275–281. A. C. Beveridge, "Childhood and Society in Eighteenth Century Scotland," in John Dwyer, ed., *New Perspectives*

on the Politics and Culture of Early Modern Scotland (Edinburgh: J. Donald, 1982), 273–274, 280–283, supplies useful comparative information on Scotland at the same time. As both Trumbach and Beveridge make clear, however, scholarship was seldom parents' sole concern. It was matched or exceeded by a concern for morals and health.

65. R. Campbell, *The London Tradesman: Being a Compendious View of all the Trades, Professions, Arts . . . Calculated for the Information of Parents, and Instruction of Youth in their Choice of Business* (London: T. Gardner, 1747), 4–5, 86, 93, 277. See also Joseph Collyer, *Parents & Guardians Directory and the Youths Guide in the Choice of a Profession or Trade* (London: R. Griffiths, 1761), 6, 21. Josiah Wedgwood, *Letters to Bentley, 1771–1780* (Didsbury, Manchester: E.J. Morten and Wedgwood Museum, 1903), 550; Wedgwood to Richard Bentley, dtd. 28 Nov. 1779. Still, after some initial reluctance, Wedgwood ended up having his own sons tutored in Latin.

66. On mercantile, professional, and trades representation at Westminster School in the eighteenth century see Trumbach, *Rise of the Egalitarian Family*, 264.

67. See for example John Heylyn (b. 1712), a Bristol copper merchant, whose educational perambulations are outlined in BRL MS B11871. Heylyn was educated initially at Marlborough School. He and his brother were then sent to Geneva to learn French, mathematics, and drawing, and Heylyn finished off learning merchants' accounts at Watts' Academy in London. He was finally apprenticed in Bristol. Heylyn's grandfather was a citizen and saddler of London who apparently made his large fortune through army contracts.

68. Dr. Williams's Library Doddridge Collection L1/7, fol. 14, Eliza Kennedy to Philip Doddridge, dtd. Edinburgh, 12 March 1747.

69. Ibid., fol. 16, same to same, dtd. 19 Dec. 1747. The boy was the son of William Kennedy of Barbados.

70. *Public Advertiser*, no. 6609 (Friday, 2 Jan. 1756).

71. For the proprietorial schools see especially Money, "Teaching in the Market-Place," 335–377.

72. Guildhall MS 11021/1, George A. Gibbs the elder to George Gibbs the younger, dtd. Exeter, 27 April 1769. For Vicary Gibbs's later career see the DNB.

73. Dr. Williams's Library Doddridge Collection MS L1/7, fol. 167, Job Orton to Mrs. Mercy Doddridge, dtd. 1 Nov. 1752.

74. BRO Acc. No. 26226, Samuel Lowder to William Prattinton, dtd. Bristol, 11 Feb. 1772.

75. For a discussion of middling reading tastes see pp. 178–182, 188–190.

76. The moral and emotional strains of sustaining this intermediary position are especially well described in Ryder, *Diary*.

77. William Mountague, *The Delights of Holland: Or a Three Months Travel About That and the Other Provinces with Observations and Reflections on their Trade, Wealth, Strength, Beauty, Policy & c. Together with a Catalogue of the Rarities in the Anatomical School at Leyden* (London, 1696), 180; see also 63–64. Mountague thought these "private bridewells" a very good idea; he also approved of Amsterdam's "fool-house" ("nowhere else to be found in the world," 172) and its perpetual labor prisons,

where criminals were forced to work by whipping, starving, or (allegedly) threat of immersion in special tanks where they had to pump constantly to keep from being drowned (174). The drowning tanks were almost certainly apocryphal. On this see Pieter Spierenburg *The Prison Experience: Disciplinary Institutions and Their Inmates in Early Modern Europe* (New Brunswick and London: Rutgers University Press, 1991), 98–104.

78. Bodleian MS Rawlinson D 34, Diary of John-Baptiste Grano, 1728–1729, fol. 5.

79. Ibid., fols. 34, 42.

80. Ibid., fol. 97.

81. Ibid., fol. 31.

82. Ibid., fol. 20. The British Library's copy of George Parker's *West-India Almanack for the Year 1719* has tipped into it the following handwritten poem, dated 4 Dec. 1719:

A Prison is a House of Care;
A Place where none can Thrive;
A Touchstone there to try a Friend;
A Grave for men Alive.

He that the worth of Friends would know,
Must for Instruction to a Prison Go;
The Want of Friends, the Worth of Friends do show.

83. Cressy, *Coming Over*, 263–295.

84. Richenda Gurney, "Journal," quoted in Janet Whitney, *Elizabeth Fry, Quaker Heroine* (Boston: Little Brown, 1936), 25. Richenda was the sister of Elizabeth Fry, the reformer.

85. Edith B. Gelles, "Gossip: An Eighteenth-Century Case," *Journal of Social History* 22 (1989):667–683.

86. For a more detailed discussion of prostitution and the way it allegedly destroyed families see pp. 112–113, 163.

87. There is not the space here to deal with this large literature. For a good recent summary see Roy Porter, "Consumption: Disease of the Consumer Society" in Brewer and Porter, *Consumption and the World of Goods*, 78n–79n. *The Onania* itself, of which numerous copies are extant, remains one of the great sources for studying eighteenth-century sexual beliefs and fears.

88. Somerset Record Office MS DD/SAS/C/1193/4, "Memoir of the Birth, Education, Life and Death of Mr. John Cannon, Sometime Officer of the Excise and Writing Master," fol. 29. The episode was said to have taken place in 1695. Cannon had probably read *Onania: Or the Heinous Sin of Self-Pollution* by the time he recounted it many years later, and he situated his retelling within a moralistic framework that stressed the divine ordination of gender complimentarity (and hence heterosexuality) and the necessity to "marry and live chaste and then shalt thou see the happy fruit of thy body to the 3d or 4th generations." I am grateful to John Brewer for bringing John Cannon's memoir to my attention. Cannon's life is wonderfully and complexly evoked in Money, "Teaching in the Market-Place," 347–366; moreover the chapter contains plates of Cannon's original manuscript (see plates 17.5 through 17.9).

89. Trumbach, *Rise of the Egalitarian Family*, 259–260.

90. Compare *The London Bawd: With her Character and Life: Discovering the Various and Subtle Intrigues of Lewd Women* (London: John Gwilliam, 1705), which features archaic-sounding tales about the cuckolding of citizens, with Edmund Curll's *Cases of Divorce for Several Causes* (London: E. Curll, 1715), a series of retrospectives about the sex life of aristocrats that includes pornographic love letters, flagellation, sex with footmen, links to the French court, and conversions to Catholicism. For more on Curll see p. 212. For "anti-aristocratic" Reformation of Manners sermons see p. 120. For advice books see, among others, James Fordyce, *The Character and Conduct of the Female Sex, and the Advantages to be Derived by Young Men from the Society of Virtuous Women* (London: T. Cadell, 1776); and Campbell, *London Tradesman*, 4–5, 86, 93, 277. For a feminist slant on the same themes see *An Essay in Defence of the Female Sex in which are Inserted the Characters of a Pedant, a Vertuoso, a Squire, a Poetaster, a Beau, a City-Critick, &c.* (New York: Source Book Press, 1970 [orig. 1696]), 66–72.

91. Michel Foucault, *The History of Sexuality* vol. 1, *An Introduction*, trans. Robert Hurley (London: Allen Lane, Penguin, 1979). On the polymorphous character of desire in the early modern period see Alan Bray, *Homosexuality in Renaissance England* (New York: Columbia University Press, 1995), especially 134–136n.

92. BL Add. MSS 19211, Diary and Letterbook of Gervase Leveland, fols. 10–12. See for example Mr. W. Day to Gervase Leveland (copy), dtd. Paris, 16 Sept. 1764: "je suis en attendant, que j'ay le plaisir de vous presse dans mes Bras, pour jamais le plus de voue de vos amis et ce luy que par l'amitie vous sera le plus attache [*sic*]."

93. Ibid., fols. 58–59, Mr. Worrell to Gervase Leveland, dtd. 18 June 1765.

94. Eve Kosofsky Sedgwick, *Between Men: English Literature and Male Homosocial Desire* (New York and Guildford: Columbia University Press, 1985); Eve Kosofsky Sedgwick, *Epistemology of the Closet* (New York and London: Harvester Wheatsheaf, 1991).

95. For a more detailed discussion of this phenomenon see p. 115.

96. BL Add. MSS 19211, fol. 17. Leveland is probably quoting here from the sayings of Confucius, a popular mid-eighteenth-century addition to the moral canon that seemed to confirm the universality of standard bourgeois morality.

97. Dr. Williams's Library Doddridge Collection, L1/3 fol. 104, William Enfield to Mr. Humphreys, undated, 1770s.

98. *A Dialogue Concerning the Subjection of Women to their Husbands . . . in Which is Interspersed Some Observations on Courtship, for the Use of the Batchelors* (London, John Wilkie: 1765), 14–15, 20.

99. Guildhall MS 11021/1, George A. Gibbs the elder to George Gibbs the younger, dtd. 27 April 1769, 9 May 1769, and 21 Jan. 1774.

100. Jeremy Bentham, *Works*, ed. John Bowring (Edinburgh: William Tait, 1843), vol. 10, 77 (from his Commonplace Book for 1774–75). Bentham was then between 21 and 23 years old.

101. The more heterodox route went through romanticism, political radicalism, free thinking, and sometimes even "free love" to an, at times, extremely critical view of "bourgeois" morality.

102. Davidoff and Hall, *Family Fortunes*.

CHAPTER 3: MIDDLING DAUGHTERS AND THE FAMILY ECONOMY

1. BRL MS 319718, Letterbook of Caleb Dickinson. Dickinson was a Jamaica merchant.

2. On the dating of the two series see Jack Lindsay, *Hogarth: His Art and His World* (New York: Taplinger, 1979), 56–61 and 82–95. The original paintings of *A Harlot's Progress*, from which the engravings were made, were destroyed by fire in 1755. The paintings of *A Rake's Progress* are in Sir John Soane's Museum, London.

3. Hogarth spent part of his adolescence in the Fleet, where his father was imprisoned for debt. See Ronald Paulson, *Popular and Polite Art in the Age of Hogarth and Fielding*, University of Notre Dame Ward-Phillips Lectures in English Language and Literature, vol. 10 (Notre Dame and London: University of Notre Dame Press, 1979), 22.

4. With one child already and another on the way, her options for employment would have been few. On the other hand, Hogarth exaggerates Moll's isolation. In "real life," prostitutes were often well integrated into their urban communities; many married, and some enjoyed the support of their families. See Judith Walkowitz, *Prostitution and Victorian Society: Women, Class, and the State* (Cambridge and New York: Cambridge University Press, 1980), 192–210. The patterns of neighborhood treatment of prostitutes described by Walkowitz as obtaining prior to the passage of the Contagious Diseases Acts (1864–1869) were almost certainly of long standing.

5. The only time Moll takes any real initiative is in plate 2, when she diverts the Jewish merchant whose mistress she is by knocking over a table, so as to permit another lover to exit unobserved. On Hogarth and antisemitism, particularly jokes about Jews being tricked by prostitutes, see Lindsay, *Hogarth*, 60; Ronald Paulson, *The Art of Hogarth* (London: Phaidon, 1975), commentary on plate 24; and Frank Felsenstein, *Anti-Semitic Stereotypes: A Paradigm of Otherness in English Popular Culture, 1660–1830* (Baltimore and London: Johns Hopkins University Press, 1995), 53–55.

6. See, for example, Edward Shorter, *The Making of the Modern Family* (London: Collins, 1976), 68–70, 74–75. Shorter insists upon the fundamental passivity of women in relation to the world outside the home, then argues, confusingly, that wives were both "all-powerful" and subservient in their own households. Roy Porter, "Rape—Does It Have a Historical Meaning?" in Sylvana Tomaselli and Roy Porter, eds. *Rape* (Oxford: Blackwell, 1986), 231, has a more "psychological" verdict:

> While men doubtless plumed themselves upon their superiority, the vast majority of women acquiesced—how willingly is hard to say—in their own subordinate status, hidden from history, acting out their own idealizations of womanhood: virgin, wife, mother.

But see also his statement, 234, "History shows women victimized but not powerless."

7. Katharine M. Rogers, *Feminism in Eighteenth-Century England* (Urbana, Chicago, and London: University of Illinois Press, 1982), 210.

8. On Addison and Steele see Shevelow, *Women and Print Culture*, 93–145; and, for a more sympathetic view, Rogers, *Feminism in Eighteenth-Century England*, 30, 60, 120–124. On David and James Fordyce see Margaret R. Hunt, "English Urban Families in Trade, 1660–1800: The Culture of Early Modern Capitalism," Ph.D. diss.,

New York University, 1986, 203–210, 246–253. Dr. Gregory is usually encountered today by way of the scathing critique of him by Mary Wollstonecraft; see *A Vindication of the Rights of Women,* ed. Carol H. Poston (New York and London: W.W. Norton, 1975 [orig. pub. 1792]), 28–34.

9. "Heterosocial" is used here to mean social and cultural interactions that include people of both sexes. (Conversely, "homosocial" refers to all-male or all-female social and cultural interactions.) In eighteenth-century advice books for women the ideal friendship in and out of marriage was invariably between a wise and benevolent older man and a grateful younger woman. Some moralists actively discouraged women from having female friends; see Shevelow, *Women and Print Culture,* 96–97.

10. Other sources were both more sympathetic to women and more genuinely informative. For example, *A Treatise of Feme Coverts, or, the Lady's Law* (London: E. and R. Nutt and R. Gosling for B. Lintot, 1732), aimed to inform "the fair Sex . . . how to preserve their Lands, Goods, and most valuable Effects, from the Incroachments of anyone" (vii). This and other sources are discussed in Amy Louise Erickson, "Common Law versus Common Practice: The Use of Marriage Settlements in Early Modern England," *Economic History Review,* 2d ser. 43 (1990):26, and in her important study, *Women and Property in Early Modern England,* 104–106.

11. Sarah Fielding, *The Governess, or Little Female Academy* (London: Pandora Press, 1987), 2.

12. Ibid., 15.

13. Ibid., 16–17, 25–28, 116.

14. Ibid., 44–52. This story actually ends happily in a sort of ménage à trois, but only because the two women manage to reconcile while the husband is away.

15. On families see ibid., 122–126. On women who envy and seek to undermine other women, see 56, 58, 64, 70–71, 97–98.

16. Ibid., 123; emphasis added.

17. The edition cited here is *The History of Little Goody Two-Shoes; Otherwise Called Mrs. Margery Twoshoes. With the Means by which she Acquired her Learning and Wisdom, and in Consequence thereof her Estate,* facsimile of a 1787 edition (New York: Meriden Gravure Co. for G. K. Hall, 1969). For the book's publication history see Wilbur Macey Stone, *The History of Little Goody Two-Shoes: An Essay and a List of Editions* (Worcester, Mass.: American Antiquarian Society, 1940), 5–6, 28–40.

18. *History of Little Goody Two-Shoes,* 46–49.

19. Ibid., 46–49.

20. Ibid., 142.

21. Ibid., 84–96.

22. For Defoe and the role of the tradesman's wife, see pp. 155–156. For Addison and Steele's view of female moral influence see *Spectator,* no. 4 (5 March 1711), Bond ed., vol. 1, 18–22; no. 10 (12 March 1711), Bond ed., vol. 1, 44–47; no. 57 (5 May 1711), Bond ed., vol. 1, 241–244; and no. 510 (15 Oct. 1712), Bond ed., vol. 4, 311–314. The Fordyce brothers probably developed the theme of women's positive moral influence most systematically. See David Fordyce, *Dialogues Concerning Education* (London: T. Cadell, 1745), vol. 1, 50, 86, 288–289, 315; and James Fordyce, *Character and Conduct of the Female Sex,* 9–10, 36, 83–85 et passim.

23. Stout, *Autobiography*, 67–68, 76. I have benefited considerably from the excellent discussion of the gender economy of the Stout family found in Hill, *Women, Work and Sexual Politics*, 32–33, 226–227.

24. Ibid., 68–70, 76. For some useful comments on the differential in education and literacy of girls versus boys see R. A. Houston, *Literacy in Early Modern Europe: Culture and Education 1500–1800* (London and New York: Longman, 1988), 7, 19–22, 38–39, 73–75 et passim.

25. Stout, *Autobiography*, 68–69, 72–73. For Ellin's prodigious capacity for work see 87, 89, 90, 96, 102, 105 et passim; on her several offers of marriage see 87; on loans to her brother see 89. Although plagued by ill health, Ellin seems to have enjoyed the very considerable respect and affection of her family, and judging from the large numbers of people who attended her burial, she was deeply respected by her coreligionists (the Quakers) as well. She was no pathetic drudge, and she clearly possessed an independent spirit. Although she devoted herself in life to assisting her brothers, on her death she bequeathed her money to her five nieces (191–192).

26. Ibid., 192. Further evidence for this pattern of keeping girls at home to work while sending boys to school is found in an occupational census of 1787, done in the county of Westmorland. It shows, over and over, farming households in which all or most of the boys were in school while the girls, almost without exception, were described as "knitters." These were relatively better-off families, but even in the families of laborers, where it was more likely that all children would have had to work, boys were much more likely to be listed in the census as "scholars." In Westmorland, where the local economy relied heavily on hand-knitting, spinning, and, increasingly, factory work, girls' disproportionate lack of formal schooling may have been more extreme than it was elsewhere. But there is no reason to think that the pattern did not hold more generally. See Willan, *An Eighteenth-Century Shopkeeper*, 62–63.

27. Lowe, *Diary*, 24.

28. Patricia Meyer Spacks, *Imagining a Self: Autobiography and Novel in Eighteenth-Century England* (Cambridge, Mass., and London: Harvard University Press, 1976), 158, suggests, on the basis of women's autobiographies and novels, that female fear is "not of absence of power but of failure of goodness and consequent loss of love." Not all the sources suggest this: for instance, court cases present very explicit instances of pursuit of power by women, along with much evidence that they feared its absence and its loss. There is a certain amount of conflicting evidence as to the *degree* of differential distribution of resources within the family. Thus, Amy Erickson finds that the value of men's bequests to sons and daughters was similar and that probate accounts do not support the notion that economies in rearing were made at the expense of girls (Erickson, *Women and Property in Early Modern Europe*, 19, 59–60, 68–78). But my sources suggest that the temporary commitment to gender equity apparently inspired by the act of drawing up a will was not necessarily sustained in more mundane transfers of resources between parents and their offspring.

29. Stout, *Autobiography*, 68–69. For Charke see p. 97.

30. Ambrose Barnes, *Memoirs of the Life of Mr. Ambrose Barnes Late Merchant and Sometime Alderman of Newcastle Upon Tyne*, Surtees Society Publications, vol. 1, ed.

"M.R." (Durham: Andrew & Co., 1867), 69. Sewing was often linked to women's alleged stay-at-home proclivities. See for example Addison and Steele, *Spectator*, no. 606 (13 Oct. 1714) Bond ed., vol. 5, 72–73. Analogies between women and animals such as tortoises and snails that, as it were, carried their homes on their backs seem to have been common. For other examples see Crawford, *Women and Religion in England*, 41–42.

31. On the importance of sewing for one woman of the lesser gentry see Amanda Vickery, "Women and the World of Goods: A Lancashire Consumer and Her Possessions, 1751–81," in Brewer and Porter, *Consumption and the World of Goods*, 282–283.

32. There is a large and diverse literature on these topics. I have benefited particularly from the following: James C. Scott, *Weapons of the Weak: Everyday Forms of Peasant Resistance* (New Haven: Yale University Press, 1985); Eugene D. Genovese, *Roll Jordan Roll: The World the Slaves Made* (London: Deutsch, 1975); Thompson, *Making of the English Working Class;* and Natalie Zemon Davis, *Society and Culture in Early Modern France* (Stanford, Calif.: Stanford University Press, 1975).

33. See pp. 157–162 for a discussion of women's separate property.

34. Hunt, "Wife-Beating, Domesticity and Women's Independence," 10–33.

35. It is an agreeable fantasy, but in the end unrealistic to think that mothers will always identify with their daughters simply because they share the same sex. This is not universally the case even in relatively sexually egalitarian societies, and it may be even less the case in more patriarchal ones, where mothers are often under heavy pressure to focus more attention and resources on boys, and where they stand, over the long run, to gain rewards for themselves by doing so.

36. David Cressy, *Literacy and the Social Order: Reading and Writing in Tudor and Stuart England* (Cambridge: Cambridge University Press, 1980), 176–177; R. S. Schofield, "Dimensions of Illiteracy, 1750–1850," *Explorations in Economic History* 10 (1973):442–443, 445–446. Efforts to quantify literacy, which are largely based upon ability to sign parish registers, petitions, or other documents, are hampered by the fact that most educational institutions taught children to read before they taught them to write. Those children likely to be taken out of school after only a year or two to work (girls, the poor) were, therefore, especially likely to be able to read but not write. A term like "literacy," although hard to dispense with, bestows a false sense of specificity upon these discussions. For a typical family in which the husband (in this case, an excise officer) was highly literate and numerate and the wife was only just able to compose a letter, see Avon Central Library, Bristol, B 25415, Letters of Badnall Family, 1720s–1730s.

37. Schofield, "Dimensions of Illiteracy," 446, 448–451; Cressy, *Literacy and the Social Order,* 176.

38. For "lumping" see Schofield, "Dimensions of Illiteracy," 450. Cressy, *Literacy and the Social Order,* 107, 113, 119–121, generally does the same although see 115–116, where he does attempt a gender breakdown, and 224n, where he discusses the very real methodological problems. Earle, "The Female Labour Market in London," 333–336, 343–344. R. A. Houston finds a similar picture outside London, observing that, among Assize deponents in the Northern Circuit between 1640 and 1750, "the literate female is an easily identifiable if not invariable type: probably a city dweller . . . , [and] the daughter, wife or widow of a gentleman, apothecary, or

high status tradesman or craftsman such as a goldsmith or merchant." R. A. Houston, "Aspects of Society in Scotland and North-east England, c. 1550–1750: Social Structure, Literacy and Geographical Mobility," Ph.D. diss., Cambridge University, 1981, 241–242.

39. Schofield, "Dimensions of Illiteracy," 445–446. Schofield found consistently rising literacy in market towns throughout England (449). On rising London literacy see Earle, "The Female Labour Market," 335. Earle found that the literacy of London women (measured by ability to sign their names) increased from 34.2 percent before 1640 to 62.5 percent after 1680; it was higher within the walls and among the London-born. According to R. A. Houston, in Central London by the 1750s, 92 percent of grooms could sign their names in full along with 74 percent of brides (Houston, *Literacy in Early Modern Europe*, 140).

40. Quaker marriage registers after 1754 show 100 percent literacy for both women and men. See Lawrence Stone, "Literacy and Education in England, 1640–1900," *Past and Present* 42 (1969):80.

41. On alleged feminine religious credulity see Natalie Zemon Davis, "City Women and Religious Change," in her *Society and Culture in Early Modern France*, 65–95, especially 65–67. For bawdy women see Wright, *Middle Class Culture*, 112–113, 277–278.

42. For the larger European context see Harry C. Payne, *The French Philosophes and the People* (New Haven and London: Yale University Press, 1976), 94–116. On the other hand, some masters and mistresses went out of their way, usually for religious reasons, to have their servants taught to read. See J. Jean Hecht, *The Domestic Servant Class in Eighteenth-Century England* (Westport, Conn.: Hyperion Press, 1981 [orig. 1956]), 99–100.

43. There was some concern about the reading matter of young men, especially during the Movement for Reformation of Manners and the later Evangelical Movement. Men's reading habits never generated the degree of interest that women's did, however. On the history of press censorship in relation to questions of gender see Margaret R. Hunt, "The De-eroticization of Women's Liberation: Social Purity Movements and the Revolutionary Feminism of Sheila Jeffreys," *Feminist Review*, no. 34 (1990):23–46.

44. Shevelow, *Women and Print Culture*, 43–49.

45. Guildhall MS 16937, fol. 4, Zelophead Wyeth Vincent to Jemima Vincent, dtd. London, 12 March 1813. The tone of Vincent's letter suggests that he may not have thought that Jemima would cooperate easily. For a sensitive discussion of girls' and women's contributions to enterprises, as well as to specifically household tasks, see Davidoff and Hall, *Family Fortunes*, 279–289. For women as teachers see 293–299; on using love to control see 329–330.

46. Guildhall MS 16937, fol. 4, Zelophead Wyeth Vincent to Jemima Vincent, dtd. London, 12 March 1813.

47. See e.g., *The Female Jockey Club or a Sketch of the Manners of the Age* (London: D. I. Eaton, 1794), 188–195, for a standard attack on bluestockings. Zelophead Vincent had a schoolteacher aunt of whom he writes, "I do not remember hearing of any offers [of marriage] my Aunt ever had; she was too learned for gentlemen in those days" (Guildhall MS 16937, "A Sketch of the History of my Maternal Ancestors by Z. W. Vincent." John Gregory, *A Father's Legacy to his Daughters* (London: W.

Strahan and T. Cadell, 1774), 31, advises learned women to "keep it a profound secret, especially from men."

48. Guildhall MS 11021/1, Eleanora Hucks to Dorothea Hucks, 25 March 1778 (unfoliated). The Huckses were related to the Gibbs family of Exeter who were merchants and professionals.

49. See Brewer, *Sinews of Power*, 68, 259n, for a woman clerk; but this was unusual. *An Essay in Defence of the Female Sex*, by "A Lady," goes so far as to suggest that women be educated to take the places of male clerks in the offices and counting houses. This is an idea with little positive resonance today, but coming at a time when secretarial work had not yet become "dead-end," it was at least partly intended to gain women an entré into the expanding world of commerce and the government bureaucracy (36).

50. For supplicatory letters by women see p. 153. Vickery, "Women and the World of Goods," 279–280, 286, 288, 290–291, shows some of the other ways literacy could affect the lives of eighteenth-century women. For a recent biography of one of the more famous polemical women of the eighteenth century see Bridget Hill, *The Republican Virago: The Life and Times of Catharine Macaulay, Historian* (Oxford and New York: Clarendon Press, 1992).

51. William Matthews, *British Diaries: An Annotated Bibliography of British Diaries Written Between 1442 and 1942* (Berkeley and Los Angeles: University of California Press, 1950), contains an impressive number of women's diaries for the late seventeenth and eighteenth centuries.

52. See especially Ruth Perry, *Women, Letters and the Novel* (New York: AMS Press, 1980); Ruth Perry, *The Celebrated Mary Astell: An Early English Feminist* (Chicago and London: University of Chicago Press, 1986); Rogers, *Feminism in Eighteenth-Century England;* and Alice Browne, *The Eighteenth-Century Feminist Mind* (Brighton: Harvester, 1987).

53. On seventeenth-century women who learned accounting see Bridget Hill, "A Refuge from Men: The Idea of a Protestant Nunnery," *Past and Present* 117 (1987):110–111.

54. *Advice to the Women and Maidens of London*, 3. See pp. 58–59 for a more extensive discussion of this tract.

55. J. C. Hodgson, ed., *Six North Country Diaries*, Surtees Society Publications, vol. 118 (Durham: Surtees Society, 1910), 92, entry dtd. 16 Nov. 1717. Thomlinson also took an interest in trade and canal projects (155).

56. Stout, *Autobiography*, 209. Such sentiments seem to have been relatively common throughout the century. In the late eighteenth century Mary Robinson, then in her teens and having fled with her profligate husband to relatives to escape their creditors, was taunted with the words "I had better think of getting my bread; women of no fortune had no right to follow the pursuits of fine ladies. Tom had better married a good tradesman's daughter than the child of a ruined merchant who was not capable of earning a living." Mary Robinson, *Memoirs of Mary Robinson "Perdita,"* ed. J. Fitzgerald Molloy (London and Philadelphia: Gibbings and Co. and J. B. Lippincott, 1895), 94.

57. Dr. Williams's Library Doddridge Collection, L1/4, fol. 102, John Birkett to Philip Doddridge, dtd. Poolbank, 12 Jan. 1744/5; see also fol. 104, J. Birkett to P. Doddridge, dtd. Kendall, 15 March 1755/6; fol. 151, Wright and S. Burkitt [*sic*] to

Mrs. Doddridge, dtd. London, 22 Jan. 1768, and L1/4 fol. 153, Miss Margaret Burkitt to Miss [Mercy] Doddridge, 15 Jan. 1777. To my knowledge, no systematic work has been done on this question, but it does seem logical that girls without brothers would fare better in terms of education, job training, and assistance in setting up in business than would girls with brothers, and this may be one such case. Middling orphan girls seem also to have been apprenticed in relatively large numbers, perhaps because set amounts had often been put aside in their parents' wills for their education and also because their room and board needed to be supplied in some way. PRO C112/165 part II, Chancery Masters' Exhibits, "Case of *Daker v. Weekes,*" contains an illustrative case. In the early 1770s one Miss Daker, orphaned daughter of a London buckram stiffener, was taught several types of sewing and given dancing lessons (although apparently no other education to speak of) before apprenticing her for two years to a mantua maker with a premium of £30. The accounts for her brother James during the same period show that he learned writing and cyphering and that he was apprenticed for seven years to a clock-case and cabinet maker with a premium of £40.

58. Snell, *Annals of the Labouring Poor,* 279–282, 293. Ilana Krausman Ben-Amos's valuable account of girls' apprenticeship in Early Modern England came to my attention after this section had been completed. It contributes new information on apprenticeship in the important city of Bristol and also contains a discussion of changes over time; see Ilana Ben-Amos, ed., *Adolescence and Youth in Early Modern England* (New Haven and London: Yale University Press, 1994), 135–150. See also Erickson, *Women and Property in Early Modern England,* 55–58.

59. Collyer, *Parents & Guardians Directory,* 100.

60. Ibid., 206–207.

61. Collyer's book is biased toward occupations that required a formal apprenticeship. Consequently it leaves out some of the most common occupations of middling women (e.g., schoolteaching and pawnbroking).

62. Ibid., 80, 84.

63. See PRO C108/132, Chancery Masters' Exhibits, Sarah Boswell to Henry Gambier, dtd. Yarmouth, 3 July 1721, a desperate letter to Henry Gambier, tea dealer and East India Company employee, from a sister-in-law, asking him to pay the security her parish demanded after she became pregnant ("my aflicons are so Grat that I have noe plase to be in as for my brother Smiter he canot secure me they will have securety for the Child he cane give none nor I have no money [*sic*]"). I am grateful to John Styles for having brought this collection to my attention.

64. Guildhall MS 557, Church Book of the Meeting House at Limestreet, 1728–1764, fols. 76–77, 21 July and 4 Aug. 1746; this record details her excommunication and reports that Sarah was "heartily grieved for the sin she had been guilty of in the light of God and the Dishonour she had been to the church and the Profession." Folio 82 (11 April 1748) records her formal request for readmission and puts off its consideration to a future meeting. However, the matter appears then to have been dropped without further discussion.

65. Rogers, *Feminism in Eighteenth-Century England,* 9, 17–18, 21, 240–242; Elaine Hobby, *Virtue of Necessity: English Women's Writing, 1649–1688* (London: Virago, 1988), 10, 57, 83.

66. Early modern European societies were accustomed to a higher degree of

oversight over *both* young men and young women than is fashionable today. But, traditionally, single women were much more carefully watched than other people. For a detailed recent study of the way this worked in late–seventeenth- and early–eighteenth-century London see Robert Shoemaker, *Prosecution and Punishment: Petty Crime and the Law in London and Rural Middlesex, c. 1660–1725* (Cambridge: Cambridge University Press, 1991), especially 179–181, 185–187. The emphasis on the difficulties single women had living independently can, however, be exaggerated. For this see especially Pamela Sharpe, "Literally Spinsters: A New Interpretation of Local Economy and Demography in Colyton in the Seventeenth and Eighteenth Centuries," *Economic History Review* 44 (1991):59–62, which shows that it was considered "normal" for poor single women, in Colyton, at any rate, to live alone or with other women. See also Erickson, *Women and Property in Early Modern England,* 187–203; and Crawford, *Women and Religion in England,* 43.

67. Porter, "Rape—Does It Have a Historical Meaning?," 222, is wrong to say that the issue of rape seldom came up in the early modern period. Rape themes, and sexual coercion more generally, were an integral part of popular culture and an institutionalized feature of male-female relations. On rape as an element of seventeenth-century humor see Hobby, *Virtue of Necessity,* 87; also BL MS Harleian 6395, "Merry Passages & Jeasts" of Nicholas L'Estrange, for, inter alia, a joke about a man who bets he can "make his instrument come out [a woman's] back" (fol. 19) and another about sex with a twelve-year-old girl (fol. 79). The L'Estrange jokebook has also been published as " 'Merry Passages & Jeasts': A Manuscript Jest-book of Sir Nicholas L'Estrange (1603–1655)," ed. H. F. Lippincott, *Library Chronicle,* University of Pennsylvania, vol. 41 (1977), 149–162.

68. Modern efforts to argue for a low incidence of rape in the early modern period (e.g., Porter's "Rape—Does It Have a Historical Meaning?") have taken eighteenth-century narratives of rape at face value and ignored the household locus of most sexual violence. But this is a very simplistic way to approach an extremely complicated and deep-rooted cultural and social phenomenon. Then as now, only a minuscule proportion of cases of rape or sexual abuse ever turned up in the courts, and those that did were generally unusual in some way. Thus J. M. Beattie, *Crime and the Courts in England, 1660–1800* (Oxford: Clarendon Press, 1986), 82, cites a case where a five-year-old girl died in the course of being raped; almost certainly the case would never have come to light had the child survived. The same was true of the vast majority of rapes and other types of sexual violence perpetrated on female servants or slaves by their masters. Generally we hear about them only if the woman became pregnant, and even then the matter was most likely hushed up. Ironically, the perspective of sexual abusers is exceptionally well documented for this period, thanks to the uncommon frankness, little sullied by remorse, of the most famous diarist in the English language. See Samuel Pepys, *The Diary of Samuel Pepys,* ed. Robert Latham and William Matthews (London: G. Bell and Sons, Ltd., 1970–1983), vol. 5, 260, 267–268, 273, 287, 313; vol. 6, 331, 336; vol. 7, 104, 123, 245, 417–419 et passim. Pepys' kissing, fondling, and efforts to initiate sexual relations with maidservants, barmaids, actresses, the wives of friends and employees, and women asking favors (such as places for their husbands, loans, etc.) are described in detail in the diary. Generations of historians have sought to minimize or explain away this aspect of Pepys' life by arguing that the women did

not mind or simply saw such depredations as part of their job. But the diary makes it very evident that many of the women *did* mind, found the experience humiliating, and tried to resist. For another revealing account, which also illuminates the racial dimensions of sexual coercion, see J. R. Ward, "A Planter and His Slaves in Eighteenth-Century Jamaica," in Smout, *Search for Wealth and Stability*, 1–20. We possess relatively little information on incest, although see Abigail Abbot Bailey, *Religion and Domestic Violence in Early New England: The Memoirs of Abigail Abbot Bailey*, ed. Ann Taves (Bloomington: Indiana University Press, 1989), for a well-documented New England case. Again from the popular culture angle, a broadside from about 1760, *A Guernsey Garland, in Three Parts* (London: Printed and Sold in Aldermary Church Yard), details a convoluted father-daughter incest case in which both father and daughter are punished, even though the daughter was coerced into sexual relations. There is a copy in the Houghton Library, Harvard University. We hear about the sexual coercion of wives only when a "forbidden" sexual act, such as heterosexual sodomy, is involved. A case of the latter is described in Thomas Ivie, *Alimony Arraigned, or, The Remonstrance and Humble Appeal of Thomas Ivie, Esq. from the High Court of Chancery, to his Highnes the Lord Protector of the Commonwealth of England, Scotland, and Ireland, &c. Wherein are Set Forth the Unheard-of Practices and Villanies of Lewd and Defamed [sic] Women, in Order to Separate Man and Wife* (London, 1654), 9. For wives being coerced into sexual relations see also Anna Clark, *Women's Silence, Men's Violence: Sexual Assault in England, 1770–1845* (London and New York: Pandora, 1987), 1, 101–103.

69. See Beveridge, "Childhood and Society in Eighteenth-Century Scotland," in Dwyer, ed., *New Perspectives on the Politics and Culture of Early Modern Scotland*, 265–290. For some typical statements of the need to keep daughters close to home see Gainsford, *Secretaries Studie*, 37; Collyer, *Parents and Guardian's Directory*, 194–195; and Gregory, *Father's Legacy to his Daughters*, 26, 51–52.

70. Stone, *Family, Sex and Marriage in England*, 304–320; Trumbach, *Rise of the Egalitarian Family*, 97–113. See also Irene Q. Brown, "Domesticity, Feminism, and Friendship: Female Aristocratic Culture and Marriage in England, 1660–1760," *Journal of Family History* 7 (1982):406–424. Two studies that suggest some of the other areas for female resistance are Prior, "Women and the Urban Economy"; and Erickson, *Women and Property in Early Modern England*.

71. Ashbridge, *Some Account of the Early Part of the Life of Elizabeth Ashbridge*, 4.

72. Ibid., 13–14, 16.

73. Ibid., 31–43, 51–53.

74. Charlotte Charke, *A Narrative of the Life of Mrs. Charlotte Charke (Youngest Daughter of Colley Cibber, Esq.) Written by Herself*. Ed. Leonard R. N. Ashley (London: Printed for W. Reeve, A. Dodd, E. Cook, 1755; Gainesville, Fla.: Scholar's Facsimiles and Reprints, 1969), 17, 25–28, 30.

75. Ibid., 17–19, 20–23, 28–30.

76. Ibid., 33.

77. Ibid., 34–35, 37–38, 40–44.

78. Ibid., 14–15, 23–25, 50–54, 117–125 et passim.

79. See ibid., 88, 144–145, 190, 192, 224–226 et passim for Charke's close relationships with woman, including one "Mrs. Brown" who passed as her "wife" for a lengthy period. For Charke's work life see pp. 142–143. For an episode in which

Charke was bailed out of debtor's prison by a group of Covent Garden coffeehouse women, see 89–95.

80. See ibid., Dedication, iii–x, also 30, 47, 125. This discussion is strongly influenced by Patricia Spacks's account of Charke in *Imagining a Self*, 75–77, 87–88, 81–83.

81. Lotte C. Van de Pol and Rudolf M. Dekker, *The Tradition of Female Transvestism in Early Modern Europe* (Basingstoke: Macmillan, 1989); Julie Wheelwright, *Amazons and Military Maids: Women Who Dressed as Men in the Pursuit of Life, Liberty and Happiness* (London: Pandora, 1989); Dianne Dugaw, *Warrior Women and Popular Balladry 1650–1850*, Cambridge Studies in Eighteenth-Century English Literature and Thought, 4 (Cambridge: Cambridge University Press, 1989), 121–142. Accounts of hundreds of these women have turned up in the European and American records; numerous others, no doubt, were never detected. None of this is to suggest that Charke did not embroider her experiences for dramatic purposes.

82. Davidoff and Hall, *Family Fortunes*, 279–289.

83. Wrigley and Schofield, *Population History of England*, 262–265. Another factor, as they point out, may be their own undercounting of remarriages. Bridget Hill's essay "The Marriage Age of Women and the Demographers," *History Workshop Journal* 28 (1989):129–147, is an important critique of the way family reconstitution studies—Wrigley and Schofield's work in particular—gloss over diversity in women's mean marriage age and fertility patterns. Hill also has a useful discussion of the complexity of the relationship between women's work and marriage choices. For a local study that questions easy correlations between rising real income and nuptiality rates, see Sharpe, "Literally Spinsters," 46–65.

84. Snell, *Annals of the Labouring Poor*, 349.

CHAPTER 4: MIDDLING MEN AND THE REFORMATION OF MANNERS

1. Dudley W. R. Bahlman, *The Moral Revolution of 1688*, Wallace Notestein Essays, no. 2 (New Haven: Yale University Press, 1957), 84–85; Tina Beth Isaacs, "Moral Crime, Moral Reform, and the State in Early Eighteenth-Century England: A Study of Piety and Politics," Ph.D. diss., University of Rochester, 1979, 56–58, 188–190, 315–316.

2. The most detailed discussions of the movement have focused on the Societies for Reformation of Manners, only one arm of the larger movement. See especially Isaacs, "Moral Crime, Moral Reform and the State"; A. G. Craig, "The Movement for the Reformation of Manners, 1688–1715," Ph.D. diss., University of Edinburgh, 1980; Tina Beth Isaacs, "The Anglican Hierarchy and the Reformation of Manners, 1688–1738," *Journal of Ecclesiastical History* 33 (1982):391–411; and Shoemaker, *Prosecution and Punishment*, 238–272. For additional information on the Reform Societies, along with other aspects of the larger movement, see W. O. B. Allen and E. MacClure, *Two Hundred Years: The History of the Society for Promoting Christian Knowledge* (London: SPCK, 1898); T. C. Curtis and W. H. Speck, "The Societies for the Reformation of Manners: A Case Study in the Theory and Practice of Moral Reform," *Literature and History* 3 (1976):45–64; Edward J. Bristow, *Vice and Vigi-*

lance: Purity Movements in Britain since 1700 (Dublin: Gill & MacMillan, 1977); Randolph Trumbach, "London's Sodomites: Homosexual Behaviour and Western Culture in the Eighteenth Century, *Journal of Social History* 11 (1977–78):1–33; and Bray, *Homosexuality in Renaissance England*, 81–104, 113–114.

3. Harold J. Perkin, *Origins of Modern English Society*, 281.

4. Curtis and Speck, "Societies for the Reformation of Manners," 60.

5. Some of these points have been made by other historians of the movement. Some time ago Dudley Bahlman compared the societies to "moral joint-stock companies" and stressed their connection to clubs and societies and to the "projecting" craze. See Bahlman, *Moral Revolution*, 101–103, 105–108. On connections to Methodism, see John Walsh, "Origins of the Evangelical Revival," in G. V. Bennett and J. D. Walsh, eds., *Essays in Modern English Church History* (London: Adam and Charles Black, 1966), 142, 144–148, 161–162. For the moral preoccupations of some of the lesser Wilkites, which were marked at times by notions of enforcement that were somewhat more libertarian than those possessed by the earlier societies, see John Brewer, "The Wilkites and the Law, 1763–74: A Study of Radical Notions of Governance," in John Brewer and John Styles, eds., *An Ungovernable People: The English and Their Law in the Seventeenth and Eighteenth Centuries* (London: Hutchinson, 1980), 170–171; and Clive Probyn, *The Sociable Humanist: The Life and Works of James Harris, 1709–1780: Provincial and Metropolitan Culture in Eighteenth-Century England* (Oxford: Clarendon Press, 1991), 194. I am grateful to Joanna Innes for bringing Probyn's study to my attention. For Wilberforce's indebtedness to the late-seventeenth- and early-eighteenth-century reformations of manners see Joanna Innes, "Politics and Morals: The Reformation of Manners Movement in Later Eighteenth-Century England," in Hellmuth, ed., *Transformation of Political Culture*, 72–73. Tina Isaacs has drawn attention to commercial elements in Reformation of Manners rhetoric and practice. See Isaacs, "Moral Crime, Moral Reform and the State," 18, 33, 349, 352, 361.

6. Ibid., 73–76.

7. Isaacs gives many details of the connections between the lower ranks of the Societies for Reformation of Manners and law enforcement officers. See ibid., 68–72, 74–75, 93, 95, 136–142.

8. Josiah Woodward, *Account of the Rise and Progress of the Religious Societies in the City of London &c. And of the Endeavours for Reformation of Manners which have been made Therein* (London, 1698), 157–178.

9. For the places where the Societies met, in London at any rate, see Bodleian MS Rawlinson D 1312, "The Names Places of Abode, Employmts & Occupacions of the Several Societys in & about the Cities of London and Westminster Belonging to the Church of England 1694." For the internal organization of one of the Societies see Guildhall MS 6479, Stewards Books of Religious Society of St. Giles, Cripplegate, 1696–1761, Orders 4–6 of the "Orders and Rules." This Society elected stewards once every half-year to oversee the collecting of dues and fines and to "keep a faithful Register of what is collected, & Distributed to be perused by any member of the Society at Request." The stewards in turn appointed six collectors, whose main job was to follow up delinquent payments. It is striking that both accountancy and debt collection were incorporated explicitly into the constitution of the organization.

10. .Guildhall MS 6478, Stewards Book of a Religious Society at Christ Church, then at Cripplegate, 1691–1753, includes lists of ministers preaching for the Society and bills of fare. This was a different Society from the one that generated what is now Guildhall MS 6479. See also F. W. B. Bullock, *Voluntary Societies 1520–1799* (St. Leonards on Sea, Sussex: Budd & Gillat, 1963), 121, 141; and Bahlman, *Moral Revolution*, 22–23, 67, 69–70.

11. Bodleian MS Rawlinson D 1312. See also Guildhall MS 6479 for the St. Giles Cripplegate Society whose membership in the early eighteenth century included the following occupations: joiner, leatherdresser, tailor (3), perukemaker (2), barber, cooper, shoemaker (2), weaver, druggist, distiller, silkman, tinman, buttonseller, needlemaker, turner, smith and ironmonger, plumber, glover, jeweler, cook, and schoolmaster. On the whole, the bent seems to be toward the skilled trades, although there were exceptions. The Societies had yet to reach their peak of membership when this list was compiled.

12. These included dinner clubs, fire insurance societies, and societies for the relief of the industrious poor, a charity to benefit the children of Anglican clergymen ejected during the Commonwealth period, and many more (the distinction between profit-making and nonprofit-making groups was quite hazy in this period). For British and Continental societies, notably the Freemasons, see Margaret C. Jacob, *The Radical Enlightenment: Pantheists, Freemasons and Republicans* (London: George Allen & Unwin, 1981). For clubs and coffeehouses see Bryant Lillywhite, *London Coffee Houses: A Reference Book of Coffee Houses of the Seventeenth, Eighteenth and Nineteenth Centuries* (London: George Allen & Unwin, 1963); and Stewart, *Rise of Public Science*, 113–117, 143–146, 172–174, 269–270 et passim.

13. For an overview see Margaret C. Jacob, *Cultural Origins of the Scientific Revolution* (Philadelphia: Temple University Press, 1988), 152–160.

14. John Leng, *The Four and Twentieth Account of the Progress Made in the Cities of London and Westminster . . . by the Societies for Promoting a Reformation of Manners.* (London: J. Downing, 1719), 3. For establishment concern about clubs devoted to sin, see Isaacs, "Moral Crime, Moral Reform and the State," 99, 227–228, 329–330.

15. Some trade associations, especially in Catholic countries, also concerned themselves with their members' virtue or, more typically, with communal religious ceremonies such as processions on saints' days. See Davis, *Society and Culture in Early Modern France*, 75, 292. Religious confraternities in England disappeared or were suppressed during the Reformation. For another nonreligious society that used the system of fines see Guildhall MS 544, "Ancient register of the Club at the Half Moon, London—The Centenary Club," a group that met from 1695 on. Some other contemporary organizations took over more than the system of fines; the Freemasons, for example, elaborated a vast body of mythicized trade lore. For this see Jacob, *Radical Enlightenment*, 116–117, 126–127.

16. It is probable that the tradesmen who entered the societies in the 1680s and '90s were living a sort of split existence: on the one hand fraternizing with agemates from all sorts of trades, on the other hand maintaining links with traditional corporate bodies. Many town guilds had by this time become extremely oligarchical, largely excluding the humbler members of each trade, certainly apprentices and journeymen, from effective power. On this see George Unwin, *Gilds and Companies of London* (London: Methuen, 1925). The predominantly young Religious Soci-

ety membership may well have found the guilds rather unresponsive to their needs. Certainly the guilds lacked any solid commitment to the kind of virtue they were seeking.

17. Guildhall MS 6479, Order 10.

18. Woodward, *Account of the Rise and Progress of the Religious Societies*, 60.

19. John Brewer, "Commercialization and Politics," in McKendrick, Brewer, and Plumb, *Birth of a Consumer Society*, 217–224, talks about the variety of commercial and mutual support functions performed by some later, more secular clubs.

20. Guildhall MS 6479, Orders 1, 2, and 8.

21. Ibid., Order 13, and Order 14, Rule 1.

22. Ibid., Order 14, Rules 1, 7, 8, 10, 15.

23. Ibid., Order 13.

24. Ibid., Order 14, Rules 5 and 16. The identification of dissent with moroseness was a commonplace of the period.

25. Guildhall MS 6479, Order 14, Rule 3 and Order 28.

26. For the expenditures on the bishop's visit see ibid., fol. 14a. There were also payments to the bishop's three coachmen and a footman (presumably vails). The total outlay was ten shillings.

27. Ibid., Order 3.

28. One of the central aims of the societies, however, was to stem the tide of conversions, and Woodward boasts, rather unconvincingly, that since the beginning of the movement "none have fal'n from the Publick communion into sects or separation." Woodward, *Account of the Rise and Progress of the Religious Societies*, 56.

29. The approach I have taken here owes much to Mary Douglas, *Purity and Danger: An Analysis of Concepts of Pollution and Taboo* (London: Routledge & Kegan Paul, 1966). In Douglas's words, "Thus we find that certain moral values are upheld and certain social rules defined by beliefs in dangerous contagion, as when the glance or touch of an adulterer is held to bring illness to his neighbours or his children." And, "I believe that ideas about separating, purifying, demarcating and punishing transgressions have as their main function to impose system on an inherently untidy experience" (4).

30. Josiah Woodward, *The Young Man's Monitor: Shewing the Great Happiness of Early Piety and the Dreadful Consequences of Indulging Youthful Lusts* (London: Joseph Downing, 1718), 32; Woodward, *Account of the Rise and Progress of the Religious Societies*, 114.

31. See Bodleian MS Rawlinson D 1312, for Thomas and Jonathan Wood, one a brassturner the other a salesman, living "Att the horse shoe Barbakin," and several youths living in groups of two and three. The Religious Society at St. Giles appears to have contained among its membership a father and son, Robert Vokins, plumber, and Joseph Vokins, tallow chandler, plus one set of brothers, George and Richard Pearce (see Guildhall MS 6479).

32. Woodward, *Young Man's Monitor*, 73.'

33. Almost all the members of St. Giles Religious Society could at least sign their names. Some displayed an extremely beautiful and clear hand which must have cost them much practice. The number of different individuals keeping accounts suggests that many of the membership were familiar with bookkeeping (see the pages of accounts in Guildhall MS 6479). On making people apply in writing

for entrance to Religious Societies see Woodward, *Account of the Rise and Progress of the Religious Societies*, 61.

34. The Freemasons also excluded women, bondsmen, and atheists. Both the Freemasons and the Religious Societies were theoretically open to all social classes; in practice, however, the entrance fees or dues kept out the poor. I am grateful to Margaret Jacob for this information.

35. The stewards' accounts, which run from 1696, show a number of other small personal charitable outlays, especially to victims of fire, that were typically agreed to by vote of the membership. Thus see Guildhall MS 6479, note for 7 June 1726, indicating an outlay of 2s 2d to a Mr. Stone "who suffer'd by the fire on London Bridge." In January 1708/09 the Society paid for the sermon at the funeral of one Lawrence Lee, who may have been a deceased member. See also the accounts for 1733, when £2.10 was paid out for the funeral of a Mr. Hathaway. Woodward, *Account of the Rise and Progress of the Religious Societies*, 103–104, mentions charity to sick members and paying for members' funeral expenses as typical Society outlays.

36. Guildhall MS 6479, fols. 15, 19, 20, 21, 22, 30. The notation on "collecting Mr. Brook's money" incidentally demonstrates the complex nature of contemporary credit relations. The Dusstys were not only debtors, but creditors. They may initially have become insolvent because of their inability to collect on a debt or series of debts owed to them.

37. Ibid., fol. 15.

38. Guildhall MS 6478; see for example James Harrison 1739, Joseph Rose 1732–1762, Samuel Salte 1741. The earlier rolls for this society have not survived. Guildhall MS 6479, Accounts for 1734.

39. Guildhall MS 6478, fols. 126, 128, 130.

40. Guildhall MS 6479, notation for 18 June 1712. On 5 April 1712 the same society gave 4d. "for the Conformity Act. Parliament."

41. It is not clear when and why this was done. Some of the Societies might have harbored dissenters or refused to sign oaths of allegiance at some point. There were persistent rumors that the Societies were Jacobite front organizations. See Isaacs, "Moral Crime, Moral Reform and the State," 22. It is unlikely that the vanished pages conceal a female membership.

42. Guildhall MS 6478.

43. See, for example, London, Friends Library, Box Meeting MSS 1671–1753, which show the membership much concerned with women setting a moral example for their children and servants. There are certain ironies to this, however. The London Women's Meeting letter for 27 May 1747 has appended to it a list of signatures of some twenty-five women, of which the first and largest is that of Tace Sowle Raylton, a prominent woman printer and hardly someone who devoted herself to staying demurely at home and setting a good example in the sense that the conduct books demanded. On the complexities of the Women's Meeting see Phyllis Mack, *Visionary Women: Ecstatic Prophecy in Seventeenth-Century England* (Berkeley, Los Angeles and Oxford: University of California Press, 1992), 319–350.

44. Bridget Hill, "A Refuge from Men," 107–130.

45. A handful of eighteenth-century woman did seek to emulate the men's groups directly—Charles and John Wesley's mother, Susanna, started a woman's

religious society in 1710 only to be forced by her husband to disband it—and, of course, John Wesley was later to champion both men's and women's sex-segregated prayer groups. See John Wesley, *The Journal of John Wesley*, ed. Nehemiah Curnock (London: Epworth Press, 1938), vol. 3, 32–34. See also Dr. Williams's Library Doddridge Collection L1/4, fol. 17, S. Clark to Mercy Doddridge (Philip Doddridge's widow), dtd. Daventry, 20 April 1757, in which Clark inquires of Mercy Doddridge after Philip Doddridge's death "whether the Dr. had left any particulr instructions w*th* respect to such Societies [i.e., Religious Societies] among the *Women* or whether he did not intend to have done something of that kind if his life had been spared & in wt. state *those Societies* are among us, as well as what Books are used by them." Jacob, *Radical Enlightenment*, 193–208, has some provocative comments on the significance of the Masonic exclusion of women. See also her "Freemasons, Women and the Paradox of the Enlightenment" in Hunt, Jacob, Mack, and Perry, *Women and the Enlightenment*, 69–93.

46. Walkowitz, *Prostitution and Victorian Society;* Leah Otis, *Prostitution in Medieval Society: The History of an Urban Institution in Languedoc* (Chicago and London: University of Chicago Press, 1985); Hunt, "De-eroticization of Women's Liberation," 23–46.

47. Josiah Woodward, *Rebuke to the Sin of Uncleanness* (London: Joseph Downing, 1720), 4, 7–8, 13–15. The scriptural references are Proverbs 5:9, Proverbs 22:14, Ecclesiastes 7:26, and Proverbs 2:18–19. Woodward's language, particularly his deliberate mixing of oral, anal, and genital metaphors, will be familiar to anyone who has perused much classical, medieval, or early modern misogynist writing. The emphasis upon predatory females, although very common in this sort of literature, was not, however, ubiquitous. Laura Gowing points out that "the Elizabethan sermon on whoredom concentrated entirely on the fornicator as a male figure, breaking up his household and marriage by his adultery; only the occasional aside addressed the adulterous woman." Laura Gowing, "Gender and the Language of Insult in Early Modern London," *History Workshop Journal,* issue 35 (1993):2. On the other hand, the evidence Gowing marshals from defamation cases suggests that, among the lay population, there was "little condemnation of men's misdeeds, even for fornication" and a great deal of condemnation of women.

48. Woodward, *Rebuke to the Sin of Uncleanness,* 10–11.

49. For more on the economics of marriage see pp. 151–156.

50. Women's reputations were much more closely identified with sexual chastity than men's were. However, men also guarded their sexual reputations and sometimes went to court to defend them. I have benefited from hearing Robert Shoemaker's "Gender and the Defence of Honor in Eighteenth-Century London" (unpublished paper, delivered at the University of London Research Seminar, British History in the Long Eighteenth Century, Institute of Historical Research, 25 May 1994). The notion of illicit sex leading to downward mobility comes from Alan Bray, who makes a similar point in relation to homosexual sex in early-eighteenth-century London. Bray, *Homosexuality in Renaissance England,* 86. For more on sexuality and disorder see pp. 162–164.

51. Woodward, *Rebuke to the Sin of Uncleanness,* 8–11. Woodward's recommendation to those who wished "to keep down the Heat of Your [sexual]

Inclinations" was the "Company of grave and sober People," a diet of bread and water, hard work, and "fervent continual Prayer and Humiliation before God" (19–20).

52. Charles Creighton, *A History of Epidemics in Britain from A.D. 664 to the Extinction of the Plague* (Cambridge: Cambridge University Press, 1891), 417–439; Charles Clayton Dennie, *A History of Syphilis* (Springfield, Ill.: Charles C. Thomas, 1962). I am grateful to Catherine Crawford for bringing these sources to my attention.

53. Beveridge, "Childhood and Society in Eighteenth Century Scotland," 275–276, discusses early modern beliefs about the erotics of mother-child relations.

54. This view was common among childrearing "experts" (see, for example, Collyer, *Parents & Guardian's Directory*, 3–4), but it was also to be found in personal accounts across the literate social spectrum. Thus William Stout, the Quaker iron-monger, gave a scathing description of his master's wife as "one who took her ease, and took no notice of trade, or anything, but indulging her children." Stout, *Autobiography*, 9. See also Ralph A. Houlbrooke, *The English Family 1450–1700* (London and New York: Longman, 1984), 140–145, 151.

55. Abelove, *Evangelist of Desire*, 49–73.

56. By the 1760s this was beginning to bear fruit in organizational terms in mixed clubs like Almack's, which was set up in 1765. See Katharine M. Rogers, *Feminism in Eighteenth-Century England* (Urbana and Chicago: University of Illinois Press, 1982), 48–49n. PRO C104/146, Chancery Masters' Exhibits, contains the minutes and accounts for 1770 to 1775 of an aristocratic club called the Ladies Club. Despite its name this was a mixed-sex club; indeed, the majority of members would appear to have been men. Earlier mixed-sex clubs may well have existed, although I am not aware of any.

57. Isaacs, "Moral Crime, Moral Reform and the State," 62.

58. Ibid., 74–76. This was how the system worked in theory. As the movement gained momentum other organizational variants appeared. Reformation of Manners groups in provincial cities were less elaborate, although several other cases of multitiered, affiliated societies can be found. On societies outside London see ibid., 73–74, 152–155.

59. See p. 163.

60. The manifesto is quoted in Bristow, *Vice and Vigilance*, 15.

61. Woodward, *Account of the Rise and Progress of the Religious Societies*, ix.

62. There has been a good deal of interest recently in the emergence of homosexual subcultures and "identities" in early-eighteenth-century cities, notably London, Paris, and Amsterdam. For London see Mary McIntosh, "The Homosexual Role," *Social Problems* 16, no. 2 (1968):182–192; Trumbach, "London's Sodomites: Homosexual Behaviour and Western Culture in the Eighteenth Century"; Bray, *Homosexuality in Renaissance England*, 8–114, 134–137n; and Randolph Trumbach, "Sodomitical Subcultures, Sodomitical Roles, and the Gender Revolution of the Eighteenth Century: The Recent Historiography," *Eighteenth-Century Life* 9 (1985):109–121. But compare Jeffrey Weeks, "Discourse, Desire and Social Deviance: Some Problems in a History of Homosexuality," in Kenneth Plummer, ed., *The Making of the Modern Homosexual* (London: Hutchinson, 1981), 76–111, which dates the emergence of a homosexual identity to the Victorian period. For descrip-

tions of raids on some twenty molly houses in the 1720s, almost certainly instigated by the Societies for Reformation of Manners, see Trumbach, "London's Sodomites," and Bray, *Homosexuality in Renaissance England*, 81–104, 113–114. There had been less ambitious raids as early as 1699.

63. The trials of mollies show, of course, that the division was not so clear and that numerous married men engaged in homosexual behavior. The identification of homosexuality with foreignness and the use of homosexual epithets to tar military and commercial rivals were very traditional, turning up in almost cyclical fashion at various points in English history. However the fears raised by the wars with Louis XIV, the arrival of a foreign dynasty in the form of William III (who was himself rumored to have homosexual proclivities), and commercial competition from the Continent, gave it a new salience. I am grateful to Alan Bray for helping me clarify this issue. Kathleen Wilson's "Empire of Virtue: The Imperial Project and Hanoverian Culture c. 1720–1785," in Stone, ed., *An Imperial Nation at War*, 128–164, came to my attention after writing this section, but her discussion of effeminacy and perceptions of military performance accords well with mine; see especially 140–142. The theme is extended further in Wilson's *Sense of the People*, 185–205. For similar themes later in the century see Gerald Newman, *The Rise of English Nationalism: A Cultural History 1740–1830* (New York: St. Martin's Press, 1987), 71–84, 115–119.

64. Isaacs, "Moral Crime, Moral Reform and the State," 76–77.

65. Bodleian MSS Rawlinson 1396–1404.

66. Shoemaker, *Prosecution and Punishment*, 251.

67. See especially Curtis and Speck, "Societies for the Reformation of Manners," 58; and Isaacs, "Moral Crime, Moral Reform and the State," 18.

68. Josiah Woodward, *Account of the Rise and Progress of the Religious Societies*, vii.

69. William Stukeley, *National Judgements the Consequence of a National Profanation of the Sabbath: A Sermon Preached Before the Honourable House of Commons at St. Margaret's, Westminster; on the 30th Day of January 1741/2* (London: T. Cooper, 1742), 9, 17. The occasion was the annual sermon commemorating the martyrdom of Charles I.

70. *The Victuallers Case, Humbly Offered to the Consideration of their Excellencies the Lords Justices, and the Rest of the Kings Ministers* (London: n.p., 1701).

71. It is not insignificant that, in its zeal to attack swearers, Sunday traders, and the like, the Societies largely ignored usury, engrossing of goods, paying employees less than they needed to live, and the like. By this time, it is true, these were essentially dead issues as far as most active traders were concerned, although they had by no means ceased to bother other people. Yet they turn up extremely infrequently in reformation literature. For a formal defense of usury from the 1690s see William Sherlock, *The Charity of Lending Without Usury and the True Notion of Usury briefly stated . . . Preach'd before the Right Honourable the Lord Mayor* (London, 1692).

72. Bodleian Rawlinson MSS 1396–1404.

73. The interest in systematic enforcement probably did the Societies no good in their campaign to win over the London judiciary. For an excellent discussion of the ways the Societies' interest in systematic law enforcement conflicted with older, more flexible methods that favored mediation, see Shoemaker, *Prosecution and Punishment*, 252–271.

74. For the scientific and other interests of some of the prominent low church clergymen who supported both the Reformation Societies and the SPCK see Jacob, *Newtonians and the English Revolution*, 92, 98, 147, 266 et passim. See also Allen and MacClure, *Two Hundred Years*, 230–231.

75. Isaacs, "Moral Crime, Moral Reform and the State," 250–251. The pamphlet was *A Help to a National Reformation—An Abstract of the Penal-Laws Against Prophaneness and Vice* (London: Printed for D. Brown, 1700). It is not known if the model page found in it originated with its author or reflected existing practice in the Societies.

76. Bodleian MS Rawlinson D 129, late-seventeenth- or early-eighteenth-century copies of various documents relating to the Societies for Reformation of Manners, fols. 4 and 10.

77. Ibid., fols. 17–23.

78. Ibid., fols. 30–31. The other main group in this Society would, presumably, have been churchwardens, with perhaps some justices of the peace. Constables and churchwardens were fairly uniformly drawn from the ranks of the middling, and in London, at any rate, an increasing number of justices of the peace (the so-called "trading justices") were, too.

79. Ibid., fols. 33–34. The registers (MSS Rawlinson 1396–1404) show that constables did occasionally take fines on the spot.

80. Ibid., fol. 26. On earlier precedents for this see Susan Brigden, "Religion and Social Obligation in Early Sixteenth-Century London," *Past & Present* 103 (May 1984):87. Hostility to the Societies often focused on procedural irregularities, which was a strong incentive to circumspection and conservatism in Society operations. Isaacs, "Moral Crime, Moral Reform and the State," 69–70, describes a particularly embarrassing scandal of 1691 that impressed the Societies with the need to be protective of their public image.

81. For the royal proclamations see Isaacs, "Moral Crime, Moral Reform and the State," 56–57. For the expanding scope of middling men's public activism, I have benefited from reading Joanna Innes' work-in-progress on William Payne, a later moral reformer who used his Reformation of Manners activism as a springboard for greater things.

82. Isaacs, "Moral Crime, Moral Reform and the State," 94; Trumbach, "London's Sodomites," 22.

83. See, for example, *The Heaven Drivers, A Poem* (London, n.p., 1701), which stresses the "mechanick" character of the reformers, suggests that they hark back to the regicides and puritans, and describes them harassing a group of gentlemen.

84. The best account of the opposition to the Societies is Isaacs, "Moral Crime, Moral Reform and the State," 174–197, and this section is largely derived from it. For Defoe see ibid., 176–178, 190. Jonathan Swift, *A Project for the Advancement of Religion and the Reformation of Manners* (London: Printed for Benj. Tooke, 1709), 18, is quoted in Isaacs, 178–179. On Sacheverell see ibid., 188–189.

85. Edward Stephens, *A Seasonable and Necessary Admonition to the Gentlemen of the First Society for Reformation of Manners* (London: n.p., 1700?), 6–8.

86. Shoemaker points out that local justices of the peace sometimes benefited financially from permitting gaming houses to stay open, and moreover that such

houses often constituted an important source of revenue for particular localities. See *Prosecution and Punishment*, 266.

87. Bahlman, *Moral Revolution*, 101, also places the movement for reform in the context of "projecting."

88. Douglas, *Purity and Danger*, 3. Douglas appears here to be using "men" in the so-called "generic" meaning of the term.

89. In fact, John Disney, a member of the SPCK, suggested in 1710 that women should get involved in Reformation of Manners activism because the "deference and respect" they enjoyed would make them especially effective moral reformers. See Shoemaker, *Prosecution and Punishment*, 213.

90. See Andrew, *Philanthropy and Police*.

91. Conversion experiences were certainly not foreign to early-eighteenth-century moral thought (see pp. 206–207 for the case of Colonel Gardiner), but they were little in evidence in the late-seventeenth-century Reformation of Manners, perhaps because of the desire to distance the movement from the charge of enthusiasm.

92. Innes, "Politics and Morals," 110–111. Both Hannah More and Sarah Trimmer, in addition to numerous lesser-known women, played important roles in the Evangelical Movement. See also Clare Midgley, *Women Against Slavery: The British Campaigns, 1780–1870* (London and New York: Routledge, 1992), 9–40.

93. Hannah More, *Strictures on the Modern System of Female Education, with a View of the Principles and Conduct Prevalent Among Women of Rank and Fortune* (London: T. Cadell and W. Davies, 1799), vol. 1, 63. The full passage reads: "This revolution of manners of the middle class [i.e., the increase in luxury] has so far altered the character of the age, as to be in danger of rendering obsolete the heretofore common saying, 'that most worth and virtue are to be found in the middle station' " (62–63). I am grateful to Dror Wahrman for pressing me to "go look at the original."

CHAPTER 5: MIDDLING WOMEN AND TRADE

1. CLRO MC6/462, City of London, Mayor's Court Interrogatories. In terms of marital status, literacy levels, and occupation these women were typical of the spread. See Earle, "Female Labour Market," 328–353. There are no indications in these records of how much the women were actually contributing to the household. Peter Earle's research suggests that many of the women engaged in petty sales and services were supporting themselves largely or entirely through these activities and that this was true of married women as well as spinsters and widows. See also Earle, *Making of the English Middle Class*, 158–174.

2. CLRO MC6/462B and MC6/462A. To establish each woman's good character it was essential to prove that she was not defying or disobeying her husband by entering into trade.

3. Many middling husbands worked out of their homes, and they had often to be at home to receive customers, oversee their journeymen and servants, and the like. Women, on the other hand, because of their distributive activities and their

responsibility for provisioning the household, were often away from home. Erickson, *Women and Property in Early Modern England*, 9–11, contains a discussion of this issue.

4. The husbands in this sample were in the middle rung of London traders. They were probably masters, and they presumably employed a maidservant in their homes and perhaps a few journeymen and an apprentice in their workshops. Most would have been entitled to vote. For an illuminating discussion of gender and occupational identity see Michael Roberts, " 'Words they are Women, and Deeds they are Men': Images of Work and Gender in Early Modern England," in Lindsey Charles and Lorna Duffin, eds., *Women and Work in Preindustrial England* (London: Croom Helm, 1985), 122–180.

5. The figures have been rounded up or down to whole numbers in the discussion.

Proportion of London Women Employed

	Wholly Maintained by Employment		Partly Maintained by Employment		No Paid Employment	
	N	%	N	%	N	%
Spinsters	187	77.6	14	5.8	40	16.6
Wives	139	32.6	117	27.4	171	40.0
Widows	134	73.2	22	12.0	27	14.8
Total	460	54.0	153	18.0	238	28.0

SOURCE: Ecclesiastical Court Depositions, 1695–1725, from Earle, "Female Labour Market in London in the Late Seventeenth and Early Eighteenth Centuries," 337.

6. Recent scholarship confirms this point, but it also draws attention to the diversity in women's work-force participation across different industries and locales. See Osamu Saito, "Who Worked When: Life-Time Profiles of Labour Force Participation in Cardington and Corfe Castle in the Late Eighteenth and Mid-Nineteenth Centuries," *Local Population Studies* 22 (1979):14–29; Snell, *Annals of the Labouring Poor*, especially 270–319; Pamela Sharpe, "Literally Spinsters," 46–65; Berg, "What Difference did Women's Work Make to the Industrial Revolution?," 22–44; and Schwarz, *London in the Age of Industrialisation*, 14–22, 45–48.

7. We should probably read this as stemming both from the force of financial necessity and from considerations of reputation: if a woman had no male worker upon whom to stake an identity, claiming the work she did on her own, even if it was low-status work, was preferable to having no occupational identity at all.

8. For the Continent see Louise Tilly and Joan Scott, *Women, Work and the Family* (New York: Holt, Rinehart and Winston, 1978); Olwen Hufton, "Women and the Family Economy in Eighteenth-Century France," *French Historical Studies* 9 (1975–76):1–22; Martha Howell, *Women, Production and Patriarchy in Late Medieval Cities* (Chicago and London: University of Chicago Press, 1986); Merry Wiesner, *Working Women in Renaissance Germany* (New Brunswick, N.J.: Rutgers University Press, 1986); and P. J. P. Goldberg, *Women, Work, and the Life Cycle in a Medieval Economy:*

Women in York and Yorkshire c. 1300–1520 (Oxford: Clarendon Press, 1992). For England see Clark, *Working Life of Women in the Seventeenth Century*, 8–13; George, *London Life in the Eighteenth Century;* Mary Prior, "Women and the Urban Economy: Oxford 1500–1800," in Mary Prior, ed., *Women in English Society 1500–1800* (London: Methuen, 1985), 93–117; Earle, "Female Labour Market in London," 339 (table 10), 348–352; Sharpe, "Literally Spinsters." See also the following chapters in Lindsey Charles and Lorna Duffin, eds., *Women and Work in Preindustrial England* (London: Croom Helm, 1985): Kay E. Lacey, "Women and Work in Fourteenth and Fifteenth Century London," 24–82; Diane Hutton, "Women in Fourteenth-Century Shrewsbury," 83–99; and Sue Wright, " 'Churmaids, Huswyfes and Hucksters': The Employment of Women in Tudor and Stuart Salisbury," 100–121. It is often suggested that opportunities for women declined over the course of the late medieval or early modern period. For a corrective to "golden age" theories of women's work-force participation see Judith M. Bennett, "Medieval Women, Modern Women: Across the Great Divide," in David Aers, ed., *Culture and History, 1350–1600: Essays on English Communities, Identities, and Writing* (New York and London: Harvester Wheatsheaf, 1992), 147–175, especially 155–158.

9. Harland, *Collectanea Relating to Manchester at Various Times*, vol. 72, 173. See also DNB. Mrs. Raffald was at work on a book on midwifery when she died.

10. Elizabeth Raffald, *The Manchester Directory For the Year 1772. Containing an Alphabetical List of the Merchants, Tradesmen, and Principal Inhabitants in the Town of Manchester, with the Situation of their Respective Warehouses, and Places of Abode* (London: Printed for the Author; and sold by R. Baldwin, and by the Author at Manchester, 1772). Raffald's directory also makes no mention of lodging-house keepers, although some Manchester women must have done this. For comparison see John Reed's *New Bristol Directory, for the Year 1792* (Bristol: John Reed, 1792), which lists some fifty-three women as lodging-house keepers; they represented close to a quarter of all the women in trade in his directory. The difference in perception presumably had to do with the "commercialization" of lodging houses in response to Bristol's large seafaring population. The entry under which Raffald subsumes her own commercial involvements is "John Raffald, Seedsman and Confectioner," in Raffald, *Manchester Directory*, 34.

11. And yet there were women sheriffs as late as the seventeenth century, and certain parish offices, notably those of churchwarden and overseer of the poor, were sometimes filled by women into the eighteenth century. Generally such women deputized men to serve for them or fined out of the appointment. On this see Rose Graham, "The Civic Position of Women at Common Law Before 1800," in Rose Graham, *English Ecclesiastical Studies, Being Some Essays in Research in Medieval History* (London: SPCK, 1929), 360–377.

12. Early voluntary associations (including moral reform associations) were, with some exceptions, notable for their nonsectarian membership policies. The Freemasons even admitted Jews. Most of these organizations (as is the case with many eighteenth-century leisure pursuits) were relatively egalitarian once one had paid an entrance fee—which effectively kept out the poor.

13. Vickery, "Women and the World of Goods," 274–301.

14. These data are based on a hand count of women's names appearing in the Economic and Social Research Council Index of approximately 40,000 Royal

Exchange Insurance policies taken out between 1775 and 1787. Obviously the "all-England" approach flattens out regional differences. For comparison see L. D. Schwarz, *London in the Age of Industrialization*, 21, table 1.2 "Female Employment," which is based in part upon the *London* policies for both the Royal Exchange Assurance and the Sun Fire between the same dates (1775–1787). The percentage of women in London trades as opposed to women in trades across England seems to have been fairly similar (within four percentage points of each other, and more usually between one and two percentage points of each other for those types of businesses that Schwarz and I survey). The sole exception seems to be millinery: Schwarz finds 85.7 percent of London milliners were women, whereas my data suggest a much lower figure (60.6 percent) for England as a whole. It is not clear whence this discrepancy comes. See also ibid., 245–247, for a discussion of the methodological challenges posed by insurance policy index.

15. An Excise Office inquiry of 1759 came up with 141,700 shops nationally. Its definition of a shop was, however, quite conservative. Thus the enumeration did *not* include purely wholesale outlets or alehouses, stalls at fairs, or "shops above stairs," and it counted homes with two shops in them as one shop. Many of the uncounted categories would have been heavily female. See Mui and Mui, *Shops and Shopkeeping*, 34–36.

16. *Baron and Feme. A Treatise of the Common Law Concerning Husbands and Wives* (London: Eliz. Nutt and R. Gosling ... for John Walthoe, 1719), 231 reads as follows:

> Two Femes Jointenants of a Lease for Years, one of them takes Husband, and dies; yet the Term shall survive; for though all Chattels real are given to the Husband if he survive, yet the Survivor between the Jointenants is the elder Title, and after the Marriage the Wife continued sole possessed; for if the Husband die, the Feme shall have it, and not the Executors of the Husband.

For evidence of purpose-built premises I am grateful to Susan Skedd for sharing with me her research on school mistresses, who at least from the 1760s on sometimes leased large houses in order to set up schools.

17. For more on the residential clustering of women see Olwen Hufton, "Women without Men: Widows and Spinsters in Britain and France in the Eighteenth Century," *Journal of Family History* 9 (1984):361 and Erickson, *Women and Property in Early Modern England*, 189–192.

18. Clark, *Working Life of Women in the Seventeenth Century*, 156–157, 302; Tilly and Scott, *Women, Work and Family*, 15, 21, 47.

19. Hill, *Women, Work and Sexual Politics*, 46. However see Prior, "Women and the Urban Economy," 96–98, for a more-than-usually candid discussion of gender inequality in the family economy.

20. For a powerful critique of idealized views of the family economy see Bennett, "Medieval Women, Modern Women."

21. Earle, "Female Labour Market in London," 338.

22. For a critique of functionalist and essentialist biases in discussions of women's work, see Charles and Duffin, eds., *Women and Work in Preindustrial England*, 18–19.

23. But see Ben-Amos, *Adolescence and Youth in Early Modern England*, 153; Wrigley and Schofield, *Population History of England*, 262–265. For a more thorough

attempt to explain this phenomenon see Jeremy Goldberg, "London Widowhood Revisited: The Decline of Female Remarriage in the Seventeenth and Early Eighteenth Centuries," *Continuity and Change* 3 (1990):323–355.

24. Moses Pitt, *The Cry of the Oppressed, Being a True and Tragical Account of the Unparallel'd Sufferings of Multitudes of Poor Imprisoned Debtors, in Most of the Gaols in England, under the Tyranny of the Gaolers, and Other Oppressors* (London: Printed for Moses Pitt, 1691), 68–69. *Feme covert* was the legal term used to designate a married woman's lack, for most intents and purposes, of a legal identity distinct from that of her husband. Susannah Taylor is using it of herself to emphasize her dependent and helpless condition.

25. Ibid., 80.

26. If he was one of the trustees he *was* within his rights, but Susannah Taylor is at least implying here that he was not a trustee. On separate settlements and married women's "rights" see pp. 157–162, 164–165.

27. For the background of the *feme sole* custom see Mary Bateson, ed., *Borough Customs*, Publications of the Selden Society; vol. 21. (London: Bernard Quaritch, 1904), 227–228. For a fairly pessimistic view of *feme sole* that accords closely with the one expressed in this chapter, see Bennett, "Medieval Women, Modern Women," 154–155.

28. PRO E112/1089/117, Court of Exchequer Bill. This was a trifling sum, amounting to little more than £5 a year. Journeyman laborers in this period made between £15 and £50 a year, depending on the trade, and middling traders such as the Browns earned £50 to £100 or more.

29. It was explicitly pointed out by the plaintiff that Sarah Brown was "possessed of or intitled to no Seperate Estate of her own."

30. What seems to have been at issue here was the principle that a married woman could operate as an independent *feme sole* trader rather than a *feme covert*, provided her husband did not meddle in any way with, or benefit directly from, his wife's trade. The significance of the *feme sole* principle for this case was that the husband of a *feme sole* trader was not liable for his wife's debts. I have not been able to determine whether Stockport actually possessed such a custom, although quite a few other towns and cities, including London, did. The plaintiff, Thomas Siddall, and the defendants, Thomas and Sarah Brown, were arguing within the terms of *feme sole* custom, although they did not use the precise term. Thomas Brown argued that he had had nothing to do with the business; Siddall argued that he had. Exchequer, as an equity court, was presumably being asked, in part, to adjudicate on the relevance of the principle for this case. Unfortunately the case does not seem to have been pursued beyond the bill stage.

31. This story is pieced together from the collection of documents that comprises PRO C105/30, Chancery Masters' Exhibits. I have been unable to locate any corresponding Chancery proceedings.

32. The assignees' side of the dispute is less well documented in the surviving records, but presumably they would have argued that Joseph Holl was more heavily involved, financially and otherwise, in Mary's business than either he or Mary would admit.

33. PRO C105/30, fol. 15, Mary Holl to Mr. Plowman, undated (1778), "Coppy to Plowman soon after my Laces was taken from me, 1778."

34. This is not to say that marital disharmony was not extremely stressful and at times damaging to men. In divorce cases the men often argued that women hurt their trade by gossiping about them or that they ruined the family finances with their extravagance. See for example GLRO, DL/C/632, Consistory Court, *Spinkes v. Spinkes* (1711–1712), fol. 172; DL/C/154, *Byfield v. Byfield* (1710), fol. 57; and DL/C/154, *Hull v. Hull* (1711), fol. 228. The entry for 7 Oct. 1758 in Turner, *Diary of Thomas Turner*, 164–165, details some of Turner's frustration and hurt when his wife refused to help him with his shop accounts.

35. There are some methodological problems with lumping all these groups together. For example, there is some evidence that spinsters had a harder time maintaining their independence than did widows. On the disproportionate number of spinsters who were prosecuted for infringing on Company monopolies see Prior, "Women and the Urban Economy," 110–113.

36. The best edition of Charke's autobiography is the original, Charlotte Charke, *A Narrative of the Life of Mrs. Charlotte Charke (Youngest Daughter of Colley Cibber, Esq.)* (London: Printed for W. Reeve, A. Dodd, E. Cook, 1755). A more recent edition is Fidelis Morgan with Charlotte Charke, *The Well-known Troublemaker: A Life of Charlotte Charke* (London and Boston: Faber and Faber, 1988), which comprises Charke's narrative alternating with background chapters by Morgan. Morgan has uncovered some useful data on Charke, but is overconcerned to "prove" that she was not a lesbian—a difficult task at this remove.

37. Charke, *Narrative of the Life of Mrs. Charlotte Charke*, 34–39, 60–66, 70.

38. Ibid., 76.

39. Ibid., 122–123, 134–136, 138–139. The suggestion in the autobiography is that Charke actually did pass as a man in addition to dressing like one.

40. See ibid., 91–92, 94, 132, 143–144, 147, 190, 223–225 et passim. It was, however, Charke's uncle, who lent her the money to open the short-lived public house, 148–149. Arrangements like the one Charke worked out with "Mrs. Brown" are turning out to be more common than was once thought. See Van de Pol and Dekker, *The Tradition of Female Transvestism*, based, in part, upon the evidence of women attempting to enter the Dutch Navy in the eighteenth century.

41. Charke, *Narrative of the Life of Mrs. Charlotte Charke*, 184, 192, 223, 231, 240. Morgan with Charke, *Well-known Troublemaker*, 217.

42. Charke, *Narrative of the Life of Mrs. Charlotte Charke*, 264–265.

43. Virtually the only traditional woman's job that Charke never tried was needlework, owing to an antipathy to it that dated from early childhood. Ibid., 33.

44. *Advice to the Women and Maidens of London*, 19.

45. A detailed description of Gertrude Rolles' stall and various of her property transactions can be found in PRO C112/181 part 2, Chancery Masters' Exhibits.

46. The will was proved 1 August, 1698, by Gertrude Rolles the younger only (PRO C112/181 part 2).

47. The sons may have been previously provided for, for it was standard practice to deduct amounts spent on sons' apprenticeship premiums, and so on, from their inheritance. Still, there is a clear intimation in this will of an ethic of female solidarity around shared work.

48. One of the standard methods in the eighteenth century for women to offset their disadvantages in terms of access to capital was to set up in business with one

or more of their sisters or another woman. This pattern manifested itself especially strongly in the two most significant and lucrative "growth" areas of eighteenth-century female entrepreneurship, millinery and the keeping of boarding schools for girls. Both these occupations demanded substantial capital and labor investment.

49. John Havill, "Eleanor Coade, Artificial Stone Manufacturer Born Exeter 1733 and died London 1821" (typescript c. 1986, copy in the Guildhall Library), contains valuable information on Coade but also some misconceptions about women's work in the eighteenth century. See also Alison Kelly, *Mrs. Coade's Stone* (Upton-upon-Severn, Worcs.: Self-Publishing Association, Ltd., in Conjunction with the Georgian Group, 1990), which includes data on Coade's designs and marketing techniques. There are thousands of extant examples of coadestone. The best known is probably the pediment of the Royal Naval College, Greenwich (discussed Havill, "Eleanor Coade," 67). A description of Coade's business premises is found in her Royal Exchange Insurance Policy of 1776 (Guildhall MS 7253/2, no. 68073. The policy was for:

> Goods in trade in her warehouse, workshop & kiln house [£]1000; adj[acent] timber built [building] having 2 kilns therein situate at Kings Arms Stairs [Lambeth]; [and] On goods in trade in the warehouse timber built having 1 kiln therein situate at Knightsbrige in the county of Middx.

Unfortunately there is no policy for her dwelling. I am grateful to Linda Semple for telling me about Eleanor Coade, for showing me several extant examples of coadestone, and for locating Eleanor Coade's insurance policies.

50. A copy of Eleanor Coade's will is PRO PROB 11/1651. The largest group (fifteen) of female legatees were spinsters. Widows accounted for five of the legatees and married women for nine, four of the latter bequests being in trust for their separate use. For ten of the female legatees marital status could not be determined, although it seems likely that the majority were not then married. Part of the reason that Coade's bequests were biased toward women (and toward spinsters and widows) was that she was, as she stated in her preamble, concerned to give money where it was most needed, and spinsters and widows tended to be poorer on average than either men or married women. On the other hand, the terms she uses to describe many of the spinsters (e.g., "my much esteemed friend Anna," "my respected friend Martha Hills," "my servant and very dear Christian friend Elizabeth Parsons") suggest that they were part of her inner circle, not simply charity cases. In another bequest she gave "[to] Mary Tozer [her spinster cousin] £200 in trust to be disposed of at her discretion for the benefit of her brother Aaron Tozer of . . . Axminster, Schoolmaster," a rare example of a woman being named a trustee for a male who is not a minor. The bequest to her long-time companion was as follows:

> Interest on 1300 of 4% bank annuities to go to Hannah Wootten or her assigns in trust during her life-time and after her death one half to go to the British & Foreign Bible Society and one half to the Society established in 1733 for the relief of necessitous widows and children of Protestant Dissenting Ministers.

One of the few extant letters referring specifically to Coade (Beavis Wood to Nathaniel, Lord Harrowby, dtd. 19 Dec. 1795) touches on the unlikelihood of her giving financial help to one of her male relatives. Wood remarks that the relative in need "has a right to expect it but I have many [doubts?] about the extent of the bounty of Miss C. She is too great a Saint to have many New Feelings for her poor Relations." In fact, in this case Eleanor asserted her influence at the India House to secure a position for him. It is clear, however, that at least some of her male relatives were nervous about the degree of her commitment to them or, perhaps, about their inability to control her decisions. The letter is quoted in Havill, "Eleanor Coade," 33. Erickson, *Women and Property in Early Modern England*, 19–20, 211–219, contains a subtle discussion of women testators' tendency to favor other women in their wills.

51. Hunt, "Hawkers, Bawlers and Mercuries," 41–68.

52. Prior, "Women and the Urban Economy," 110–113. But the loosening of controls also played a role in the proletarianization of a number of trades.

53. Alison Adburgham, *Shops and Shopping, 1800–1914: Where and in What Manner the Well-Dressed Englishwoman Bought her Clothes* (London: Allen and Unwin, 1964), 5–6; Dorothy Davis, *A History of Shopping* (London and Toronto: Routledge & Kegan Paul and University of Toronto Press, 1966), 191–203.

54. There is much evidence of women's investments scattered across the archives. The Guildhall Library's unrivaled collection of insurance policies contains copious evidence of women's *rentier* activity. Some of these are discussed in Earle, *Making of the English Middle Class*, 171–174. Chancery and Exchequer records show some of women's other investments. See, for example, PRO C114/182 part 2, Chancery Masters' Exhibits, for the accounts of Judith DuBuc (1720s and 1730s); C112/46 part 1, Papers and Accounts relating to the estate of Hannah Bayly, 1756–1759; and E112/1241, Exchequer Bills, piece 3666, Eliz. Fitzmaurice vs. Edmund Brown. Divorce Cases in Consistory Court sometimes made mention of the ways women (or their trustees) invested their separate estates. For women investors in the Bank of England, East India Company, South Sea Company, and long annuities see Dickson, *Financial Revolution*, 278, 280, 281–282.

55. In the Sun Insurance Policy book for 1720/1721 (Guildhall MS 11936/13), there were thirty-six rentier women out of a total of ninety-two women policy holders. Some of these women owned buildings broken into tiny tenements and densely occupied.

CHAPTER 6: THE BONDS OF MATRIMONY

1. Barnes, *Memoirs*, 67–68, 71. For more on sauces see Campbell, *London Tradesman*, 277.

2. Ambrose Barnes, *The Life of Ambrose Barnes, Sometime Alderman of Newcastle* (Newcastle: Printed by T. & J. Hodgson for Emerson Charnley, 1828), 33. This earlier, privately printed version of parts of the Barnes manuscript is different from the Surtees Society version and a good deal less authoritative, although it does contain some material not found in the later edition. The original manuscript of the memoirs perished in a fire at the Literary and Philosophical Society of Newcastle upon Tyne in 1893.

3. Barnes, *Memoirs* (1867), 68, 101.

4. Ibid., 71–72, 169.

5. Barnes, *Life* (1828), 29–30.
6. Barnes, *Memoirs* (1867), 46.
7. Ibid., 72, 68, 70.
8. Ibid., 71, 73.
9. The cynical among us will be reassured to find that, in later years, Barnes's children intrigued among themselves for his money and affection, and antipathies developed. For example, one son, who had gone into the law, conceived a violent dislike for all members of the clergy, including his own brother. See ibid., 75–76.
10. For more on the allegely disordered lives of elites see pp. 197–202.
11. Barnes, *Memoirs* (1867), 117, 210. For a discussion of Barnes's republicanism see pp. 194–195.
12. BL Sloane MS 4460.7, fols. 61–62. The item apparently dates from 1693–1694.
13. A fine overview of eighteenth-century courtship is found in Hill, *Women, Work and Sexual Politics,* 174–186.
14. For more on Samuel Marriott's life and family difficulties see pp. 27–29.
15. "[M]y want of Spirit which I thought to be my Misfortune only, I found to be now charged upon me as my Fault," Marriott wrote dejectedly after an interview with her. Bodleian, MS Rawlinson D 114, fol. 63.
16. Thomas Wright, *The Autobiography of Thomas Wright of Birkenshaw in the County of York. 1736–1797,* ed. Thomas Wright (London: John Russell Smith, 1864), 47–48.
17. Ibid., 48, 90–108.
18. Dr. Williams's Library Doddridge Collection L1/4, fol. 151, Wright and S. Burkitt to Mrs. Doddridge, 22 Jan. 1768.
19. For an account of the use of dowries as starting capital, see Earle, *Making of the English Middle Class,* 110, 190, 194, 196–198. For the later eighteenth century and the early nineteenth century see Davidoff and Hall, *Family Fortunes,* 123. For a discussion of the dowry system and marital egalitarianism or the lack thereof, see Susan Moller Okin, "Patriarchy and Married Women's Property in England: Questions about Some Current Views," *Eighteenth-Century Studies* 17 (1983–1984):121–138.
20. On the uses to which portions were put in aristocratic families see Okin, "Patriarchy and Married Women's Property," 131; see also Trumbach, *Rise of the Egalitarian Family,* 81.
21. Guildhall MS 12,017, "Some Account of the Life &c of John Fryer & of Several of his Relations written by himself 1715 &c," fols. 22–23.
22. Jonathan Priestley, "Some Memoirs Concerning the Family of the Priestleys, Written at the Request of a Friend. (1696)," in Charles Jackson, ed., *Yorkshire Diaries and Autobiographies,* Surtees Society Publications, vol. 77 (Durham: Surtees Society, 1886), 12–13. The Priestleys and their kin included cloth factors and manufacturers, grocers, merchants, and a maltster. One of the aunts was a professional moneylender.
23. For an account of one such protracted negotiation in a rural setting see Leonard Wheatcroft, *The Courtship Narrative of Leonard Wheatcroft, Derbyshire Yeoman,*

ed. George Parfitt and Ralph Houlbrooke (Reading: Whiteknights Press, 1986), 25–26, 54, 62, 79–80. In this case some land was involved.

24. On aristocratic marriage settlements and the methods by which portions and jointures were financed see Beckett, *Aristocracy in England,* 107–108, 296–297.

25. Earle, *Making of the English Middle Class,* 187.

26. Nor was this a problem only in middling families. See Peter Roebuck, *Yorkshire Baronets, 1640–1760: Families, Estates and Fortunes* (Oxford: Oxford University Press, 1980), 330, cited in Susan Staves, *Married Women's Separate Property in England, 1660–1833* (Cambridge, Mass.: Harvard University Press, 1990), 118.

27. The papers of John Moore (1620–1702), grocer and sometime Lord Mayor of London, include a typical letter of this type from the widow of a haberdasher, who was trying to get her six-year-old daughter into Christ's hospital and who wrote that her husband had left her with "a charge of children and . . . no Imployment wherebye to maintayne her said children." The petition is accompanied by a letter signed by nine churchwardens of St. Swithins, which testifies that the petitioner is "a very honest and Industrious woman to the best of our knowledge and hath been alwaies very willing to worke for a livelyhood." This gives some sense of the kind of resolve a woman had to display to get support. (Guildhall MS 507, Mary Moss to John Moore, dtd. 14 Dec. 1686.) Less respectable and less literate was Sarah Bosswell of Yarmouth who, between 1720 and 1721, wrote, or had written on her behalf, a series of pathetic appeals for financial help to her brother-in-law, Henry Gambier, an employee of the East India Company. See p. 253, nn. 63–64. Donna Andrew has recently completed an article on supplicant's letters to Margaret, Lady Spencer, that illuminates many of the gendered aspects of the practice. See Donna T. Andrew, "*Noblesse Oblige:* Female Charity in an Age of Sentiment," in John Brewer and Susan Staves, eds., *Early Modern Conceptions of Property* (London and New York: Routledge, 1995). I am grateful to Donna Andrew for permitting me to read this article before publication.

28. GLRO DL/C/154, Consistory Court of London Proceedings, fols. 51, 56–57, Statement of Elizabeth Byfield.

29. DL/C/154, fol. 247, Statement of Hester Pitts; and DL/C/632, fol. 124, Deposition of Joseph Wilson, Elizabeth Spinke's brother-in-law. All the quotations are taken from actions for divorce *a mensa et thoro* (actually, legal separation) brought before the court in the years 1711 to 1713. For a more detailed discussion of these and other cases see Hunt, "Wife-beating, Domesticity and Women's Independence," 10–33. For cultural attitudes to wife-beating see Roderick Phillips, *Putting Asunder: A History of Divorce in Western Society* (Cambridge: Cambridge University Press, 1988), 324–330; and Hill, *Women, Work and Sexual Politics,* 198–200.

30. Defoe, *Complete English Tradesman,* vol. 1, 140.

31. Ibid., vol. 1, 143–144.

32. Guildhall MS 11021/1, Eleanora Hucks to Nelly Hucks, undated (probably April 1774).

33. Ibid., Hucks to Hucks, undated (1774).

34. Ibid., Hucks to Hucks, undated (1774).

35. Dr. Williams's Library MS L1/2, fol. 95, Miss Mercy Doddridge to Mrs. Mercy Doddridge, dtd. 27 Dec. 1752. Miss Mercy's rather unenthusiastic views of marriage can be surmised from her correspondence with another spinster, a Miss

E. Clark. See MS L1/5, fols. 46 and 48, E. Clark to Miss Mercy Doddridge, dtd. 26 Nov. 1762; E. Clark to Miss Mercy Doddridge, dtd. 19 Feb. 1763.

36. [Sarah Chapone], *The Hardships of the English Laws in Relation to Wives* (London: George Faulkner, 1735), 47. I am grateful to Jan Thaddeus for uncovering the authorship of this tract.

37. When other sorts of assistance failed, it was not uncommon for women to place advertisements in the newspapers describing their plight and asking for donations from the reading public. The following advertisement, which appeared in the *Public Advertiser,* no. 6611 (5 Jan. 1756) is typical of a fairly extensive genre:

> A Gentlewoman of a good Family is now reduced to the greatest Poverty, and must be utterly undone and made incapable of helping herself if she cannot raise six pounds to pay her Rent and another debt of forty-four shillings. . . . She has no other way left but to implore the assistance of all Charitable and well-disposed People, that will be pleased to send their Benevolence for O.P. with Mrs. Jane Philips in the Upper Ground, facing the Royal Oak, by Marygold Stairs, near Christ Church in Surry.

Other advertisements dwelt on the depredations of extravagant men. See for example the *Public Advertiser,* no. 6616 (10 Jan. 1756). Most women who placed ads referred to themselves as "gentlewomen" but this need not be taken too literally. For a stimulating discussion of the phenomenon of women telling their tales of woe in print see Shevelow, *Women and Print Culture,* 58–92.

38. This formula is adapted from Lee Holcombe, *Wives and Property: Reform of the Married Women's Property Law in Nineteenth-Century England* (Toronto and Buffalo: University of Toronto Press, 1983), 40. On separate settlements see especially Staves, *Married Women's Separate Property in England;* Amy Louise Erickson, "Common Law versus Common Practice," 21–39; and Erickson, *Women and Property;* 102–155. The "trust" part of the separate settlement could be a serious part of the arrangement, or it could be purely nominal, or mention of trustees could be omitted, in which case, at least in theory, the woman administered her own funds. Staves, *Married Women's Separate Property in England,* 133, notes that by 1725 the courts had decided that women *could* possess separate property without the intermediary trustees. Many agreements retained trustees, however.

39. A marriage settlement is not synonymous with a separate settlement. A marriage settlement might provide for any or all of the following: the jointure (the amount of money a woman would be awarded for her support on her husband's death), portions and/or maintenance for children of a previous marriage, the allowance a woman might expect for clothes ("pin money"), a married woman's right to dispose of property by will, or a separate settlement for the wife. Many marriage settlements did *not* include provisions for a separate settlement.

40. For a discussion of patterns of bequests among female testators see Erickson, *Women and Property,* 209–221. For separate estates by bequest see ibid., 124, 214. My impression is that the practice of establishing separate estates by bequest was a good deal more common in the eighteenth than the seventeenth century.

41. For a discussion of Richard Steele and pin money see Edmund Leites, "Good Humor at Home, Good Humor Abroad: The Intimacies of Marriage and the Civilities of Social Life in the Ethic of Richard Steele," in Edward A. Bloom, Lillian D. Bloom, and Edmund Leites, eds., *Educating the Audience: Addison, Steele*

and Eighteenth-Century Culture, Papers Presented to the Clark Library Seminar, 15 November 1980 (Los Angeles: William Andrews Clark Memorial Library, University of California, 1984), 51–89. In fact, attacks on separate settlements considerably predate Richard Steele; see for instance Richard Allestree, *The Ladies Calling* (Oxford: Printed at the Theater, 1705 [orig. 1673]), 186. The middling separate settlements encountered in the course of the present study virtually never involved pin money in the strict sense, although the issue admittedly is complicated by the fact that the term was sometimes understood to mean separate settlements more generally. See Staves, *Married Women's Separate Property in England,* 155–156, on the difficulty of distinguishing pin money from separate settlements.

42. Erickson, "Common Law versus Common Practice," 26–27, 31–33, 37. The median value of these men's estates was a mere £160, and that of the settlement was £40, with the range being £13 to £640 for the value of the estates and £5 to £528 for the value of the settlements. Three-quarters of the settlements involved sums of money under £100. There were two gentlemen in Erickson's sample of thirty-nine, but there were also at least three husbandmen and a weaver. Probate accounts of this type would not be likely to make mention of property or monies disposed of years before. And they would not be likely to indicate separate estates acquired by wives through bequests.

43. Davidoff and Hall, *Family Fortunes,* 209–210.

44. Historians who study separate settlements generally agree that they arose initially as a way to safeguard the wife's family's money and to provide for the welfare of children rather than to promote female autonomy; after that, consensus breaks down. Basically the debate boils down to the following question: did separate settlements, notwithstanding their original intent, promote women's independence and improve their status, or were they merely a negligible drop in the patriarchal bucket? For an optimistic view see Stone, *Family, Sex and Marriage in England,* 330–333; for a pessimistic view see Okin, "Patriarchy and Married Women's Property in England," 121–138. Okin thinks that, in practice, a woman had little control over her separate estate, because she had a legal and religious obligation to obey her husband and because he could bully her into giving up what control she possessed.

45. Peter Briggins (1666–1717) of London, a rich, well-connected grocer, makes a matter-of-fact reference to investing his wife's separate estate in hops. There is no mention at all of any involvement on the part of his wife. Howard, ed., *Eliot Papers,* vol. 2, 54.

46. Bruce H. Mann, *Neighbors and Strangers: Law and Community in Early Connecticut* (Chapel Hill and London: University of North Carolina Press, 1987), 162–169, deals with the use of formal credit instruments within families and the potentially alienating effects of abstract "legal formalism" on neighborly and intrafamilial financial arrangements.

47. PRO C114/182 part 2, Chancery Masters' Exhibits, "A Book of Receipts, Payments and Disbursements." Notations like the following suggest someone who administers her own money:

> I have lent Mr. Armiger [her husband] my 300 £: he is to alow me 5 pd percent till returned. I have his note. I have borrowed of Madame Dehais one 100 for Mr. Armiger.

He is to pay me 5 percent he made me a Bond att Mr. Strasy, the [notary?].” (fol. 170)

Later DuBuc writes

Jay finy de conte avec Mr. Armiger a avril 1722 jay acorde de prandre sur le bien en morgege ce que il ne me peut rendre de ce que luy ay preste a condition quand il aura ventre son bien qui il me le Rendra.” (fol. 170)

A notation from the early 1720s reads

recu . . . Warant de mon stok dans la Compagnie du Sude de 1051:17-6 qui Estoit du a Xmas 1723-4 [amount] 31:11:1.” (fol. 172)

One for July 22, 1732 reads

I have sold all my South Sea Stock. I have [bought?] one thousand pound of 3 per cent annuity at the bank of the Lottery 1731.” (fol. 81)

Trustees for her separate estate are nowhere in evidence in this woman's accounts.

48. PRO E112/1241 piece 3666, Court of Exchequer, *Elizabeth Fitzmaurice, widow, v. Edmund Brown.* By the time the case was brought both Elinor and William Fitzmaurice were dead. Elizabeth Fitzmaurice was a later wife of Fitzmaurice's, while Edmund Brown was Elinor Fitzmaurice's grandson and, presumably, heir.

49. When the bookseller, real-estate speculator, and prison reformer Moses Pitt was imprisoned for debt in the late seventeenth century, he signed over his wife's estate to his creditor as a matter of course. We are not told what she thought of this. See Pitt, *Cry of the Oppressed,* 119. There is much evidence of conflict over separate settlements in the sources. For three quite disparate cases see Guildhall MS 10823/1, Commonplace Book of George Boddington, Levant merchant, fols. 30–32, for the troubled marriage of his daughter and financial machinations of his son-in-law; and BL Add. MSS 45718, fols. 40–47 et passim, for the autobiography and the accounts of a gentlewoman, Elizabeth Freke, which detail two decades of battles with her husband over her separate settlement. The Bodleian Library possesses a letter from John Dunton, the bookseller, to his estranged wife, seeking to coerce her into giving up her jointure in order to pay his debts (MS Rawlinson D 72, fols. 137–142, undated, ca. 1718).

50. GLRO DL/C/154, fol. 508, Statement of Elizabeth Spinkes. The threat of confinement in a madhouse was a standard one, and some men, like Spinkes, actually delivered on the threat. This case casts a somewhat equivocal light on Dr. James Newton, for whose career see the DNB.

51. GLRO DL/C/154 fol. 228, Statement of Mary Hull.

52. GLRO DL/C/154, fol. 247, Statement of Rebecca Hudson. These cases are contained in the interrogatory books for 1711–1713.

53. See M. R. Chesterman, “Family Settlements on Trust: Landowners and the Rising Bourgeoisie,” in G. R. Rubin and David Sugarman, eds., *Law, Economy and Society, 1750–1914: Essays in the History of English Law* (Abingdon, Oxon.: Professional Books, 1984), 124–167, i–xii. On the other hand, Davidoff and Hall show that separate settlements still continued to be used by male relatives for their own investment purposes (*Family Fortunes,* 209). Susan Staves discusses juridical efforts, dating for the most part from the late eighteenth century, that were designed to stop women (or their husbands) from “sinking the fund” and dissipating the

capital that was supposed to be used for her support and that of her children. See Staves, *Married Women's Separate Property in England*, 150–153. Even in the present day women in the wealthier classes still have a much more passive relationship to money than do their fathers, brothers, and husbands, and this state of affairs is still often enforced structurally via the trust.

54. Nicolas de Venette, *The Mysteries of Conjugal Love Reveal'd*, translated from the French (London: n.p., 1712), 136–137. This is an abridged translation of one of the editions of de Venette's *Tableau de l'amour considéré dans l'estat du mariage*, originally published in Amsterdam in 1687.

55. Ibid., 141.

56. For the flow of resources from kin see pp. 151–153.

57. See pp. 112–115 for a discussion of Reformation of Manners activists' attacks on prostitutes. An excellent discussion of eighteenth-century charities for reformed prostitutes that gives due attention to notions about out-of-control sexuality among poor women is Andrew, *Philanthropy and Police*, 119–127, 187–194.

58. *The London Bawd*, 35–54. On the long history of efforts, juridical and otherwise, to separate "whores" from other women (including forcing the former to wear distinctive headgear, live in different parts of town, wear badges, etc.), see Otis, *Prostitution in Medieval Society*. "Respectable" women often collaborated enthusiastically with these projects.

59. See for example William Hazeland, *A Sermon Preached in the Chapel of the Asylum, Near Westminster Bridge on the Sunday Before Christmas-day, 1760* (London: J. Beecroft, 1761), which dwells at inflammatory length upon the huge number of debauched women working the London streets, the virtual impossibility of reforming them, and their well-nigh irresistible appeal: "Your Sons, Yourselves might possibly have been led astray by her harlot lure" (12).

60. The prize for the most involved series of sexual accusations in a divorce case probably should go to Ivie v. Ivie, which came through Chancery during the interregnum. It gives a good sense of the range of possible sexual incompatibilities, miscommunications, and abuses. See Ivie, *Alimony Arraigned*. Thomas Ivie accused his wife Theodosia of keeping low company, refusing to give him any account of what she spent (a woman friend is said to have advised her that "what was her Husbands, was her own, and why should she account for her own" (11); if true, a most creative approach to the principle of coverture), withholding herself from him sexually so there would be no issue, threatening to abort their child, being "too familiar" with her own father, and consulting fortune-tellers to find out when Ivie would die. She is also said to have complained to other women "that her first Husband had done the part of a man, twelve times [on] the marriage night. But that this husband [i.e., Ivie] had done but eight" (12). Thomas also claimed that he never received her portion and had to pay for her extravagant lifestyle.

Theodosia Ivie, for her part, accused her husband of beating her, infecting her with venereal disease, trying to sodomize her, and sleeping with her maid-servant, as well as dissipating her separate estate. Her side of the story is told in such a way as to refute it in *Alimony Arraigned;* it is recounted more sympathetically by one of her relatives in John Bramston, *The Autobiography of Sir John Bramston, K.B., of Skreens, in the Hundred of Chelmsford*, Camden Society Publications, vol. 32 (London: Printed for the Camden Society, 1845), 15–19, 279–281. The luxuriant variety of the accusations in this case is unusual, but taken individually, most of the sexual (and nonsexual) allegations on both sides were fairly commonplace, and combinations of them could be found in middling as well as elite divorce cases throughout the period.

61. BL Add. MSS 4264, fol. 216, Catharine Cockburn to Anne Arbuthnot, dtd. 18 April 1741.

62. Earle, *Making of the English Middle Class*, 195. The presence of a jointure agreement took precedence over and had the effect of barring the traditional right of dower. As Susan Staves points out, the jointure often ended up being for considerably less than what the widow would have gotten in dower; see Staves, *Married Women's Separate Property in England*, 27–32, 94–130). Moreover, jointures were susceptible to being broken by impecunious husbands, just as separate estates were. Conversely, Amy Erickson suggests that a jointure might be preferable if the man's estate was heavily burdened by debts. Whereas dower was computed on the basis of the man's estate *after* all his debts had been paid, jointure was treated as an ordinary debt, and the widow, who was often the executrix, tended to pay herself first. See Erickson, "Common Law versus Common Practice," 33–34.

63. Testators and others sometimes sought legal means of forcing their relations to support them or their dependents. For instance, bequests might come with the condition that the inheritor support his or her aged parents until they died. Such arrangements were ancient practice in the countryside; they have been little studied for urban people. For an example of the latter see PRO C112/76, Chancery Master's Exhibits, an assignment of a lease on property in Lambeth by one Jane Franklin, tallow chandler, who was passing the trade to her son William. The condition of the transfer was that he pay her £20 rent each year. After her death, £8 a year was to go to his spinster sister, also named Jane, up to the time the ground lease expired or she married. If the son refused to pay he was to be expelled from the property. See Hill, *Women, Work and Sexual Politics*, 251, for a typical rural case; and Erickson, *Women and Property*, 164–165, for a discussion of regional variations.

64. Hufton, "Women and the Family Economy in Eighteenth-Century France," 21.

65. See GLRO A/CSC/8, General Index to the Court Books, Corporation of the Sons of the Clergy. An especially large number of women seem to have given to the maiden daughters' fund, which, unlike some other spinsters' charities, gave a pension rather than a lump-sum payment—thus acting as a disincentive to marriage. Granted, a good many of the pensioners were probably well beyond marriageable age.

66. For an influential argument about the Evangelical Revival and the rise of the middle class, see Davidoff and Hall, *Family Fortunes*, 71–192. For a dissenting voice see Wahrman, " 'Middle-Class' Domesticity goes Public," 396–432.

67. (Mrs.) Edwin [Almyra] Gray, ed., *Papers and Diaries of a York Family, 1764–1839* (London: Sheldon Press, 1927), 21, 31–33, 70.

68. Ibid., 33–34.

69. Ibid., 35–37, 72.

70. Ibid., 74–76.

71. In 1809 her daughter Lucy made a special note in a book she was reading of the line "Every hour comes to us charged with duty and the moment it is past

returns to heaven to register itself, how spent." Daily plans for the employment of *her* daughter's (Faith Gray's grandaughter's) time survive from 1825 and 1826 (ibid., 44, 257).

72. Mrs. Gray took a very dim view of the poor laws, which were, she thought, "so constituted and so administered as to hold out a certain support to the idle and profligate" (ibid., 58). Such criticisms had been around since medieval times. They are especially interesting in this context, however, because indiscriminate giving was thought by some to be a particular vice of women, especially elite women. Compare Perkin, *Origins of Modern English Society*, 224–225, on Cobden's disdain for the "maternal" charity of the squire's wife and daughters when compared with a "masculine species of charity" designed to inculcate in the labouring classes "the love of independence, the privilege of self respect, the disdain of being patronized or petted, the desire to accumulate and the ambition to rise."

73. Gray, *Papers and Diaries*, 52, 55.

74. Ibid., 54–66. These women's commitment to "scientific" charity is very clear, from their close accounting and their use of work incentives to their adoption of some of the dietary recommendations of Count Rumford, a contemporary Continental reformer. For an overview of the Sunday School Movement and other charitable efforts of the period, including a discussion of "scientific" charity, see Andrew, *Philanthropy and Police*, 170–172, 174–177, 181, 183. Sarah Trimmer's *The Oeconomy of Charity; or, an Address to Ladies Concerning Sunday Schools, the Establishment of Schools of Industry under Female Inspection* (London: T. Bensley, 1787) is an effort to publicize activities like those of Faith Gray's circle. Trimmer's own contribution to more scientific philanthropy was the inclusion in her tract of a detailed fold-out plan for a newly invented spinning wheel "at which twelve little girls can spin at once" (72). Middle-class female philanthropy converged readily with the factory system.

75. Gray, *Papers and Diaries*, 75, 89.

CHAPTER 7: PRINT CULTURE AND THE MIDDLING CLASSES

1. Adam Smith, *An Inquiry into the Nature and Causes of The Wealth of Nations*, ed. Edwin Cannan (New York: Modern Library, 1937), 117–118.

2. See pp. 27–28, 39–40.

3. R. H. Tawney, *Religion and the Rise of Capitalism: A Historical Study*, Scott Holland Memorial Lectures, 1922 (London: J. Murray, 1926); Schlatter, *Social Ideas of Religious Leaders*. See also Weber, *Protestant Ethic*.

4. Bartholemew Ashwood, *The Heavenly Trade or the Best Merchandizing: The Only Way to Live Well in Impoverishing Times* (London: Printed for Samuel Lee, 1679), 353, 334. The book is dedicated to Mr. Jeremy Holwey, a Bristol merchant, in whose house it is said to have been written.

5. Ibid., 350, 353.

6. See, for example, John Warner, *The Gayne of Losse* (London: 1645); and Thomas Tisser, *A Sermon Preached at St. Bartholemew Exchange, on Wednesday the 3d of December, 1701. Before the Honourable Company of Merchants Trading into the Levant-Seas* (London: Samuel Keble, 1702). See also Thomas R. Preston, "Biblical Criticism, Literature and the Eighteenth-Century Reader," in Isabel Rivers, ed., *Books and*

Their Readers in Eighteenth-Century England (Leicester and New York: Leicester University Press and St. Martin's Press, 1982), 97–126, especially 111–112.

7. The volitional spirit of accumulating things in a bank is somewhat more akin to a doctrine that permits "works" to play some role in salvation (Arminianism) than it is to orthodox Calvinist predestinarianism. On Arminian trends in this period see Norman Sykes, *From Sheldon to Secker: Aspects of English Church History, 1660–1760* (Cambridge: Cambridge University Press, 1959), 144–151, 186–187, 219.

8. For a recent discussion of this issue see Donald Davie, *The Eighteenth-Century Hymn in England,* Cambridge Studies in Eighteenth-Century English Literature and Thought, 19 (Cambridge: Cambridge University Press, 1993).

9. The original *Collection for Improvement of Husbandry and Trade* appeared in London between 1692 and 1703 in the form of unpaginated single sheets. The edition used here is the reassembled (and retitled) reprint: John Houghton, *Husbandry and Trade Improv'd: Being a Collection of Many Valuable Materials Relating to Corn, Cattle, Coals, Hops, Wood, &c.,* ed. R. Bradley, 4 vols. (London: Woodman and Lyon, 1728).

10. Ibid., vol. 1, 18.

11. Houghton's approach derives from an older genre of compendia of exchange rates, distances between cities, trading fairs, and the like, that were designed mainly for merchants and commercial travelers. See for example Lewes Roberts, *The Merchants Mappe of Commerce: Wherein, the Vniversall Manner and Matter of Trade, is Compendiously Handled. The Standerd and Currant Coines of Sundry Princes, Observed. The Reall and Imaginary Coines of Accompts and Exchanges, Expressed. The Naturall and Artificiall Commodities of all Countries for Transportation Declared. The Weights and Measures of all Eminent Cities and Townes of Traffique, Collected and Reduced One into Another; and all to the Meridian of Commerce Practised in the Famous Citie of London* (London: 1638). Louis B. Wright, *Middle Class Culture in Elizabethan England* (Chapel Hill: University of North Carolina Press, 1935), 162–164, lists examples going back to the 1570s.

12. Houghton, *Husbandry and Trade Improv'd,* vol. 1, 261–263, 275, 439–445; vol. 2, 48, 97–99, 326.

13. The scientists and virtuosi were not strangers to the profit principle, although many of them were ambivalent on the subject. Houghton's zeal, however, is unadulterated by doubts. On early science and commerce see Jacob, *Newtonians and the English Revolution,* 20, 51, 53–54, 68, 160, 272.

14. For more detail on seventeenth- and eighteenth-century projects see Stewart, *Rise of Public Science,* 166–182, 257–283. For Houghton's views on slavery and labor exploitation more generally see Hunt, "Racism, Imperialism and the Traveler's Gaze in Eighteenth-Century England," 333–357. For Houghton's other activities see, once again, Stewart, *Rise of Public Science,* 16, 22, 167n.

15. Quoted in Christopher Hill, *The Century of Revolution: 1603–1714* (Edinburgh: Thomas Nelson, 1961), 219. See Dickson, *Financial Revolution,* 15–35, for post-Restoration ambivalence toward banks and bankers.

16. See *Spectator,* no. 69 (19 May 1711), Bond ed., vol. 1, 292–296; see also no. 3 (3 March 1711), Bond ed., vol. 1, 14–17; no. 174 (19 Sept. 1711), Bond, ed. vol. 2, 185–189; and no. 552 (3 Dec. 1712), Bond, ed., vol. 4, 478–483; among others.

17. Burnet's book is of additional interest because, as W. A. Speck has shown, it

was especially popular among M.P.s with merchant backgrounds. See W. A. Speck, "Politicians, Peers, and Publication by Subscription, 1700–50," in Isabel Rivers, ed., *Books and Their Readers in Eighteenth-Century England* (Leicester and New York: Leicester University Press and St. Martin's Press, 1982), 63–64. One would not want to read too much significance into this finding. As Speck points out, the books that this particular group of (former) merchants bought in the largest numbers were not, in other respects, very different from those preferred by more traditional elites.

18. Gilbert Burnet, *Bishop Burnet's History of His Own Time*, 6 vols. (Oxford: Oxford University Press, 1833), vol. 1, 223–224, 124, 140, 144–145, 155, 163, 170, 208, 318; vol. 2., 211–212, 214, 225; vol. 6, 57–58.

19. For an influential discussion of books and non-elite readers, particularly in relation to religious sectarianism, see Christopher Hill, *The World Turned Upside Down: Radical Ideas During the English Revolution* (Harmondsworth, Sussex: Penguin, 1975), especially 17–19, 92–94, 161–162, 363. See also Margaret Spufford, *Small Books and Pleasant Histories: Popular Fiction and Its Readership in Seventeenth-Century England* (Cambridge: Cambridge University Press, 1981).

20. See p. 85.

21. Jeake, *Astrological Diary*, 2.

22. Micheal Hunter and Annabel Gregory, in Jeake, *Astrological Diary*, 40–50, give a fine overview of Jeake's reading. Jeake may well have been intended for one of the professions; this is suggested by his early training in Latin and apparently abortive start on Hebrew at the age of thirteen (88).

23. Ibid., 99, entry for 20 March, 1668.

24. Ibid., 149, entry for 1 Jan. 1680. This page is reproduced in facsimile, ibid., p. 77 (figure 1).

25. Ibid., 261.

26. Ibid., 232, entry for 13 April 1694.

27. Ibid., 232, entry for 13 April 1694.

28. Ibid., 72, 254–259, shorthand entries for April through Sept., 1699.

29. Ibid., 186, entry for 18 July 1687. Jeake's correspondence with his wife during this period shows him acting on some of the news. See for example East Sussex RO, FRE 5301, Samuel Jeake to his wife Elizabeth, dtd. 26 March 1696, informing her of the parliamentary vote on clipped money and advising her not to take in any debts in bad coin.

30. Jeake, *Astrological Diary*, 255.

31. Hunter and Gregory (ibid., 261n) discuss the reference tables, or *ephemerides*, that Jeake used. For a detailed discussion of another provincial man with astrological interests see Money, "Teaching in the Market-Place," 356–360. See also Bernard Capp, *Astrology and the Popular Press: English Almanacs, 1500–1800* (London: Faber, 1979); and Patrick Curry, *Prophecy and Power: Astrology in Early Modern England* (Princeton, N.J.: Princeton University Press, 1989).

32. Jeake, *Astrological Diary*, 11–21, 73–76. Hunter and Gregory offer a compelling discussion of the ways astrological interests could complement commercial and religious trends. On providentialism among the members of the Royal Society (on the fringe of which Samuel Jeake moved) see Jacob, *Newtonians and the England Revolution*, 44, 95–96. See also Stewart, *Rise of Public Science*, 385–388.

33. Guildhall MS 3041/9, "Catalog of My Books Dec. 1711," Thomas Bowrey.

34. Thomas Bowrey, *The Papers of Thomas Bowrey, 1669–1713* . . . Part I: *Diary of a Six Weeks' Tour in 1698 in Holland and Flanders,* ed. Richard Carnac Temple (London: Printed for the Hakluyt Society, 1927), 12, 34, 38–41.

35. See for example William Mountague, *The Delights of Holland: or a Three Months Travel About That and the Other Provinces with Observations and Reflections on their Trade, Wealth, Strength, Beauty, Policy & c. Together with a Catalogue of the Rarities in the Anatomical School at Leyden* (London, 1696).

36. For a provocative discussion of the spread of books on architecture, initially reading matter for the elite but soon filtering down to the middling ranks, see Borsay, *English Urban Renaissance,* 49–51, 290–291, 306–307.

37. Money, "Teaching in the Market-Place," 336–339, 343–346, contains a lively, well-contextualized account of the eclectic reading interests of one Cannon, an officer in His Majesty's Excise. David Vaisey's edition of *The Diary of Thomas Turner 1745–1765* contains an invaluable appendix that lists Turner's books, including large numbers of how-to books. See 347–353 (Appendix D, "Thomas Turner's Reading"). See also Money, *Experience and Identity,* 121–130; and J. Paul Hunter, *Before Novels: The Cultural Contexts of Eighteenth-Century English Fiction* (New York and London: Norton, 1990). For a discussion of reading (and writing) and the middle class in a later period see Davidoff and Hall, *Family Fortunes,* 155–162.

38. See *The Course of the Exchange* (London: John Castaing and others, 1698–1810). For other similar items see Dickson, *Financial Revolution in England,* 544–548.

39. Lotteries are complicated, since their appeal is based on the notion that only some individuals will win. However, the government lotteries of the early eighteenth century were generally organized so that most entrants benefited to a degree, via an annuity plan, and some won larger prizes. See Dickson, *Financial Revolution,* 72–73. On the innovatory role of the printing industry in the development of techniques of mass production in the early modern period see Elizabeth Eisenstein, *The Printing Press as an Agent of Change: Communications and Cultural Transformations in Early-Modern Europe,* 2 vols. (Cambridge and New York: Cambridge University Press, 1979), vol. 1, 80–113.

40. Houghton, *Husbandry and Trade Improv'd,* vol. 1, 257–275.

41. *The Public Advertiser,* no. 6609 (Friday, 2 Jan. 1756). I am grateful to Phyllis Mack and Linda Semple for introducing me to the filofax and for several stimulating discussions on the moral and cosmological significance of new time-management techniques in the early modern period.

42. Samuel Lee, *A Collection of the Names of the Merchants Living in and about the City of London* (London, 1677). On the early history of directories see J. E. Norton, *Guide to the National and Provincial Directories of England and Wales, Excluding London, Published Before 1856* (London: Royal Historical Society, 1950); and P. J. Atkins, *The Directories of London, 1677–1987* (London and New York: Mansell, 1990).

43. See especially Penelope Corfield, with Serena Kelly, " 'Giving Directions to the Town': The Early Town Directories," *Urban History Yearbook* (1984):22–35; and Corfield, *Impact of English Towns,* 73, 76, 171, 187–188.

44. Raffald, *Manchester Directory,* 47–60.

45. *Norwich Directory or Gentlemen and Tradesmen's Assistant* (Norwich, 1783), 48.

46. Daniel Baugh, "Poverty, Puritanism and Political Economy: English Attitudes Toward the Poor, 1660–1800," in Stephen B. Baxter, ed., *England's Rise to Greatness, 1660–1763* (Berkeley and Los Angeles: University of California Press, 1983), 63–107; Deborah Valenze, "Charity, Custom and Humanity: Changing Attitudes Toward the Poor in Eighteenth-Century England," in Jane Garnett and Colin Matthew, eds., *Revival and Religion Since 1700: Essays for John Walsh* (London and Rio Grande: The Hambledon Press, 1993), 21–39.

47. For William Dugdale see David C. Douglas, *English Scholars, 1660–1730* (London: Eyre & Spottiswoode, 1951), 45–46, and also the DNB.

48. The "truth," at least as regarded local government, was somewhat more complex. For useful and sometimes conflicting accounts of municipal politics in the eighteenth century see Cannadine, *Lords and Landlords;* Corfield, *Impact of English Towns,* 146–167; and DeKrey, *A Fractured Society.* For an illuminating eighteenth-century account see T. H. B. Oldfield, *An Entire and Complete History, Political and Personal, of the Boroughs of Great Britain,* 3 vols. (London: G. Riley, 1792).

49. A much more detailed discussion of travel narratives is to be found in Hunt, "Racism, Imperialism and the Traveler's Gaze," from which this section is largely derived.

50. Among Bristol library users between the years 1773 and 1784 (a period for which we have library borrowing records) books in the category comprising history, antiquities, and geography (the bulk of these being travel narratives), stood far ahead of those in any other category in popularity. *Belles lettres* were a distant second and theology and ecclesiastical history a dismal fifth. Three out of the ten most-borrowed books, including the most popular book of all, were travel or exploration books. The top book was John Hawkesworth's *Account of the Voyages . . . for making discoveries in the southern hemisphere* (1773). See Paul Kaufman, *Borrowings from the Bristol Library 1773–1784: A Unique Record of Reading Vogues* (Charlottesville: Bibliographical Society of the University of Virginia, 1960), 121–122.

51. Hunt, "Racism, Imperialism and the Traveler's Gaze."

52. For more on Bowrey see pp. 181–182. I have benefited from a talk given by Geoffrey Holmes titled "The Discovery of England in the late Seventeenth Century" (Institute of Historical Research, 22 Feb. 1983), which, among other things, made it clear that it was not *only* mercantile travelers who noticed trade and industry.

53. Josiah Tucker, *Instructions for Travellers* (Dublin: William Watson, 1758), 15, 17, 19, 27, 29–30. For a discussion of travel narratives and their tendency to focus on commercial possibilities in general, and labor supply in particular, see Mary Louise Pratt, *Imperial Eyes: Travel Writing and Transculturation* (London and New York: Routledge, 1992).

54. Alexander Carlyle, *Anecdotes and Characters of the Times,* ed. James Kinsley (London, New York and Toronto: Oxford University Press, 1973), 38. I am grateful to Joanna Innes for bringing these passages to my attention.

55. Hiroshi Mizuta, *Adam Smith's Library: A Supplement to Bonar's Catalogue with a Checklist of the Whole Library* (Cambridge: University Press for the Royal Economic Society, 1967); see also Smith, *Wealth of Nations,* index 2, "Table of Authorities Cited," 971–976.

56. Ryder, *Diary,* 52 (entry for 12 July 1715). For more on Dudley Ryder see pp. 4, 229 n.9.

57. Carlyle, *Anecdotes and Characters of the Time,* 38.

CHAPTER 8: PRIVATE ORDER AND POLITICAL VIRTUE

1. John Locke, *The Two Treatises of Government,* ed. Peter Laslett (New York: New American Library, 1966). In effecting this split, Locke is building on a much older tradition. For this see Susan Moller Okin, *Women in Western Political Thought* (Princeton, N.J.: Princeton University Press, 1992), 73–96. Okin also shows that only partially concealed behind Locke's rhetoric of individualism and "separate spheres" is a deep commitment to patriarchal forms (ibid., 199–201, 249–250, 282). For valuable discussions of the permeable, some would say nonexistent, barriers between public and private, the family and state governance, see Susan Dwyer Amussen, *An Ordered Society: Gender and Class in Early Modern England* (Oxford: Basil Blackwell, 1988), 34–66; and Crawford, *Women and Religion in England,* 49–50.

2. See pp. 147–149.

3. Barnes, *Memoirs,* 225.

4. Ibid., 48.

5. See Caroline Robbins, *The Eighteenth-Century Commonwealthman: Studies in the Transmission, Development and Circumstances of English Liberal Thought from the Restoration of Charles II until the War with the Thirteen Colonies* (Cambridge, Mass.: Harvard University Press, 1959); J. G. A. Pocock, *The Machiavellian Moment: Florentine Political Thought and the Atlantic Republican Tradition* (Princeton, N.J.: Princeton University Press, 1975); and H. T. Dickinson, *Liberty and Property: Political Ideology in Eighteenth-Century Britain* (London: Weidenfeld & Nicolson, 1977).

6. Barnes, *Memoirs,* 47.

7. Ibid., 49. For Commonwealth arguments against stock-jobbers see Pocock, *Machiavellian Moment,* 426–427; and for the larger context see Stewart, *Rise of Public Science,* 261–265.

8. Pocock, *Machiavellian Moment,* 460–461.

9. Barnes, *Memoirs,* 210–216. Extracts from Barnes's political writing appear, much abridged, in the printed version of the *Memoirs.* The original Barnes manuscript was probably still extant in 1811, since a letter from William Turner in Newcastle to the Reverend Joseph Hunter written in that year contains notes said to have been taken from it (BL Add. MSS 24607/4, fols. 75–76; and Add. MSS 24607/5). Presumably the political writings too were destroyed in the 1893 fire at the Literary and Philosophical Society of Newcastle Upon Tyne.

10. Barnes, *Memoirs,* 213. I am grateful to Amanda Collins for explaining to me the subtle differences between *virtus* and *virtù.*

11. Ibid., 214.

12. See pp. 59, 66.

13. Mountague, *Delights of Holland,* 161–163.

14. Thompson, "Argument: Eighteenth-Century English Society," 133–165.

15. Pocock, *Machiavellian Moment,* 56–57, 89–90 et passim.

16. Alexander Hamilton, *A New Account of the East Indies, Being the Observations and Remarks of Captain Alexander Hamilton Who Spent his Time there from the year 1688 to 1723*, 2 vols. (Edinburgh: J. Mosman, 1727), vol. 1, 232–233. The letter was to a Mr. Vaux, newly appointed to an Indian civil judgeship at Child's behest, and was written some time between 1684 and 1696.

17. GLRO Acc. 1128/177–8, "Sir Francis Child's Journal of his Visit to the Low Countries (1697)." Francis Child was the most prominent banker of his day and was elected Lord Mayor of London in 1698.

18. Samuel Wright, *A Sermon Preach'd Before the Societies for Reformation of Manners at Salters-Hall, June 25, 1715* (London: John Clark and Eman. Matthews, 1715), 13.

19. See pp. 120–121.

20. Daniel Defoe, *Conjugal Lewdness; or, Matrimonial Whoredom: A Treatise Concerning the Use and Abuse of the Marriage Bed*, ed. Maximillian E. Novak (Gainesville, Fla.: Scholars' Facsimiles and Reprints, 1967 [orig. 1727]), 133–134, 252, 257.

21. See Novak's preface to Defoe's *Conjugal Lewdness*, vi.

22. See pp. 73–75.

23. Henry Hamilton, "The Failure of the Ayr Bank, 1772," *Economic History Review* (2d ser.) 7 (1956):405–417.

24. See D. Fordyce, *Dialogues Concerning Education*, vol. 1, 33, 37.

25. Ibid., vol. 1, 15.

26. Ibid., vol. 1, 90. See also J. Fordyce, *Character and Conduct of the Female Sex*, 30–31, 71–72.

27. D. Fordyce, *Dialogues Concerning Education*, vol. 1, 88. A tradition of publishing *libelles*, that is, scurrilous and illegal exposés of the sex lives of royalty and aristocracy, did not arise in England in quite the way that it did in France. Still, these themes were often expressed in more restrained ways. Compare Robert Darnton, *The Literary Underground of the Old Regime* (Cambridge, Mass.: Harvard University Press, 1982).

28. Guildhall MS 11021/1, George A. Gibbs to Anne Vicary, dtd. Exeter, 2 July 1746.

29. See pp. 148, 167.

30. Guildhall MS 11021/1, George A. Gibbs to Anne Vicary, dtd. Exeter, 8 Sept. 1744.

31. Ibid., George A. Gibbs to Anne Vicary, dtd. Exeter, 16 May 1747.

32. See Langford, *A Polite and Commercial People*, 125–134, for a discussion of the moral reformism of the 1740s and '50s.

33. John Taylor, *A Kicksey Winsey: Or a Lerry Come-Twang: Wherein Iohn Taylor hath Satyrically Suited 800 of his Bad Debtors that will not Pay him for his Returne of his Iourney from Scotland* (London: 1619), sig. B4. The career of Taylor, also known as "The Water Poet," is described in Wallace Notestein, *Four Worthies, John Chamberlain, Anne Clifford, John Taylor, Oliver Heywood* (London: Jonathan Cape, 1956), 169–208.

34. BL Egerton MS 2395, fol. 501, quoted in K. G. Davies, *The Royal African Company* (London: Longmans, Green and Co., 1957), 64.

35. BRO HA/C/3 Acc. No. 14581, Elizabeth Cornish to Richard Haynes, dtd. 30 Oct. 1789. For the Cornishes' vicissitudes in trade and debts to their relatives

and others see *idem,* also E. Cornish to R. Haynes dtd. 9 Dec. 1788 and 30 Nov. 1789, and an undated fragment of another letter from E. Cornish to R. Haynes about the possibility of Mr. Cornish going as a shopman while she goes to lodgings.

36. On the sons of mercantile and professional families attending the elite schools see Trumbach, *Rise of the Egalitarian Family,* 264.

37. Joseph Addison and Richard Steele, *Spectator,* no. 15 (17 March 1710/11), Bond ed., vol. 1, 68.

38. This topic is well covered in Trumbach, *Rise of the Egalitarian Family,* 197–224. For a classic contemporary discussion see William Gouge, *Of Domesticall Duties; Eight Treatises,* The English Experience, no. 83 (Norwood, N.J. and Amsterdam: Walter J. Johnson, Inc. and Theatrum Orbis, 1976 [facs. 1622 edition]), 507–518.

39. This is the subject of *Spectator,* no. 246 (12 Dec. 1711), Bond ed. vol. 2, 454–458, cited in Trumbach, *Rise of the Egalitarian Family,* 203.

40. James Nelson, *Essay on the Government of Children,* 3d. ed. (London: R. & J. Dodsley, 1763), unpaginated dedication. Nelson's readers were supposed to grasp from the wording of the dedication ("the Office of a tender Mother," "cherishing", "charmed with the pleasing Task you have undertaken," etc.) that the Countess also breastfed her children. For specific reference to aristocratic breastfeeding see 43.

41. Other childrearing books have tended to be aimed at one class only, says Nelson, "as Princes, etc.," and have thus proved "too narrow to instruct the Whole, and too confined to become general Rules" (ibid., unpaginated preface).

42. D. with J. Fordyce, *Temple of Virtue,* 84–91. In the British Museum copy some of the figures have been identified in a contemporary hand, although not this exemplary servant of his sovereign. Portions of *The Temple of Virtue* had been completed a good deal before this, but this is presumably an idealized portrait of the elder Pitt.

43. The British Library catalog lists sixteen editions of *Some Remarkable Passages* before 1800, including a French translation and at least another seventeen editions in the nineteenth century.

44. Philip Doddridge, *Some Remarkable Passages in the Life of the Honourable Col. James Gardiner Who Was Slain at the Battle of Preston-Pans, September 21, 1745* (London: Printed for James Buckland, 1747), 3–4. A less idealized account of Gardiner is to be found in Carlyle, *Anecdotes and Characters of the Times,* 9–11, 26, 66, 68–69, 72–74. I am grateful to Joanna Innes for this reference.

45. Doddridge, *Some Remarkable Passages,* 8, 15, 21–23, 32–36, 62–63.

46. Ibid., 88–89, 92–93, 133.

47. Ibid., 99.

48. Ibid., 99, 124–126.

49. I have benefited much from discussions with Joanna Innes on this point. See also Vickery, "Golden Age to Separate Spheres," 396–397; and Langford, *Polite and Commercial People,* 121, 721–725.

50. Our knowledge of the eighteenth-century gentry and aristocracy has advanced significantly in the last thirty years. See especially G. E. Mingay, *English Landed Society in the Eighteenth Century* (London: Routledge & Kegan Paul, 1963); Mingay, *Gentry;* Stone, *Family, Sex and Marriage in England;* Trumbach, *Rise of the Egalitarian Family;* Cannadine, *Lords and Landlords;* Michael Bush, *Noble Privilege*

(New York: Holmes & Meier, 1983); Bush, *English Aristocracy;* Cannon, *Aristocratic Century;* and Stone and Stone, *An Open Elite?*

51. Mingay, *Gentry,* 2.

52. Stone and Stone, *An Open Elite?,* 49–133, 148–180 et passim.

53. See pp. 29–34.

54. Stone and Stone in *An Open Elite?,* 222–239, find that the movement of younger sons of the best families into trade has been, in their words, "grossly exaggerated" (237). One exception to this was Hertfordshire, where a goodly number of well-born youths entered the extremely lucrative brewing business. Younger sons did, however, move readily into the professions.

55. An excellent picture of the proximity of factories and warehouses to homes, even among quite prosperous commercial families, can be gained from looking at eighteenth-century fire insurance policies. See Guildhall MS 11936, Sun Insurance Office Policy Registers (old series), vols. 1–413, 1710–1799; Guildhall MS 7252, Royal Exchange Assurance Company Policy Registers (Agents' Books) (first orig. series), vols. 1–7, 1753–1759; Guildhall MS 7253, Royal Exchange Assurance Company Policy Registers (Agents' Books) (second orig. series), vols 1–98, 1773–1833.

56. Roger North, *The Lives of the Right Hon. Francis North, Baron Guildford; The Hon. Sir Dudley North; and the Hon. and Rev. Dr. John North . . . Together with the Autobiography of the Author,* ed. Augustus Jessopp, 3 vols. (London: George Bell and Sons, 1890): vol. 3, 6. For North's brother Dudley, apprenticed to a Turkey merchant after a heavy dose of accounting and attention to writing skills, see vol. 2, 3–4, 7. Susan Whyman's work on John Verney suggests a similar sort of ambidexterity in that family. Susan E. Whyman, "Land and Trade Reconsidered: John Verney, Merchant and Baronet, 1660–1720," paper delivered at the Institute of Historical Research, London, 27 April 1994.

57. See p. 115. See also Jacob, *Radical Enlightenment,* 144–151; and Joseph Klaits, *Printed Propaganda under Louis XIV: Absolute Monarchy and Public Opinion* (Princeton, N.J.: Princeton University Press, 1978).

58. Alexander Lindsay, *The Lives of the Lindsays* (London: J. Murray, 1849), vol. 2, 302–303, quoted in A. C. Beveridge, "Childhood and Society in Eighteenth-Century Scotland," in John Dwyer, ed., *New Perspectives on the Politics and Culture of Early Modern Scotland, 1560–1800* (Edinburgh: J. Donald, 1982), 283.

59. In this period effeminacy was at least as closely identified with heterosexual libertinism as it was with homosexuality. On this see especially Bray, *Homosexuality in Renaissance England,* 130–131n. Compare as well Trumbach "London's Sodomites," and Trumbach, "Sodomitical Subcultures, Sodomitical roles."

60. Terry Eagleton, *The Function of Criticism: From the Spectator to Post-Structuralism* (London: Verso, 1984). See also Nancy Armstrong, *Desire and Domestic Fiction: A Political History of the Novel* (New York and Oxford: Oxford University Press, 1987). I have benefited from discussions with Judith Frank on this issue.

61. *The Levellers, A Dialogue Between Two Young Ladies, Concerning Matrimony, Proposing an Act for Enforcing Marriage, for the Equality of Matches, and Taxing Single Persons; with the Danger of Celibacy to a Nation* (London: J. How, 1703). Reprinted in *Harleian Miscellany,* vol. 5, 418–420.

62. Curll, *Cases of Divorce for Several Causes,* vii–viii. See also Addison and Steele, *Spectator,* no. 57 (5 May 1711), Bond ed., vol. 1, 241–244.

63. *Dialogue Concerning the Subjection of Women to their Husbands*, 17–18, 20, 25.

64. David Kuchta and Dror Wahrman are both working on studies that bear centrally on the history of masculinity in eighteenth-century England.

65. See pp. 43–44.

66. Brown, "Domesticity, Feminism, and Friendship," 406–424.

67. For the increase in companionate marriage among the aristocracy beginning in the late seventeenth century see Stone, *Family, Sex and Marriage in England*, 298–315 and 367–374; and Trumbach, *Rise of the Egalitarian Family*, 83–87, 97–113.

68. Dr. Williams's Library Doddridge Collection L1/5, fol. 43, S. Clark to Mrs. Mercy Doddridge, dtd. Birmingham, 13 Sept. 1762. The Doddridge correspondence abounds with appeals for ordered families. See for example, L1/7, Nathaniel Neal to Philip Doddridge Jr., dtd. the Million Bank, 3 April 1753; and L1/4, fol. 181., S. Clark to Philip Doddridge, Jr., dtd. 28 April 1753.

69. My emphasis.

70. See pp. 166–170.

CONCLUSION

1. K. Davies, "The Mess of the Middle Class," *Past and Present* 22 (1962): 77–83.

2. This is from a broadside, probably dating from 1696, entitled *A New Ballad Upon the Land Bank: Or Credit Restored*. There is a copy in the London Guildhall Library.

3. G. R. Rubin, "Law, Poverty and Imprisonment for Debt, 1869–1914," in G. R. Rubin and David Sugarman, eds., *Law, Economy and Society, 1750–1914: Essays in the History of English Law* (Abingdon, Oxon: Professional Books, 1984), 241–245.

SELECTED BIBLIOGRAPHY

MANUSCRIPT SOURCES

Bodleian Library, Oxford

MS Rawlinson C 861. Diary of an Anonymous Wigmaker. 1707.

MS Rawlinson D 34. Prison Diary of John-Baptiste Grano. 1728–1729.

MS Rawlinson D 72. Correspondence of John Dunton. Early eighteenth century.

MS Rawlinson D 114. "A Narrative . . . of Certain Particular Transactions and Events . . . Relating to the Transcriber of them. S[amuel] M[arriott]." 1728.

MS Rawlinson D 129. Copies of various documents relating to the Societies for Reformation of Manners. Late seventeenth–early eighteenth centuries.

MS Rawlinson D 908, fol. 118. "Fragment of a preface to some tract exposing the conduct of one Capt. W. M., a prisoner in Newgate for a debt of £750 to a younger brother; written by that brother in the strongest terms of virulent abuse, shortly after the year 1724."

MS Rawlinson D 1312. "The Names Places of Abode, Employmts & Occupacions of the Several Societys in & about the Cities of London and Westminster Belonging to the Church of England 1694."

MSS Rawlinson 1396–1404. Societies for Reformation of Manners, "Names of Persons Making Complaints." 1710–1715.

Bristol Record Office

HA/C/3 Acc. No. 14581. Letters of Elizabeth Cornish to Richard Haynes. 1788–1789.

Acc. No. 26226. Letters of Samuel Lowder of Bristol. 1769–1776.

Bristol Reference Library

MS 319718. Letterbook of Caleb Dickinson. 1757–1758.

MS B 11871. Autobiography and Journal of John Heylyn. 1741–1765.

British Library

Add. MSS 15627. Journal of Thomas Wright. 1711–1762.
Add. MSS 19211. Diary and Letterbook of Gervase Leveland. 1764–1765.
Add. MSS 24607/4. Letter of William Turner to Joseph Hunter. 1811.
Add. MSS 24607/5. Extracts Copied from the MS Life of Ambrose Barnes. Early nineteenth century.
Add. MSS 4264/21. Correspondence of Catherine Cockburn and Anne Hepburn, afterwards Arbuthnot. 1731–1748.
Add. MSS 4460 Extracts from the Day Books of Henry Sampson. 1693–1694.
Add. MSS 45718. Commonplace Book of Elizabeth Freke. 1684?–1714.
Egerton MS 2227. Letter and Memorandum Book of David Mendez da Costa. 1757–1759.
Harleian MS 6395. "Merry Passages and Jeasts" of Nicholas L'Estrange. Ca. 1660–1680.

Brotherton Library, Leeds

MS Marriner 37. Correspondence of Lister Family. 1750s–1770s.

Corporation of London Record Office

Mayor's Court Interrogatories MC6/462. Cryer v. Jonaway. 1686.

Dr. Williams's Library, London

MS 24.157. Correspondence of Samuel Kenrick and James Wodrow. 1809.
Doddridge MSS L/4, L/5, L/7. Doddridge Collection. Eighteenth century.
Henry MSS 90.4. Letterbook of Sarah Savage. 1712–1715.

East Sussex Record Office

FRE 5301–5305. Correspondence of Samuel Jeake and his wife, Elizabeth. 1696–1697.

Friends Library, London

MS Vol. S 193/3, 193/4, 194/1, 194/2, 194/3, 193/5. Diaries and Letterbooks of John Kelsall. Ca. 1700–1730.
Box Meeting MSS 1671–1753. Records of the Women's Meetings. 1671–1753.

Greater London Record Office

Acc. 1128/177–178. Sir Francis Child's Journal of his Visit to the Low Countries. 1697.
A/CSC/8. General Index to the Court Books, Corporation of the Sons of the Clergy. Eighteenth century.

A/CSC/13/1. Committee Minute Books, Corporation of the Sons of the Clergy. Eighteenth century.

A/CSC/390/3. Miscellaneous Petitions from Widows, Corporation of the Sons of the Clergy. Eighteenth century.

DL/C/154. Consistory Court of London Interrogatory Books. 1711–1713.

DL/C/632. Consistory Court Depositions. 1710–1712.

Guildhall Library, London

MS 205. Diaries of Stephen Monteage, 9 vols. 1733, 1738, 1739, 1740, 1741, 1743, 1746, 1757–1760, 1762–1764.

MS 507. Correspondence of John Moore. 1680s.

MS 544. Ancient Register of the Club at the Half Moon, London–The Centenary Club. 1695 on.

MS 557. Church Book of the Meeting House at Limestreet. 1728–1764.

MS 3041/4. Papers of the Bowrey Family. Early eighteenth century.

MS 3041/9. Miscellaneous Papers of Thomas and Mary Bowrey. Early eighteenth century.

MS 6478. Stewards Book of a Religious Society at Christ Church, then at Cripplegate. 1691–1753.

MS 6479. Stewards Books of a Religious Society at St. Giles, Cripplegate. 1696–1761.

MS 9939. Diaries of William Mawhood the elder. 49 vols. 1764–1790.

MS 9941. Estate, Legal and Family Papers of the Mawhood Family. 1709–1796.

MS 7252. Royal Exchange Assurance Company Policy Registers, Agents' Books. First orig. series, vols. 1–7. 1753–1759.

MS 7253. Royal Exchange Assurance Company Policy Registers, Agents' Books. Second orig. series, vols. 1–98. 1773–1833.

MS 10823/1. Commonplace and Memo Book Kept by George Boddington (1646–1719) with Additional Notes by Thomas Boddington (1678–1755) and Thomas Boddington the younger (1722–1779). Late seventeenth–eighteenth centuries.

MS 11021/1. Papers of the Gibbs Family. 1744–1782.

MS 11936. Sun Insurance Office Policy Registers. Old series, vols. 1–413. 1710–1799.

MS 12017. "Some Account of the Life &c of John Fryer & of Several of his Relations Written by Himself." 1715.

MS 16927. Letterbook of Edward Baker. 1757–ca. 1820.

MS 16937. Papers of Zelophead Vincent. Late eighteenth–early nineteenth centuries.

Public Record Office
Court of Chancery

C105/30. Papers relating to Mary Holl. 1770s.

C105/5 part 1. Inventory of the Shop of Mrs Martha Braithwaite. 1744.

C106/65. "The History of the Profligate Son." Late eighteenth–early nineteenth centuries.

C108/132. Correspondence of Henry Gambier. 1720–1721.

C112/165 part II. Papers Relating to the Case of Daker v. Weekes. 1730s–1770s.

C112/181 part 1. Lease and other documents relating to Gertrude Rolles. 1681–1703.

C112/76. Letters and Papers Relating to the Estate of Jane Franklin. 1716–1723.

C112/99. Copybook of Esther Praeger and Mark Praeger the elder. Late eighteenth century.

C114/182 part 2. Accounts of Judith DuBuc. 1710s–1730s.

Court of Exchequer

E112/1089 piece 117. Documents relating to Sarah Brown's Grocer's Shop. 1750s.

E112/1241 piece 3666. Elizabeth Fitzmaurice v. Edmund Brown. 1761.

Somerset Record Office

DD/SAS/C/1193/4. "Memoir of the Birth Education Life and Death of Mr. John Cannon Sometime Officer of the Excise and Writing Master"

PRINTED PRIMARY SOURCES

Addison, Joseph, and Richard Steele. *The Spectator.* Ed. Donald F. Bond. 5 vols. Oxford: Clarendon Press, 1965.

Advice to the Women and Maidens of London. Shewing, that Instead of their Usual Pastime; and Education in Needlework, Lace and Point-making, it were Far more Necessary and Profitable to Apply Themselves to the Right Understanding and Practice of the Method of Keeping Books of Account: Whereby, Either Single, or Married, They may Know their Estates, Carry on their Trades, and Avoid the Danger of a Helpless and Forlorn Condition, Incident to Widows. By One of that Sex. London, 1678.

Allestree, Richard. *The Ladies Calling.* Oxford: Printed at the Theater, 1705. Originally published 1673.

Ashbridge, Elizabeth. *Some Account of the Early Part of the Life of Elizabeth Ashbridge, Who Departed this Life in Truth's Service, in Ireland, the 16th of the 5th Month, 1755, Written by Herself,* with additional biographical material by her third husband. Dublin: C. Bentham, 1820.

Ashwood, Bartholemew. *The Heavenly Trade or the Best Merchandizing: The Only Way to Live Well in Impoverishing Times.* London, 1679.

Astell, Mary. *Reflections Upon Marriage.* 3rd ed. London: printed for R. Wilkin, 1706.

Bailey, Abigail Abbot. *Religion and Domestic Violence in Early New England: The Memoirs of Abigail Abbot Bailey.* Ed. Ann Taves. Bloomington, Ind.: Indiana University Press, 1989.

Barnes, Ambrose. *Memoirs of the Life of Mr. Ambrose Barnes Late Merchant and Sometime Alderman of Newcastle Upon Tyne.* Surtees Society Publications, vol. 50. Durham: Andrew & Co., 1867.

Baron and Feme. A Treatise of the Common Law Concerning Husbands and Wives. London: Eliz. Nutt and R. Gosling for John Walthoe, 1719.

Baxter, Richard. *Faithful Souls shall be with Christ: The Certainty Proved and their Christianity Described and Exemplified in the Truly Christian Life and Death of that Excellent, Amiable Saint, Henry Ashurst, Esq., Citizen of London.* In his *Works*, vol. 18. London: 1681.

Bentham, Jeremy. *Works.* Ed. John Bowring. 11 vols. Edinburgh: William Tait, 1843.

Blackall, Ofspring. *Practical Discourses upon Our Saviour's Sermon on the Mount.* 2 vols. London: Thomas Ward, 1718.

Bowrey, Thomas. *The Papers of Thomas Bowrey, 1669–1713 . . . Part I: Diary of a Six Weeks' Tour in 1698 in Holland and Flanders.* Ed. Richard Carnac Temple. London: Printed for the Hakluyt Society, 1927.

Bradford, Samuel. *Honest and Dishonest Ways of Getting Wealth.* London: Printed for John Wyat, 1720.

Bramston, John. *The Autobiography of Sir John Bramston, K. B., of Skreens, in the Hundred of Chelmsford.* Camden Society Publications, 32. London: Printed for the Camden Society, 1845.

Burnet, Gilbert. *Bishop Burnet's History of His Own Time.* 6 vols. Oxford: Oxford University Press, 1833. Originally published 1724.

Bury, Samuel. *Account of the Life and Death of Elizabeth Bury Who Died May the 11th, 1720, Aged 76. Chiefly Collected Out of her Own Diary.* Bristol: J. Penn, 1721.

Campbell, R. *The London Tradesman: Being a Compendious View of all the Trades, Professions, Arts . . . Calculated for the Information of Parents, and Instruction of Youth in their Choice of Business.* London: T. Gardner, 1747.

Carlyle, Alexander. *Anecdotes and Characters of the Times.* Ed. James Kinsley. London, New York, and Toronto: Oxford University Press, 1973.

Chalmers, George. *An Estimate of the Comparative Strength of Great Britain.* Reprints of Economic Classics. New York: Augustus M. Kelley, 1969. Facsimile of 1794 edition.

[Chapone, Sarah]. *The Hardships of the English Laws in Relation to Wives.* London: George Faulkner, 1735.

Charke, Charlotte. *The Lover's Treat: Or Unnatural Hatred, Being a True Narrative as Deliver'd to the Author by One of the Family Who was Principally Concern'd in the Following Account.* London: Bailey's Printing Office, ca. 1758.

———. *A Narrative of the Life of Mrs. Charlotte Charke (Youngest Daughter of Colley Cibber, Esq.) Written by Herself.* Ed. Leonard R. N. Ashley. London: Printed for W. Reeve, A. Dodd, E. Cook, 1755. Reprinted Gainesville, Fla.: Scholar's Facsimiles and Reprints, 1969.

Child, Josiah. *Brief Observations Concerning Trade and Interest of Money.* London, 1668.

A Collection of the Best Pieces in Prose and Verse, Against the Naturalization of the Jews. London: M. Cooper, 1753.

Collyer, Joseph. *Parents & Guardians Directory and the Youth's Guide in the Choice of a Profession or Trade.* London: R. Griffiths, 1761.

A Compleat Guide to All Persons who have any Trade or Concern with the City of London and Parts Adjacent. London: J. Osborn, 1750.

The Course of the Exchange. London: John Castaing and others, 1698–1810.

Crowne, John. *City Politiques. A Comedy.* London, 1683.

Curll, Edmund. *Cases of Divorce for Several Causes.* London: E. Curll, 1715.

Defoe, Daniel. *The Compleat English Gentleman*. Ed. Karl Bulbring. London: David Nutt, 1890. Originally published 1729.

———. *The Complete English Tradesman in Familiar Letters, Directing him in all the Several Parts and Progressions of Trade*. 2d ed. 2 vols. London: Printed for Charles Rivington, 1727. Reprinted New York: Augustus M. Kelley, 1969, in facsimile.

———. *Conjugal Lewdness; or, Matrimonial Whoredom: A Treatise Concerning the Use and Abuse of the Marriage Bed*. Ed. Maximillian E. Novak. Gainesville, Fla.: Scholars' Facsimiles and Reprints, 1967. Originally published 1727.

———. *A Review of the State of the British Nation*. London: n.p., 1704–1713.

D'Ewes, Simonds. *The Autobiography and Correspondence of Sir Simonds D'Ewes*. Ed. James Orchard Halliwell. 2 vols. London: R. Bentley, 1845.

A Dialogue Concerning the Subjection of Women to their Husbands . . . in Which is Interspersed Some Observations on Courtship, for the Use of the Batchelors. London: John Wilkie, 1765.

Doddridge, Philip. *Sermons to Young Persons*. London: R. Hett, 1734.

———. *Some Remarkable Passages in the Life of the Honourable Col. James Gardiner Who was Slain at the Battle of Preston-Pans, September 21, 1745*. London: Printed for James Buckland, 1747.

An Essay in Defence of the Female Sex. In Which are Inserted the Characters of a Pedant, a Vertuoso, a Squire, a Poetaster, a Beau, a City-Critick & c. New York, Source Book Press, 1970. Originally published 1696.

The Female Jockey Club, or a Sketch of the Manners of the Age. London: D. I. Eaton, 1794.

Fennor, William. *The Compter's Common-Wealth, or a Voiage made to an Infernall Iland long since Discovered by many Captaines, Seafaring-men, Gentlement, Marchants, and other Tradesmen; But the Conditions, Nature, and Qualities of the People there Inhabiting, and those that Trafficke with them, were Never so Truly Expressed or Lively set foorth*. London, 1617.

Fielding, Sarah. *The Governess, or Little Female Academy*. London: Pandora Press, 1987. Originally published 1749.

Fiennes, Celia. *The Journeys of Celia Fiennes*. London: MacDonald, 1983.

Fleetwood, William. *Chronicon Preciosum: Or an Account of English Money, the Price of Corn, and Other Commodities for the Last 600 Years*. London: C. Harper, 1707.

———. *The Relative Duties of Parents and Children, Husbands and Wives, Masters and Servants, Consider'd in Sixteen Sermons: with Three More upon the Case of Self-Murther*. London: C. Harper, 1705.

———. *Two Sermons; the One Before the King on March the 2nd 1717 Being the First Sunday in Lent and Publish'd by His Majesty's Special Command. The Other Preach'd in the City on the Justice of Paying Debts*. London: Printed by W. C. for J. Wyat, 1718.

Fordyce, David. *Dialogues Concerning Education*. 2 vols. London: T. Cadell, 1745.

Fordyce, David, with additional material by James Fordyce. *The Temple of Virtue: A Dream*. London: James Magee, 1759.

Fordyce, Henrietta. *Memoirs of the Late Mrs. Henrietta Fordyce, Relict of James Fordyce, D.D.; Containing Original Letters, Anecdotes and Pieces of Poetry. To Which is Added a Sketch of the Life of James Fordyce, D. D.* London: Hurst, Robinson & Co., 1823.

Fordyce, James. *The Character and Conduct of the Female Sex, and the Advantages to be Derived by Young Men from the Society of Virtuous Women*. London: T. Cadell, 1776.

———. *Sermons to Young Women*. 2 vols. London: A. Millar and T. Cadell, 1767.

Freke, Elizabeth. *Mrs. Freke, Her Diary*. Ed. Mary Carbery. Cork: Privately Printed, 1913.

Gainsford, Thomas. *The Secretaries Studie: Containing New Familiar Epistles or Directions for the Formall, Orderly, and Iudicious Inditing of Letters*. The English Experience, no. 658. Amsterdam and Norwood, N.J.: Walter Johnson, Inc. and Theatrum Orbis Terrarum, Ltd., 1974. Originally published 1616.

Gibbon, Edward. *The Autobiographies of Edward Gibbon*. Ed. John Murray. London: John Murray, 1907.

Gouge, William. *Of Domesticall Duties; Eight Treatises*. The English Experience, no. 83. Norwood, N.J. and Amsterdam: Walter J. Johnson and Theatrum Orbis, 1976. Facsimile of 1622 edition.

Gough, Richard. *The History of Myddle*. Firle, Sussex: Caliban Books, 1979.

Gray, Mrs. Edwin [Almyra], ed. *Papers and Diaries of a York Family, 1764–1839*. London: Sheldon Press, 1927.

Gregory, John. *A Father's Legacy to his Daughters*. London: W. Strahan and T. Cadell, 1774.

A Guernsey Garland, in Three Parts. London: Printed and Sold in Aldermary Church Yard, ca. 1760.

Hamilton, Alexander. *A New Account of the East Indies, Being the Observations and Remarks of Captain Alexander Hamilton who Spent his Time there from the Year 1688 to 1723*. 2 vols. Edinburgh: J. Mossman, 1727.

Harland, John, ed. *Collectanea Relating to Manchester at Various Times*. Chetham Society Publications, vols. 68 and 72. Manchester: Chetham Society, 1866–1867.

Harrold, Edmund. "Edmund Harrold: His Book of Remks and Obs'ns. 1712." In John Harland, ed., *Collectanea Relating to Manchester and its Neighbourhood, at Various Periods*. Chetham Society Publications 68. Manchester: Chetham Society, 1866.

Hayes, Richard. *The Gentleman's Complete Book-keeper*. London: J. Noon, 1741.

Hays, Mary. *Letters and Essays, Moral and Miscellaneous*. London: T. Knott, 1793.

Hazeland, William. *A Sermon Preached in the Chapel of the Asylum, Near Westminster Bridge on the Sunday Before Christmas-day, 1760*. London: J. Beecroft, 1761.

The Heaven Drivers, A Poem. London: n.p., 1701.

A Help to a National Reformation—An Abstract of the Penal-Laws Against Prophaneness and Vice. London: Printed for D. Brown (etc.), 1700.

Heywood, Oliver. *The Rev. Oliver Heywood, B. A., 1630–1702, his Autobiography, Diaries, Anecdote and Event Books*. Ed. J. Horsfall Turner. 4 vols. Brighouse: Printed for the Editor, 1881–1885.

The History of Little Goody Two-Shoes; Otherwise Called Mrs. Margery Twoshoes. With the Means by which she Acquired her Learning and Wisdom, and in Consequence thereof her Estate. New York: Meriden Gravure Co. for G. K. Hall, 1969. Facsimile of 1787 ed.

Hodgson, J. C., ed. *Six North Country Diaries.* Surtees Society Publications, vols. 118 and 124, 2 vols. Durham: Surtees Society, 1910.

Houghton, John. *Husbandry and Trade Improv'd: Being a collection of Many Valuable Materials Relating to Corn, Cattle, Coals, Hops, Wool, &c.* Ed. R. Bradley. 4 vols. London: Woodman and Lyon, 1728.

Howard, Eliot, ed. *The Eliot Papers.* 2 vols. Gloucester: Privately Printed by J. Bellows, 1893–1894.

Ivie, Thomas. *Alimony Arraign'd, or, The Remonstrance and Humble Appeal of Thomas Ivie, Esq. from the High Court of Chancery, to his Highnes the Lord Protector of the Commonwealth of England, Scotland, and Ireland, &c.: Wherein are Set Forth the Un-heard-of Practices and Villanies of Lewed and Defamed [sic] Women, in Order to Separate Man and Wife.* London, 1654.

Jeake, Samuel. *An Astrological Diary of the Seventeenth Century: Samuel Jeake of Rye, 1652–1699.* Ed. Michael Hunter and Annabel Gregory. Oxford: Oxford University Press, 1988.

Johnson, Joshua. *Joshua Johnson's Letterbook 1771–1774: Letters from a Merchant in London to His Partners in Maryland.* Ed. Jacob M. Price. London: London Record Society, 1979.

Johnson, Samuel. *The Idler.* London: Jones & Co., 1826. Originally published 1758–1760.

Lee, Samuel. *A Collection of the Names of the Merchants Living in and about the City of London.* London, 1677.

Leng, John. *The Four and Twentieth Account of the Progress Made in the Cities of London and Westminster . . . by the Societies for Promoting a Reformation of Manners.* London: J. Downing, 1719.

The Levellers: A Dialogue Between Two Young Ladies, Concerning Matrimony; Proposing an Act for Enforcing Marriage, for the Equality of Matches, and Taxing Single Persons; with the Danger of Celibacy to a Nation. London: J. How, 1703. Reprinted in the *Harleian Miscellany* 5 (1810):416–433.

Lippincott, H. F. " 'Merry Passages & Jeasts' A Manuscript Jestbook of Sir Nicholas L'Estrange, (1603–1655)." *Library Chronicle University of Pennsylvania,* 41, Dept. Pamphlet 2376 (1977):149–162.

Locke, John. *John Locke on Education.* Classics in Education, no. 20. Ed. Peter Gay. New York: Bureau of Publications, Teachers' College, Columbia University, 1964.

———. *The Two Treatises of Government.* Ed. Peter Laslett. New York: New American Library, 1966.

The London Bawd: With her Character and Life: Discovering the Various and Subtle Intrigues of Lewd Women. London: John Gwilliam, 1705.

Longden, Henry. *The Life of Henry Longden, Late of Sheffield, Compiled from his Own Memoirs.* Liverpool: Thomas Kaye, 1813.

Lowe, Roger. *Diary of Roger Lowe of Ashton-in-Makerfield, Lancashire, 1663–74.* London: Longmans, Green and Co., 1938.

Mackworth, Humphrey. *England's Glory or the Great Improvement of Trade in General . . . by a Royal Bank, or Office of Credit to be Erected in London.* London, 1694.

Mandeville, Bernard. *The Fable of the Bees.* Ed. Phillip Harth. Harmondsworth: Penguin, 1970.

Mawhood, William. *The Mawhood Diary. Selections from the Diary Notebooks of William Mawhood, Woollen-Draper of London, for the Years 1764–1790*. Publications of the Catholic Record Society, vol. 50. Ed. E. E. Reynolds. London: Privately Printed for the Society, 1956.

More, Hannah. *Strictures on the Modern System of Female Education; with a View of the Principles and Conduct Prevalent Among Women of Rank and Fortune*. 2 vols. London: T. Cadell and W. Davies, 1799.

Mountague, William. *The Delights of Holland: Or, a Three Months Travel About That and the Other Provinces with Observations and Reflections on their Trade, Wealth, Strength, Beauty, Policy &c. Together with a Catalogue of the Rarities in the Anatomical School at Leyden*. London, 1696.

Nelson, James. *Essay on the Government of Children*. 3d ed. London: R. & J. Dodsley, 1763.

A New Ballad Upon the Land Bank: Or Credit Restored. London: n.p., ca. 1696.

North, Roger. *The Gentleman Accomptant; An Essay to Unfold the Mystery of Accompts. By Way of Debtor or Creditor, Commonly Called Merchants Accompts, and Applying the Same to the Concerns of the Nobility and Gentry of England. Shewing I. The Great Advantages of Gentlemens Keeping their own Accompts, with Directions to Persons of Quality and Fortune. II. The Ruin that Attends Men of Estate by Neglect of Accompts. III. The Usefulness of the Knowledge of Accompts, to Such as are Any Way Employed in the Publick Affairs of the Nation. IV. Of Banks . . . V. Of Stocks and Stock-Jobbing . . . VI. A Short and Easy Vocabulary*. London: E. Curll, 1714.

———. *The Lives of the Right Hon. Francis North, Baron Guildford; The Hon. Sir Dudley North; and the Hon. and Rev. Dr. John North . . . Together with the Autobiography of the Author*. Ed. Augustus Jessopp. 3 vols. London: George Bell and Sons, 1890.

Norwich Directory, or Gentlemen and Tradesmen's Assistant. Norwich: n.p., 1783.

Oakes, James. *The Oakes Diaries: Business, Politics and the Family in Bury St. Edmunds 1778–1827*. Suffolk Records Society, vols. 32 and 33. Ed. Jane Fiske. Woodbridge: Boydell, 1990–1991.

Oldfield, T. H. B. *An Entire and Complete History, Political and Personal, of the Boroughs of Great Britain*. 3 vols. London: G. Riley, 1792.

Onania; or the Heinous Sin of Self-Pollution, 8th ed. London: T. Crouch, 1723.

Osborne, Francis. *Advice to a Son*. London, 1656.

Pepys, Samuel. *The Diary of Samuel Pepys*. Ed. Robert Latham and William Matthews. 11 vols. London: Bell & Hyman, 1970–1983.

Pitt, Moses. *The Cry of the Oppressed. Being a True and Tragical Account of the Unparallel'd Sufferings of Multitudes of Poor Imprisoned Debtors, in most of the Gaols in England, under the Tyranny of Gaolers, and Other Oppressors*. London: Printed for Moses Pitt, 1691.

Priestley, Jonathan. "Some Memoirs Concerning the Family of the Priestleys, Written at the Request of a Friend. (1696)." In Charles Jackson, ed., *Yorkshire Diaries and Autobiographies*, Surtees Society Publications, vol. 77. Durham: Surtees Society, 1886.

Pryme, Abraham de la. *The Diary of Abraham de la Pryme, The Yorkshire Antiquary*. Surtees Society Publications, vol. 54. Durham: Surtees Society, 1870.

Raffald, Elizabeth. *The Manchester Directory for the Year 1772. Containing an Alphabetical List of the Merchants, Tradesmen, and Principal Inhabitants in the Town of*

Manchester, with the Situation of their Respective Warehouses, and Places of Abode. London: Printed for the Author, and sold by R. Baldwin, and by the Author at Manchester, 1772.

Reed, John. *New Bristol Directory for the Year 1792.* Bristol: John Reed, 1792.

Roberts, Lewes. *The Merchants Mappe of Commerce: Wherein, the Vniversall Manner and Matter of Trade, is Compendiously Handled. The Standerd and Currant Coines of Sundry Princes, Observed. The Reall and Imaginary Coines of Accompts and Exchanges, Expressed. The Naturall and Artificiall Commodities of all Countries for Transportation Declared. The Weights and Measures of all Eminent Cities and Townes of Traffique, Collected and Reduced One into Another; and all to the Meridian of Commerce Practised in the Famous Citie of London.* London, 1638.

Robinson, Mary. *Memoirs of Mary Robinson "Perdita".* Ed. J. Fitzgerald Molloy. London and Philadelphia: Gibbings and Co. and J. B. Lippincott, 1895.

Ryder, Dudley. *The Diary of Dudley Ryder, 1715–1716.* Ed. William Matthews. London: Methuen & Co., 1939.

Scott, Sarah. *A Description of Millenium Hall and the Country Adjacent.* Virago Modern Classics, no. 214. Intro. Jane Spencer. London: Virago, 1986.

Scott, William. *An Essay of Drapery: Or, the Compleate Citizen. Trading Iustly. Pleasingly. Profitably.* Kress Library of Business and Economics, no. 9. Ed. Sylvia Thrupp. Boston: Baker Library, Harvard Graduate School of Business Administration, 1953. Originally published 1635.

Sedley, Charles. *The Mulberry Garden, A Comedy.* London, 1668.

Sherlock, William. *The Charity of Lending Without Usury and the True Notion of Usury Briefly Stated . . . Preach'd Before the Right Honourable the Lord Mayor.* London, 1692.

Smith, Adam. *An Inquiry into the Nature and Causes of the Wealth of Nations.* Ed. Edwin Cannan. New York: Modern Library, 1937.

Steele, Richard. *The Trades-man's Calling. Being a Discourse Concerning the Nature, Necessity, Choice &c. of a Calling in General. Directions for the Right Managing of the Tradesman's Calling in Particular.* London, 1684.

Stephens, Edward. *A Collection of Modern Relations of Matter of Fact, Concerning Witches and Witchcraft Upon the Persons of People To Which is Prefixed a Meditation . . . by the late Lord Chief Justice Hale Upon Occasion of a Tryal of Several Witches Before Him.* London, 1693.

———. *A Seasonable and Necessary Admonition to the Gentlemen of the First Society for Reformation of Manners.* London: n.p., ca. 1700.

Stout, William. *Autobiography of William Stout of Lancaster, 1665–1752.* Ed. J. D. Marshall. Manchester and New York: Manchester University Press and Barnes & Noble, 1967.

Stukeley, William. *The Family Memoirs of the Rev. William Stukeley, M.D.* Surtees Society Publications, vol. 73. Ed. W. C. Lukis. 3 vols. Durham: Andrews & Co., 1882.

———. *National Judgements the Consequence of a National Prophanation of the Sabbath: A Sermon Preached Before the Honourable House of Commons at St. Margaret's, Westminster; on the 30th Day of January 1741/2.* London: T. Cooper, 1742.

Sutton, Christopher. *Disce Mori: Learne to Die.* 2 vols. London, 1600.

Swift, Jonathan. *Collected Poems of Jonathan Swift,* vol. 2. Ed. Joseph Horrell. London: Routledge & Kegan Paul, 1958.

Taylor, John. *A Kicksey Winsey: Or a Lerry Come-Twang: Wherein Iohn Taylor hath Satyrically Suited 800 of his Bad Debtors that will not Pay him for his Returne of his Iourney from Scotland.* London, 1619.

Tisser, Thomas. *A Sermon Preached at St. Bartholemew Exchange, on Wednesday the 3d of December, 1701. Before the Honourable Company of Merchants Trading into the Levant-Seas.* London: Samuel Keble, 1702.

A Treatise of Feme Coverts, or, the Lady's Law. London: E. and R. Nutt and R. Gosling for B. Lintot, 1732.

Trimmer, Sarah. *An Easy Introduction to the Knowledge of Nature, and Reading the Holy Scriptures. Adapted to the Capacities of Children.* London: T. Longman, 1793.

———. *The Oeconomy of Charity; or, an Address to Ladies Concerning Sunday Schools, the Establishment of Schools of Industry under Female Inspection.* London: T. Bensley, 1787.

Tucker, Josiah. *Instructions for Travellers.* Dublin: William Watson, 1758.

———. *A Letter to a Friend Concerning Naturalizations.* London: Thomas Trye, 1753.

Turner, Thomas. *The Diary of Thomas Turner, 1754–1765.* Ed. Donald Vaisey. Oxford: Oxford University Press, 1984.

Venette, Nicolas de. *The Mysteries of Conjugal Love Reveal'd.* London: n.p., 1712. Abridged translation of *Tableau de l'amour considéré dans l'estat du mariage,* originally published in Amsterdam, 1687.

The Victuallers Case, Humbly Offered to the Consideration of their Excellencies the Lords Justices, and the Rest of the Kings Ministers. London: n.p., 1701.

Ward, J. R. "A Planter and his Slaves in Eighteenth-century Jamaica." In T. C. Smout, ed., *The Search for Wealth and Stability: Essays in Economic and Social History Presented to M. W. Flinn.* London: Macmillan, 1979.

Warner, John. *The Gayne of Losse, or, Temporall Losses Spiritually Improved.* London, 1645.

Wedgwood, Josiah. *Letters to Bentley, 1771–1780.* Didsbury, Manchester: E. J. Morten and Wedgwood Museum, 1903.

Wesley, John. *The Journal of John Wesley.* Ed. Nehemiah Curnock. 8 vols. London: Epworth Press, 1938.

Wheatcroft, Leonard. *The Courtship Narrative of Leonard Wheatcroft, Derbyshire Yeoman.* Ed. George Parfitt and Ralph Houlbrooke. Reading: Whiteknights Press, 1986.

Wollstonecraft, Mary. *A Vindication of the Rights of Women.* Ed. Carol H. Poston. New York and London: W. W. Norton, 1975. Originally published 1792.

Woodward, Josiah. *An Account of the Rise and Progress of the Religious Societies in the City of London &c. And of the Endeavours for Reformation of Manners which have been made Therein.* London, 1698.

———. *A Rebuke to the Sin of Uncleanness.* London: John Downing, 1720.

———. *Sodom's Vices Destructive to Other Cities and States: A Sermon Preached before the Right Honourable the Lord Mayor of the City of London at the Chappel of Guildhall.* London, 1697.

———. *The Young Man's Monitor: Shewing the Great Happiness of Early Piety and the Dreadful Consequences of Indulging Youthful Lusts.* London: Joseph Downing, 1718.

Wright, Samuel. *A Sermon Preach'd Before the Societies for Reformation of Manners at Salters-Hall, June 25, 1715.* London: John Clark and Eman. Matthews, 1715.

Wright, Thomas. *The Autobiography of Thomas Wright of Birkenshaw in the County of York. 1736–1797.* Ed. Thomas Wright. London: John Russell Smith, 1864.

SECONDARY SOURCES

Abelove, Henry. *Evangelist of Desire: John Wesley and the Methodists.* Stanford, Calif.: Stanford University Press, 1990.

Adburgham, Alison. *Shops and Shopping, 1800–1914: Where and In What Manner the Well-Dressed Englishwoman Bought her Clothes.* London: Allen and Unwin, 1964.

Aers, David, ed. *Culture and History, 1350–1600: Essays on English Communities, Identities, Writing.* New York and London: Harvester Wheatsheaf, 1992.

Allen, W. O. B., and E. MacClure. *Two Hundred Years: The History of the Society for Promoting Christian Knowledge.* London: SPCK, 1898.

Amussen, Susan Dwyer. *An Ordered Society: Gender and Class in Early Modern England.* Oxford: Basil Blackwell, 1988.

Anderson, B. L. "Money and the Structure of Credit in the Eighteenth Century." *Business History* 12(1970):85–101.

Andrew, Donna T. "Aldermen and the Big Bourgeoisie of London Reconsidered." *Social History* 6(1981):356–364.

———. "The Code of Honour and Its Critics: The Opposition to Duelling in England, 1700–1850." *Social History* 5(1980):409–434.

———. "*Noblesse Oblige:* Female Charity in an Age of Sentiment." In John Brewer and Susan Staves, eds., *Early Modern Conceptions of Property.* London and New York: Routledge, 1995.

———. *Philanthropy and Police: London Charity in the Eighteenth Century.* Princeton: Princeton University Press, 1989.

Appleby, Joyce Oldham. *Economic Thought and Ideology in Seventeenth-Century England.* Princeton: Princeton University Press, 1978.

Armstrong, Nancy. *Desire and Domestic Fiction: A Political History of the Novel.* New York and Oxford: Oxford University Press, 1987.

Atkins, P. J. *The Directories of London, 1677–1987.* London and New York: Mansell, 1990.

Bahlman, Dudley W. R. *The Moral Revolution of 1688.* Wallace Notestein Essays, no. 2. New Haven: Yale University Press, 1957.

Bailyn, Bernard. *New England Merchants in the Seventeenth Century.* New York: Harper Torchbooks, 1964.

Bateson, Mary, ed. *Borough Customs.* Publications of the Selden Society, vols. 18 and 21. London: Bernard Quaritch, 1904–1906.

Baugh, Daniel A., ed. *Aristocratic Government and Society in Eighteenth-Century England.* New York: New Viewpoints, 1975.

———. "Poverty, Puritanism and Political Economy: English Attitudes Toward the Poor, 1660–1800." In Stephen B. Baxter, ed., *England's Rise to Greatness, 1660–1763.* Berkeley: University of California Press, 1983.

Baumgarten, Deborah. *The Fruit of Her Hands: Esther Prager, an Anglo-Jewish Woman in Eighteenth-Century Trade.* Senior thesis, Amherst College, 1992.

Baxter, Stephen B., ed. *England's Rise to Greatness, 1660–1763.* Berkeley and Los Angeles: University of California Press, 1983.

Beattie, J. M. *Crime and the Courts in England, 1660–1800.* Oxford: Clarendon Press, 1986.

Beckett, J. V. *The Aristocracy in England, 1660–1914.* Oxford: Basil Blackwell, 1986.

Ben-Amos, Ilana Krausman. *Adolescence and Youth in Early Modern England.* New Haven and London: Yale University Press, 1994.

Bennett, G. V., and J. D. Walsh, eds. *Essays in Modern English Church History.* London: Adam and Charles Black, 1966.

Bennett, Judith M. "History That Stands Still: Women's Work in the European Past." *Feminist Studies* 14(1988):269–283.

———. "Medieval Women, Modern Women: Across the Great Divide." In David Aers, ed., *Culture and History, 1350–1600: Essays on English Communities, Identities, and Writing.* New York and London: Harvester Wheatsheaf, 1992.

Berg, Maxine. *The Age of Manufactures: Industry, Innovation and Work in Britain, 1700–1820.* London: Blackwell/Fontana, 1985.

———. "Women's Work, Mechanization and the Early Phases of Industrialization in England." In R. E. Pahl, ed., *On Work: Historical, Comparative and Theoretical Approaches.* Oxford: Basil Blackwell, 1988.

———. *The Machinery Question and the Making of Political Economy, 1815–1848.* Cambridge: Cambridge University Press, 1980.

———. "What Difference Did Women's Work Make to the Industrial Revolution?" *History Workshop Journal* 35(1993):22–44.

Berg, Maxine, Pat Hudson, and Michael Sonenscher, eds. *Manufacture in Town and Country Before the Factory.* Cambridge: Cambridge University Press, 1983.

Beveridge, A. C. "Childhood and Society in Eighteenth-Century Scotland." In John Dwyer, ed., *New Perspectives on the Politics and Culture of Early Modern Scotland, 1560–1800.* Edinburgh: J. Donald, 1982.

Birks, Michael. *Gentlemen of the Law.* London: Steven & Sons, Ltd., 1960.

Black, Jeremy. *The English Press in the Eighteenth Century.* London: Croom Helm, 1987.

Bloom, Edward A., Lillian D. Bloom, and Edmund Leites, eds. *Educating the Audience: Addison, Steele and Eighteenth-Century Culture.* Papers Presented to the Clark Library Seminar, 15 November 1980. Los Angeles: William Andrews Clark Memorial Library, University of California, 1984.

Borsay, Peter. *The English Urban Renaissance: Culture and Society in the Provincial Town, 1660–1770.* Oxford: Clarendon Press, 1989.

———. "The English Urban Renaissance: The Development of Provincial Urban Culture, c. 1680–1760." *Social History* 2(1977):581–603.

Bourdieu, Pierre. "Social Space and Symbolic Power." *Sociological Theory* 7(1989):14–25.

Bowen, H. V. "The Pests of Human Society: Stockbrokers, Jobbers and Speculators in Mid-Eighteenth-Century Britain." *History* 78 (1993):38–53.

Bray, Alan. *Homosexuality in Renaissance England.* New York: Columbia University Press, 1995.

Brewer, John. *Party Ideology and Popular Politics at the Accession of George III.* Cambridge: Cambridge University Press, 1976.

————. *The Sinews of Power: War, Money and the English State, 1688–1783.* New York: Alfred A. Knopf, 1989.

————. "The Wilkites and the Law, 1763–74: A Study of Radical Notions of Governance." In John Brewer and John Styles, eds., *An Ungovernable People: The English and Their Law in the Seventeenth and Eighteenth Centuries.* London: Hutchinson, 1980.

Brewer, John, and Roy Porter, eds. *Consumption and the World of Goods.* London: Routledge, 1993.

Brewer, John, and Susan Staves, eds. *Early Modern Conceptions of Property.* London and New York: Routledge, 1995.

Brewer, John, and John Styles, eds. *An Ungovernable People: The English and Their Law in the Seventeenth and Eighteenth Centuries.* London: Hutchinson, 1980.

Brigden, Susan. "Religion and Social Obligation in Early Sixteenth-Century London." *Past & Present* 103(1984):66–112.

————. "Youth and the English Reformation." *Past & Present* 95 (1982):37–67.

Bristow, Edward J. *Vice and Vigilance: Purity Movements in Britain since 1700.* Dublin: Gill & MacMillan, 1977.

Brown, Irene Q. "Domesticity, Feminism, and Friendship: Female Aristocratic Culture and Marriage in England, 1660–1760." *Journal of Family History* 7(1982): 406–424.

Browne, Alice. *The Eighteenth-Century Feminist Mind.* Brighton: Harvester, 1987.

Bullock, F. W. B. *Voluntary Societies 1520–1799.* St. Leonards on Sea, Sussex: Budd & Gillat, 1963.

Burman, Sandra, ed. *Fit Work for Women.* London: Croom Helm, in Association with Oxford University Womens' Studies Committee, 1979.

Bush, Michael L. *The English Aristocracy: A Comparative Synthesis.* Manchester: Manchester University Press, 1984.

————. *Noble Privilege.* New York: Holmes & Meier, 1983.

Cadwallader, Francis J. J. "In Pursuit of the Merchant Debtor and Bankrupt, 1066–1732." Ph.D. diss. (Laws), University of London, 1965.

Cannadine, David. *Lords and Landlords: The Aristocracy and the Towns, 1774–1967.* Leicester: Leicester University Press, 1980.

Cannon, John. *Aristocratic Century: The Peerage in Eighteenth-Century England.* Cambridge: Cambridge University Press, 1984.

Capp, Bernard. *Astrology and the Popular Press: English Almanacs, 1500–1800.* London: Faber, 1979.

Carswell, John. *The South Sea Bubble.* London: Alan Sutton, 1993. Originally published 1960.

Carus-Wilson, Eleanora Mary, ed. *Essays in Economic History.* 3 vols. London: E. Arnold, 1954.

Charles, Lindsey, and Lorna Duffin, eds. *Women and Work in Preindustrial England.* London: Croom Helm, 1985.

Chaytor, Miranda. "Household and Kinship, Ryton in the Late Sixteenth and Early Seventeenth Centuries." *History Workshop Journal* 10(1980):25–60.

Chesterman, M. R. "Family Settlements in Trust: Landowners and the Rising Bourgeoisie." In G. R. Rubin and David Sugarman, eds., *Law, Economy and Society,*

1750–1914: Essays in the History of English Law. Abingdon, Oxon.: Professional Books, 1984.

Clark, Alice. *Working Life of Women in the Seventeenth Century,* London, New York: Routledge, 1992. Originally published 1919.

Clark, Anna. *The Struggle for the Breeches: Gender and the Making of the British Working Class.* Berkeley: University of California Press, 1995.

———. *Women's Silence, Men's Violence: Sexual Assault in England, 1770–1845.* London and New York: Pandora, 1987.

Clark, J. C. D. *English Society 1688–1832: Ideology, Social Structure and Political Practice During the Ancien Regime.* Cambridge: Cambridge University Press, 1985.

Clark, Peter, and Paul Stack, eds. *Crisis and Order in England Towns 1500–1700: Essays in Urban History.* London: Routledge & Kegan Paul, 1972.

Clay, C. G. A. *Economic Expansion and Social Change: England, 1500–1700.* 2 vols. Cambridge: Cambridge University Press, 1984.

Cohen, Patricia Cline. "Reckoning with Commerce: Numeracy in Eighteenth-Century America." In John Brewer and Roy Porter, eds., *Consumption and the World of Goods.* London and New York: Routledge, 1993.

Coleman, D. C. *The Economy of England, 1450–1750.* London and New York: Oxford University Press, 1977.

Colley, Linda. *Britons: Forging the Nation, 1707–1837.* New Haven and London: Yale University Press, 1992.

———. *In Defiance of Oligarchy: The Tory Party, 1714–60.* Cambridge: Cambridge University Press, 1982.

Corfield, Penelope. "Class by Name and Number in Eighteenth-Century Britain." *History* 72(1987):38–61.

———. *The Impact of English Towns, 1700–1800.* Oxford: Oxford University Press, 1982.

Corfield, Penelope, with Serena Kelly. " 'Giving Directions to the Town': The Early Town Directories." *Urban History Yearbook* (1984):22–35.

Crafts, Nicholas. *British Economic Growth During the Industrial Revolution.* Oxford: Clarendon Press, 1985.

Craig, A. G. "The Movement for the Reformation of Manners, 1688–1715." Ph.D. diss., University of Edinburgh, 1980.

Crawford, Patricia. *Women and Religion in England 1500–1720.* London and New York: Routledge, 1993.

Creighton, Charles. *A History of Epidemics in Britain from A.D. 664 to the Extinction of the Plague.* Cambridge: Cambridge University Press, 1891.

Cressy, David. *Coming Over: Migration and Communication Between England and New England in the Seventeenth Century.* Cambridge: Cambridge University Press, 1987.

———. *Literacy and the Social Order: Reading and Writing in Tudor and Stuart England.* Cambridge: Cambridge University Press, 1980.

———. "Literacy in Context: Meaning and Measurement in Early Modern England." In John Brewer and Roy Porter, eds., *Consumption and the World of Goods.* London and New York: Routledge, 1993.

Curry, Patrick. *Prophecy and Power: Astrology in Early Modern England.* Princeton: Princeton University Press, 1989.

———. "Towards a Post-Marxist Social History: Thompson, Clark and Beyond." In

Adrian Wilson, ed., *Rethinking Social History: English Society 1570–1920 and Its Interpretation.* Manchester and New York: Manchester University Press, 1993.

Curtis, T. C., and W. H. Speck. "The Societies for the Reformation of Manners: A Case Study in the Theory and Practice of Moral Reform." *Literature and History* 3(1976):45–64.

Davidoff, Leonore, and Catherine Hall. *Family Fortunes: Men and Women of the English Middle Class, 1780–1850.* Chicago: University of Chicago Press, 1987.

Davie, Donald. *The Eighteenth-Century Hymn in England.* Cambridge Studies in Eighteenth-Century English Literature and Thought, 19. Cambridge: Cambridge University Press, 1993.

Davies, K. "The Mess of the Middle Class." *Past & Present* 22 (1962):77–83.

Davies, K. G. *The Royal African Company.* London: Longmans, Green and Co., 1957.

Davis, Dorothy. *A History of Shopping.* London and Toronto: Routledge & Kegan Paul and University of Toronto Press, 1966.

Davis, Natalie Zemon. *Society and Culture in Early Modern France.* Stanford, Calif.: Stanford University Press, 1975.

Davis, Ralph. *Aleppo and Devonshire Square: English Traders in the Levant in the Eighteenth Century.* London: Macmillan, 1967.

———. *The Rise of the English Shipping Industry in the Seventeenth and Eighteenth Centuries.* Newton Abbot: David and Charles, 1972.

Davison, Lee Krim. "Public Policy in an Age of Economic Expansion: The Search for Commercial Accountability in England, 1690–1750." Ph.D. diss. Harvard University, 1990.

d'Cruze, Shani. *Our Time in God's Hands: Religion and the Middling Sort in Eighteenth-Century Colchester.* Chelmsford: Essex Record Office and Local History Centre, University of Essex, 1991.

DeKrey, Gary. *A Fractured Society: The Politics of London in the First Age of Party, 1688–1715.* Oxford: Clarendon Press, 1985.

Dennie, Charles Clayton. *A History of Syphilis.* Springfield, Ill.: Charles C. Thomas, 1962.

Derrida, Jacques. *Of Grammatology.* Trans. Gayatri Chakravorty Spivak. Baltimore: Johns Hopkins University Press, 1976.

Dickinson, H. T. *Liberty and Property: Political Ideology in Eighteenth-Century Britain.* London: Weidenfeld & Nicolson, 1977.

Dickson, P. G. M. *The Financial Revolution in England: A Study in the Development of Public Credit 1688–1756.* London: St. Martin's Press, 1967.

———. *The Sun Insurance Office, 1710–1960.* London: Oxford University Press, 1960.

Douglas, David C. *English Scholars, 1660–1730.* London: Eyre & Spottiswoode, 1951.

Douglas, Mary. *Purity and Danger: An Analysis of Concepts of Pollution and Taboo.* London: Routledge & Kegan Paul, 1966.

Dugaw, Dianne. *Warrior Women and Popular Balladry 1650–1850.* Cambridge Studies in Eighteenth-Century English Literature and Thought, 4. Cambridge: Cambridge University Press, 1989.

Dwyer, John, ed. *New Perspectives on the Politics and Culture of Early Modern Scotland, 1560–1800.* Edinburgh: J. Donald, 1982.

Eagleton, Terry. *The Function of Criticism: From the Spectator to Post-Structuralism.* London: Verso, 1984.

Earle, Alice. *Child Life in Colonial Days.* New York: Macmillan, 1961. Originally published 1899.

Earle, Peter. "The Female Labour Market in London in the Late Seventeenth and Early Eighteenth Centuries." *Economic History Review* (2d ser.) 42(1989):328–353.

————. *The Making of the English Middle Class: Business, Society and Family Life in London, 1660–1730.* Berkeley and Los Angeles: University of California Press, 1989.

————. *The World of Defoe.* London: Weidenfeld & Nicolson, 1976.

Eisenstein, Elizabeth. *The Printing Press as an Agent of Change: Communications and Cultural Transformations in Early-Modern Europe.* 2 vols. Cambridge and New York: Cambridge University Press, 1979.

Erickson, Amy Louise. "Common Law versus Common Practice: The Use of Marriage Settlements in Early Modern England." *Economic History Review* (2d ser.) 43(1990):21–39.

————. *Women and Property in Early Modern England.* London and New York: Routledge, 1993.

Federer, Andrew. "Payment, Credit and the Organization of Work in Eighteenth-Century Westminster." Unpublished paper given at the SSRC Conference, "Manufacture in Town and Country before the Factory," Balliol College, Oxford, September 1980.

Felsenstein, Frank. *Anti-Semitic Stereotypes: A Paradigm of Otherness in English Popular Culture, 1660–1830.* Baltimore and London: Johns Hopkins University Press, 1995.

Flinn, M. W. *Men of Iron: The Crowleys in the Early Iron Industry.* Edinburgh: Edinburgh University Press, 1962.

Foucault, Michel. *The History of Sexuality, Vol. I: An Introduction.* Trans. Robert Hurley. London: Allen Lane, Penguin, 1979.

Fryer, Peter. *Staying Power: Black People in Britain since 1504.* Atlantic Highlands, N.J.: Humanities Press, 1984.

Garnett, Jane, and Colin Matthew, eds. *Revival and Religion Since 1700: Essays for John Walsh.* London and Rio Grande: The Hambledon Press, 1993.

George, M. Dorothy. *London Life in the Eighteenth Century.* New York: Harper & Row, 1964.

Gelles, Edith B. "Gossip: An Eighteenth-Century Case." *Journal of Social History* 22(1989):667–683.

Gillis, John. *For Better, For Worse: British Marriage, 1600 to the Present.* New York and Oxford: Oxford University Press, 1985.

————. *Youth and History: Traditions and Change in European Age Relations, 1770–Present.* New York: Academic Press, 1981.

Glass, D. V. "Socio-economic Status and Occupations in the City of London at the End of the Seventeenth Century." In A. E. J. Hollaender and William Kellaway, eds., *Studies in London History Presented to Philip Edmund Jones.* London: Hodder and Stoughton, 1969.

Goldberg, Jeremy. "London Widowhood Revisited: The Decline of Female

Remarriage in the Seventeenth and Early Eighteenth Centuries." *Continuity and Change* 3(1990):323–355.

Goldberg, P. J. P. *Women, Work, and the Life Cycle in a Medieval Economy: Women in York and Yorkshire c. 1300–1520.* Oxford: Clarendon Press, 1992.

Gowing, Laura. "Gender and the Language of Insult in Early Modern London." *History Workshop Journal*, 35(1993):1–21.

Graham, Rose, ed. *English Ecclesiastical Studies, Being Some Essays in Research in Medieval History.* London: SPCK, 1929.

Hall, Catherine. "The Early Formation of Victorian Domestic Ideology." In Sandra Burman, ed., *Fit Work for Women.* London: Croom Helm, in Association with Oxford University Women's Studies Committee, 1979.

———. "Gender Divisions and Class Formation in the Birmingham Middle Class, 1780–1850." In Raphael Samuel, ed., *People's History and Socialist Theory,* History Workshop Series. London and Boston: Routledge & Kegan Paul, 1981.

———. "Private Persons Versus Public Someones: Class, Gender and Politics in England, 1780–1850." In Carolyn Steedman, Cathy Urwin, and Valerie Walkerdine, eds., *Language, Gender and Childhood.* London and Boston: Routledge & Kegan Paul, 1985.

Hamilton, Henry. "The Failure of the Ayr Bank, 1772." *Economic History Review* (2d ser.) 8(1956):405–417.

Harlan, Robert Dale. "William Strahan: Eighteenth-Century London Printer." Ph.D. diss., University of Michigan, 1960.

Harris, Michael. "Moses Pitt and Insolvency in the London Book Trade in the Late Seventeenth Century." In Robin Myers, ed., *Economics of the British Booktrade, 1605–1939.* Cambridge: Chadwick-Healey, 1985.

Havill, John. "Eleanor Coade, Artificial Stone Manufacturer Born Exeter 1733 and Died London 1821." Typescript, copy in the Guildhall Library, 1986.

Hecht, J. Jean. *The Domestic Servant Class in Eighteenth-Century England.* Westport, Conn.: Hyperion Press, 1981. Originally published 1956.

Hellmuth, Eckhart, ed. *The Transformation of Political Culture: England and Germany in the Late Eighteenth Century.* Oxford and London: Oxford University Press and the German Historical Institute, 1990.

Hexter, J. H. "The Myth of the Middle Class in Tudor England." In J. H. Hexter, ed., *Reappraisals in History.* London: Longman, 1961.

———. *Reappraisals in History.* London: Longmans, 1961.

Hill, Bridget. "The Marriage Age of Women and the Demographers." *History Workshop Journal* 28(1989):129–147.

———. "A Refuge from Men: The Idea of a Protestant Nunnery." *Past & Present* 117 (1987):107–130.

———. *The Republican Virago: The Life and Times of Catharine Macaulay, Historian.* Oxford and New York: Clarendon Press, 1992.

———. *Women, Work and Sexual Politics in Eighteenth-Century England.* Oxford, New York: Basil Blackwell, 1989.

Hill, Christopher. "A Bourgeois Revolution?" In J. G. A. Pocock, ed., *Three British Revolutions: 1641, 1688, 1776.* Princeton: Princeton University Press, 1980.

———. *The Century of Revolution: 1603–1714.* New York: Norton, 1980.

———. *The World Turned Upside Down: Radical Ideas During the English Revolution.* Harmondsworth: Penguin, 1975.

Hirschman, A. O. *The Passions and the Interests: Political Arguments for Capitalism Before its Triumph.* Princeton, N.J.: Princeton University Press, 1977

Hobby, Elaine. *Virtue of Necessity: English Women's Writing, 1649–1688.* London: Virago, 1988.

Holcombe, Lee. *Wives and Property: Reform of the Married Women's Property Law in Nineteenth-Century England.* Toronto and Buffalo: University of Toronto Press, 1983.

Holdsworth, William. *A History of English Law.* 15 vols. London: Methuen & Co., 1937–1965.

Hollaender, A. E. J., and William Kellaway, eds. *Studies in London History Presented to Philip Edmund Jones.* London: Hodder and Stoughton, 1969.

Holmes, Geoffrey. *Augustan England: Professions, State and Society, 1680–1730.* London: George Allen and Unwin, 1982.

Hoppit, Julian. "Financial Crises in Eighteenth-Century England." *Economic History Review* (2d ser.) 39 (1986):39–58.

———. *Risk and Failure in English Business, 1700–1800.* Cambridge: Cambridge University Press, 1987.

Horwitz, Henry. " 'The Mess of the Middle Class' Revisited: The Case of the 'Big Bourgeoisie' of Augustan London." *Continuity and Change* 2(1987):263–296.

Houlbrooke, Ralph A. *The English Family 1450–1700.* London and New York: Longman, 1984.

Houston, R. A. "Aspects of Society in Scotland and North-east England, c. 1550–1750: Social Structure, Literacy and Geographical Mobility." Ph.D. diss., Cambridge University, 1981.

———. *Literacy in Early Modern Europe: Culture and Education 1500–1800.* London and New York: Longman, 1988.

Howell, Martha. *Women, Production and Patriarchy in Late Medieval Cities.* Chicago and London: University of Chicago Press, 1986.

Howson, Geoffrey. *A History of Mathematics Education in England.* Cambridge: Cambridge University Press, 1982.

Hufton, Olwen. "Women and the Family Economy in Eighteenth-Century France." *French Historical Studies* 9(1975–1976):1–22.

———. "Women Without Men: Widows and Spinsters in Britain and France in the Eighteenth Century." *Journal of Family History* 9 (1984):355–376.

Hughes, Edward. *North Country Life in the Eighteenth Century.* 2 vols. London: Oxford University Press, 1952–1965.

———. "The Professions in the Eighteenth Century." In Daniel A. Baugh, ed., *Aristocratic Government and Society in Eighteenth-Century England.* New York: New Viewpoints, 1975.

Hunt, Margaret R. "The De-eroticization of Women's Liberation: Social Purity Movements and the Revolutionary Feminism of Sheila Jeffreys." *Feminist Review*, no. 34(1990):23–46.

———. "English Urban Families in Trade, 1660–1800: The Culture of Early Modern Capitalism." Ph.D. diss., New York University, 1986.

————. "Hawkers, Bawlers and Mercuries: Women and the London Press in the Early Enlightenment." In Margaret R. Hunt, Margaret Jacob, Phyllis Mack, and Ruth Perry, eds., *Women and the Enlightenment.* Women and History, no. 9. New York: The Institute for Research in History and The Haworth Press, 1984.

————. "Racism, Imperialism and the Traveler's Gaze in Eighteenth-Century England." *Journal of British Studies* 32 (1993):333–357.

————. "Time-Management, Writing, and Accounting in the Eighteenth-Century English Trading Family: A Bourgeois Enlightenment?" *Business and Economic History* (2d ser.) 18 (1989):150–159.

————. "Wife-beating, Domesticity and Women's Independence in Eighteenth-Century London." *Gender and History* 4(1992):10–33.

Hunt, Margaret, Margaret Jacob, Phyllis Mack, and Ruth Perry, eds. *Women and the Enlightenment.* Women and History, no. 9. New York: The Institute for Research in History and The Haworth Press, 1984.

Hunter, J. Paul. *Before Novels: The Cultural Contexts of Eighteenth-Century English Fiction.* New York and London: Norton, 1990.

Innes, Joanna. "King's Bench Prison in the Late Eighteenth Century: Law, Order and Authority in a London Debtor's Prison." In John Brewer and John Styles, eds., *An Ungovernable People.* London: Hutchinson, 1981.

————. "Parliament and the Shaping of Eighteenth-Century English Social Policy." *Transactions of the Royal Historical Society* (5th ser.) 40 (1990):63–92.

————. "Politics and Morals: The Reformation of Morals Movement in Later Eighteenth-Century England." In Eckhart Hellmuth, ed., *The Transformation of Political Culture: England and Germany in the Late Eighteenth Century.* Oxford and London: Oxford University Press and the German Historical Institute, 1990.

Isaacs, Tina Beth. "The Anglican Hierarchy and the Reformation of Manners, 1688–1738." *Journal of Ecclesiastical History* 33 (1982):391–411.

————. "Moral Crime, Moral Reform and the State in Early Eighteenth-Century England: A Study of Piety and Politics." Ph.D. diss., University of Rochester, 1979.

Jacob, Margaret C. *Cultural Origins of the Scientific Revolution.* Philadelphia: Temple University Press, 1988.

————. "Freemasons, Women and the Paradox of the Enlightenment." In Margaret Hunt, Margaret C. Jacob, Phyllis Mack, and Ruth Perry, eds., *Women and the Enlightenment.* Women and History, No. 9. New York: The Institute for Research in History and the Haworth Press, 1984.

————. *The Newtonians and the English Revolution, 1689–1720.* Hassocks, Sussex: Harvester Press, 1976.

————. *The Radical Enlightenment: Pantheists, Freemasons and Republicans.* London: George Allen & Unwin, 1981.

James, Patricia. *Population Malthus, His Life and Times.* London: Routledge & Kegan Paul, 1979.

Jones, D. W. "London Merchants and the Crisis of the 1690s." In Peter Clark and Paul Stack, eds., *Crisis and Order in England Towns 1500–1700: Essays in Urban History.* London: Routledge & Kegan Paul, 1972.

Jones, Mary Gwladys. *The Charity School Movement: A Study of Eighteenth-Century Puritanism in Action.* Cambridge: The University Press, 1938.

Katz, Michael B., Michael J. Doucet, and Mark J. Stern. *The Social Organization of Early Industrial Capitalism.* Cambridge, Mass.: Harvard University Press, 1982.

Kaufman, Paul. *Borrowings from the Bristol Library, 1773–1784: A Unique Record of Reading Vogues.* Charlottesville: Bibliographical Society of the University of Virginia, 1960.

Kelly, Alison. *Mrs. Coade's Stone.* Upton-upon-Severn, Worcs.: Self-Publishing Association, Ltd. in Conjunction with the Georgian Group, 1990.

Klaits, Joseph. *Printed Propaganda under Louis XIV: Absolute Monarchy and Public Opinion.* Princeton, N.J.: Princeton University Press, 1978.

Landau, Norma. *The Justices of the Peace, 1679–1760.* Berkeley: University of California Press, 1984.

Landes, David. *Revolution in Time: Clocks and the Making of the Modern World.* Cambridge, Mass.: Belknap Press of Harvard University Press, 1983.

Langford, Paul. *A Polite and Commercial People: England 1727–1783.* Oxford: Oxford University Press, 1992.

———. *Public Life and the Propertied Englishman, 1689–1798.* Oxford: Clarendon Press, 1991.

Langford, Paul, and Christopher Harvie. *The Eighteenth Century and the Age of Industry.* The Oxford History of Britain, vol. 4. Oxford: Oxford University Press, 1992.

Laurence, Anne. *Women in England, 1500–1760: A Social History.* London: Weidenfeld and Nicolson, 1995.

Lears, Jackson. "The Concept of Cultural Hegemony: Problems and Possibilities." *American Historical Review* 90(1985):567–593.

Leites, Edmund. "Good Humor at Home, Good Humor Abroad: The Intimacies of Marriage and the Civilities of Social Life in the Ethic of Richard Steele." In Edward A. Bloom, Lillian D. Bloom, and Edmund Leites, eds., *Educating the Audience: Addison, Steele and Eighteenth-Century Culture.* Papers Presented to the Clark Library Seminar, 15 November 1980. Los Angeles: William Andrews Clark Memorial Library, University of California, 1984.

Lillywhite, Bryant. *London Coffee Houses: A Reference Book of Coffee Houses of the Seventeenth, Eighteenth and Nineteenth Centuries.* London: George Allen & Unwin, 1963.

Lindsay, Jack. *Hogarth: His Art and His World.* New York: Taplinger, 1979.

Mack, Phyllis. *Visionary Women: Ecstatic Prophecy in Seventeenth-Century England.* Berkeley, Los Angeles, and Oxford: University of California Press, 1992.

Malmgreen, Gail. *Silk Town: Industry and Culture in Macclesfield, 1750–1835.* Hull: The University of Hull Press, 1985.

Mann, Bruce H. *Neighbors and Strangers: Law and Community in Early Connecticut.* Chapel Hill and London: University of North Carolina Press, 1987.

Matthews, William. *British Diaries: An Annotated Bibliography of British Diaries Written Between 1442 and 1942.* Berkeley and Los Angeles: University of California Press, 1950.

McIntosh, Mary. "The Homosexual Role." *Social Problems* 16, no. 2(1968):182–92.

McKendrick, Neil, ed. *Historical Perspectives: Studies in English Thought and Society in Honour of J. H. Plumb.* London: Europa, 1974.

———. "Home Demand and Economic Growth: A New View of the Role of Women and Children in the Industrial Revolution." In Neil McKendrick, ed., *Historical*

Perspectives: Studies in English Thought and Society in Honour of J. H. Plumb. London: Europa, 1974.

———. "Josiah Wedgwood, Cost Accounting and the Industrial Revolution." *Economic History Review* (2d ser.) 23(1970):45–67.

McKendrick, Neil, John Brewer, and J. H. Plumb. *The Birth of a Consumer Society: The Commercialization of Eighteenth-Century England.* London: Hutchinson, 1983.

Medick, Hans. "Plebeian Culture in the Transition to Capitalism." In Raphael Samuel and Gareth Stedman Jones, eds., *Culture, Ideology and Politics: Essays for Eric Hobsbawm.* London: Routledge and Kegan Paul, 1982.

———. "The Transition from Feudalism to Capitalism: Renewal of a Debate." In Raphael Samuel, ed., *People's History and Socialist Theory.* London: Routledge and Kegan Paul, 1981.

Melling, Joseph, and Jonathan Barry, eds. *Culture in History: Production, Consumption and Values in Historical Perspective.* Exeter: University of Exeter Press, 1992.

———. "The Problem of Culture: An Introduction." In Joseph Melling and Jonathan Barry, eds., *Culture in History: Production, Consumption and Values in Historical Perspective.* Exeter: University of Exeter Press, 1992.

Miller, Perry. *The New England Mind: The Seventeenth Century.* Cambridge, Mass., Harvard University Press, 1954.

Mingay, G. E. *English Landed Society in the Eighteenth Century.* London: Routledge & Kegan Paul, 1963.

———. *The Gentry: The Rise and Fall of a Ruling Class.* London and New York: Longman, 1976.

Mizuta, Hiroshi. *Adam Smith's Library: A Supplement to Bonar's Catalogue with a Checklist of the Whole Library.* Cambridge: Cambridge University Press for the Royal Economic Society, 1967.

Money, John. *Experience and Identity: Birmingham and the West Midlands, 1760–1800.* Manchester: Manchester University Press, 1977.

———. "Teaching in the Market-Place, or 'Caesar adsum jam forte Pompey aderat': The Retailing of Knowledge in Provincial England During the Eighteenth Century." In John Brewer and Roy Porter, eds., *Consumption and the World of Goods.* London and New York: Routledge, 1993.

Morris, R. J. *Class and Class Consciousness in the Industrial Revolution, 1780–1850.* London and Basingstoke: Macmillan, 1979.

Mui, Hoh-Cheung, and Lorna H. Mui. *Shops and Shopkeeping in Eighteenth-Century England.* Kingston, Ont.: McGill-Queen's University Press, 1989.

Newman, Gerald. *The Rise of English Nationalism: A Cultural History 1740–1830.* New York: St. Martin's Press, 1987.

Norton, J. E. *Guide to the National and Provincial Directories of England and Wales, Excluding London, Published Before 1856.* London: Royal Historical Society, 1950.

Notestein, Wallace. *Four Worthies, John Chamberlain, Anne Clifford, John Taylor, Oliver Heywood.* London: Jonathan Cape, 1956.

Nussbaum, Felicity. *The Brink of All We Hate: English Satires on Women, 1660–1750.* Lexington Ky.: The University Press of Kentucky, 1984.

Okin, Susan Moller. "Patriarchy and Married Women's Property in England: Questions about Some Current Views." *Eighteenth-Century Studies* 17(1983–1984): 121–138.

————. *Women in Western Political Thought.* Princeton, N.J.: Princeton University Press, 1992.

Otis, Leah. *Prostitution in Medieval Society: The History of an Urban Institution in Languedoc.* Chicago, London: University of Chicago Press, 1985.

Ozment, Steven. *When Fathers Ruled: Family Life in Reformation Europe.* Cambridge, Mass.: Harvard University Press, 1983.

Pahl, R. E., ed. *On Work: Historical, Comparative and Theoretical Approaches.* Oxford: Basil Blackwell, 1988.

Paulson, Ronald. *The Art of Hogarth.* London: Phaidon, 1975.

————. *Popular and Polite Art in the Age of Hogarth and Fielding.* University of Notre Dame Ward-Phillips Lectures in English Language and Literature, vol. 10. Notre Dame, Ind.: University of Notre Dame Press, 1979.

Pears, Iain. *The Discovery of Painting: The Growth of Interest in the Arts in England, 1680–1768.* New Haven and London: Published for the Paul Mellon Centre for Studies in British Art by Yale University Press, 1988.

Perkin, Harold J. *The Origins of Modern English Society, 1780–1880.* London: Routledge & Kegan Paul, 1969.

Perry, Ruth. *The Celebrated Mary Astell: An Early English Feminist.* Chicago and London: University of Chicago Press, 1986.

————. *Women, Letters and the Novel.* New York: AMS Press, 1980.

Phillips, Roderick. *Putting Asunder: A History of Divorce in Western Society.* Cambridge: Cambridge University Press, 1988.

Pinchbeck, Ivy. *Women Workers and the Industrial Revolution, 1750–1850.* London: Frank Cass, 1977. Originally published 1930.

Plumb, J. H. *The Commercialisation of Leisure in Eighteenth-Century England.* The Stenton Lecture. Reading: University of Reading, 1973.

Plummer, Kenneth, ed. *The Making of the Modern Homosexual.* London: Hutchinson, 1981.

Pocock, J. G. A. *The Machiavellian Moment: Florentine Political Thought and the Atlantic Republican Tradition.* Princeton: Princeton University Press, 1975.

————, ed. *Three British Revolutions: 1641, 1688, 1776.* Princeton: Princeton University Press, 1980.

————. *Virtue, Commerce and History: Essays on Political Thought and History, Chiefly in the Eighteenth Century.* Cambridge: Cambridge University Press, 1985.

Pollard, Sidney. *The Genesis of Modern Management: A Study of the Industrial Revolution in Great Britain.* London: Edward Arnold, 1965.

Poovey, Mary. *The Proper Lady and the Woman Writer: Ideology as Style in the Works of Mary Wollstonecraft, Mary Shelley and Jane Austen.* Chicago and London: University of Chicago Press, 1984.

Porter, Roy. "Consumption: Disease of the Consumer Society." In John Brewer and Roy Porter, eds., *Consumption and the World of Goods.* London and New York: Routledge, 1993.

————. *English Society in the Eighteenth Century.* London: Penguin-Allen Lane, 1982.

————. "Rape—Does It Have a Historical Meaning?" In Roy Porter and Sylvana Tomaselli, eds., *Rape: An Historical and Social Enquiry.* Oxford: Blackwell, 1986.

Porter, Roy, and Sylvana Tomaselli, eds. *Rape: An Historical and Social Enquiry.* Oxford: Blackwell, 1986.

Postan, M. M. "Credit in Medieval Trade." In Eleanora Mary Carus-Wilson, ed., *Essays in Economic History,* vol. 1. London: Edward Arnold, 1954.

Power, Eileen. *Medieval Women.* Cambridge: Cambridge University Press, 1975.

Preston, Thomas R. "Biblical Criticism, Literature and the Eighteenth-century Reader." In Isabel Rivers, ed., *Books and their Readers in Eighteenth-Century England.* Leicester and New York: Leicester University Press and St. Martin's Press, 1982.

Price, Jacob M. *Capital and Credit in British Overseas Trade: The View from the Chesapeake, 1700–1776.* Cambridge, Mass.: Harvard University Press, 1980.

———. "The Excise Affair Revisited: The Administrative and Colonial Dimensions of a Parliamentary Crisis." In Stephen B. Baxter, ed., *England's Rise to Greatness, 1660–1763.* Berkeley, Los Angeles, and London: University of California Press, 1983.

Prior, Mary. "Women and the Urban Economy: Oxford 1500–1800." In Mary Prior, ed., *Women in English Society 1500–1800.* London: Methuen, 1985.

———, ed. *Women in English Society 1500–1800.* London: Methuen, 1985.

Probyn, Clive. *The Sociable Humanist: The Life and Works of James Harris, 1709–1780: Provincial and Metropolitan Culture in Eighteenth-Century England.* Oxford: Clarendon Press, 1991.

Quataert, Jean. "The Shaping of Women's Work in Manufacturing, Guilds, Households and the State in Central Europe, 1648–1870." *American Historical Review* 90(1985):1122–1148.

Rattray-Taylor, Gordon. *The Angel Makers: A Study in the Psychological Origins of Historical Change, 1750–1850.* New York: E. P. Dutton & Co., 1974.

Rich, E. E., and C. H. Wilson, eds. *The Cambridge Economic History of Europe,* vol. 5. Cambridge: Cambridge University Press, 1977.

Rivers, Isabel, ed. *Books and their Readers in Eighteenth-Century England.* Leicester and New York: Leicester University Press and St. Martin's Press, 1982.

Robbins, Caroline. *The Eighteenth-Century Commonwealthman: Studies in the Transmission, Development and Circumstances of English Liberal Thought from the Restoration of Charles II until the War with the Thirteen Colonies.* Cambridge, Mass.: Harvard University Press, 1959.

Roberts, Michael. " 'Words they are Women, and Deeds they are Men': Images of Work and Gender in Early Modern England." In Lindsey Charles and Lorna Duffin, eds., *Women and Work in Preindustrial England.* London: Croom Helm, 1985.

Rodgers, Betsy. *Cloak of Charity: Studies in Eighteenth-Century Philanthropy.* London: Methuen & Co., 1949.

Rogers, Katharine M. *Feminism in Eighteenth-Century England.* Urbana and Chicago: University of Illinois Press, 1982.

Rogers, Nicholas. "Money, Land and Lineage: The Big Bourgeoisie of Hanoverian London." *Social History* 4(1979):437–454.

———. *Whigs and Cities: Popular Politics in the Age of Walpole and Pitt.* Oxford: Clarendon Press, 1989.

Roth, Cecil. *Anglo-Jewish Letters (1158–1917).* London: The Socino Press, 1938.

————. *A History of the Jews in England.* Oxford: Oxford University Press, 1949.

Rowlands, Marie B. *Masters and Men in the West Midland Metalware Trades Before the Industrial Revolution.* Manchester: Manchester University Press, 1975.

Rubin, G. R. "Law, Poverty and Imprisonment for Debt, 1869–1914." In G. R. Rubin and David Sugarman, eds., *Law, Economy and Society, 1750–1914: Essays in the History of English Law.* Abingdon, Oxon.: Professional Books, 1984.

Rubin, G. R., and David Sugarman, eds. *Law, Economy and Society, 1750–1914: Essays in the History of English Law.* Abingdon, Oxon.: Professional Books, 1984.

Ryan, Mary P. *Cradle of the Middle Class: The Family in Oneida County, New York, 1790–1865.* Cambridge: Cambridge University Press, 1981.

Saito, Osamu. "Who Worked When: Life-Time Profiles of Labour Force Participation in Cardington and Corfe Castle in the Late Eighteenth and Mid-Nineteenth Centuries." *Local Population Studies* 22(1979):14–29.

Samuel, Raphael, ed. *People's History and Socialist Theory.* History Workshop Series. London and Boston: Routledge & Kegan Paul, 1981.

Samuel, Raphael, and Gareth Stedman Jones, eds. *Culture, Ideology and Politics: Essays for Eric Hobsbawm.* London: Routledge & Kegan Paul, 1982.

Schaffer, Simon. "A Social History of Plausibility: County, City and Calculation in Augustan Britain." In Adrian Wilson, ed., *Rethinking Social History: English Society 1570–1920 and Its Interpretation.* Manchester and New York: Manchester University Press, 1993.

Schlatter, Richard. *The Social Ideas of Religious Leaders, 1660–1688.* Oxford and London: Oxford University Press and Humphrey Milford, 1940.

Schofield, R. S. "Dimensions of Illiteracy, 1750–1850." *Explorations in Economic History* 10(1973):437–454.

Schwarz, L. D. "Conditions of Life and Work in London, c. 1770–1820, with Special Reference to East London." Ph.D. diss., Oxford, 1976.

————. "Income Distribution and Social Structure in London in the Late Eighteenth Century." *Economic History Review* (2d ser.) 32(1979):250–259.

————. *London in the Age of Industrialisation: Entrepreneurs, Labour Force and Living Conditions 1700–1850.* Cambridge Studies in Population, Economy and Society in Past Time, 19. Cambridge: Cambridge University Press, 1992.

————. "Social Class and Social Geography: The Middle Classes in London at the End of the Eighteenth Century." *Social History* 7(1982):167–185.

Schwarz, L. D., and L. J. Jones. "Wealth, Occupations and Insurance in the Late Eighteenth Century: The Policy Registers of the Sun Fire Office." *Economic History Review* (2d ser.) 36 (1983):365–373.

Scott, Joan Wallach. *Gender and the Politics of History.* New York: Columbia University Press, 1988.

Scribner, Sylvia, and Michael Cole. *The Psychology of Literacy.* Cambridge, Mass.: Harvard University Press, 1981.

Seaver, Paul S. *Wallington's World: A Puritan Artisan in Seventeenth-Century London.* Stanford, Calif.: Stanford University Press, 1985.

Sedgwick, Eve Kosofsky. *Between Men: English Literature and Male Homosocial Desire.* New York and Guildford: Columbia University Press, 1985.

Sedgwick, Eve Kosofsky. *The Epistemology of the Closet.* New York and London: Harvester Wheatsheaf, 1991.

Seed, John. "From 'Middling Sort' to Middle Class in Late Eighteenth- and Early Nineteenth-Century England." In Michael L. Bush, ed., *Social Order and Social Classes in Europe Since 1500: Studies in Social Stratification*. London and New York: Longman, 1992.

Sekora, John. *Luxury: The Concept in Western Thought, Eden to Smollett*. Baltimore, Md.: Johns Hopkins Press, 1977.

Shannon, H. A. "The Coming of General Limited Liability." In Eleanora Mary Carus-Wilson, ed., *Essays in Economic History*, vol. 1. London: Edward Arnold, 1954.

Sharpe, Pamela. "Literally Spinsters: A New Interpretation of Local Economy and Demography in Colyton in the Seventeenth and Eighteenth Century." *Economic History Review* (2d ser.) 44(1991):46–65.

Shevelow, Kathryn. *Women and Print Culture: The Construction of Femininity in the Early Periodical*. London and New York: Routledge, 1989.

Shoemaker, Robert B. *Prosecution and Punishment: Petty Crime and the Law in London and Rural Middlesex, c. 1660–1725*. Cambridge: Cambridge University Press, 1991.

Shorter, Edward. *The Making of the Modern Family*. London: Collins, 1976.

Slater, Miriam. *Family Life in the Seventeenth Century: The Verneys of Claydon House*. London: Routledge & Kegan Paul, 1984.

Smail, John. *The Origins of Middle-Class Culture: Halifax, Yorkshire, 1660–1780*. Ithaca, N.Y.: Cornell University Press, 1994.

Smout, T. C., ed., *The Search for Wealth and Stability: Essays in Economic and Social History Presented to M. W. Flinn*. London: Macmillan, 1979.

Snell, K. D. M. *Annals of the Labouring Poor: Social Change and Agrarian England, 1660–1900*. Cambridge: Cambridge University Press, 1985.

Sombart, Werner. *The Quintessence of Capitalism: A Study of the History and Psychology of the Modern Business Man*. Trans. M. Epstein. New York: E. P. Dutton & Co., 1915.

Sommerville, C. John. "English Puritans and Children: A Socio-Cultural Explanation." *Journal of Psychohistory* 6(1978):113–137.

Spacks, Patricia Meyer. *Imagining a Self: Autobiography and Novel in Eighteenth-Century England*. Cambridge, Mass., and London: Harvard University Press, 1976.

Spadafora, David. *The Idea of Progress in Eighteenth-Century Britain*. New Haven and London: Yale University Press, 1990.

Speck, W. A. "Political Propaganda in Augustan England." *Transactions of the Royal Historical Society* (5th ser.) 22(1972):17–32.

———. "Politicians, Peers, and Publication by Subscription, 1700–50." In Isabel Rivers, ed., *Books and their Readers in Eighteenth-Century England*. Leicester and New York: Leicester University Press and St. Martin's Press, 1982.

Spierenburg, Pieter. *The Prison Experience: Disciplinary Institutions and Their Inmates*. New Brunswick, N.J.: Rutgers University Press, 1991.

Spufford, Margaret. *Contrasting Communities: English Villages in the Sixteenth and Seventeenth Centuries*. Cambridge: Cambridge University Press, 1974.

———. *The Great Reclothing of Rural England: Petty Chapmen and Their Wares in the Seventeenth Century*. History Series, no. 33. Ronceverte, W.V.: Hambledon Press, 1984.

———. *Small Books and Pleasant Histories: Popular Fiction and Its Readership in Seventeenth-Century England.* Cambridge: Cambridge University Press, 1981.

Stack, Carol. *All Our Kin: Strategies for Survival in a Black Community.* New York: Harper & Row, 1974.

Staves, Susan. *Married Women's Separate Property in England, 1660–1833.* Cambridge, Mass.: Harvard University Press, 1990.

———. "Pin Money." *Studies in Eighteenth-Century Culture* 14 (1985):47–77.

Steedman, Carolyn, Cathy Urwin, and Valerie Walkerdine, eds. *Language, Gender and Childhood.* London, Boston: Routledge & Kegan Paul, 1985.

Stewart, Larry. *The Rise of Public Science: Rhetoric, Technology, and Natural Philosophy in Newtonian Britain, 1660–1750.* Cambridge: Cambridge University Press, 1992.

Stone, Lawrence. *The Family, Sex and Marriage in England, 1500–1800.* London: Weidenfeld & Nicolson, 1977.

———. ed. *An Imperial State at War: Britain from 1689 to 1815.* London: Routledge, 1994.

———. "Literacy and Education in England, 1640–1900." *Past & Present* 42(1969):69–139.

———. *Uncertain Unions: Marriage in England, 1660–1753.* Oxford and New York: Oxford University Press, 1992.

Stone, Lawrence, and Jeanne C. Fawtier Stone. *An Open Elite? England 1540–1880.* Oxford: Clarendon Press, 1984.

Stone, Wilbur Macey. *The History of Little Goody Two-Shoes: An Essay and a List of Editions.* Worcester, Mass.: American Antiquarian Society, 1940.

Supple, Barry. *The Royal Exchange Assurance: A History of British Insurance 1720–1970.* Cambridge: Cambridge University Press, 1970.

Sykes, Norman. *From Sheldon to Secker: Aspects of English Church History, 1660–1760.* Cambridge: Cambridge University Press, 1959.

Tawney, R. H. *Religion and the Rise of Capitalism: A Historical Study.* Scott Holland Memorial Lectures, 1922. London: J. Murray, 1926.

Thirsk, Joan, ed. *Agrarian History of England and Wales,* vols. 5 (1–2), 6. Cambridge: Cambridge University Press, 1984–1985.

Thomas, Keith. *Religion and the Decline of Magic.* New York: Scribner's, 1971.

Thompson, E. P. "Argument: Eighteenth-Century English Society: Class Struggle Without Class?" *Social History* 3(1978):133–165.

———. *The Making of the English Working Class.* London: Gollancz, 1963.

———. *The Poverty of Theory and Other Essays.* London: Merlin Press, 1978.

———. "Time, Work-Discipline, and Industrial Capitalism." *Past & Present* 38(1967):58–97.

Thrupp, Sylvia. *The Merchant Class of Medieval London, 1300–1500.* Ann Arbor: University of Michigan Press, 1962. Originally published 1948.

Tilly, Louise, and Joan Scott. *Women, Work and the Family.* New York: Holt, Rinehart and Winston, 1978.

Trumbach, Randolph. "London's Sodomites: Homosexual Behaviour and Western Culture in the Eighteenth Century." *Journal of Social History* 11(1977–78):1–33.

———. *The Rise of the Egalitarian Family: Aristocratic Kinship and Domestic Relations in Eighteenth-Century England.* New York: Academic Press, 1978.

———. "Sodomitical Subcultures, Sodomitical Roles, and the Gender Revolution of the Eighteenth Century: The Recent Historiography." *Eighteenth-Century Life* 9(1985):109–121.

Unwin, George. *Gilds and Companies of London*. London: Methuen, 1925.

Valenze, Deborah. "Charity, Custom and Humanity: Changing Attitudes Toward the Poor in Eighteenth-Century England." In Jane Garnett and Colin Matthew, eds., *Revival and Religion Since 1700: Essays for John Walsh*. London and Rio Grande: The Hambledon Press, 1993.

Van de Pol, Lotte C., and Rudolf M. Dekker. *The Tradition of Female Transvestism in Early Modern Europe*. Basingstoke: Macmillan, 1989.

Vickery, Amanda. "Golden Age to Separate Spheres? A Review of the Categories and Chronology of English Women's History." *Historical Journal* 36(1993):383–414.

———. "Women and the World of Goods: A Lancashire Consumer and her Possessions, 1751–81." In John Brewer and Roy Porter, eds., *Consumption and the World of Goods*. London and New York: Routledge, 1993.

Vincent, W. A. L. *The Grammar Schools: Their Continuing Tradition, 1660–1714*. London: John Murray, 1969.

Wahrman, Dror. " 'Middle-Class' Domesticity Goes Public: Gender, Class, and Politics from Queen Caroline to Queen Victoria." *Journal of British Studies* 32(1993):396–432.

Walkowitz, Judith. *Prostitution and Victorian Society: Women, Class and the State*. Cambridge and New York: Cambridge University Press, 1980.

Walsh, John. "Origins of the Evangelical Revival." In G. V. Bennett and J. D. Walsh, eds., *Essays in Modern English Church History*. London: Adam and Charles Black, 1966.

———. "Religious Societies: Methodist and Evangelical, 1738–1800." In William J. Sheils and Diana Woods, eds., *Voluntary Religion*. Oxford: Published for the Ecclesiastical History Society by Basil Blackwell, 1986.

Ward, John R. *The Finance of Canal Building in Eighteenth-Century England*. Oxford: Oxford University Press, 1974.

Watts, Michael R. *The Dissenters: From the Reformation to the French Revolution*. Oxford: Clarendon Press, 1978.

Weatherill, Lorna. *Consumer Behavior and Material Culture in Britain, 1660–1760*. London: Routledge, 1988.

Weber, Max. *The Protestant Ethic and the Spirit of Capitalism*. Trans. Talcott Parsons. New York: Charles Scribner's Sons, 1958. Originally published 1904–1905.

Weeks, Jeffrey. "Discourse, Desire and Social Deviance: Some Problems in a History of Homosexuality." In Kenneth Plummer, ed., *The Making of the Modern Homosexual*. London: Hutchinson, 1981.

Wheelwright, Julie. *Amazons and Military Maids: Women Who Dressed as Men in the Pursuit of Life, Liberty and Happiness*. London: Pandora, 1989.

Whitney, Janet. *Elizabeth Fry, Quaker Heroine*. Boston: Little Brown, 1936.

Wiesner, Merry. *Working Women in Renaissance Germany*. New Brunswick, N.J.: Rutgers University Press, 1986.

Wildeblood, Joan, and Peter Brinson. *The Polite World: A Guide to English Manners and Deportment from the Thirteenth to the Nineteenth Century*. London: Oxford University Press, 1965.

Wiles, Roy McKeen. "The Relish for Reading in Provincial England Two Centuries Ago." In Paul J. Korshin, ed., *The Widening Circle: Essays on the Circulation of Literature in Eighteenth-Century Europe.* Philadelphia: University of Philadelphia Press, 1976.

Willan, T. S. *An Eighteenth-Century Shopkeeper: Abraham Dent of Kirkby Stephen.* Manchester: Manchester University Press, 1970.

Williams, D. "Morals, Markets and the English Crowd in 1766." *Past & Present* 104(1984):56–73.

Wilson, Adrian, ed. *Rethinking Social History: English Society 1570–1920 and Its Interpretation.* Manchester and New York: Manchester University Press, 1993.

Wilson, Kathleen. "Empire of Virtue: The Imperial Project and Hanoverian Culture c. 1720–1785." In Lawrence Stone, ed., *An Imperial State at War: Britain from 1689 to 1815.* London: Routledge, 1994.

———. "Empire, Trade and Popular Politics in Mid-Hanoverian Britain: The Case of Admiral Vernon." *Past & Present* 121(1988):74–109.

———."The Rejection of Deference: Urban Political Culture in England 1715–1785." Ph.D. diss., Yale University, 1985.

———. *The Sense of the People: Politics, Culture, and Imperialism in England, 1715–1785.* Cambridge and New York: Cambridge University Press, 1995.

———. "Urban Culture and Political Activism in Hanoverian England: The Example of Voluntary Hospitals." In Eckhart Hellmuth, ed., *The Transformation of Political Culture: England and Germany in the Late Eighteenth Century.* Oxford and London: Oxford University Press and the German Historical Institute, 1990.

Wolff, Janet, and John Seed, eds. *The Culture of Capital: Art, Power, and the Nineteenth-Century Middle Class.* Manchester: Manchester University Press, 1988.

Wright, Louis B. *Middle Class Culture in Elizabethan England.* Chapel Hill: University of North Carolina Press, 1935.

Wright, Sue. "Churmaids, Huswyfes and Hucksters: The Employment of Women in Tudor and Stuart Salisbury." In Lindsey Charles and Lorna Duffin, eds., *Women and Work in Preindustrial England.* London: Croom Helm, 1985.

Wrigley, E. A. *People, Cities and Wealth: The Transformation of Traditional Society.* Oxford: Basil Blackwell, 1987.

Wrigley, E. A., and R. S. Schofield. *The Population History of England 1541–1871: A Reconstruction.* London: Edward Arnold, 1981.

Yamey, Basil. *Historical Accounting Literature: A Catalogue of the Collection of Early Works on Book-keeping and Accounting in the Library of the Institute of Chartered Accountants in England and Wales, Together with a Bibliography of Literature on the Subject Published Before 1750 and Not in the Institute Library.* London: Mansell, 1975.

Yamey, Basil S., H. C. Edey, and Hugh W. Thomson. *Accounting in England and Scotland: 1543–1800: Double Entry in Exposition and Practice.* London: Sweet & Maxwell, 1963.

INDEX

Abelove, Henry, 241 n.35, 262 n.55

Aberdeen, 200

Accounting, 12, 58–62; accountants in novels, 60; alleged superiority of Dutch in, 59; double-entry, history of, 239 n.11; God and, 148, 172–175; linked to respectability, 61, 89; manuals, 43, 58, 60, 143, 242 n.45; as metaphor, 61, 148, 162, 173–175; national prosperity and, 59; rationality and, 61–62, 175, 208; replaces magic, 58; in seventeenth- and eighteenth-century businesses, 31, 35, 54, 60, 127, 233 n.32, 270 n.34; women and, 58–59, 89, 91, 243 n.50, 252 n.53

Actresses, 82, 96

Adburgham, Alison, 272 n.53

Addison, Joseph, 175, 205, 287 n.37, 288 n.62

Addison, Joseph, and Richard Steele: *Tatler* and *Spectator*, 75, 80, 101, 177, 204, 241 n.37, 281 n.16, 287 nn.37, 39, 288 n.62

Adultery and fornication, 44; bastard-bearing, 67, 73, 74, 92; cuckoldry as humorous, 246 n.90; Elizabethan views of, 261 n.47; excommunication for, 92, 253 n.64; likely to bring down "collective judgements," 112; said to be officially sanctioned during Restoration, 113; social and monetary costs of, 162–163

Advice books: on family relations, 26, 149; for girls and women, 75–80, 159, 246

n.90, 248 n.9; for landed classes, 59; for tradesmen, 25–26, 35, 246 n.90; on training and education of youth, 49, 62, 69, 90–91

Advice to the Women and Maidens of London, 58–59, 89, 242 n.45, 243 n.50

Africa, 79, 189

Africans, 189

Albury Park, 4

Aldermen, 147, 194

Alehousekeepers, 136

Alehouses, 54

Allen, W. O. B., 256 n.2, 264 n.74

Allestree, Richard (clergyman): *Ladies Calling*, 276 n.41

Almack's Club, 262 n.56

America, North, 30

American Indians: 189

Amsterdam, 63, 66; Bourse, 181; homosexual subculture in, 262 n.62; municipal institutions of, 181, 244 n.77; Stock Exchange, 182, 196; "wanton republican expressions" by brokers in, 196

Amussen, Susan Dwyer, 285 n.1

Anderson, B. L., 230 n.4, 232 n.29

Anderson, Elizabeth (silk seller), 126

Andrew, Donna T., 74–75, 123, 221 n.4, 223 n.17, 226–227 n.36, 272 n.27, 278 n.57, 280 n.74

Animals, prevention of cruelty to, 77, 79

Anne I, Queen, 119

Apothecaries, 175, 205, 258 n.11

Printed in the United Kingdom
by Lightning Source UK Ltd.
129094UK00001B/223/A